T0181587

Low-Level Programming

C, Assembly, and Program Execution on
Intel® 64 Architecture

Igor Zhirkov

Apress®

Low-Level Programming: C, Assembly, and Program Execution on Intel® 64 Architecture

Igor Zhirkov
Saint Petersburg, Russia

ISBN-13 (pbk): 978-1-4842-2402-1   ISBN-13 (electronic): 978-1-4842-2403-8
DOI 10.1007/978-1-4842-2403-8

Library of Congress Control Number: 2017945327

Cover image designed by Freepik

Managing Director: Welmoed Spahr
Editorial Director: Todd Green
Acquisitions Editor: Robert Hutchinson
Development Editor: Laura Berendson
Technical Reviewer: Ivan Loginov
Coordinating Editor: Rita Fernando
Copy Editor: Lori Jacobs
Compositor: SPi Global
Indexer: SPi Global

Distributed to the book trade worldwide by Springer Science+Business Media New York, 233 Spring Street, 6th Floor, New York, NY 10013. Phone 1-800-SPRINGER, fax (201) 348-4505, e-mail orders-ny@springer-sbm.com, or visit www.springeronline.com. Apress Media, LLC is a California LLC and the sole member (owner) is Springer Science + Business Media Finance Inc (SSBM Finance Inc). SSBM Finance Inc is a **Delaware** corporation.

For information on translations, please e-mail rights@apress.com, or visit http://www.apress.com/rights-permissions.

Apress titles may be purchased in bulk for academic, corporate, or promotional use. eBook versions and licenses are also available for most titles. For more information, reference our Print and eBook Bulk Sales web page at http://www.apress.com/bulk-sales.

Any source code or other supplementary material referenced by the author in this book is available to readers on GitHub via the book's product page, located at www.apress.com/9781484224021. For more detailed information, please visit http://www.apress.com/source-code.

Printed on acid-free paper

Contents at a Glance

Contents

About the Author

Igor Zhirkov teaches his highly successful "System Programming Languages" course in ITMO University in Saint-Petersburg, which is a six-time winner of the ACM-ICPC Intercollegiate World Programming Championship. He studied at Saint Petersburg Academic University and received his master's degree from ITMO University. Currently he is doing research in verified C refactorings as part of his PhD thesis and formalization of Bulk Synchronous Parallelism library in C at IMT Atlantique in Nantes, France. His main interests are low-level programming, programming language theory, and type theory.

His other interests include playing piano, calligraphy, art, and the philosophy of science.

About the Technical Reviewer

Ivan Loginov is a researcher and lecturer at ITMO University of Saint Petersburg, Russia (University of Information Technologies, Mechanics and Optics), teaching the course "Introduction to Programming Languages" to bachelor degree students of computer science.

He received his master's degree from ITMO University. His research focuses on compiler theory, language workbenches, and distributed and parallel programming as well as new teaching techniques and their application to IT (information technology).

Currently, he is writing his PhD dissertation on a cloud-based modeling toolkit for system dynamics.

His hobbies include playing the trumpet and reading classic (Russian) literature.

Acknowledgments

I was blessed to meet a great number of persons, both very gifted and extremely dedicated, who helped me and often guided me toward the areas of knowledge I could never have imagined myself.

I thank Vladimir Nekrasov, my most beloved math teacher, for his course and his influence on me, which enabled me to think better and more logically.

I thank Andrew Dergachev, who entrusted me to create and teach my course and helped me so much during these years, Boris Timchenko, Arkady Kluchev, Ivan Loginov (who also kindly agreed to be the technical reviewer for this book), and all my colleagues from ITMO university, who helped me to shape this course in one way or another.

I thank all my students who provided feedback or even helped me in teaching. You are the very reason I am doing this. Several students helped by reviewing the draft of this book, I want to note the most useful remarks of Dmitry Khalansky and Valery Kireev.

For me, the years I have spent in Saint-Petersburg Academic University are easily the best of my life. Never have I had more opportunities to study with world-class specialists working in the leading companies along with other students, much smarter than me. I want to express my deepest gratitude to Alexander Omelchenko, Alexander Kulikov, Andrey Ivanov, and everyone contributing to the quality of computer science education in Russia. I also thank Dmitry Boulytchev, Andrey Breslav, and Sergey Sinchuk from JetBrains, my supervisors who have taught me a lot.

I am also very grateful to my french colleagues: Ali Ed-Dbali, Frédéric Loulergue, Rémi Douence, and Julien Cohen.

I also want to thank Sergei Gorlatch and Tim Humernbrum for providing much necessary feedback on Chapter 17, which helped me shape it into a much more consistent and understandable version. Special thanks go to Dmitry Shubin for his most useful impact on fixing the imperfections of this book.

I am very grateful to my friend Alexey Velikiy and to his agency CorpGlory.com, which focused on data visualizations and infographics and crafted the best illustrations in this book.

Behind every little success of mine is an infinite amount of support from my family and friends. I would not have achieved anything without you.

Last, but not least, I thank the Apress team, including Robert Hutchinson, Rita Fernando, Laura Berendson, and Susan McDermott, for putting their trust in me and this project and doing everything they could to bring this book into reality.

Introduction

This book aims to help you develop a consistent vision of the domain of low-level programming. We want to enable a careful reader to

- Freely write in assembly language.

- Understand the Intel 64 programming model.

- Write maintainable and robust code in C11.

- Understand the compilation process and decipher assembly listings.

- Debug errors in compiled assembly code.

- Use appropriate models of computation to greatly reduce program complexity.

- Write performance-critical code.

There are two kinds of technical books: those used as a reference and those used to learn. This book is, without doubt, the second kind. It is pretty dense on purpose, and in order to successfully digest the information we highly suggest continuous reading. To quickly memorize new information you should try to connect it with the information with which you are already familiar. That is why we tried, whenever possible, to base our explanation of each topic on the information you received from previous topics.

This book is written for programming students, intermediate-to-advanced programmers, and low-level programming enthusiasts. The prerequisites are a basic understanding of binary and hexadecimal systems and a basic knowledge of Unix commands.

Questions and Answers   Throughout this book you will encounter numerous questions. Most of them are meant to make you think again about what you have just learned, but some of them encourage you to do additional research, pointing to the relevant keywords.

We propose the answers to these questions in our GitHub page, which also hosts all listings and starting code for assignments, updates and other goodies.

Refer to the book's page on Apress site for additional information: http://www.apress.com/us/book/9781484224021.

There you can also find several preconfigured virtual machines with Debian Linux installed, with and without a graphical user interface (GUI), which allows you to start practicing right away without spending time setting up your system. You can find more information in section 2.1.

We start with the very simple core ideas of what a computer is, explaining concepts of model of computation and computer architecture. We expand the core model with extensions until it becomes adequate enough to describe a modern processor as a programmer sees it. From Chapter 2 onward we start programming in the real assembly language for Intel 64 without resorting to older 16-bit architectures, that are often taught for historical reasons. It allows us to see the interactions between applications and operating system through the system calls interface and the specific architecture details such as endianness. After a brief overview of legacy architecture features, some of which are still in use, we study virtual memory in great detail and illustrate its usage with the help of procfs and examples of using mmap system call in assembly. Then we dive into the process of compilation, overviewing preprocessing, static, and dynamic linking. After exploring interrupts and system calls mechanisms in greater detail, we finish the first part with a chapter about different models of computations, studying examples of finite state machines, stack machines, and implementing a fully functional compiler of Forth language in pure assembly.

The second part is dedicated to the C language. We start from the language overview, building a core understanding of its model of computation necessary to start writing programs. In the next chapter we study the type system of C and illustrate different kinds of typing, ending with about a discussion of polymorphism and providing exemplary implementations for different kinds of polymorphism in C. Then we study the ways of correctly structuring the program by splitting it into multiple files and also viewing its effect on the linking process. The next chapter is dedicated to the memory management, input and output. After that, we elaborate three facets of each language: syntax, semantics, and pragmatics and concentrate on the first and the third ones. We see how the language propositions are transformed into abstract syntax trees, the difference between undefined and unspecified behavior in C, and the effect of language pragmatics on the assembly code produced by the compiler. In the end of the second part, we dedicate a chapter to the good code practices to give readers an idea of how the code should be written depending on its specific requirements. The sequence of the assignments for this part is ended by the rotation of a bitmap file and a custom memory allocator.

The final part is a bridge between the two previous ones. It dives into the translation details such as calling conventions and stack frames and advanced C language features, requiring a certain understanding of assembly, such as volatile and restrict keywords. We provide an overview of several classic low-level bugs such as stack buffer overflow, which can be exploited to induce an unwanted behavior in the program. The next chapter tells about shared objects in great details and studies them on the assembly level, providing minimal working examples of shared libraries written in C and assembly. Then, we discuss a relatively rare topic of code models. The chapter studies the optimizations that modern compilers are capable of and how that knowledge can be used to produce readable and fast code. We also provide an overview of performance-amplifying techniques such as specialized assembly instructions usage and cache usage optimization. This is followed by an assignment where you will implement a sepia filter for an image using specialized SSE instructions and measure its performance. The last chapter introduces multithreading via pthreads library usage, memory models, and reorderings, which anyone doing multithreaded programming should be aware of, and elaborates the need for memory barriers.

The appendices include short tutorials on gdb (debugger), make (automated build system), and a table of the most frequently used system calls for reference and system information to make performance tests given throughout the book easier to reproduce. They should be read when necessary, but we recommend that you get used to gdb as soon as you start assembly programming in Chapter 2.

Most illustrations were produced using VSVG library aimed to produce complex interactive vector graphics, written by Alexey Velikiy (http://www.corpglory.com). The sources for the library and book illustrations are available at VSVG Github page: https://github.com/corpglory/vsvg.

We hope that you find this book useful and wish you an enjoyable read!

PART I

Assembly Language and Computer Architecture

CHAPTER 1

▓ ▓ ▓

Basic Computer Architecture

This chapter is going to give you a general understanding of the fundamentals of computer functioning. We will describe a core model of computation, enumerate its extensions, and take a closer look at two of them, namely, registers and hardware stack. It will prepare you to start assembly programming in the next chapter.

1.1 The Core Architecture

1.1.1 Model of Computation

What does a programmer do? A first guess would probably be "construction of algorithms and their implementation." So, we grasp an idea, then we code, and this is the common way of thinking.

Can we construct an algorithm to describe some daily routine, like going out for a walk or shopping? The question does not sound particularly hard, and many people will gladly provide you with their solutions.

However, all these solutions will be fundamentally different. One will operate with such actions as "opening the door" or "taking the key"; the other will rather "leave the house," omitting details. The third one, however, will go rogue and provide a detailed description of the movement of his hands and legs, or even describe his muscle contraction patterns.

The reason those answers are so different is the *incompleteness of the initial question*.

All ideas (including algorithms) need a way to be expressed. To describe a new notion we use other, simpler notions. We also want to avoid vicious cycles, so the explanation will follow the shape of a pyramid. Each level of explanation will grow horizontally. We cannot build this pyramid infinitely, because the explanation has to be finite, so we stop at the level of basic, primitive notions, which we have deliberately chosen not to expand further. So, choosing the basics is a fundamental requirement to express anything.

It means that algorithm construction is impossible unless we have fixed a set of basic actions, which act as its building blocks.

Model of computation is a set of basic operations and their respective costs.

The costs are usually integer numbers and are used to reason about the algorithms' complexity via calculating the combined cost of all their operations. We are not going to discuss computational complexity in this book.

Most models of computation are also **abstract machines**. It means that they describe a hypothetical computer, whose instructions correspond to the model's basic operations. The other type of models, decision trees, is beyond the scope of this book.

1.1.2 von Neumann Architecture

Now let us imagine we are living in 1930s, when today's computers did not yet exist. People wanted to automate calculations somehow, and different researchers were coming up with different ways to achieve such automation. Common examples are Church's Lambda calculus or the Turing machine. These are typical abstract machines, describing imaginary computers.

© Igor Zhirkov 2017
I. Zhirkov, *Low-Level Programming*, DOI 10.1007/978-1-4842-2403-8_1

One type of machine soon became dominant: the von Neumann architecture computer.

Computer architecture describes the functionality, organization, and implementation of computer systems. It is a relatively high-level description, compared to a calculation model, which does not omit even a slight detail.

von Neumann architecture had two crucial advantages: it was robust (in a world where electronic components were highly unstable and short-lived) and easy to program.

In short, this is a computer consisting of one processor and one memory bank, connected to a common bus. A **central processing unit (CPU)** can execute instructions, fetched from **memory** by a **control unit**. The **arithmetic logic unit (ALU)** performs the needed computations. The memory also stores data. See Figures 1-1 and 1-2.

Following are the key features of this architecture:

- Memory stores only bits (a unit of information, a value equal to 0 or 1).

- Memory stores both encoded instructions and data to operate on. There are no means to distinguish data from code: both are in fact bit strings.

- Memory is organized into cells, which are labeled with their respective indices in a natural way (e.g., cell #43 follows cell #42). The indices start at 0. Cell size may vary (John von Neumann thought that each bit should have its address); modern computers take one byte (eight bits) as a memory cell size. So, the 0-th byte holds the first eight bits of the memory, etc.

- The program consists of instructions that are fetched one after another. Their execution is sequential unless a special jump instruction is executed.

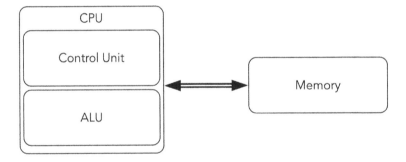

Figure 1-1. *von Neumann architecture—Overview*

Assembly language for a chosen processor is a programming language consisting of mnemonics for each possible binary encoded instruction (machine code). It makes programming in machine codes much easier, because the programmer then does not have to memorize the binary encoding of instructions, only their names and parameters.

Note, that instructions can have parameters of different sizes and formats.

An architecture does not always define a precise instruction set, unlike a model of computation.

A common modern personal computer have evolved from old von Neumann architecture computers, so we are going to investigate this evolution and see what distinguishes a modern computer from the simple schematic in Figure 1-2.

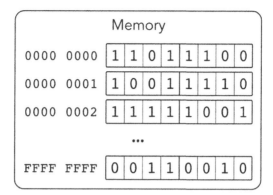

Figure 1-2. *von Neumann architecture—Memory*

■ **Note**   Memory state and values of registers fully describe the CPU state (from a programmer's point of view). Understanding an instruction means understanding its effects on memory and registers.

1.2   Evolution

1.2.1   Drawbacks of von Neumann Architecture

The simple architecture described previously has serious drawbacks.

First of all, this architecture is not interactive at all. A programmer is limited by manual memory editing and visualizing its contents somehow. In the early days of computers, it was pretty straightforward, because the circuits were big and bits could have been flipped literally with bare hands.

Moreover, this architecture is not multitask friendly. Imagine your computer is performing a very slow task (e.g., controlling a printer). It is slow because a printer is much slower than the slowest CPU. The CPU then has to wait for a device reaction a percentage of time close to 99%, which is a waste of resources (namely, CPU time).

Then, when everyone can execute any kind of instruction, all sorts of unexpected behavior can occur. The purpose of an operating system (OS) is (among others) to manage the resources (such as external devices) so that user applications will not cause chaos by interacting with the same devices concurrently. Because of this we would like to prohibit all user applications from executing some instructions related to input/output or system management.

Another problem is that memory and CPU performance differ drastically.

Back in the old times, computers were not only simpler: they were designed as integral entities. Memory, bus, network interfaces—everything was created by the same engineering team. Every part was specialized to be used in this specific model. So parts were not destined to be interchangeable. In these circumstances none tried to create a part capable of higher performance than other parts, because it could not possibly increase overall computer performance.

But as the architectures became more or less stable, hardware developers started to work on different parts of computers independently. Naturally, they tried to improve their performance for marketing purposes. However, not all parts were easy *and cheap*[1] to speed up. This is the reason CPUs soon became *much* faster than memory. It is possible to speed up memory by choosing other types of underlying circuits, but it would be much more expensive [12].

---

[1]Note how often solutions the engineers come up with are dictated by economic reasons rather than technical limitations.

When a system consists of different parts and their performance characteristics differ a lot, the slowest part can become a **bottleneck**. It means that if is the slowest part is replaced with a faster analogue, the overall performance will increase significantly. That's where the architecture had to be heavily modified.

1.2.2   Intel 64 Architecture

In this book we only describe the Intel 64 architecture.[2]

Intel has been developing its main processor family since the 1970s. Each model was intended to preserve the binary compatibility with older models. It means that even modern processors can execute code written and compiled for older models. It leads to a tremendous amount of legacy. Processors can operate in a number of modes: real mode, protected, virtual, etc. If not specified explicitly, we will describe how a CPU operates in the newest, so-called **long mode**.

1.2.3   Architecture Extensions

Intel 64 incorporates multiple extensions of von Neumann's architecture. The most important ones are listed here for a quick overview.

Registers These are memory cells placed directly on the CPU chip. Circuit-wise they are much faster, but they are also more complicated and expensive. Register accesses do not use the bus. The response time is quite small and usually equals a couple of CPU cycles. See section 1.3 "Registers".

Hardware stack A stack in general is a data structure. It supports two operations: *push*ing an element on top of it and *pop*ping the topmost element. A hardware stack implements this abstraction on top of memory through special instructions and a register, pointing at the last stack element. A stack is used not only in computations but to store local variables and implement function call sequence in programming languages. See section 1.5 "Hardware stack".

Interrupts This feature allows one to change program execution order based on events external to the program itself. After a signal (external or internal) is caught, a program's execution is suspended, some registers are saved, and the CPU starts executing a special routine to handle the situation. Following are exemplary situations when an interrupt occurs (and an appropriate piece of code is executed to handle it):

- A signal from an external device.

- Zero division.

- Invalid instruction (when CPU failed to recognize an instruction by its binary representation).

- An attempt to execute a privileged instruction in a non-privileged mode.
  See section 6.2 "Interrupts" for a more detailed description.

Protection rings A CPU is always in a state corresponding to one of the so-called protection rings. Each ring defines a set of allowed instructions. The zero-th ring allows executing any instruction from the entire CPU's instruction set, and thus it is the most privileged. The third allows only the safest ones. An attempt to execute a privileged instruction results in an interrupt. Most applications are working inside the third ring to ensure that they do not modify crucial system data structures (such as page tables) and do not work with external devices, bypassing the OS. The other two rings (first and second) are intermediate, and modern operating systems are not using them.

See section 3.2 "Protected mode" for a more detailed description.

Virtual memory This is an abstraction over physical memory, which helps distribute it between programs in a safer and more effective way. It also isolates programs from one another.

---

[2]Also known as x86_64 and AMD64.

See section 4.2 "Motivation" for a more detailed description.

Some extensions are not directly accessible by a programmer (e.g., caches or shadow registers). We will mention some of them as well.

Table 1-1 summarizes information about some von Neumann architecture extensions seen in modern computers.

Table 1-1. *von Neumann Architecture: Modern Extensions*

Problem	Solution
Nothing is possible without querying slow memory	Registers, caches
Lack of interactivity	Interrupts
No support for code isolation in procedures, or for context saving	Hardware stack
Multitasking: any program can execute any instruction	Protection rings
Multitasking: programs are not isolated from one another	Virtual memory

▪ **Sources of information**   No book should cover the instruction set and processor architecture completely. Many books try to include exhaustive information about instruction set. It gets outdated quite soon; moreover, it bloats the book unnecessarily.

We will often refer you to Intel® 64 and IA-32 Architectures Software Developer's Manual available online: see [15]. Get it now!

There is no virtue in copying the instruction descriptions from the "original" place they appear in; it is much more mature to learn to work with the source.

The second volume covers instruction set completely and has a very useful table of contents. Please, always use it to get information about instruction set: it is not only a very good practice, but also a quite reliable source.

Note, that many educational resources devoted to assembly language in the Internet are often heavily outdated (as few people program in assembly these days) and do not cover the 64-bit mode at all. The instructions present in older modes often have their updated counterparts in long mode, and those are working in a different way. This is a reason we strongly discourage using search engines to find instruction descriptions, as tempting as it might be.

1.3   Registers

The data exchange between CPU and memory is a crucial part of computations in a von Neumann computer. Instructions have to be fetched from memory, operands have to be fetched from memory; some instructions store results also in memory. It creates a bottleneck and leads to wasted CPU time when it waits for the data response from the memory chip. To avoid constant wait, a processor was equipped with its own memory cells, called registers. These are few but fast. Programs are usually written in such a way that most of the time the working set of memory cells is small enough. This fact suggests that programs can be written so that most of the time the CPU will be working with registers.

Registers are based on transistors, while main memory uses condensers. We could have implemented main memory on transistors and gotten a much faster circuit. There are several reasons engineers prefer other ways of speeding up computations.

- Registers are more expensive.

- Instructions encode the register's number as part of their codes. To address more registers the instructions have to grow in size.

- Registers add complexity to the circuits to address them. More complex circuits are harder to speed up. It is not easy to set up a large register file to work on 5 GHz.

Naturally, register usage slows down computers in the worst case. If everything has to be fetched into registers before the computations are made and flushed into memory after, where's the profit?

The programs are usually written in such a way, that they have one particular property. It is a result of using common programming patterns such as loops, function, and data reusage, not some law of nature. This property is called **locality of reference** and there are two main types of it: temporal and spatial.

Temporal locality means that accesses to one address are likely to be close in time.

Spatial locality means that after accessing an address X the next memory access will likely to be close to X, (like $X - 16$ or $X + 28$).

These properties are not binary: you can write a program exhibiting stronger or weaker locality.

Typical programs are using the following pattern: the data working set is small and can be kept inside registers. After fetching the data into registers once we will work with them for quite some time, and then the results will be flushed into memory. The data stored in memory will rarely be used by the program. In case we need to work with this data we will lose performance because

- We need to fetch data into the registers.

- If all registers are occupied with data we still need later on, we will have to spill some of them, which means save their contents into temporally allocated memory cells.

■ **Note**   A widespread situation for an engineer: decreasing performance in the worst case to improve it in average case. It does work quite often, but it is prohibited when building real-time systems, which impose constraints on the worst system reaction time. Such systems are required to issue a reaction to events in no more than a certain amount of time, so decreasing performance in the worst case to improve it in other cases is not an option.

1.3.1   General Purpose Registers

Most of the time, programmer works with **general purpose registers**. They are interchangeable and can be used in many different commands.

These are 64-bit registers with the names r0, r1, ..., r15. The first eight of them can be named alternatively; these names represent the meaning they bear for some special instructions. For example, r1 is alternatively named rcx, where c stands for "cycle." There is an instruction loop, which uses rcx as a cycle counter but *accepts no operands explicitly*. Of course, such kind of special register meaning is reflected in documentation for corresponding commands (e.g., as a counter for loop instruction). Table 1-2 lists all of them; see also Figure 1-3.

> ▪ **Note** Unlike the hardware stack, which is implemented on top of the main memory, registers are a completely different kind of memory. Thus they do not have addresses, as the main memory's cells do!

The alternate names are in fact more common for historical reasons. We will provide both for reference and give a tip for each one. These semantic descriptions are given for a reference; you don't have to memorize them right now.

Table 1-2. *64-bit General Purpose Registers*

Name	Alias	Description
r0	rax	Kind of an "accumulator," used in arithmetic instructions. For example, an instruction div is used to divide two integers. It accepts one operand and uses rax implicitly as the second one. After executing div rcx a big 128-bit wide number, stored in parts in two registers rdx and rax is divided by rcx and the result is stored again in rax.
r3	rbx	Base register. Was used for base addressing in early processor models.
r1	rcx	Used for cycles (e.g., in loop).
r2	rdx	Stores data during input/output operations.
r4	rsp	Stores the address of the topmost element in the hardware stack. See section 1.5 "Hardware stack".
r5	rbp	Stack frame's base. See section 14.1.2 "Calling convention".
r6	rsi	Source index in string manipulation commands (such as movsd)
r7	rdi	Destination index in string manipulation commands (such as movsd)
r8		
r9 ... r15	no	Appeared later. Used mostly to store temporal variables (but sometimes used implicitly, like r10, which saves the CPU flags when syscall instruction is executed. See Chapter 6 "Interrupts and system calls").

You usually *do not want* to use rsp and rbp registers because of their very special meaning (later we will see how they corrupt stack and stack frame). However, you can perform arithmetic operations on them directly, which makes them general purpose.

Table 1-3 shows registers sorted by their names following an indexing convention.

Table 1-3. *64-Bit General Purpose Registers—Different Naming Conventions*

r0	r1	r2	r3	r4	r5	r6	r7
rax	rcx	rdx	rbx	rsp	rbp	rsi	rdi

Addressing a part of a register is possible. For each register you can address its lowest 32 bits, lowest 16 bits, or lowest 8 bits.

When using the names r0,...,r15 it is done by adding an appropriate suffix to a register's name:

- d for double word—lower 32 bits;

- w for word—lower 16 bits;

- b for byte—lower 8 bits.

For example,

- r7b is the lowest byte of register r7;

- r3w consists of the lowest two bytes of r3; and

- r0d consists of the lowest four bytes of r0.

The alternate names also allow addressing the smaller parts.

Figure 1-4 shows decomposition of wide general purpose registers into smaller ones.

The naming convention for accessing parts of rax, rbx, rcx, and rdx follows the same pattern; only the middle letter (a for rax) is changing. The other four registers do not allow an access to their second lowest bytes (like rax does by the name of ah). The lowest byte naming differs slightly for rsi, rdi, rsp, and rbp.

- The smallest parts of rsi and rdi are sil and dil (see Figure 1-5).

- The smallest parts pf rsp and rbp are spl and bpl (see Figure 1-6).

In practice, the names r0-r7 are rarely seen. Usually programmers stick with alternate names for the first *eight* general purpose registers. It is done for both legacy and semantic reasons: rsp relates a lot more information, than r4. The other eight (r8-r15) can only be named using an indexed convention.

■ **Inconsistency in writes**   All reads from smaller registers act in an obvious way. The writes into 32-bit parts, however, fill the upper 32 bits of the full register with sign bits. For example, zeroing eax will zero the entire rax, storing -1 into eax will fill the upper 32 bits with ones. Other writes (e.g., in 16-bit parts) act as intended: they leave all other bits unaffected. See section 3.4.2 "CISC and RISC" for the explanation.

1.3.2   Other Registers

The other registers have special meaning. Some registers have system-wide importance and thus cannot be modified except by the OS.

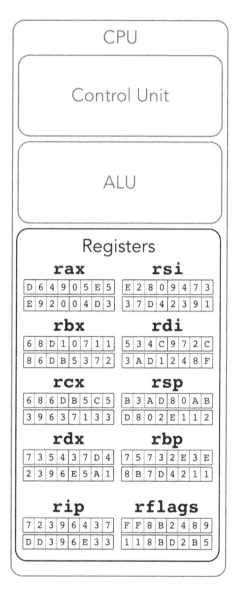

Figure 1-3. *Approximation of Intel 64: general purpose registers*

A programmer has access to rip register. It is a 64-bit register, which always stores an address of the next instruction to be executed. Branching instructions (e.g., jmp) are in fact modifying it. So, every time any instruction is being executed, rip stores the address of the next instruction to be executed.

■ **Note** All instructions have different size!

Another accessible register is called rflags. It stores flags, which reflect the current program state—for example, what was the result of the last arithmetic instruction: was it negative, did an overflow happened, etc. Its smaller parts are called eflags (32 bit) and flags (16 bit).

■ **Question 1** It is time to do preliminary research based on the documentation [15]. Refer to section 3.4.3 of the first volume to learn about register rflags. What is the meaning of flags CF, AF, ZF, OF, SF? What is the difference between OF and CF?

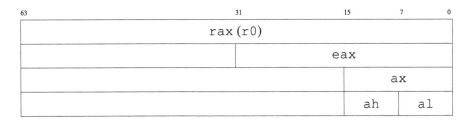

Figure 1-4. rax decomposition

In addition to these core registers there are also registers used by instructions working with floating point numbers or special parallelized instructions able to perform similar actions on multiple pairs of operands at the same time. These instructions are often used for multimedia purposes (they help speed up multimedia decoding algorithms). The corresponding registers are 128-bit wide and named xmm0 - xmm15. We will talk about them later.

Some registers have appeared as non-standard extensions but became standardized shortly after. These are so-called **model-specific registers**. See section 6.3.1 "Model specific registers" for more details.

1.3.3 System Registers

Some registers are designed specifically to be used by the OS. They do not hold values used in computations. Instead, they store information required by system-wide data structures. Thus their role is supporting a framework, born from a symbiosis of the OS and CPU. All applications are running inside this framework. The latter ensures that applications are well isolated from the system itself and from one another; it also manages resources in a way more or less transparent for a programmer.

It is extremely important that these registers are inaccessible by applications themselves (at least the applications should not be able to modify them). This is the goal of privileged mode (see section 3.2).

We will list some of these registers here. Their meaning will be explained in detail later.

- cr0, cr4 store flags related to different processor modes and virtual memory;

- cr2, cr3 are used to support virtual memory (see sections 4.2 "Motivation", 4.7.1 "Virtual address structure");

- cr8 (aliased as tpr) is used to perform a fine tuning of the interrupts mechanism (see section 6.2 "Interrupts").

- efer is another flag register used to control processor modes and extensions (e.g., long mode and system calls handling).

- idtr stores the address of the interrupt descriptors table (see section 6.2 "Interrupts").

- gdtr and ldtr store the addresses of the descriptor tables (see section 3.2 "Protected mode").

- cs, ds, ss, es, gs, fs are so-called **segment registers**. The segmentation mechanism they provide is considered legacy for many years now, but a part of it is still used to implement privileged mode. See section 3.2 "Protected mode".

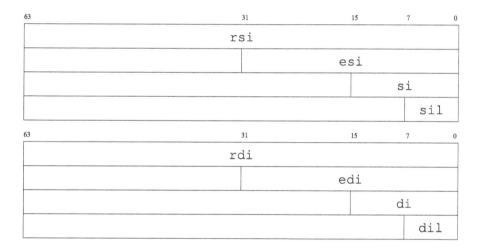

Figure 1-5. rsi *and* rdi *decomposition*

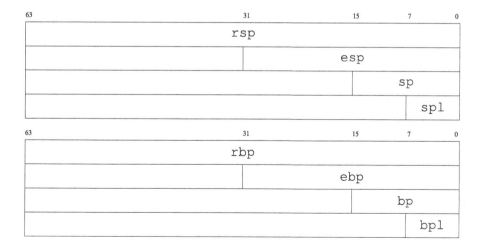

Figure 1-6. rsp *and* rbp *decomposition*

1.4 Protection Rings

Protection rings are one of the mechanisms designed to limit the applications' capabilities for security and robustness reasons. They were invented for Multics OS, a direct predecessor of Unix. Each ring corresponds to a certain privilege level. Each instruction type is linked with one or more privilege levels and is not executable on others. The current privilege level is stored somehow (e.g., inside a special register).

Intel 64 has four privilege levels, of which *only two* are used in practice: ring-0 (the most privileged) and ring-3 (the least privileged). The middle rings were planned to be used for drivers and OS services, but popular OSs did not adopt this approach.

In long mode, the current protection ring number is stored in the lowest two bits of register cs (and duplicated in those of ss). It can only be changed when handling an interrupt or a system call. So an application cannot execute an arbitrary code with elevated privilege levels: it can only call an interrupt handler or perform a system call. See Chapter 3 "Legacy" for more information.

1.5 Hardware Stack

If we are talking about data structures in general, a stack is a data structure, a container with two operations: a new element can be placed on top of the stack (push); the top element can be taken away from the stack (pop).

There is a hardware support for such data structure. It does not mean there is also a separate stack memory. It is just sort of an emulation implemented with two machine instructions (push and pop) and a register (rsp). The rsp register holds an address of the topmost element of the stack. The instructions perform as follows:

- push argument

  1. Depending on argument size (2, 4, and 8 bytes are allowed), the rsp value is decreased by 2, 4, or 8.

  2. An argument is stored in memory starting at the address, taken from the modified rsp.

- pop argument

  1. The topmost stack element is copied into the register/memory.

  2. rsp is increased by the size of its argument. An augmented architecture is represented in Figure 1-7.

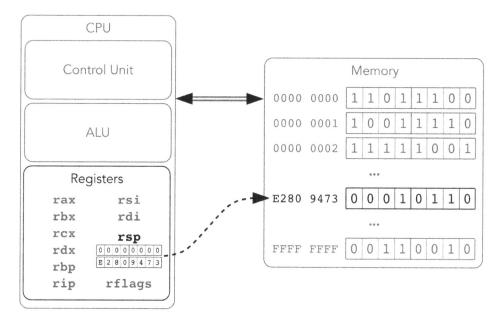

Figure 1-7. *Intel 64, registers and stack*

The hardware stack is most useful to implement function calls in higher-level languages. When a function *A* calls another function *B*, it uses the stack to save the context of computations to return to it after *B* terminates.

Here are some important facts about the hardware stack, most of which follow from its description:

1. There is no such situation as an empty stack, even if we performed push zero times. A pop algorithm can be executed anyway, probably returning a garbage "topmost" stack element.

2. Stack grows toward zero address.

3. Almost all kinds of its operands are considered signed integers and thus can be expanded with sign bit. For example, performing push with an argument $B9_{16}$ will result in the following data unit being stored on the stack:

   0xff b9, 0xffffffb9 or 0xff ff ff ff ff ff ff b9.

   By default, push uses an 8-byte operand size. Thus an instruction push -1 will store 0xff ff ff ff ff ff ff ff on the stack.

4. Most architectures that support stack use the same principle with its top defined by some register. What differs, however, is the meaning of the respective address. On some architectures it is the address of the *next element*, which will be written on the next push. On others it is the address of the *last element* already pushed into the stack.

■ **Working with Intel docs: How to read instruction descriptions**   Open the second volume of [15]. Find the page corresponding to the `push` instruction. It begins with a table. For our purpose we will only investigate the columns OPCODE, INSTRUCTION, 64-BIT MODE, and DESCRIPTION. The OPCODE field defines the machine encoding of an instruction (operation code). As you see, there are options and each option corresponds to a different DESCRIPTION. It means that sometimes not only the operands vary but also the operation codes themselves.

INSTRUCTION describes the instruction mnemonics and allowed operand types. Here R stands for any general purpose register, M stands for memory location, IMM stands for immediate value (e.g., integer constant like 42 or 1337). A number defines operand size. If only specific registers are allowed, they are named. For example:

- `push r/m16`—push a general purpose 16-bit register or a 16-bit number taken from memory into the stack.

- `push CS`—push a segment register `cs`.

The DESCRIPTION column gives a brief explanation of the instruction's effects. It is often enough to understand and use the instruction.

- Read the further explanation of `push`. When is the operand not sign extended?

- Explain all effects of the instruction `push rsp` on memory and registers.

1.6   Summary

In this chapter we provided a quick overview of von Neumann architecture. We have started adding features to this model to make it more adequate for describing modern processors. So far we took a closer look at registers and the hardware stack. The next step is to start programming in assembly, and that is what the next chapter is dedicated to. We are going to view some sample programs, pinpoint several new architectural features (such as endianness and addressing modes), and design a simple input/output library for *nix to ease interaction with a user.

■ **Question 2**   What are the key principles of von Neumann architecture?

■ **Question 3**   What are registers?

■ **Question 4**   What is the hardware stack?

■ **Question 5**   What are the interrupts?

■ **Question 6**   What are the main problems that the modern extensions of the von Neumann model are trying to solve?

■ **Question 7**   What are the main general purpose registers of Intel 64?

■ **Question 8**   What is the purpose of the stack pointer?

■ **Question 9**   Can the stack be empty?

■ **Question 10**   Can we count elements in a stack?

CHAPTER 2

Assembly Language

In this chapter we will start practicing assembly language by gradually writing more complex programs for Linux. We will observe some architecture details that impact the writing of all kinds of programs (e.g., endianness).

We have chosen a *nix system in this book because it is much easier to program in assembly compared to doing so in Windows.

2.1 Setting Up the Environment

It is impossible to learn programming without trying to program. So we are going to start programming in assembly right now.

We are using the following setup in order to complete assembler and C assignments:

- Debian GNU\Linux 8.0 as an operating system.

- NASM 2.11.05 as an assembly language compiler.

- GCC 4.9.2 as C language compiler. This exact version is used to produce assembly from C programs. Clang compiler can be used as well.

- GNU Make 4.0 as a build system.

- GDB 7.7.1 as a debugger.

- The text editor you like (preferably with syntax highlighting). We advocate ViM usage.

If you want to set up your own system, install any Linux distribution you like and make sure you install the programs just listed. To our knowledge, Windows Subsystem for Linux is also well suited to do all the assignments. You can install it and then install necessary packages using `apt-get`. Refer to the official guide located at: `https://msdn.microsoft.com/en-us/commandline/wsl/install_guide`.

On Apress web site for this book, `http://www.apress.com/us/book/9781484224021`, you can find the following:

- Two preconfigured virtual machines with the whole toolchain installed. One of them has a desktop environment; the other one is just the minimal system that can be accessed through SSH (Secure Shell). The installation instructions and other usage information is located in the `README.txt` file in the downloaded archive.

- A link to GitHub page with all the book's listings, answers to the questions, and solutions.

© Igor Zhirkov 2017
I. Zhirkov, *Low-Level Programming*, DOI 10.1007/978-1-4842-2403-8_2

2.1.1   Working with Code Examples

Throughout this chapter, you will see numerous code examples. Compile them and if you have difficulty grasping their logic, try to execute them step by step using gdb. It is a great help in studying code. See Appendix A for a quick tutorial on gdb.

Appendix D provides more information about the system used for performance tests.

2.2   Writing "Hello, world"

2.2.1   Basic Input and Output

Unix ideology postulates that "everything is a file." A **file**, in a large sense, is anything that looks like a stream of bytes. Through files one can abstract such things as

- data access on a hard drive/SSD;

- data exchange between programs; and

- interaction with external devices.

We will follow the tradition of writing a simple "Hello, world!" program for a start. It displays a welcome message on screen and terminates. However, such a program must show characters on screen, which cannot be done directly if a program is not running on bare metal, without an operating system babysitting its activity. An operating system's purpose is, among other things, to abstract and manage resources, and display is surely one of them. It provides a set of routines to handle communication with external devices, other programs, file systems, and so on. A program usually *cannot bypass* the operating system and interact directly with the resources it controls. It is limited to **system calls**, which are routines provided by an operating system to user applications.

Unix identifies a file with its **descriptor** as soon as it is opened by a program. A descriptor is nothing more than an integer value (like 42 or 999). A file is opened explicitly by invoking the **open** system call; however, three important files are opened as soon as a program starts and thus should not be managed manually. These are **stdin**, **stdout**, and **stderr**. Their descriptors are 0, 1, and 2, respectively. **stdin** is used to handle input, **stdout** to handle output, and **stderr** is used to output information about the program execution process but not its results (e.g., errors and diagnostics).

By default, keyboard input is linked to **stdin** and terminal output is linked to **stdout**. It means that "Hello, world!" should *write into* **stdout**.

Thus we need to invoke the **write** system call. It writes *a given amount of bytes* from memory starting at *a given address* to *a file with a given descriptor* (in our case, 1). The bytes will encode string characters using a predefined table (ASCII-table). Each entry is a character; an index in the table corresponds to its code in a range from 0 to 255.

See Listing 2-1 for our first complete example of an assembly program.

Listing 2-1. hello.asm

```
global _start

section .data
message: db 'hello, world!', 10

section .text
_start:
    mov     rax, 1          ;system call number should be stored in rax
    mov     rdi, 1          ; argument #1 in rdi: where to write (descriptor)?
```

```
mov     rsi, message    ; argument #2 in rsi: where does the string start?
mov     rdx, 14         ; argument #3 in rdx: how many bytes to write?
syscall                 ; this instruction invokes a system call
```

This program invokes a **write** system call with correct arguments on lines 6-9. It is really the only thing it does. The next sections will explain this sample program in greater detail.

2.2.2   Program Structure

As we remember from the von Neumann machine description, there is only one memory, for both code and data; those are indistinguishable. However, a programmer wants to separate them. An assembly program is usually divided into **sections**. Each section has its use: for example, .text holds instructions, .data is for **global variables** (data available in every moment of the program execution). One can switch back and forth between sections; in the resulting program all data, corresponding to each section, will be gathered in one place.

To get rid of numeric address values programmers use **labels**. They are just readable names and addresses. They can precede any command and are usually separated from it by a colon. There is one label in this program at line 5, _start.

A notion of variable is typical for higher-level languages. In assembly language, in fact, notions of variables and procedures are quite subtle. It is more convenient to speak about labels (or addresses).

An assembly program can be divided into multiple files. One of them should contain the _start label. It is the **entry point**; it marks the first instruction to be executed.

This label should be declared global (see line 1). The meaning of it will be evident later.

Comments start with a semicolon and last until the end of the line.

Assembly language consists of commands, which are directly mapped into machine code. However, not all language constructs are commands. Others control the translation process and are usually called **directives.**[1]

In the "Hello, world!" example there are three directives: global, section, and db.

■ **Note**   Assembly language is, in general, case insensitive, but label names are not!

mov, mOV, Mov are all the same thing, but global _start and global _START are not! Section names are case sensitive too: section .DATA and section .data differ!

The db directive is used to create byte data. Usually data is defined using one of these directives, which differ by data format:

- db—bytes;
- dw—so-called words, equal to 2 bytes each;
- dd—double words, equal to 4 bytes; and
- dq—quad words, equal to 8 bytes.

Let's see an example, in Listing 2-2.

Listing 2-2. data_decl.asm

```
section .data
    example1: db 5, 16, 8, 4, 2, 1
    example2: times 999 db 42
    example3: dw 999
```

---

[1]The NASM manual also uses the name "pseudo instruction" for a specific subset of directives.

`times` *n* cmd is a directive to repeat `cmd` *n* times in program code. As if you copy-pasted it *n* times. It also works with central processor unit (CPU) instructions.

Note that you can create data inside any section, including `.text`. As we told you earlier, for a CPU data and instructions are all alike and the CPU will try to interpret data as encoded instructions when asked to.

These directives allow you to define several data objects one by one, as in Listing 2-3, where a sequence of characters is followed by a single byte equal to 10.

Listing 2-3. `hello.asm`

```
message: db 'hello, world!', 10
```

Letters, digits, and other characters are encoded in ASCII. Programmers have agreed upon a table, where each character is assigned a unique number—its *ASCII-code*. We start at address corresponding to the label message. We store the ASCII codes for all letters of string `"hello, world!"`, then we add a byte equal to 10. Why 10? By convention, to start a new line we output a special character with code 10.

■ **Terminological chaos**   It is quite common to refer to the integer format most native to the computer as **machine word**. As we are programming a 64-bit computer, where addresses are 64-bit, general purpose registers are 64-bit, it is pretty convenient to take the machine word size as 64 bits or 8 bytes.

In assembly programming for Intel architecture the term **word** was indeed used to describe a 16-bit data entry, because on the older machines it was exactly the machine word. Unfortunately, for legacy reasons, it is still used as in old times. That's why 32-bit data is called double words and 64-bit data is referred to as quad words.

2.2.3   Basic Instructions

The `mov` instruction is used to write a value into either register or memory. The value can be taken from other register or from memory, or it can be an immediate one. However,

1. `mov` cannot copy data from memory to memory;

2. the source and the destination operands must be of the same size.

The `syscall` instruction is used to perform **system calls** in *nix systems. The input/output operations depend on hardware (which can be also used by multiple programs at the same time), so programmers are not allowed to control them directly, bypassing the operating system.

Each system call has a unique number. To perform it

1. The `rax` register has to hold system call's number;

2. The following registers should hold its arguments: `rdi`, `rsi`, `rdx`, `r10`, `r8`, and `r9`.

   System call cannot accept more than six arguments.

3. Execute `syscall` instruction.

It does not matter in which order the registers are initialized.

Note, that the `syscall` instruction changes `rcx` and `r11`! We will explain the cause later. When we wrote the "Hello, world!" program we used a simple `write` syscall. It accepts

1. **File descriptor**;

2. The buffer address. We start taking consecutive bytes for writing from here;

3. The amount of bytes to write.

To compile our first program, save the code in hello.asm[2] and then launch these commands in the shell:

```
> nasm -felf64 hello.asm -o hello.o
> ld -o hello hello.o
> chmod u+x hello
```

The details of compilation process along with compilation stages will be discussed in Chapter 5. Let's launch "Hello, world!"

```
> ./hello
hello, world!
Segmentation fault
```

We have clearly output what we wanted. However, the program seems to have caused an error. What did we do wrong? After executing a system call, the program continues its work. We did not write any instructions after syscall, but the memory holds indeed some random values in the next cells.

■ **Note** If you did not put anything at some memory address, it will certainly hold some kind of garbage, not zeroes or any kind of valid instructions.

A processor has no idea whether these values were intended to encode instructions or not. So, following its very nature, it tries to interpret them, because rip register points at them. It is highly unlikely these values encode correct instructions, so an interrupt with code 6 will occur (invalid instruction).[3]

So what do we do? We have to use the exit system call, which terminates the program in a correct way, as shown in Listing 2-4.

Listing 2-4. hello_proper_exit.asm

```
section .data
message: db 'hello, world!', 10

section .text
global _start

_start:
    mov     rax, 1          ; 'write' syscall number
    mov     rdi, 1          ; stdout descriptor
    mov     rsi, message    ; string address
    mov     rdx, 14         ; string length in bytes
    syscall

    mov     rax, 60         ; 'exit' syscall number
    xor     rdi, rdi
    syscall
```

---

[2]Remember: all source code, including listings, can be found on www.apress.com/us/book/9781484224021 and is also stored in the home directory of the preconfigured virtual machine!
[3]Even if not, soon the sequential execution will lead the processor to the end of allocated virtual addresses, see section 4.2. In the end, the operating system will terminate the program because it is unlikely that the latter will recover from it.

Question 11   What does instruction xor rdi, rdi do?

Question 12   What is the program return code?

Question 13   What is the first argument of the exit system call?

2.3   Example: Output Register Contents

Time to try something a bit harder. Let's output rax value in hexadecimal format, as shown in Listing 2-5.

Listing 2-5.   Print rax Value: print_rax.asm

```
section .data
codes:
    db      '0123456789ABCDEF'

section .text
global _start
_start:
    ; number 1122... in hexadecimal format
    mov rax, 0x1122334455667788

    mov rdi, 1
    mov rdx, 1
    mov rcx, 64
    ; Each 4 bits should be output as one hexadecimal digit
    ; Use shift and bitwise AND to isolate them
    ; the result is the offset in 'codes' array
.loop:
    push rax
    sub rcx, 4
    ; cl is a register, smallest part of rcx
    ; rax -- eax -- ax -- ah + al
    ; rcx -- ecx -- cx -- ch + cl
    sar rax, cl
    and rax, 0xf

    lea rsi, [codes + rax]
    mov rax, 1

    ; syscall leaves rcx and r11 changed
    push rcx
    syscall
    pop rcx

    pop rax
    ; test can be used for the fastest 'is it a zero?' check
    ; see docs for 'test' command
    test rcx, rcx
    jnz .loop
```

```
mov     rax, 60 ;           invoke 'exit' system call
xor     rdi, rdi
syscall
```

By shifting rax value and logical ANDing it with mask 0xF we transform the whole number into one of its hexadecimal digits. Each digit is a number from 0 to 15. Use it as an index and add it to the address of the label codes to get the representing character.

For example, given rax = 0x4A we will use indices 0x4 = 4_{10} and 0xA = 10_{10}.[4] The first one will give us a character '4' whose code is 0x34. The second one will result into character 'a' whose code is 0x61.

■ **Question 14**   Check that the ASCII codes mentioned in the last example are correct.

We can use a hardware stack to save and restore register values, like around syscall instruction.

■ **Question 15**   What is the difference between sar and shr? Check Intel docs.

■ **Question 16**   How do you write numbers in different number systems in a way understandable to NASM? Check NASM documentation.

■ **Note**   When a program starts, the value of most registers is not well defined (it can be absolutely random). It is a great source of rookie mistakes, as one tends to assume that they are zeroed.

2.3.1   Local Labels

Notice the unusual label name .loop: it starts with a dot. This label is local. We can reuse the label names without causing name conflicts as long as they are local.

The last used dotless global label is a base one for all subsequent local labels (until the next global label occurs). The full name for .loop label is _start.loop. We can use this name to address it from anywhere in the program, even after other global labels occurs.

2.3.2   Relative Addressing

This demonstrates how to address memory in a more complex way than just by immediate address.

Listing 2-6. Relative Addressing: print_rax.asm

```
lea rsi, [codes + rax]
```

Square brackets denote **indirect addressing;** the address is written inside them.

- mov rsi, rax—copies rax into rsi

- mov rsi, [rax]—copies memory contents (8 sequential bytes) starting at address, stored in rax, into rsi. How do we know that we have to copy exactly 8 bytes? As we know, mov operands are of the same size, and the size of rsi is 8 bytes. Knowing these facts, the assembler is able to deduce that exactly 8 bytes should be taken from memory.

---

[4]The subscript denotes the number system's base.

The instructions lea and mov have a subtle difference between their meanings. lea means "load effective address."

It allows you to calculate an address of a memory cell and store it somewhere. This is not always trivial, because there are tricky address modes (as we will see later): for example, the address can be a sum of several operands.

Listing 2-7 provides a quick demonstration of what lea and mov are doing.

Listing 2-7. lea_vs_mov.asm

```
; rsi <- address of label 'codes', a number
mov rsi, codes

; rsi <- memory contents starting at 'codes' address
; 8 consecutive bytes are taken because rsi is 8 bytes long
mov rsi, [codes]

; rsi <- address of 'codes'
; in this case it is equivalent of mov rsi, codes
; in general the address can contain several components
lea rsi, [codes]

; rsi <- memory contents starting at (codes+rax)
mov rsi, [codes + rax]

; rsi <- codes + rax
; equivalent of combination:
; -- mov rsi, codes
; -- add rsi, rax
; Can't do it with a single mov!
lea rsi, [codes + rax]
```

2.3.3   Order of Execution

All commands are executed consecutively except when special jump instructions occur. There is an unconditional jump instruction jmp addr. It can be viewed as a substitute of mov rip, addr.[5]

Conditional jumps rely on contents of rflags register. For example, jz address jumps to address only if zero flag is set.

Usually one uses either a test or a cmp instruction to set up necessary flags coupled with conditional jump instruction.

cmp subtracts the second operand from the first; it does not store the result anywhere, but it sets the appropriate flags based on it (e.g., if operands are equal, it will set zero flag). test does the same thing but uses logical AND instead of subtraction.

An example shown in Listing 2-8 incorporates writing 1 in rbx if rax < 42, and 0 otherwise.

---

[5]This action is impossible to encode using the mov command. Check Intel docs to verify that it is not implemented.

Listing 2-8. `jumps_example.asm`

```
    cmp rax, 42
    jl yes
    mov rbx, 0
    jmp ex
yes:
    mov rbx, 1
ex:
```

It is a common (and fast) way to test register value for being zero with `test reg,reg` instruction.

At least two commands exist for each arithmetic flag *F*: `jF` and `jnF`. For example, sign flag: `js` and `jns`. Other useful commands include

1. `ja` (jump if above)/`jb` (jump if below) for a jump after a comparison of *unsigned numbers* with `cmp`.

2. `jg` (jump if greater)/`jl` (jump if less) for *signed*.

3. `jae` (jump if above or equal), `jle` (jump if less or equal) and similar. Some of common jump instructions are shown in Listing 2-9.

Listing 2-9. Jump Instructions: `jumps.asm`

```
mov rax, -1
mov rdx, 2

cmp rax, rdx
jg location
ja location            ; different logic!

cmp rax, rdx
je  location           ; if rax equals rdx
jne location           ; if rax is not equal to rdx
```

■ **Question 17** What is the difference between `je` and `jz`?

2.4 Function Calls

Routines (functions) allow one to isolate a piece of program logic and use it as a black box. It is a necessary mechanism to provide abstraction. Abstraction allows you to build more complex systems by encapsulating complex algorithms under opaque interfaces.

Instruction `call <address>` is used to perform calls. It does exactly the following:

```
push rip
jmp <address>
```

The address now stored in the stack (former `rip` contents) is called **return address**.

Any function can accept an unlimited number of arguments. The first six arguments are passed in `rdi`, `rsi`, `rdx`, `rcx`, `r8`, and `r9`, respectively. The rest is passed on to the stack in reverse order.

What we consider an end to a routine is unclear. The most straightforward thing to say is that `ret` instruction denotes the function end. Its semantic is fully equivalent to `pop rip`.

Apparently, the fragile mechanism of `call` and `ret` only works when the state of the stack is carefully managed. One should not invoke `ret` unless the stack is exactly in the same state as when the function started. Otherwise, the processor will take whatever is on top of the stack as a return address and use it as the new `rip` content, which will certainly lead to executing garbage.

Now let's talk about how functions use registers. Obviously, executing a function *can change registers*. There are two types of registers.

- **Callee-saved registers** must be restored by the procedure being called. So, if it needs to change them, it has to change them back.

  These registers are callee-saved: `rbx`, `rbp`, `rsp`, `r12-r15`, a total of seven registers.

- **Caller-saved registers** should be saved before invoking a function and restored after. One does not have to save and restore them if their value will not be of importance after.

  All other registers are caller-saved.

These two categories *are a convention*. That is, a programmer must follow this agreement by

- Saving and restoring callee-saved registers.

- Being always aware that caller-saved registers can be changed during function execution.

▓ **A source of bugs** A common mistake is not saving caller-saved registers before `call` and using them after returning from function. Remember:

1. If you change `rbx`, `rbp`, `rsp`, or `r12-r15`, change them back!

2. If you need *any* other register to survive function call, save it yourself before calling!

Some functions can **return a value**. This value is usually the very essence of why the function is written and executed. For example, we can write a function that accepts a number as its argument and returns it squared.

Implementation-wise, we are returning values by storing them in `rax` before the function ends its execution. If you need to return two values, you are allowed to use `rdx` for the second one.

So, the pattern of calling a function is as follows:

- Save all caller-saved registers you want to survive function call
  (you can use `push` for that).

- Store arguments in the relevant registers (`rdi`, `rsi`, etc.).

- Invoke function using `call`.

- After function returns, `rax` will hold the return value.

- Restore caller-saved registers stored before the function call.

▓ **Why do we need conventions?** A function is used to abstract a piece of logic, forgetting completely about its internal implementation *and changing it when necessary*. Such changes should be completely transparent to the outside program. The convention described previously allows you to call any function from any given place and be sure about its effects (may change any caller-saved register; will keep callee-saved registers intact).

Some system calls also return values—be careful and read the docs!

You should never use `rbp` and `rsp`. They are implicitly used during the execution. As you already know, `rsp` is used as a stack pointer.

■ **On system call arguments**   The arguments for system calls are stored in a different set of registers than those for functions. The fourth argument is stored in r10, while a function accepts the fourth argument in rcx!

The reason is that syscall instruction implicitly uses rcx. System calls cannot accept more than six arguments.

If you do not follow the described convention, you will be unable to change your functions without introducing bugs in places where they are called.

Now it is time to write two more functions: print_newline will print the newline character; print_hex will accept a number and print it in hexadecimal format (see Listing 2-10).

Listing 2-10. print_call.asm

```asm
section .data

newline_char: db 10
codes: db '0123456789abcdef'

section .text
global _start

print_newline:
    mov rax, 1              ; 'write' syscall identifier
    mov rdi, 1              ; stdout file descriptor
    mov rsi, newline_char ; where do we take data from
    mov rdx, 1              ; the amount of bytes to write
    syscall
  ret

print_hex:
    mov rax, rdi

    mov rdi, 1
    mov rdx, 1
    mov rcx, 64            ; how far are we shifting rax?
iterate:
    push rax               ; Save the initial rax value
    sub rcx, 4
    sar rax, cl            ; shift to 60, 56, 52, ... 4, 0
                           ; the cl register is the smallest part of rcx
    and rax, 0xf           ; clear all bits but the lowest four
    lea rsi, [codes + rax]; take a hexadecimal digit character code

    mov rax, 1             ;

    push rcx               ; syscall will break rcx
    syscall                ; rax = 1 (31) -- the write identifier,
                           ;   rdi = 1 for stdout,
                           ; rsi = the address of a character, see line 29
```

```
    pop rcx

    pop rax                 ; ^ see line 24 ^
    test rcx, rcx           ; rcx = 0 when all digits are shown
    jnz iterate

    ret
_start:
    mov rdi, 0x1122334455667788
    call print_hex
    call print_newline

    mov rax, 60
    xor rdi, rdi
    syscall
```

2.5   Working with Data

2.5.1   Endianness

Let's try to output a value stored in memory using the function we just wrote. We are going to do it in two
different ways: first we will enumerate all its bytes separately and then we will type it as usual (see Listing 2-11).

Listing 2-11. endianness.asm

```
section .data
demo1: dq 0x1122334455667788
demo2: db 0x11, 0x22, 0x33, 0x44, 0x55, 0x66, 0x77, 0x88

section .text

_start:
    mov rdi, [demo1]
    call print_hex
    call print_newline

    mov rdi, [demo2]
    call print_hex
    call print_newline

    mov rax, 60
    xor rdi, rdi
    syscall
```

When we launch it, to our surprise, we get completely different results for demo1 and demo2.

```
> ./main
1122334455667788
8877665544332211
```

As we see, multi-byte numbers are stored in *reverse* order!

The bits in each byte are stored in a straightforward way, but the bytes are stored from the least significant to the most significant.

This applies only to memory operations: in registers, the bytes are stored in a natural way. Different processors have different conventions on how the bytes are stored.

- **Big endian** multibyte numbers are stored in memory starting with the *most* significant bytes.

- **Little endian** multibyte numbers are stored in memory starting with the *least* significant bytes.

As the example shows, Intel 64 is following the little endian convention. In general, choosing one convention over the other is a matter of choice, made by hardware engineers.

These conventions do not concern arrays and strings. However, if each character is encoded using 2 bytes rather than just 1, those bytes will be stored in reverse order.

The advantage of little endian is that we can discard the most significant bytes effectively converting the number from a wider format to a narrower one, like 8 bytes.

For example, `demo3: dq 0x1234`. Then, to convert this number into `dw` we have to read a `dword` number starting at the same address `demo3`. See Table 2-1 for a complete memory layout.

Table 2-1. *Little Endian and Big Endian for quad word number 0x1234*

ADDRESS	VALUE – LE	VALUE – BE
demo3	0x34	0x00
demo3 + 1	0x12	0x00
demo3 + 2	0x00	0x00
demo3 + 3	0x00	0x00
demo3 + 4	0x00	0x00
demo3 + 5	0x00	0x00
demo3 + 6	0x00	0x12
demo3 + 7	0x00	0x34

Big endian is a native format often used inside network packets (e.g., TCP/IP). It is also an internal number format for Java Virtual Machine.

Middle endian is a not very well-known notion. Assume we want to create a set of routines to perform arithmetic with 128-bit numbers. Then the bytes can be stored as follows: first will be the 8 least significant bytes in reversed order and then the 8 most significant bytes also in reverse order:

7 6 5 4 3 2 1 0, 16 15 14 13 12 11 10 9 8

2.5.2   Strings

As we already know, the characters are encoded using the ASCII table. A code is assigned to each character. A string is obviously a sequence of character codes. However, it does not say anything about how to determine its length.

1. Strings start with their explicit length.

```
db 27, 'Selling England by the Pound'
```

2. A special character denotes the string ending. Traditionally, the zero code is used. Such strings are called **null-terminated.**

```
db 'Selling England by the Pound', 0
```

2.5.3   Constant Precomputation

It is not uncommon to see such code:

```
lab: db 0
...
   mov rax, lab + 1 + 2*3
```

NASM supports arithmetic expressions with parentheses and bit operations. Such expressions can only include constants known to the compiler. This way it can precompute all such expressions and insert the computation results (as constant numbers) in executable code. So, such expressions are NOT calculated at runtime.

A runtime analogue would need to use such instructions as add or mul.

2.5.4   Pointers and Different Addressing Types

Pointers are addresses of memory cells. They can be stored in memory or in registers.

The pointer size is 8 bytes. Data usually occupies several memory cells (i.e., several consecutive addresses). The pointers hold no information about the pointed data length. When trying to write somewhere a value whose size is not specified and can not be deduced (for example, mov [myvariable], 4), we can get compilation errors. In such cases we have to provide size explicitly as shown below:

```
section .data
test: dq -1

section .text

mov byte[test], 1 ;1
mov word[test], 1 ;2
mov dword[test], 1 ;4
mov qword[test], 1 ;8
```

Question 18   What is test equal to after each of the commands listed previously?

Let's see how one can encode operands in instructions.

1. Immediately:

   An instruction is itself contained in memory. The operands in some form are its parts; those parts have addresses of their own. Many instructions can contain the operand values themselves.

   This is the way to move a number 10 into rax.

   ```
   mov rax, 10
   ```

2. Through a register:

This instruction transfers rbx value into rax.

```
mov rax, rbx
```

3. By direct memory addressing:

This instruction transfers 8 bytes starting at the tenth address into rax:

```
mov rax, [10]
```

We can also take the address from register:

```
mov r9, 10
mov  rax, [r9]
```

We can use precomputations:

```
buffer: dq 8841, 99, 00
...
mov rax, [buffer+8]
```

The address inside this instruction was precomputed, because both base and offset are constants in control of compiler. Now it is just a number.

4. Base-indexed with scale and displacement

Most addressing modes are generalized by this mode. The address here is calculated based on the following components:

$$Address = base + index * scale + displacement$$

- Base is either immediate or a register;

- Scale can only be immediate equal to 1, 2, 4, or 8;

- Index is immediate or a register; and

- Displacement is always immediate.

Listing 2-12 shows examples of different addressing types.

Listing 2-12. addressing.asm

```
mov rax, [rbx + 4* rcx + 9]
mov rax, [4*r9]
mov rdx, [rax + rbx]
lea rax, [rbx + rbx * 4]      ; rax = rbx * 5
add r8, [9 + rbx*8 + 7]
```

A big picture You can think about byte, word, etc. as about type specifiers. For instance, you can either push 16-, 32-, or 64-bit numbers into the stack. Instruction push 1 is unclear about how many bits wide the operand is. In the same way mov word[test], 1 signifies, that [test] is a word; there is an information about number format encoded in push word 1.

2.6 Example: Calculating String Length

Let's start by writing a function to calculate the length of a null-terminated string.

As we do not have a routine to print something to standard output, the only way to output value is to return it as an exit code through exit system call. To see the exit code of the last process use the $? variable.

```
> true
> echo $?
0
> false
> echo $?
1
```

Let's write an assembly program that mimics the false shell command, as shown in Listing 2-13.

Listing 2-13. false.asm

```
global _start

section .text
_start:
    mov rdi, 1
    mov rax, 60
    syscall
```

Now we have everything needed to calculate string length. Listing 2-14 shows the code.

Listing 2-14. String Length: strlen.asm

```
global _start

section .data

test_string: db "abcdef", 0

section .text

strlen:                     ; by our convention, first and the only argument
                            ; is taken from rdi
    xor rax, rax            ; rax will hold string length. If it is not
                            ; zeroed first, its value will be totally random

.loop:                      ; main loop starts here
    cmp byte [rdi+rax], 0   ; Check if the current symbol is null-terminator.
                            ; We absolutely need that 'byte' modifier since
                            ; the left and the right part of cmp should be
                            ; of the same size. Right operand is immediate
                            ; and holds no information about its size,
                            ; hence we don't know how many bytes should be
                            ; taken from memory and compared to zero
    je .end                 ; Jump if we found null-terminator
```

```
    inc rax                 ; Otherwise go to next symbol and increase
                            ; counter
    jmp .loop

.end:
    ret                     ; When we hit 'ret', rax should hold return value

_start:

    mov rdi, test_string
    call strlen
    mov rdi, rax

    mov rax, 60
    syscall
```

The important part (and the only part we will leave) is the strlen function. Notice, that

1. strlen changes registers, so after performing call strlen the registers *can* change their values.

2. strlen does not change rbx or any other callee-saved registers.

■ **Question 19**   Can you spot a bug or two in Listing 2-15? When will they occur?

Listing 2-15. Alternative Version of strlen: strlen_bug1.asm

```
global _start

section .data
test_string: db "abcdef", 0

section .text

strlen:
.loop:
    cmp byte [rdi+r13], 0
    je .end
    inc r13
    jmp .loop
.end:
    mov rax, r13
    ret

_start:
    mov rdi, test_string
    call strlen
    mov rdi, rax

    mov rax, 60
    syscall
```

2.7 Assignment: Input/Output Library

Before we start doing anything cool looking, we are going to ensure we won't have to code the same basic routines over and over again. As for now, we do not have anything; even getting keyboard input is a pain. So, let's build a small library for basic input and output functions.

First you have to read Intel docs [15] for the following instructions (remember, they are all described in details in the second volume):

- `xor`
- `jmp`, `ja`, and similar ones
- `cmp`
- `mov`
- `inc`, `dec`
- `add`, `imul`, `mul`, `sub`, `idiv`, `div`
- `neg`
- `call`, `ret`
- `push`, `pop`

These commands are core to us and you should know them well. As you might have noticed, Intel 64 supports thousands of commands. Of course, there is no need for us to dive there. Using system calls together with instructions listed earlier will get us pretty much anywhere.

You also have to read docs for the `read` system call. Its code is 0; otherwise it is similar to `write`. Refer to the Appendix C in case of difficulties.

Edit `lib.inc` and provide definitions for the functions instead of stub `xor rax, rax` instructions. Refer to Table 2-2 for the required functions' semantics. We do recommend implementing them in the given order because sometimes you will be able to reuse your code by calling functions you have already written.

Table 2-2. *Input/Output Library Functions*

Function	Definition
exit	Accepts an exit code and terminates current process.
string_length	Accepts a pointer to a string and returns its length.
print_string	Accepts a pointer to a null-terminated string and prints it to **stdout**.
print_char	Accepts a character code directly as its first argument and prints it to **stdout**.
print_newline	Prints a character with code 0xA.
print_uint	Outputs an unsigned 8-byte integer in decimal format.
	We suggest you create a buffer on the stack[6] and store the division results there. Each time you divide the last value by 10 and store the corresponding digit inside the buffer. Do not forget, that you should transform each digit into its ASCII code (e.g., 0x04 becomes0x34).
print_int	Output a signed 8-byte integer in decimal format.
read_char	Read one character from **stdin and return it**. If the end of input stream occurs, return 0.
read_word	Accepts a buffer address and size as arguments. Reads next word from **stdin** (skipping whitespaces[7] into buffer). Stops and returns 0 if word is too big for the buffer specified; otherwise returns a buffer address.
	This function should null-terminate the accepted string.
parse_uint	Accepts a null-terminated string and tries to parse an unsigned number from its start.
	Returns the number parsed in rax, its characters count in rdx.
parse_int	Accepts a null-terminated string and tries to parse a signed number from its start. Returns the number parsed in rax; its characters count in rdx (including sign if any). No spaces between sign and digits are allowed.
string_equals	Accepts two pointers to strings and compares them. Returns 1 if they are equal, otherwise 0.
string_copy	Accepts a pointer to a string, a pointer to a buffer, and buffer's length. Copies string to the destination. The destination address is returned if the string fits the buffer; otherwise zero is returned.

Use test.py to perform automated tests of correctness. Just run it and it will do the rest.

Remember, that a string of *n* characters needs *n* + 1 bytes to be stored in memory because of a null-terminator.

Read Appendix A to see how you can execute the program step by step observing the changes in register values and memory state.

2.7.1 Self-Evaluation

Before testing or when facing an unexpected result, check the following quick list:

1. Labels denoting functions should be global; others should be local.

2. You do not assume that registers hold zero "by default."

3. You save and restore callee-saved registers if you are using them.

---

[6]In fact, by decreasing rsp you allocate memory on the stack.

[7]We consider spaces, tabulation, and line breaks as whitespace characters. Their codes are 0x20, 0x9, and 0x10, respectively.

4. You save caller-saved registers you need before `call` and restore them after.

5. You do not use buffers in `.data`. Instead, you allocate them on the stack, which allows you to adapt multithreading if needed.

6. Your functions accept arguments in `rdi`, `rsi`, `rdx`, `rcx`, `r8`, and `r9`.

7. You do not print numbers digit after digit. Instead you transform them into strings of characters and use `print_string`.

8. `parse_int` and `parse_uint` are setting `rdx` correctly. It will be really important in the next assignment.

9. All parsing functions and `read_word` work when the input is terminated via Ctrl-D.

Done right, the code will not take more than 250 lines.

Question 20　Try to rewrite `print_newline` without calling `print_char` or copying its code. Hint: read about tail call optimization.

Question 21　Try to rewrite `print_int` without calling `print_uint` or copying its code. Hint: read about tail call optimization.

Question 22　Try to rewrite `print_int` without calling `print_uint`, copying its code, or using `jmp`. You will only need one instruction and a careful code placement.

Read about co-routines.

2.8　Summary

In this chapter we started to do real things and apply our basic knowledge about assembly language. We hope that you have overcome any possible fear of assembly. Despite being verbose to an extreme, it is not a hard language to use. We have learned to make branches and cycles and perform basic arithmetic and system calls; we have also seen different addressing modes, little and big endian. The following assembly assignments will use the little library we have built to facilitate interaction with user.

Question 23　What is the connection between `rax`, `eax`, `ax`, `ah`, and `al`?

Question 24　How do we gain access to the parts of `r9`?

Question 25　How can you work with a hardware stack? Describe the instructions you can use.

Question 26　Which ones of these instructions are incorrect and why?

```
mov [rax], 0
cmp [rdx], bl
mov bh, bl
mov al, al
```

```
add bpl, 9
add [9], spl
mov r8d, r9d
mov r3b, al
mov r9w, r2d
mov rcx, [rax + rbx + rdx]
mov r9, [r9 + 8*rax]
mov [r8+r7+10], 6
mov [r8+r7+10], r6
```

Question 27 Enumerate the callee-saved registers

Question 28 Enumerate the caller-saved registers

Question 29 What is the meaning of `rip` register?

Question 30 What is the SF flag?

Question 31 What is the ZF flag?

Question 32 Describe the effects of the following instructions:

- `sar`
- `shr`
- `xor`
- `jmp`
- `ja, jb,` and similar ones.
- `cmp`
- `mov`
- `inc,dec`
- `add`
- `imul, mul`
- `sub`
- `idiv, div`
- `call, ret`
- `push, pop`

■ **Question 33**   What is a label and does it have a size?

■ **Question 34**   How do you check whether an integer number is contained in a certain range (*x, y*)?

■ **Question 35**   What is the difference between `ja`/`jb` and `jg`/`jl`?

■ **Question 36**   What is the difference between `je` and `jz`?

■ **Question 37**   How do you test whether `rax` is zero without the `cmp` command?

■ **Question 38**   What is the program return code?

■ **Question 39**   How do we multiply `rax` by 9 using exactly one instruction?

■ **Question 40**   By using exactly two instructions (the first is `neg`), take an absolute value of an integer stored in `rax`.

■ **Question 41**   What is the difference between little and big endian?

■ **Question 42**   What is the most complex type of addressing?

■ **Question 43**   Where does the program execution start?

■ **Question 44**   `rax = 0x112233445567788`. We have performed `push rax`. What will be the contents of byte at address `[rsp+3]`?

CHAPTER 3

Legacy

This chapter will introduce you to the legacy processor modes, which are no longer used, and to their *mostly* legacy features, which are still relevant today. You will see how processors evolved and learn the details of protection rings implementation (privileged and user mode). You will also understand the meaning of Global Descriptor Table. While this information helps you understanding the architecture better, it is not crucial for assembly programming in user space.

As processors evolved, each new mode increased the machine word's length and added new features. A processor can function in one of the following modes:

- Real mode (the most ancient, 16-bit one);

- Protected (commonly referred as 32-bit one);

- Virtual (to emulate real mode inside protected);

- System management mode (for sleep mode, power management, etc.);

- Long mode, with which we are already a bit familiar.

We are going to take a closer look at real and protected mode.

3.1 Real mode

Real mode is the most ancient. It lacks virtual memory; the physical memory is addressed directly and general purpose registers are 16-bit wide.

So, neither rax nor eax exist yet, but ax, al, and ah do.

Such registers can hold values from 0 to 65535, so the amount of bytes we can address using one of them is 65536 bytes. Such memory region is called **segment**. Do not confuse it with protected mode segments or ELF (Executable and Linkable Format) file sections!

These are the registers usable in real mode:

- ip, flags;

- ax, bx, cx, dx, sp, bp, si, di;

- Segment registers: cs, ds, ss, es, (later also gs and fs).

As it was not straightforward to address more than 64 kilobytes of memory, engineers came up with a solution to use special **segment registers** in the following way:

- Each physical address consists of 20 bits (so, 5 hexadecimal digits).

© Igor Zhirkov 2017

I. Zhirkov, *Low-Level Programming*, DOI 10.1007/978-1-4842-2403-8_3

- Each logical address consists of two components. One is taken from a segment register and encodes the segment start. The other is an offset inside this segment. The hardware calculates the physical address from these components the following way:

  physical address = segment base * 16 + offset

  You can often see addresses written in form of `segment:offset`, for example: `4a40:0002, ds:0001, 7bd3:ah`.

As we already stated, programmers want to separate code from data (and stack), so they intend to use different segments for these code sections. Segment registers are specialized for that: `cs` stores the code segment start address, `ds` corresponds to data segment, and `ss` to stack segment. Other segment registers are used to store additional data segments.

Note that strictly speaking, the segment registers do not hold segments' starting addresses but rather their parts (the four most significant hexadecimal digits). By adding another zero digit to multiply it by 16_{10} we get the real segment starting address.

Each instruction referencing memory implicitly assumes usage of one of segment registers. Documentation clarifies the default segment registers for each instruction. However, common sense can help as well. For instance, `mov` is used to manipulate data, so the address is relative to the data segment.

```
mov al, [0004]    ; === mov al, ds:0004
```

It is possible to redefine the segment explicitly:

```
mov al, cs:[0004]
```

When the program is loaded, the loader sets `ip`, `cs`, `ss`, and `sp` registers so that `cs:ip` corresponds to the entry point, and `ss:sp` points on top of the stack.

The central processing unit (CPU) always starts in real mode, and then the main loader usually executes the code to explicitly switch it to protected mode and then to the long mode.

Real mode has numerous drawbacks.

- It makes multitasking very hard. The same address space is shared between all programs, so they should be loaded at different addresses. Their relative placement should usually be decided during compilation.

- Programs can rewrite each other's code or even operating system as they all live in the same address space.

- Any program can execute any instruction, including those used to set up the processor's state. Some instructions should only be used by the operating system (like those used to set up virtual memory, perform power management, etc.) as their incorrect usage can crash the whole system.

The protected mode was intended to solve these problems.

3.2   Protected Mode

Intel 80386 was the first processor implementing protected 32-bit mode.

It provides wider versions of registers (`eax`, `ebx`, ..., `esi`, `edi`) as well as new protection mechanisms: protection rings, virtual memory, and an improved segmentation.

These mechanisms isolated programs from one another, so an abnormal termination of one of them did not harm the others. Furthermore, programs were not able to corrupt other processes' memory.

The way of obtaining a segment starting address has changed compared to real mode. Now the start is calculated based on an entry in a special table, not by direct multiplication of segment register contents.

Linear address = segment base (taken from system table) + offset

Each of segment registers cs, ds, ss, es, gs, and fs stores so-called **segment selector**, containing an index in a special segment descriptor table and a little additional information. There are two types of segment descriptor tables: possibly numerous **LDT (Local Descriptor Table)** and only one **GDT (Global Descriptor Table)**.

LDTs were intended for a hardware task-switching mechanism; however, operating system manufacturers did not adapt it. Today programs are isolated by virtual memory, and LDTs are not used.

GDTR is a register to store GDT address and size.

Segment selectors are structured as shown in Figure 3-1.

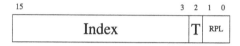

Figure 3-1. *Segment selector (contents of any segment register)*

Index denotes descriptor position in either GDT or LDT. The T bit selects either LDT or GDT. As LDTs are no longer used, it will be zero in all cases.

The table entries in GDT/LDT also store information about which privilege level is assigned to the described segment. When a segment is accessed through segment selector, a check of **Request Privilege Level** (RPL) value (stored in selector = segment register) against **Descriptor Privilege Level** (stored in descriptor table) is performed. If RPL is not privileged enough to access a high privileged segment, an error will occur. This way we could create numerous segments with various permissions and use RPL values in segment selectors to define which of them are accessible to us right now (given our privilege level).

Privilege levels are the same thing as protection rings!

It is safe to say that current privilege level (e.g., current ring) is stored in the lowest two bits of cs or ss (these numbers should be equal). This is what affects the ability to execute certain critical instructions (e.g., changing GDT itself).

It's easy to deduce that for ds, changing these bits allows us to override the current privilege level to be less privileged specifically for data access to a selected segment.

For example, we are currently in ring0 and ds= 0x02. Even though the lowest two bits of cs and ss are 0 (as we are inside ring0), we can't access data in a segment with privilege level higher than 2 (like 1 or 0).

In other words, the RPL field stores how privileged we are when requesting access to a segment. Segments in turn are assigned to one of four protection rings. When requesting access with a certain privilege level, the privilege level should be higher than the privilege level attributed to segment itself.

■ **Note** You can't change cs directly.

Figure 3-2 shows the GDT descriptor format[1].

---

[1]In this book we are approximating things a bit because certain data structures can have a different format based on page size, etc. The documentation will give you most precise answers (read volume 3, chapter 3 of [15]

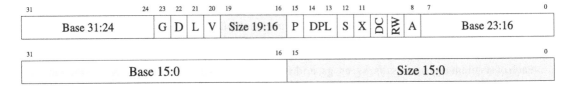

31		24	23	22	21	20	19		16	15	14	13	12	11				8	7			0
Base 31:24			G	D	L	V	Size 19:16			P	DPL		S	X	DC	RW	A		Base 23:16			

31		16	15		0
Base 15:0			Size 15:0		

Figure 3-2. Segment descriptor (inside GDT or LDT)

G—Granularity, e.g., size is in 0 = bytes, 1 = pages of size 4096 bytes each.
D—Default operand size (0 = 16 bit, 1 = 32 bit).
L—Is it a 64-bit mode segment?
V—Available for use by system software.
P—Present in memory right now.
S—Is it data/code (1) or is it just some system information holder (0).
X—Data (0) or code (1).
RW—For data segment, is writing allowed? (reading is always allowed); for code segment, is reading allowed? (writing is always prohibited).
DC—Growth direction: to lower or to higher addresses? (for data segment); can it be executed from higher privilege levels? (if code segment)
A—Was it accessed?
DPL—Descriptor Privilege Level (to which ring is it attached?)

The processor always (even today) starts in real mode. To enter protected mode one has to create GDT and set up gdtr; set a special bit in cr0 and make a so-called **far jump**. Far jump means that the segment (or segment selector) is explicitly given (and thus can be different from default), as follows:

```
jmp 0x08:addr
```

Listing 3-1 shows a small snippet of how we can turn on protected mode (assuming start32 is a label on 32-bit code start).

Listing 3-1. Enabling Protected Mode loader_start32.asm

```
lgdt cs:[_gdtr]

mov eax, cr0              ; !! Privileged instruction
or al, 1                 ; this is the bit responsible for protected mode
mov cr0, eax             ; !! Privileged instruction

    jmp (0x1 << 3):start32  ; assign first seg selector to cs

align 16
_gdtr:                   ; stores GDT's last entry index + GDT address
dw 47
dq _gdt

align 16

_gdt:
; Null descriptor (should be present in any GDT)
dd 0x00, 0x00
```

```
; x32 code descriptor:
db 0xFF, 0xFF, 0x00, 0x00, 0x00, 0x9A, 0xCF,    0x00 ; differ by exec bit
; x32 data descriptor:
db 0xFF, 0xFF, 0x00, 0x00, 0x00, 0x92, 0xCF,    0x00 ; execution off (0x92)
;  size  size  base  base  base  util  util|size base
```

Align directives control alignment, the essence of which we explain later in this book.

■ **Question 45**   Decipher this segment selector: 0x08.

You might think that every memory transaction needs another one now to read GDT contents. This is not true: for each segment register there is a so-called **shadow register**, which cannot be directly referenced. It serves as a cache for GDT contents. It means that once a segment selector is changed, the corresponding shadow register is loaded with the corresponding descriptor from GDT. Now this register will serve as a source of all information needed about this segment.

The D flag needs a little explanation, because it depends on segment type.

- It is a code segment: default address and operand sizes. One means 32-bit addresses and 32-bit or 8-bit operands; zero corresponds to 16-bit addresses and 16-bit or 8-bit operands. We are talking about encoding of machine instructions here. This behavior can be altered by preceding an instruction by a prefix 0x66 (to alter operand size) or 0x67 (to alter address size).

- Stack segment (it is a data segment AND we are talking about one selected by ss).[2] It is again default operand size for call, ret, push/pop, etc. If the flag is set, operands are 32-bit wide and instructions affect esp; otherwise operands are 16-bit wide and sp is affected.

- For data segments, growing toward low addresses, it denotes their limits (0 for 64 KB, 1 for 4 GB). This bit should always be set in long mode.

As you see, the segmentation is quite a cumbersome beast. There are reasons it was not largely adopted by operating systems and programmers alike (and is now pretty much abandoned).

- No segmentation is easier for programmers;

- No commonly used programming language includes segmentation in its memory model. It is always flat memory. So it is a compiler's job to set up segments (which is hard to implement).

- Segments make memory fragmentation a disaster.

- A descriptor table can hold up to 8192 segment descriptors. How can we use this small amount efficiently?

After the introduction of long mode segmentation was purged from processor, but not completely. It is still used for protection rings and thus a programmer should understand it.

---

[2]In this case, documentation names this flag B.

3.3   Minimal Segmentation in Long Mode

Even in long mode each time an instruction is selected, the processor is using segmentation. It provides us with a flat linear virtual address, which is then turned into a physical one by virtual memory routines (see section 4.2).

LDT is a part of a hardware context-switching mechanism that no one really adopted; for this reason it was disabled in long mode completely.

All memory addressing through *main* segment registers (cs, ds, es, and ss) do not consider the GDT values of base and offset anymore. The segment base is always fixed at 0x0 no matter the descriptor contents; the segment sizes are not limited at all. The other descriptor fields, however, are not ignored.

It means, that in long mode *at least three descriptors should be present in GDT*: the null descriptor (should be always present in any GDT), code, and data segments. If you want to use protection rings to implement privileged and user modes, you need also code and data descriptors for user-level code.

▪ **Why do we need separate descriptors for code and data?**   No combination of descriptor flags allows a programmer to set up read/write permissions and execution permission simultaneously.

Even with the very small experience in assembly language we already have, it is not hard to decipher this loader fragment, showing an exemplary GDT. It is taken from Pure64, an open source operating system loader. As it is executed before the operating system, it does not contain user-level code or data descriptors (see Listing 3-2).

Listing 3-2. A Sample GDT gdt64.asm

```
align 16  ; This ensures that the next command or data element is
; stored starting at an address divisible by 16 (even if we need
; to skip some bytes to achieve that).

; The following will be copied to GDTR via LGDTR instruction:

GDTR64:                     ; Global Descriptors Table Register
    dw gdt64_end - gdt64 - 1 ; limit of GDT (size minus one)
    dq 0x0000000000001000    ; linear address of GDT

; This structure is copied to 0x0000000000001000
gdt64:
SYS64_NULL_SEL equ $-gdt64       ; Null Segment
    dq 0x0000000000000000
; Code segment, read/exec, nonconforming
SYS64_CODE_SEL equ $-gdt64
    dq 0x0020980000000000        ; 0x00209A0000000000
; Data segment, read/write, expand down
SYS64_DATA_SEL equ $-gdt64
    dq 0x0000900000000000        ; 0x0020920000000000
gdt64_end:

; Dollar sign denotes the current memory address, so
; $-gdt64 means an offset from `gdt64` label in bytes
```

3.4 Accessing Parts of Registers

3.4.1 An Unexpected Behavior

We are usually thinking about eax, rax, ax, etc. as parts of a same physical register. The observable behavior mostly supports this hypothesis unless we are writing into a 32-bit part of a 64-bit register. Let us take a look at the example shown in Listing 3-3.

Listing 3-3. The Land of Registry Wonders risc_cisc.asm

```
mov rax, 0x1122334455667788    ; rax = 0x1122334455667788
mov eax, 0x42                  ; !rax = 0x00 00 00 00 00 00 00 42
                               ; why not rax = 0x1122334400000042 ??

mov rax, 0x1122334455667788    ; rax = 0x1122334455667788
mov ax, 0x9999                 ; rax = 0x1111222233339999, as expected
                               ; this works as expected

mov rax, 0x1122334455667788    ; rax = 0x1122334455667788
xor eax, eax                   ; rax = 0x0000000000000000
                               ; why not rax = 0x1122334400000000?
```

As you see, writing in 8-bit or 16-bit parts leaves the rest of bits intact. Writing to 32-bit parts, however, fills the upper half of a wide register with sign bit!

The reason is that how programmers are used to perceiving a processor is much different from how things are really done inside. In reality, registers rax, eax, and all others do not exist as fixed physical entities.

To explain this inconsistency, we have to first elaborate two types of instruction sets: CISC and RISC.

3.4.2 CISC and RISC

One of possible processors' classification divides processors based on their instruction set. When designing one there are two extremes.

- Make loads of specialized, high-level instructions. It corresponds to **CISC (Complete Instruction Set Computer)** architectures.

- Use only few primitive instructions, making a **RISC (Reduced Instruction Set Computer)** architecture.

CISC instructions are usually slower but also do more; sometimes it is possible to implement complex instructions in a better way, than by combining primitive RISC instructions (we will see an example of that later in this book when studying SSE (Streaming SIMD Extensions) in Chapter 16). However, most programs are written in high-level languages and thus depend on compilers. It is very hard to write a compiler that makes a good use of a rich instruction set.

RISC eases the job of compilers and is also friendlier to optimizations on a lower, microcode level, such as pipelines.

■ **Question 46**   Read about microcode in general and processor pipelines.

The Intel 64 instruction set is indeed a CISC one. It has thousands of instructions—just look at the second volume of [15]! However, these instructions are decoded and translated into a stream of simpler microcode instructions. Here various optimizations take effect; the microcode instructions are reordered and some of them can even be executed simultaneously. This is not a native feature of processors but rather an adaptation aimed at better performance together with backward compatibility with older software.

It is quite unfortunate that there is not much information available on the microcode-level details of modern processors. By reading technical reviews such as [17] and optimization manuals such as the one provided by Intel, you can develop a certain intuition about it.

3.4.3   Explanation

Now back to the example shown in Listing 3-3. Let's think about instruction decoding. The part of a CPU called instruction decoder is constantly translating commands from an older CISC system to a more convenient RISC one. Pipelines allow for a simultaneous execution of up to six smaller instructions. To achieve that, however, the notion of registers should be virtualized. During microcode execution, the decoder chooses an available register from a large bank of physical registers. As soon as the bigger instruction ends, the effects become visible to programmer: the value of some physical registers may be copied to those, currently assigned to be, let's say, rax.

The data interdependencies between instructions stall the pipeline, decreasing performance. The worst cases occur when the same register is read and modified by several consecutive instructions (think about rflags!).

If modifying eax means keeping upper bits of rax intact, it introduces an additional dependency between current instruction and whatever instruction modified rax or its parts before. By discarding upper 32 bits on each write to eax we eliminate this dependency, because we do not care anymore about previous rax value or its parts.

This kind of a new behavior was introduced with the latest general purpose registers' growth to 64 bits and does not affect operations with their smaller parts for the sake of compatibility. Otherwise, most older binaries would have stopped working because assigning to, for example, bl, would have modified the entire ebx, which was not true back when 64-bit registers had not yet been introduced.

3.5   Summary

This chapter was a brief historical note on processor evolution over the last 30 years. We have also elaborated on the intended use of segments back in the 32-bit era, as well as which leftovers of segmentation we are stuck with for legacy reasons. In the next chapter we are going to take a closer look at the virtual memory mechanism and its interaction with protection rings.

CHAPTER 4

Virtual Memory

This chapter covers virtual memory as implemented in Intel 64. We are going to start by motivating an abstraction over physical memory and then getting a general understanding of how it looks like from a programmer's perspective. Finally, we will dive into implementation details to achieve a more complete understanding.

4.1 Caching

Let's start with a truly omnipresent concept called caching.

The Internet is a big data storage. You can access any part of it, but the delay after you made a query can be significant. To smoothen your browsing experience, web browser caches web pages and their elements (images, style sheets, etc.). This way it does not have to download the same data over and over again. In other words, the browser saves the data on the hard drive or in RAM (random access memory) to give much faster access to a local copy. However, downloading the whole Internet is not an option, because the storage on your computer is very limited.

A hard drive is much bigger than RAM but also a great deal slower. This is why all work with data is done after preloading it in RAM. Thus main memory is being used as a cache for data from external storage.

Anyway, a hard drive also has a cache on its own...

On CPU crystal there are several levels of data caches (usually three: L1, L2, L3). Their size is much smaller than the size of main memory, but they are much faster too (the closest level to the CPU is almost as close as registers). Additionally, CPUs possess at least an **instruction cache** (queue storing instructions) and a **Translation Lookaside Buffer** to improve virtual memory performance.

Registers are even faster than caches (and smaller) so they are a cache on their own.

Why is this situation so pervasive? In information system, which does not need to give strict guarantees about its performance levels, introducing caches often *decreases the average access time* (the time between a request and a response). To make it work we need our old friend **locality**: in each moment of time we only have a small working set of data.

The virtual memory mechanism allows us, among other things, to use physical memory as a cache for chunks of program code and data.

4.2 Motivation

Naturally, given a single task system where there is only one program running at any moment of time, it is wise just to put it directly into physical memory starting at some fixed address. Other components (device drivers, libraries) can also be placed into memory in some fixed order.

© Igor Zhirkov 2017
I. Zhirkov, *Low-Level Programming*, DOI 10.1007/978-1-4842-2403-8_4

In a multitasking-friendly system, however, we prefer a framework supporting a parallel (or pseudo parallel) execution of multiple programs. In this case an operating system needs some kind of memory management to deal with these challenges:

- Executing programs of arbitrary size (maybe even greater than physical memory size). It demands an ability to load only those parts of program we need in the near future.

- Having several programs in memory at the same time.

   Programs can interact with external devices, whose response time is usually slow. During a request to a slow piece of hardware that may last thousands of cycles, we want to lend precious CPUs to other programs. Fast switching between programs is only possible if they are already in memory; otherwise we have to spend much time retrieving them from external storage.

- Storing programs in any place of physical memory.

   If we achieve that, we can load pieces of programs in any free part of the memory, even if they are using absolute addressing.

   In case of absolute addressing, like `mov rax, [0x1010ffba]`, all addresses including starting address become fixed: all exact address values are written into machine code.

- Freeing programmers from memory management tasks as much as possible.

   While programming, we do not want to think about how different memory chips on our target architectures can function, what is the amount of physical memory available, etc. Programmers should pay closer attention to program logic instead.

- Effective usage of shared data and code.

   Whenever several programs want to access the same data or code (libraries) files, it is a waste to duplicate them in memory for each additional user.

Virtual memory usage addresses these challenges.

4.3 Address Spaces

Address space is a range of addresses. We see two types of address spaces:

- Physical address, which is used to access the bytes on the real hardware. Naturally, there is a certain memory capacity a processor cannot exceed. It is based on addressing capabilities. For example, a 32-bit system cannot address more than 4GB of memory per process, because 2^{32} different addresses roughly correspond to 4GB of addressed memory. However, we could put less memory inside the machine capable of addressing 4GB, like, 1GB or 2GB. In this case some addresses of the physical address space will become forbidden, because there are no real memory cells behind them.

- Logical address is the address as an application sees it.

  In instruction `mov rax, [0x10bfd]` there is a logical address: `0x10bfd`.

  A programmer has an illusion that he is the *sole memory user*. Whatever memory cell he addresses, he never sees data or instructions of other programs, which are running with his own in parallel. Physical memory holds several programs at time, however.

  In our circumstances **virtual address** is synonymous to logical address.

Translation between these two address types is performed by a hardware entity called **Memory Management Unit (MMU)** with help of multiple translation tables, residing in memory.

4.4 Features

Virtual memory is an abstraction over physical memory. Without it we would work directly with physical memory addresses.

In the presence of virtual memory we can pretend that every program is the only memory consumer, because it is isolated from others in its own address space.

The address space of a single process is split into **pages** of equal length (usually 4KB). These pages are then dynamically managed. Some of them can be backed up to external storage (in a **swap file**), and brought back in case of a need.

Virtual memory offers some useful features, by assigning an unusual meaning to memory operations (read, write) on certain memory pages.

- We can communicate with external devices by means of Memory Mapped Input/ Output (e.g., by writing to the addresses, assigned to some device, and reading from them).

- Some pages can correspond to files, taken from external storage with the help of the operating system and file system.

- Some pages can be shared among several processes.

- Most addresses are **forbidden**—their value is not defined, and an attempt to access them results in an error.[1] This situation usually results in abnormal termination of program.

  Linux and other Unix-based systems use a **signal** mechanism to notify applications of exceptional situations. It is possible to assign a handler to almost all types of signals.

  Accessing a forbidden address will be intercepted by the operating system, which will throw a `SIGSEGV` signal at the application. It is quite common to see an error message, `Segmentation fault`, in this situation.

- Some pages correspond to files, taken from storage (executable file itself, libraries, etc.), but some do not. These **anonymous pages** correspond to memory regions of stack and **heap** —dynamically allocated memory. They are called so because there are no names in file system to which they correspond. To the contrary, an image of the running executable data files and devices (which are abstracted as files too) all have names in the file system.

---

[1]An interrupt #PF (Page Fault) occurs.

A continuous area of memory is called a **region** if:

- It starts at an address, which is multiple of a page size (e.g., 4KB).

- All its pages have the same permissions.

If the free physical memory is over, some pages can be swapped to external storage and stored in a swap file, or just discarded (in case they correspond to some files in file system and were not changed, for example). In Windows, the file is called PageFile.sys, in *nix systems a dedicated partition is usually allocated on disk. The choice of pages to be swapped is described by one of the **replacement strategies**, such as:

- Least recently used.

- Last recently used.

- Random (just pick a random page).

Any kind of a system with caching has a replacement strategy.

■ **Question 47**   Read about different replacement strategies. What other strategies exist?

Each process has a **working set** of pages. It consists of his exclusive pages present in physical memory.

■ **Allocation**   What happens when a process needs more memory? It cannot get more pages on its own, so it asks the operating system for more pages. The system provides it with additional *addresses*.

Dynamic memory allocation in higher-level languages (C++, Java, C#, etc.) eventually ends up querying pages from the operating system, using the allocated pages until the process runs out of memory and then querying more pages.

4.5   Example: Accessing Forbidden Address

Now we are going to see a **memory map** of a single process with our own eyes. It shows which pages are available and what they correspond to. We will observe different kinds of memory regions:

1. Corresponding to executable file, loaded into memory, itself.

2. Corresponding to code libraries.

3. Corresponding to stack and heap (**anonymous pages**).

4. Just empty regions of forbidden addresses.

Linux offers us an easy-to-use mechanism to explore various useful information about processes, called procfs. It implements a special purpose file system, where by navigating directories and viewing files, one can get access to any process's memory, environment variables, etc. This file system is mounted in the /proc directory.

Most notably, the file /proc/PID/maps shows a memory map of process with identifier PID.[2]

---

[2]To find the process identifier, use such standard programs as ps or top.

Let's write a simple program, which enters a loop (and thus does not terminate) (Listing 4-1). It will allow us to see its memory layout while it is running.

Listing 4-1. `mappings_loop.asm`

```
section .data
correct: dq -1
section .text

global _start
_start:
jmp _start
```

Now we have to launch a file `/proc/?/maps`, where ? is the process ID. See the complete terminal contents in Listing 4-2.

Listing 4-2. `mappings_loop`

```
> nasm -felf64 -o main.o mappings_loop.asm
> ld -o main main.o
> ./main &
[1] 2186
> cat /proc/2186/maps
00400000-00401000 r-xp 00000000 08:01 144225 /home/stud/main
00600000-00601000 rwxp 00000000 08:01 144225 /home/stud/main
7fff11ac0000-7fff11ae1000 rwxp 00000000 00:00 0 [stack]
7fff11bfc000-7fff11bfe000 r-xp 00000000 00:00 0 [vdso]
7fff11bfe000-7fff11c00000 r--p 00000000 00:00 0 [vvar]
ffffffffff600000-ffffffffff601000 r-xp 00000000 00:00 0 [vsyscall]
```

Left column defines the memory region range. As you may notice, all regions are contained between addresses ending with three hexadecimal zeros. The reason is that they are composed of pages whose size is 4KB each (= 0x1000 bytes).

We observe that different sections defined in the assembly file were loaded as different regions. The first region corresponds to the code section and holds encoded instructions; the second corresponds to data.

As you see, the address space is huge and spans from 0-th to $2^{64} - 1$-th byte. However, only a few addresses are allocated; the rest are being forbidden.

The second column shows read, write, and execution permissions on pages. It also indicates whether the page is **shared** among several processes or it is **private** to this specific process.

▓ **Question 48**   Read about meaning of the fourth (`08:01`) and fifth (`144225`) column in `man procfs`.

So far we did nothing wrong. Now let's try to write into a forbidden location.

Listing 4-3. Producing segfault: `segfault_badaddr.asm`

```
section .data
correct: dq -1
section .text
global _start
_start:
mov rax, [0x400000-1]
```

```
; exit
mov rax, 60
xor rdi, rdi
syscall
```

We are accessing memory at address 0x3fffff, which is one byte before the code segment start. This address is forbidden and hence the writing attempt results in a segmentation fault, as the message suggests.

```
> ./main Segmentation fault
```

4.6   Efficiency

Loading a missing page into physical memory from a swap file is a very costly operation, involving a huge amount of work from operating system. How come this mechanism turned out not only to be effective memory-wise but also to perform adequately? The key success factors are:

1. Thanks to locality, the need to load additional pages occurs rarely. In the worst case we have indeed very slow access; however, such cases are extremely rare. Average access time stays low.

   In other words, we rarely try to access a page which is not loaded in physical memory.

2. It is clear that efficiency could not be achieved without the help of special hardware. Without a cache of translated page addresses **TLB (Translation Lookaside Buffer)** we would have to use a translation mechanism all the time. TLB stores the starting physical addresses for some pages we will likely to work with. If we translate a virtual address inside one of these pages, the page start will be immediately fetched from TLB.

   In other words, we rarely try to translate an address from a page, that we did not recently locate in physical memory.

Remember that a program that uses less memory can be faster because it produces fewer page faults.

■ **Question 49**   What is an associative cache? Why is TLB one?

4.7   Implementation

Now we are going to dive into details and see how exactly the translation happens.

■ **Note**   For now we are only talking about a dominant case of 4KB pages. Page size can be tuned and other parameters will change accordingly; refer to section 4.7.3 and [15] for additional details.

4.7.1   Virtual Address Structure

Each virtual 64-bit address (e.g., ones we are using in our programs) consists of several fields, as shown in Figure 4-1.

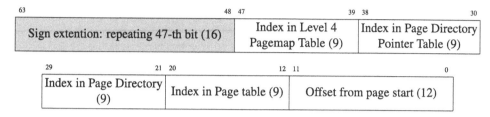

Figure 4-1. *Structure of virtual address*

The address itself is in fact only 48 bits wide; it is sign-extended to a 64-bit **canonical address**. Its characteristic is that its 17 left bits are equal. If the condition is not satisfied, the address gets rejected immediately when used.

Then 48 bits of virtual address are transformed into 52 bits of physical address with the help of special tables.[3]

■ **Bus Error**   When occasionally using a non-canonical address you will see another error message: `Bus error`.

Physical address space is divided into slots to be filled with virtual pages. These slots are called **page frames**. There are no gaps between them, so they always start from an address ending with 12 zero bits.

The least significant 12 bits of virtual address and of physical page correspond to the address offset inside page, so they are equal.

The other four parts of virtual address represent indexes in translation tables. Each table occupies exactly 4KB to fill an entire memory page. Each record is 64 bits wide; it stores a part of the next table's starting address as well as some service flags.

4.7.2   Address Translation in Depth

Figure 4-2 reflects the address translation process.

---

[3]Theoretically we could support all 64 bits of physical addresses, but we do not need that many addresses yet.

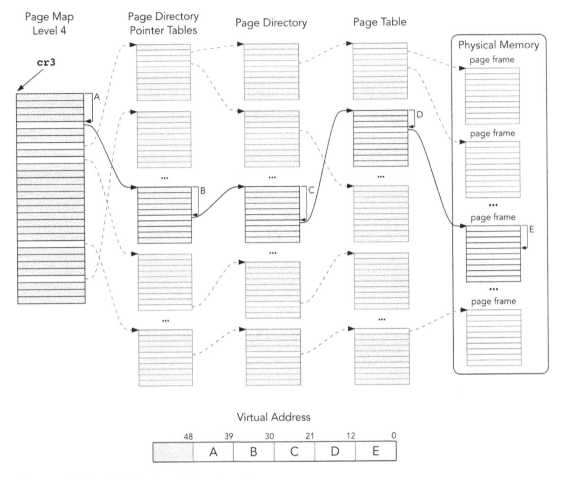

Figure 4-2. *Virtual address translation schematic*

First, we take the first table starting address from `cr3`. The table is called **Page Map Level 4 (PML4)**. Fetching elements from PML4 is performed as follows:

- Bits 51:12 are provided by `cr3`.

- Bits 11:3 are bits 47:39 of the virtual address.

- The last three bits are zeroes.

The entries of PML4 are referred as PML4E. The next step of fetching an entry from the Page Directory Pointer table mimics the previous one:

- Bits 51:12 are provided by selected PML4E.

- Bits 11:3 are bits 38:30 of the virtual address.

- The last three bits are zeroes.

The process iterates through two more tables until at last we fetch the page frame address (to be precise, its 51:12 bits). The physical address will use them and 12 bits will be taken directly from the virtual address.

Are we going to perform so many memory reads instead of one now? Yes, it does look bulky. However, thanks to the page address cache, **TLB**, we usually access memory on already translated and memorized pages. We should only add the correct offset inside page, which is blazingly fast.

As TLB is an associative cache; it is quickly providing us with translated page addresses given a starting virtual address of the page.

Note that translation pages can be cached for a faster access. Figure 4-3 specifies the Page Table Entry format.

63	62	61	60	59	58	57	56	55	54	53	52	51	50	49	48	47	46	45	44	43	42	41	40	39	38	37	36	35	34	33	32
EXB				Reserved																Page frame 47:32											

31	30	29	28	27	26	25	24	23	22	21	20	19	18	17	16	15	14	13	12	11	10	9	8	7	6	5	4	3	2	1	0
Page frame 31:12																				AVL			misc			D	A	PCD	PWT	U	W	P

Figure 4-3. *Page table entry*

P   Present (in physical memory)
W   Writable (writing is allowed)
U   User (can be accessed from ring3)
A   Accessed
D   Dirty (page was modified after being loaded—e.g., from disk)
EXB   Execution-Disabled Bit (forbids executing instructions on this page)
AVL   Available (for operating system developers)
PCD   Page Cache Disable
PWT   Page Write-Through (bypass cache when writing to page)

If P is not set, an attempt to access the page results in an interrupt with code #PF (Page fault). The operating system can handle it and load the respective page. It can also be used to implement lazy file memory mapping. The file parts will be loaded in memory as needed.

The operating system uses W bit to protect the page from being modified. It is needed when we want to share code or data between processes, avoiding unnecessary doubling. Shared pages marked with W can be used for data exchange between processes.

Operating system pages have U bit cleared. If we try to access them from ring3, an interrupt will occur.

In absence of segment protection the virtual memory is the ultimate memory guarding mechanism.

▪ **On segmentation faults**   In general, segmentation faults occurs when there is an attempt to access memory with insufficient permissions (e.g., writing into read-only memory). In case of forbidden addresses we can consider them to have no valid permissions, so accessing them is just a particular case of memory access with insufficient permissions.

EXB (also called NX) bit forbids code execution. The **DEP** (Data Execution Prevention) technology is based on it. When a program is being executed, parts of its input can be stored in a stack or its data section. A malicious user can exploit its vulnerabilities to mix encoded instructions into the input and then execute them. However, if data and stack section pages are marked with EXB, no instructions can be executed from them. The .text section, however, will remain executable, but it is usually protected from any modifications by W bit anyway.

4.7.3   Page Sizes

The structure of tables of a different hierarchy level is very much alike. The page size may be tuned to be 4KB, 2MB, or 1GB. Depending on the structure, this hierarchy can shrink to a minimum of two levels. In this case PDP will function as a page table and will store part of a 1GB frame. See Figure 4-4 to see how the entry format changes depending on page size.

PDP partial format: either maps 1GB pages or transfers to the next level

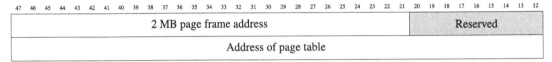

PD partial format: either maps 2MB pages or transfers to the next level

Figure 4-4. *Page Directory Pointer table and Page Directory table entry format*

This is controlled by the 7-th bit in the respective PDP or PD entry. If it is set, the respective table maps pages; otherwise, it stores addresses of the next level tables.

4.8   Memory Mapping

Mapping means "projection," making correspondence between entities (files, devices, physical memory), and virtual memory regions. When the loader fills the process's address space, when a process requests pages from the operating system, when the operating system projects files from a disk into processes' address spaces—these are examples of memory mapping.

A system call mmap is used for all types of memory mapping. To perform it we follow the same simple steps described in Chapter 2. Table 4-1 shows its arguments.

Table 4-1. *mmap System Call*

REGISTER	VALUE	MEANING
rax	9	System call identifier
rdi	addr	An operating system attempts to map into pages starting from this specific address. This address should correspond to a page start. A zero address indicates that the operating system is free to choose any start.
rsi	len	Region size
rdx	prot	Protection flags (read, write, execute...)
r10	flags	Utility flags (shared or private, anonymous pages, etc.)
r8	fd	Optional descriptor of a mapped file. The file should therefore be opened.
r9	offset	Offset in file.

After a call to `mmap`, `rax` will hold a pointer to the newly allocated pages.

4.9 Example: Mapping File into Memory

We need another system call, namely, `open`. It is used to open a file by name and to acquire its **descriptor**. See Table 4-2 for details.

Table 4-2. *open System Call*

REGISTER	VALUE	MEANING
rax	2	System call identifier
rdi	file name	Pointer to a null-terminated string, `name.holding` file
rsi	flags	A combination of permission flags (read only, write only, or both).
rdx	mode	If `sys open` is called to create a file, it will hold its file system permissions.

Mapping file in memory is done in three simple steps:

- Open file using `open` system call. `rax` will hold file descriptor.

- Call `mmap` with relevant arguments. One of them will be the file descriptor, acquired at step 1.

- Use `print_string` routine we have created in Chapter 2. For the sake of brevity we omit file closing and error checks.

4.9.1 Mnemonic Names for Constants

Linux was written in C, so to ease interaction with it some useful constants are predefined in a C way. The line

```
#define NAME 42
```

defines a substitution performed in compile time. Whenever a programmer writes `NAME`, the compiler substitutes it with 42. This is useful to create mnemonic names for various constants. NASM provides similar functionality using

```
%define directive
%define NAME  42
```

See section 5.1 "Preprocessor" for more details on how such substitutions are made.

Let's take a look at a man page for `mmap` system call, describing its third argument `prot`.

The prot argument describes the desired memory protection of the mapping (and must not conflict with the open mode of the file). It is either `PROT_NONE` or the bitwise OR of one or more of the following flags:

```
PROT_EXEC  Pages may be executed.

PROT_READ  Pages may be read.
```

PROT_WRITE Pages may be written.

PROT_NONE Pages may not be accessed.

PROT_NONE and its friends are examples of such mnemonic names for integers used to control mmap behavior. Remember that both C and NASM allow you to perform compile-time computations on constant values, including bitwise AND and OR operations. Following is an example of such computation:

```
%define PROT_EXEC 0x4
%define PROT_READ 0x1

  mov rdx, PROT_READ | PROT_EXEC
```

Unless you are writing in C or C++, you will have to check these predefined values somewhere and copy them to your program.

Following is how to know the specific values of these constants for Linux:

1. Search them in header files of the Linux API in /usr/include.

2. Use one of the Linux Cross Reference (lxr) online, like: http://lxr.free-electrons.com.

We do recommend the second way for now, as we do not know C yet. You may even use a search engine like Google and type lxr PROT_READ as a search query to get relevant results immediately after following the first link.

For example, here is what LXR shows when being queried PROT_READ:

PROT_READ

```
Defined as a preprocessor macro in:
arch/mips/include/uapi/asm/mman.h, line 18
arch/xtensa/include/uapi/asm/mman.h, line 25
arch/alpha/include/uapi/asm/mman.h, line 4
arch/parisc/include/uapi/asm/mman.h, line 4
include/uapi/asm-generic/mman-common.h, line 9
```

By following one of these links you will see

```
18 #define PROT_READ      0x01          /* page can be read */
```

So, we can type %define PROT_READ 0x01 in the beginning of the assembly file to use this constant without memorizing its value.

4.9.2   Complete Example

Create a file test.txt with any contents and then compile and launch the file listed in Listing 4-4 in the same directory. You will see file contents written to stdout.

Listing 4-4. mmap.asm

```
; These macrodefinitions are copied from linux sources
; Linux is written in C, so the definitions looked a bit
; different there.
; We could have just looked up their values and use
; them directly in right places
; However it would have made the code much less legible

%define O_RDONLY 0
%define PROT_READ 0x1
%define MAP_PRIVATE 0x2

section .data
; This is the file name. You are free to change it.
fname: db 'test.txt', 0

section .text
global _start

; These functions are used to print a null terminated string
print_string:
    push rdi
    call string_length
    pop rsi
    mov rdx, rax
    mov rax, 1
    mov rdi, 1
    syscall
    ret
string_length:
    xor rax, rax
.loop:
    cmp byte [rdi+rax], 0
    je .end
    inc rax
    jmp .loop
.end:
    ret

_start:
; call open
mov rax, 2
mov rdi, fname
mov rsi, O_RDONLY       ; Open file read only
mov rdx, 0              ; We are not creating a file
                       ; so this argument has no meaning
syscall
```

```
; mmap
mov r8, rax            ; rax holds opened file descriptor
                       ; it is the fourth argument of mmap
mov rax, 9             ; mmap number
mov rdi, 0             ; operating system will choose mapping destination
mov rsi, 4096          ; page size
mov rdx, PROT_READ     ; new memory region will be marked read only
mov r10, MAP_PRIVATE   ; pages will not be shared

mov r9, 0              ; offset inside test.txt
syscall                ; now rax will point to mapped location

mov rdi, rax
call print_string

mov rax, 60            ; use exit system call to shut down correctly
xor rdi, rdi
syscall
```

4.10 Summary

In this chapter we have studied the concept and the implementation of virtual memory. We have elaborated it as a particular case of caching. Then we have reviewed the different types of address spaces (physical, virtual) and the connection between them through a set of translation tables. Then we dived into the virtual memory implementation details.

Finally, we have provided a minimal working example of the memory the mapping using Linux system calls. We will use it again in the assignment for Chapter 13, where we will base our dynamic memory allocator on it. In the next chapter we are going to study the process of translation and linkage to see how an operating system uses the virtual memory mechanism to load and execute programs.

Question 50   What is virtual memory region?

Question 51   What will happen if you try to modify the program execution code during its execution?

Question 52   What are forbidden addresses?

Question 53   What is a canonical address?

Question 54   What are the translation tables?

Question 55   What is a page frame?

Question 56   What is a memory region?

Question 57   What is the virtual address space? How is it different from the physical one?

Question 58   What is a Translation Lookaside Buffer?

Question 59   What makes the virtual memory mechanism performant?

Question 60   How is the address space switched?

Question 61   Which protection mechanisms does the virtual memory incorporate?

Question 62   What is the purpose of EXB bit?

Question 63   What is the structure of the virtual address?

Question 64   Does a virtual and a physical address have anything in common?

Question 65   Can we write a string in `.text` section? What happens if we read it? And if we overwrite it?

Question 66   Write a program that will call `stat`, `open`, and `mmap` system calls (check the system calls table in Appendix C). It should output the file length and its contents.

Question 67   Write the following programs, which all map a text file `input.txt` containing an integer x in memory using a `mmap` system call, and output the following:

1. $x!$ (factorial, $x! = 1 \cdot 2 \cdot \cdots \cdot (x-1) \cdot x$). It is guaranteed that $x \geq 0$.

2. 0 if the input number is prime, 1 otherwise.

3. Sum of all number's digits.

4. x-th Fibonacci number.

5. Checks if x is a Fibonacci number.

CHAPTER 5

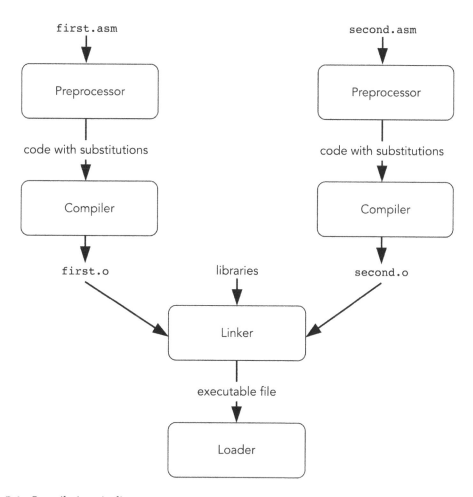

Compilation Pipeline

This chapter covers the compilation process. We divide it into three main stages: preprocessing, translation, and linking. Figure 5-1 shows an exemplary compilation process. There are two source files: first.asm and second.asm. Each is treated separately before linking stage.

Figure 5-1. *Compilation pipeline*

© Igor Zhirkov 2017
I. Zhirkov, *Low-Level Programming*, DOI 10.1007/978-1-4842-2403-8_5

Preprocessor transforms the program source to obtain other program in the same language. The transformations are usually substitutions of one string instead of others.

Compiler transforms each source file into a file with encoded machine instructions. However, such a file is not yet ready to be executed because it lacks the right connections with the other separately compiled files. We are talking about cases in which instructions address data or instructions, which are declared in other files.

Linker establishes connections between files and makes an executable file. After that, the program is ready to be run. Linkers operate with object files, whose typical formats are ELF (Executable and Linkable Format) and COFF (Common Object File Format).

Loader accepts an executable file. Such files usually have a structured view with metadata included. It then fills the fresh address space of a newborn process with its instructions, stack, globally defined data, and runtime code provided by the operating system.

5.1 Preprocessor

Each program is created as a text. The first stage of compilation is called preprocessing. During this stage, a special program is evaluating preprocessor directives found in the program source. According to them, textual substitutions are made. As a result we get a modified source code without preprocessor directives *written in the same programming language*. In this section we are going to discuss the usage of the NASM macro processor.

5.1.1 Simple Substitutions

One of the basic preprocessor directives is called %define. It performs a simple substitution.

Given the code shown in Listing 5-1, a preprocessor will substitute cat_count by 42 whenever it encounters such a substring in the program source.

Listing 5-1. define_cat_count.asm

```
%define cat_count 42

mov rax, cat_count
```

To see the preprocessing results for an input file.asm, run nasm -E file.asm. It is often very useful for debug purposes. Let's see the result in Listing 5-2 for the file in Listing 5-1.

Listing 5-2. define_cat_count_preprocessed.asm

```
%line 2+1 define_cat_count.asm

mov rax, 42
```

The commands to declare substitutions are called **macros**. During a process called **macro expansion** their occurrences are replaced with pieces of text. The resulting text fragments are called **macro instances**. In Listing 5-2, a number 42 in line mov rax, cat_count is a macro instance. Names such as cat_count are often referred to as **preprocessor symbols**.

■ **Redefinition** NASM allows you to redefine existing preprocessor symbols.

It is important that the preprocessor knows little to nothing about the programming language *syntax*. The latter defines valid language constructions.

For example, the code shown in Listing 5-3 is correct. It doesn't matter if neither a nor b alone constitutes a valid assembly construction; as long as the final result of substitutions is syntactically valid, the compiler is fine with it.

Listing 5-3. macro_asm_parts.asm

```
%define a mov rax,
    %define b rbx


    a b
```

In another example, in higher-level languages, an *if* statement has a form of *if (<expression>) then <statement> else <statement>*. Macros can operate parts of this construction which on their own are not syntactically correct (e.g., a sole *else <statement>* clause). As long as the result is syntactically correct, the compiler will have no problems with it.

Contrarily, other types of macros exist, namely, syntactic macros, tied to the language structure and operating with its constructions. Such macros modify them in a structured way. Languages like LISP, OCaml, and Scala use syntactic macros.

Why are we using macros at all? Apart from automation, which we will see later, they provide mnemonics for pieces of code.[1]

For constants, it allows us distinguish occurrences of 42 which are used to count cats from those used to count dogs or whatever else. Otherwise, certain program modifications would be more painful and error prone, since we would have had to make more decisions based on what this specific number means.

For packs of language constructs, it provides us with a certain automatization just as subroutines do. Macros are expanded at compile time, while routines are executed in runtime. The choice is up to you.

For assembly, no optimizations are performed on programs. However, in higher-level languages people use global *constant* variables for that matter. A good compiler will substitute its occurrences with its value. A bad one, however, cannot be aware of optimizations, which can be the case when programming microcontrollers or applications for exotic operating systems. In such cases people often do a compiler's job by using macros as in assembly language.

■ **Style**   It is a good practice to name all constants in your program.

In assembly and C people usually define global constants using macro definitions.

5.1.2   Substitutions with Arguments

Macros are better than that: they can have arguments. Listing 5-4 shows a simple macro with three arguments.

---

[1]D. Knuth takes this idea to extreme in his approach called **Literate Programming**

Listing 5-4. `macro_simple_3arg.asm`

```
%macro test 3
dq %1
dq %2
dq %3
%endmacro
```

Its action is simple: for each argument it will create a quad word data entry. As you see, arguments are referred by their indices starting at 1. When this macro is defined, a line `test 666, 555, 444` will be replaced by those shown in Listing 5-5

Listing 5-5. `macro_simple_3arg_inst.asm`

```
dq 666
dq 555
dq 444
```

■ **Question 68**   Find more examples of `%define` and `%macro` usage in NASM documentation.

5.1.3   Simple Conditional Substitution

Macros in NASM support various conditionals. The simplest of them is `%if`. Listing 5-6 shows a minimal example.

Listing 5-6. `macroif.asm`

```
BITS 64
%define x 5

%if x == 10

mov rax, 100

%elif x == 15

mov rax, 115

%elif x == 200
mov rax, 0
%else
mov rax, rbx
%endif
```

Listing 5-7 shows an instantiated macro. Remember, you can check the preprocessing result using `nasm -E`.

Listing 5-7. `macroif_preprocessed.asm`

```
%line 1+1 if.asm
[bits 64]
```

```
%line 15+1 if.asm
mov rax, rbx
```

The condition is an expression similar to what you might see in high-level languages: arithmetics and logical conjectures (and, or, not).

5.1.4   Conditioning on Definition

It is possible to decide in compile time whether a part of file should be assembled or not. One of many %if counterparts is %ifdef. It works in a similar way, but the condition is satisfied if a certain preprocessor symbol is defined. An example shown in Listing 5-8 incorporates such a directive.

Listing 5-8. defining_in_cla.asm

```
%ifdef flag
hellostring: db "Hello",0
%endif
```

As you can see, the symbol flag is not defined here using %define directive. Thus, we have the line labeled by hellostring.

It is worth mentioning that preprocessor symbols can be defined directly when calling NASM thanks to -d key. For example, the macro condition in Listing 5-8 will be satisfied when NASM is called with -d myflag argument.

■ **Question 69**   Check the preprocessor output on file, shown in Listing 5-8.

In the next sections we are going to see more preprocessor directives similar to %if.

5.1.5   Conditioning on Text Identity

%ifidn is used to test if two text strings are equal (spacing differences are not taken into account). Depending on the comparison result the subsequent code will or will not be assembled.

This allows us to create very flexible macros which will depend, for example, on the argument name.

To illustrate, let's create a pushr macro instruction (see Listing 5-9). It will function exactly the same way as a push assembly instruction but will also accept rip and rflags registers.

Listing 5-9. pushr.asm

```
%macro pushr 1
%ifidn %1, rflags
pushf
%else
push %1
%endif
%endmacro

pushr rax
pushr rflags
```

Listing 5-10 shows what the two macros in Listing 5-9 become after instantiation.

Listing 5-10. `pushr_preprocessed.asm`

```
%line 8+1 pushr/pushr.asm

push rax
pushf
```

As you can see, the macro adjusted its behavior based on the argument's text representation. Notice that `%else` clauses are allowed just like for regular `%if`. To make the comparison case insensitive, use the `%ifidni` directive instead.

5.1.6   Conditioning on Argument Type

The NASM preprocessor is a bit aware of the assembly language elements (token types). It can distinguish quoted strings from numbers and identifiers. There is a triple of `%if` counterparts for this purpose: `%ifid` to check whether its argument is an identifier, `%ifstr` for a string check, and `%ifnum` to check whether it is a number or not.

Listing 5-11 shows an example of a macro, which prints either a number or a string (using an identifier). It uses several routines developed during the first assignment to calculate string length, output string, and output integer.

Listing 5-11. `macro_arg_types.asm`

```
%macro print 1
   %ifid %1
      mov rdi, %1
      call print_string
   %else

     %ifnum %1
        mov rdi, %1
        call print_uint
     %else
        %error "String literals are not supported yet"
     %endif
   %endif

%endmacro

myhello: db 'hello', 10, 0
_start:
   print myhello
   print 42
   mov rax, 60
   syscall
```

The indentation is completely optional and is done for the sake of readability.

In case the argument is neither string nor identifier, we use the %error directive to force NASM into throwing an error. If we had used %fatal instead, we would have stopped assembling completely and any further errors would be ignored; a simple %error, however, will give NASM a chance to signal about following errors too before it stops processing input files.

Let's observe the macro instantiations in Listing 5-12

Listing 5-12. macro_arg_types_preprocessed.asm

```
%line 73+1 macro_arg_types/macro_arg_types.asm

myhello: db 'hello', 10, 0
_start:
 mov rdi, myhello
%line 76+0 macro_arg_types/macro_arg_types.asm
 call print_string

%line 77+1 macro_arg_types/macro_arg_types.asm

%line 77+0 macro_arg_types/macro_arg_types.asm
 mov rdi, 42
 call print_uint

%line 78+1 macro_arg_types/macro_arg_types.asm
 mov rax, 60
 syscall
```

5.1.7   Evaluation Order: Define, xdefine, Assign

All programming languages have a notion of evaluation strategy. It describes the order of evaluation in complex expressions. How should we evaluate $f(g(1), h(4))$? Should we evaluate $g(1)$ and $h(4)$ first and then let f act on the results? Or should we inline $g(1)$ and $h(4)$ inside the body of f and defer their own evaluations until they are really needed?

Macros are evaluated by NASM macroprocessor, and they do have a complex structure, as any macro instantiation can include other macros to be instantiated. A fine tuning of evaluation order is possible, because NASM provides slightly different versions of macro definition directives, namely

- %define for a deferred substitution. If macro body contains other macros, they will be expanded after the substitution.

- %xdefine performs substitutions when being defined. Then the resulting string will be used in substitutions.

- %assign is like %xdefine, but it also forces the evaluation of arithmetic expressions and throws an error if the computation result is not a number.

To better understand the subtle difference between %define and %xdefine take a look at the example shown in Listing 5-13.

Listing 5-13. `defines.asm`

```
%define i 1

%define d i * 3
%xdefine xd i * 3
%assign a i * 3

mov rax, d
mov rax, xd
mov rax, a

; let's redefine i
%define i 100
mov rax, d
mov rax, xd
mov rax, a
```

Listing 5-14 shows the preprocessing result.

Listing 5-14. `defines_preprocessed.asm`

```
%line 2+1 defines.asm

%line 6+1 defines.asm

mov rax, 1 * 3
mov rax, 1 * 3
mov rax, 3

mov rax, 100 * 3
mov rax, 1 * 3
mov rax, 3
```

The key differences are that

- `%define` **may change its value between instantiations if parts of it are redefined.**

- `%xdefine` has other macros on which it directly depends glued to it after being defined.

- `%assign` forces evaluation and substitutes values. Where xdefine would have left you with the preprocessor symbol equal to 4+2+3, `%assign` will compute it and assign value 9 to it.

We will use the wonderful properties of `%assign` to show some magic after becoming familiar with macro repetitions.

5.1.8   Repetition

The `times` directive is executed after all macro definitions are fully expanded and thus cannot be used to repeat pieces of macros.

But there is another way NASM can make macro loops: by placing the loop body between %rep and %endrep directives. Loops can be executed only a fixed amount of times, specified as %rep argument. An example in Listing 5-15 shows how a preprocessor calculates a sum of integers from 1 to 10 and then uses this value to initialize a global variable `result`.

Listing 5-15. `rep.asm`

```
%assign x 1
%assign a 0
%rep 10
%assign a x + a
%assign x x + 1
%endrep

result: dq a
```

After preprocessing the `result` value is correctly initialized to 55 (see Listing 5-16). You can check it manually.[2]

Listing 5-16. `rep_preprocessed.asm`

```
%line 7+1 rep/rep.asm

result: dq 55
```

We can use `%exitrep` to immediately leave the cycle. It is thus analogous to break instruction in high-level languages.

5.1.9 Example: Computing Prime Numbers

The macro shown in Listing 5-17 is used to produce a sieve of prime numbers. It means that it defines a static array of bytes, where each *i*-th byte is equal to 1 if and only if *i* is a prime number.

A **prime number** is a natural number greater than 1 such that it has no positive divisors other than 1 and itself.

The algorithm is simple:

- **0 and 1 are not primes.**

- 2 is a prime number.

- For each *current* up to *limit* we check whether no *i* from 2 up to *n*/2 is *n*'s divisor.

Listing 5-17. `prime.asm`

```
%assign limit 15
is_prime: db 0, 0, 1
%assign n 3
%rep limit
    %assign current 1
    %assign i 1
        %rep n/2
            %assign i i+1
            %if n % i = 0
                %assign current 0
                %exitrep
```

---

[2]A simple formula for the sum of first *n* natural numbers is: $\dfrac{n(n+1)}{2}$

```
        %endif
      %endrep
db current ; n
    %assign n n+1
%endrep
```

By accessing the *n*-th element of the is_prime array we can find out whether *n* is a prime number or not. After preprocessing the following code in Listing 5-18 will be generated:

Listing 5-18. prime_preprocessed.asm

```
%line 2+1 prime/prime.asm
is_prime: db 0, 0, 1
%line 16+1 prime/prime.asm
db 1
%line 16+0 prime/prime.asm
db 0
db 1
db 0
db 1
db 0
db 0
db 0
db 1
db 0
db 1
db 0
db 0
db 0

db 1
```

By reading the *i*-th byte starting at is_prime we get 1 if *i* is prime; 0 otherwise.

■ **Question 70** Modify the macro the way it would produce a bit table, taking eight times less space in memory. Add a function that will check number for primarily and return 0 or 1, based on this precomputed table.

■ **Hint** for the macro you will probably have to copy and paste a lot.

5.1.10 Labels Inside Macros

There is not much we can do in assembly without labels. Using fixed label names inside macros is not quite common. When the macro is instantiated many times inside the same file, the multiply defined labels can produce clashes which stop compilation.

There is an option to use macro local labels, which is a label you cannot access outside current macro instantiation. In order to do that, you can prefix such label name with double percent, as follows: %%labelname. Each macro local label will get a random prefix, which will change between macro instances but will remain the same inside one instance. Listing 5-19 shows an example. Listing 5-20 contains the preprocessing results.

Listing 5-19. `macro_local_labels.asm`

```
%macro mymacro 0
%%labelname:
%%labelname:
%endmacro


Mymacro


Mymacro


mymacro
```

The macro mymacro is instantiated three times. Each time the local label gets a unique name. The base name (after double percent) becomes prepended with a numerical prefix different in each instance. The first prefix is `..@0.`, the second is `..@1.`, and so on.

Listing 5-20. `macro_local_labels_inst.asm`

```
%line 5+1 macro_local_labels/macro_local_labels.asm

..@0.labelname:
%line 6+0 macro_local_labels/macro_local_labels.asm
..@0.labelname:
%line 7+1 macro_local_labels/macro_local_labels.asm

..@1.labelname:
%line 8+0 macro_local_labels/macro_local_labels.asm
..@1.labelname:
%line 9+1 macro_local_labels/macro_local_labels.asm

..@2.labelname:
%line 10+0 macro_local_labels/macro_local_labels.asm
..@2.labelname:
```

5.1.11 Conclusion

You can think about macros as about a programming meta-language executed during compilation. It can do quite complex computations and is limited in two ways:

- These computations cannot depend on user input (so they can only operate constants).

- The cycles can be executed no more than a fixed amount of times. It means that while-like constructions are impossible to encode.

5.2 Translation

A compiler usually translates source code from one language into another language. In case of translation from high-level programming languages into machine code, this process incorporates multiple inner steps. During these stages we gradually push the code **IR (Intermediate Representation)** toward the target language. Each push of IR is closer to the target language. Right before producing assembly code the **IR** will be very close to assembly, so we can flush the assembly into a readable listing instead of encoding instructions.

Not only is translation a complex process, it also loses information about source code structure, so reconstructing readable high-level code from the assembly file is impossible.

A compiler works with atomic code entities called **modules**. A module usually corresponds to a code source file (but not a header or include file). Each module is compiled independently from the other modules. The **object file** is produced from each module. It contains binary encoded instructions but usually cannot be executed right away. There are several reasons.

For instance, the object file is completed separately from other files but refers to outside code and data. It is not yet clear whether that code or data will reside in memory, or the position of the object file itself.

The assembly language translation is quite straightforward because the correspondence between assembly mnemonics and machine instructions is almost one to one. Apart from label resolution there is not much nontrivial work. Thus, for now we will concentrate on the following compilation stage, namely, linking.

5.3 Linking

Let's return to our first examples of assembly programs. To transform a "Hello, world!" program from source code to executable file, we used the following two commands:

```
> nasm -f elf64 -o hello.o hello.asm
> ld -o hello hello.o
```

We used NASM first to produce an **object file**. Its format, elf64, was specified by the -f key. Then we used another program, ld (a linker), to produce a file ready to be executed. We will take this file format as an example to show you what the linker really does.

5.3.1 Executable and Linkable Format

ELF (Executable and Linkable Format) is a format for object files quite typical for *nix systems. We will limit ourselves to its 64-bit version.

ELF allows for three types of files.

1. **Relocatable object files** are .o-files, produced by compiler.

   Relocation is a process of assigning definitive addresses to various program parts and changing the program code the way all links are attributed correctly. We are speaking about all kinds of memory accesses by absolute addresses. Relocation is needed, for example, when the program consists of multiple modules, which are referencing one another. The order in which they will be placed in memory is not yet fixed, so the absolute addresses are not determined. Linkers can combine these files to produce the next type of object files.

2. **Executable object file** can be loaded in memory and executed right away. It is essentially a structured storage for code, data, and utility information.

3. **Shared object files** can be loaded when needed by the main program. They are linked to it dynamically. In Windows OS these are well known dll-files; in *nix systems their names often end with .so.

The purpose of any linker is to make an executable (or shared) object file, given a set of relocatable ones. In order to do it, a linker must perform the following tasks:

- **Relocation**

- **Symbol resolution**. Each time a symbol (function, variable) is dereferenced, a linker has to modify the object file and fill the instruction part, corresponding to the operand address, with the correct value.

5.3.1.1 Structure

An ELF file starts with the main header, which stores global meta-information.

See Listing 5-21 for a typical ELF header. The hello file is a result of compiling a "Hello, world!" program shown in Listing 2-4.

Listing 5-21. hello_elfheader ELF Header:

```
ELF Header:
  Magic:   7f 45 4c 46 02 01 01 00 00 00 00 00 00 00 00 00
  Class:                             ELF64
  Data:                              2's complement, little endian
  Version:                           1 (current)
  OS/ABI:                            UNIX - System V
  ABI Version:                       0
  Type:                              EXEC (Executable file)
  Machine:                           Advanced Micro Devices X86-64
  Version:                           0x1
  Entry point address:               0x4000b0
  Start of program headers:          64 (bytes into file)
  Start of section headers:          552 (bytes into file)
  Flags:                             0x0
  Size of this header:               64 (bytes)
  Size of program headers:           56 (bytes)
  Number of program headers:         2
  Size of section headers:           64 (bytes)
  Number of section headers:         6
  Section header string table index: 3
```

ELF files then provide information about a program that can be observed from two points of view:

- **Linking view**, consisting of sections.

  It is described by section table, which is accessible through readelf -S.

  Each section in turn can be:

  - Raw data to be loaded into memory.

  - Formatted metadata about other sections, used by loader (e.g., **.bss**), linker (e.g., **relocation tables**), or debugger (e.g., **.line**).

Code and data are stored inside sections.

- **Execution view**, consisting of segments.

   It is described by a **Program Header Table**, which can be studied using `readelf -l`. We will take a closer look at it in section 5.3.5.

   Each entry can describe

   – Some kind of information the system needs to execute the program.

   – An ELF segment, containing zero or more sections. They have the same set of permissions (read, write, execute) enforced by virtual memory. Each segment has a starting address and is loaded in a separate **memory region**, consisting of consecutive pages.

After revising Listing 5-21, we notice, that it describes precisely the position and dimensions of program headers and section headers.

We start with the sections view since the linker works mainly with them.

5.3.1.2   Sections in ELF Files

Assembly language allows manual section controls. NASM's `section` corresponds to object file sections. You have already seen a couple of those, namely, `.text` and `.data`. The list of the most used sections follows; the full list can be found in [24].

.text stores machine instructions.

.rodata stores read only data.

.data stores initialized global variables.

.bss stores readable and writable global variables, initialized to zero. There is no need to dump their contents into an object file as they are all filled with zeros anyway. Instead, a total section size is stored. An operating system may know faster ways of initializing such memory than zeroing it manually.

   In assembly, you can put data here by placing `resb`, `resw`, and similar directives after the `section .bss`.

.rel.text stores **relocation table** for the `.text` section. It is used to memorize places where a linker should modify `.text` after choosing the loading address for this specific object file.

.rel.data stores a relocation table for data referenced in **module**.

.debug stores a symbol table used to debug program. If the program was written in C or C++, it will store information not only about global variables (as **.symtab** does) but also about local variables.

.line defines correspondence with pieces of code and line numbers in source code. We need it because the correspondence between lines of source code in higher-level languages and assembly instructions is not straightforward. This information allows one to debug a program in a higher-level language line by line.

.strtab stores character strings. It is like an array of strings. Other sections, such, as **.symtab** and **.debug**, use not immediate strings but their indices in **.strtab**.

.symtab stores a symbol table. Whenever a programmer defines a label, NASM will create a **symbol** for it.[3] This table also stores utility information, which we are going to examine later.

   Now that we have a general understanding of the ELF file linking view, we will observe some examples to show particularities of three different ELF file types.

5.3.2   Relocatable Object Files

Let's investigate an object file, obtained by compiling a simple program, shown in Listing 5-22.

---

[3]Not to be confused with preprocessor symbols!

Listing 5-22. `symbols.asm`

```
section .data
datavar1: dq 1488
datavar2: dq 42

section .bss
bssvar1: resq 4*1024*1024
bssvar2: resq 1

section .text

extern somewhere
global _start
    mov rax, datavar1
    mov rax, bssvar1
    mov rax, bssvar2
    mov rdx, datavar2
_start:
jmp _start
    ret
textlabel: dq 0
```

This program uses extern and global directives to mark **symbols** in a different way. These two directives control the creation of a **symbol table**. By default, all symbols are local to the current module. extern defines a symbol that is defined in other modules but referenced in the current one. On the other hand, global defines a globally available symbol that other modules can refer to by defining it as extern inside them.

■ **Avoid confusion**   Do not confuse global and local symbols with global and local labels!

The GNU binutils is a collection of binary tools used to work with object files. It includes several tools used to explore the object file contents. Several of them are of particular interest for us.

- If you only need to look up the symbol table, use nm.

- Use objdump as a universal tool to display general information about an object file. In addition to ELF, it does support other object file formats.

- If you know that the file is in ELF format, readelf is often the best and most informative choice.

Let's feed this program to objdump to produce the results shown in Listing 5-23.

Listing 5-23. Symbols

```
> nasm -f elf64 main.asm && objdump -tf -m intel main.o
main.o:     file format elf64-x86-64

architecture: i386:x86-64, flags 0x00000011:
HAS_RELOC, HAS_SYMS
start address 0x0000000000000000
```

```
SYMBOL TABLE:
0000000000000000 l   df *ABS*  0000000000000000 main.asm
0000000000000000 l   d  .data  0000000000000000 .data
0000000000000000 l   d  .bss   0000000000000000 .bss
0000000000000000 l   d  .text  0000000000000000 .text
0000000000000000 l      .data  0000000000000000 datavar1
0000000000000008 l      .data  0000000000000000 datavar2
0000000000000000 l      .bss   0000000000000000 bssvar1
0000000002000000 l      .bss   0000000000000000 bssvar2
0000000000000029 l      .text  0000000000000000 textlabel
0000000000000000        *UND*  0000000000000000 somewhere
0000000000000028 g      .text  0000000000000000 _start
```

We are shown a symbol table, where each symbol is annotated with useful information. What do its columns mean?

1. Virtual address of the given symbol. For now we do not know the section starting addresses, so all virtual addresses are given *relative to section start*. For example, datavar1 is the first variable stored in .data, its address is 0, and its size is 8 bytes. The second variable, datavar2, is located in the same section with a greater offset of 8, next to datavar1. As somewhere is defined as extern, it is obviously located in some other module, so for now its address has no meaning and is left zero.

2. A string of seven letters and spaces; each letter characterizes a symbol in some way. Some of them are of interest to us.

   (a) l, g, - - local, global, or neither.

   (b) ...

   (c) ...

   (d) ...

   (e) I, - - a link to another symbol or an ordinary symbol.

   (f) d, D, - - debug symbol, dynamic symbol, or an ordinary symbol.

   (g) F, f, O, - - function name, file name, object name, or an ordinary symbol.

3. What section does this label correspond to? *UND* for unknown section (symbol is referenced, but not defined here), *ABS* means no section at all.

4. Usually, this number shows an alignment (or its absence).

5. Symbol name.

For example, let's investigate the first symbol shown in Listing 5-23. It is

f a file name,
d only necessary for debug purposes,
l local to this module.

The global label _start (which is also an **entry point**) is marked with the letter g in the second column.

■ **Note**   Symbol names are case sensitive: _start and _STaRT are different.

As the addresses in the symbol table are not yet the *real* virtual addresses but ones relative to sections, we might ask ourselves: how do these look in machine code? NASM has already performed its duty, and the machine instructions should be assembled. We can look inside interesting sections of object files by invoking objdump with parameters -D (disassemble) and, optionally, -M intel-mnemonic (to make it show Intel-style syntax rather than AT&T one). Listing 5-24 shows the results.

■ **How to read disassembly dumps** The left column usually is the absolute address where the data will be loaded. Before linking, it is an address relative to the section start.

The second column shows raw bytes as hexadecimal numbers.

The third column can contain the results of disassembling the assembly command mnemonics.

Listing 5-24. objdump_d

```
> objdump -D -M intel-mnemonic main.o
main.o:     file format elf64-x86-64
Disassembly of section .data:
0000000000000000 <datavar1>:    ...
0000000000000008 <datavar2>:    ...
Disassembly of section .bss:
0000000000000000 <bssvar1>:     ...
0000000002000000 <bssvar2>:     ...
Disassembly of section .text:
0000000000000000 <_start-0x28>:
   0:   48 b8 00 00 00 00 00    movabs rax,0x0
   7:   00 00 00
   a:   48 b8 00 00 00 00 00    movabs rax,0x0
  11:   00 00 00
  14:   48 b8 00 00 00 00 00    movabs rax,0x0
  1b:   00 00 00
  1e:   48 ba 00 00 00 00 00    movabs rdx,0x0
  25:   00 00 00
0000000000000028 <_start>:
  28:   c3                      ret
0000000000000029 <textlabel>:
```

The mov operand in section .text with offsets 0 and 14 relative to section start should be datavar1 address, but it is equal to zero! The same thing happened with bssvar. It means that the linker has to change compiled machine code, filling the right absolute addresses in instruction arguments. To achieve that, for each symbol all references to it are remembered in **relocation table**. As soon as the linker understands what its true virtual address will be, it goes through the list of symbol occurrences and fills in the holes.

A separate relocation table exists for each section in need of one.

To see the relocation tables use readelf --relocs. See Listing 5-25.

Listing 5-25. readelf_relocs

```
> readelf --relocs  main.o
Relocation section '.rela.text' at offset 0x440 contains 4 entries:
  Offset          Info      Type            Sym. Value      Name+Addend
000000000002   000200000001 R_X86_64_64    0000000000000000 .data + 0
00000000000c   000300000001 R_X86_64_64    0000000000000000 .bss + 0

000000000016   000300000001 R_X86_64_64    0000000000000000 .bss + 2000000
000000000020   000200000001 R_X86_64_64    0000000000000000 .data + 8
```

An alternative way to display the symbol table is to use a more lightweight and minimalistic nm utility. For each symbol it shows the symbol's virtual address, type, and name. Note that the type flag is in different format compared to objdump. See Listing 5-26 for a minimal example.

Listing 5-26. nm

```
> nm main.o
0000000000000000 b bssvar
0000000000000000 d datavar
                 U somewhere
000000000000000a T _start
000000000000000b t textlabel
```

5.3.3   Executable Object Files

The second type of object file can be executed right away. It retains its structure, but the addresses are now bound to exact values.

We shall take a look at another example, shown in Listing 5-27. It includes two global variables, somewhere and private, one of which is available to all modules (marked global). Additionally, a symbol func is marked as global.

Listing 5-27. executable_object.asm

```
global somewhere
global func

section .data

somewhere: dq 999
private: dq 666

section .text

func:
    mov rax, somewhere
    ret
```

We are going to compile it as usual using nasm -f elf64, and then link it using ld with the previous object file, obtained by compiling the file shown in Listing 5-22. Listing 5-28 shows the changes in objdump output.

Listing 5-28. `objdump_tf`

```
> nasm -f elf64 symbols.asm
> nasm -f elf64  executable_object.asm
> ld symbols.o executable_object.o -o main
> objdump -tf main

main:      file format elf64-x86-64
architecture: i386:x86-64, flags 0x00000112:
EXEC_P, HAS_SYMS, D_PAGED

start address 0x0000000000000000

SYMBOL TABLE:
00000000004000b0 l    d  .code  0000000000000000 .code
00000000006000bc l    d  .data  0000000000000000 .data
0000000000000000 l    df *ABS*  0000000000000000 executable_object.asm
00000000006000c4 l       .data  0000000000000000 private
00000000006000bc g       .data  0000000000000000 somewhere
0000000000000000         *UND*  0000000000000000 _start
00000000006000cc g       .data  0000000000000000 __bss_start
00000000004000b0 g     F .code  0000000000000000 func
00000000006000cc g       .data  0000000000000000 _edata
00000000006000d0 g       .data  0000000000000000 _end
```

The flags are different: now the file can be executed (EXEC_P); there are no more relocation tables (the HAS_RELOC flag is cleared). Virtual addresses are now intact, and so are addresses in code. This file is ready to be loaded and executed. It retains a symbol table, and if you want to cut it out making the executable smaller, use the `strip` utility.

▓ **Question 71**   Why does `ld` issue a warning if `_start` is not marked global? Look the entry point address in this case by using `readelf` with appropriate arguments.

▓ **Question 72**   Find out the `ld` option to automatically strip the symbol table after linking.

5.3.4   Dynamic Libraries

Almost every program uses code from libraries. There are two types of libraries: static and dynamic.

Static libraries consist of several relocatable object files. These are linked to the main program and are merged with the result executable file.

> In the Windows world, these files have an extension `.lib`.

> In the Unix world, these are either `.o` files or `.a` archives holding several `.o` files inside.

Dynamic libraries are also known as **shared object files** the third of three object file types we have defined previously.

> They are linked with the program during its execution.

> In the Windows world, these are the infamous `.dll` files.

> In the Unix world, these files have an `.so` extension (shared objects).

While static libraries are just undercooked executables without entry points, dynamic libraries have some differences which we are going to look at now.

Dynamic libraries are loaded when they are needed. As they are object files on their own, they have all kind of meta-information about which code they provide for external usage. This information is used by a loader to determine the exact addresses of exported functions and data.

Dynamic libraries can be shipped separately and updated independently. It is both good and bad. While the library manufacturer can provide bug fixes, he can also break backward compatibility by, for example, changing functions arguments, effectively shipping a delayed action mine.

A program can work with any amount of shared libraries. Such libraries should be loadable at any address. Otherwise they would be stuck at the same address, which puts us in exactly the same situation as when we are trying to execute multiple programs in the same physical memory address space. There are two ways to achieve that:

- We can perform a relocation in runtime, when the library is being loaded. However, it steals a very attractive feature from us: the possibility to reuse library code in physical memory without its duplication when several processes are using it. If each process performs library relocation to a different address, the corresponding pages become patched with different address values and thus become different for different processes.

  Effectively the **.data** section would be relocated anyway because of its mutable nature. Renouncing global variables allows us to throw away both the section and the need to relocate it.

  Another problem is that **.text** section must be left writable in order to perform its modification during the relocation process. It introduces certain security risks, leaving its modification possible by malicious code. Moreover, changing **.text** of every shared object when multiple libraries are required for an executable to run can take a great deal of time.

- We can write **PIC (Position Independent Code)**. It is now possible to write code which can be executed no matter where it resides in memory. For that we have to get rid of absolute addresses completely. These days processors support `rip`-relative addressing, like `mov rax, [rip + 13]`. This feature facilitates PIC generation.

  This technique allows for **.text** section sharing. Today programmers are strongly encouraged to use PIC instead of relocations.

■ **Note** Whenever you are using non-constant global variables, you prevent your code from being reenterable, that is, being executable inside multiple threads simultaneously without changes. Consequently, you will have difficulties reusing it in a shared library. It is one of many arguments against a global mutable state in program.

Dynamic libraries spare disk space and memory. Remember that pages may be either marked private or shared among several processes. If a library is used by multiple processes, most parts of it are not duplicated in physical memory.

We will show you how to build a minimal shared object now. However, we will defer the explanation of things like Global Offset Tables and Procedure Linkage Tables until Chapter 15.

Listing 5-29 shows minimal shared object contents. Notice the external symbol `_GLOBAL_OFFSET_TABLE` and `:function` specification for the global symbol `func`. Listing 5-30 shows a minimal launcher that calls a function in a shared object file and exits correctly.

Listing 5-29. `libso.asm`

```
Extern _GLOBAL_OFFSET_TABLE_

global func:function

section .rodata
message: db "Shared object wrote this", 10, 0

section .text
func:
    mov     rax, 1
    mov     rdi, 1
    mov     rsi, message
    mov     rdx, 14
    syscall
ret
```

Listing 5-30. `libso_main.asm`

```
global _start

extern func

section .text
_start:
    mov rdi, 10
    call func
    mov rdi, rax
    mov rax, 60
    syscall
```

Listing 5-31 shows build commands and two views of an ELF file.

Notice that dynamic library has more specific sections such as `.dynsym`. Sections `.hash`, `.dynsym`, and `.dynstr` are necessary for relocation.

.dynsym stores symbols visible from outside the library.

.hash is a hash table, needed to decrease the symbol search time for **.dynsym.**

.dynstr stores strings, requested by their indices from **.dynsym.**

Listing 5-31. `libso`

```
> nasm -f elf64 -o main.o main.asm
> nasm -f elf64 -o libso.o libso.asm
> ld -o main main.o -d libso.so
> ld -shared -o libso.so libso.o --dynamic-linker=/lib64/ld-linux-x86-64.so.2
> readelf -S libso.so
There are 13 section headers, starting at offset 0x5a0:
```

```
Section Headers:
  [Nr] Name               Type              Address           Offset
       Size               EntSize           Flags  Link  Info  Align
  [ 0]                    NULL              0000000000000000  00000000
       0000000000000000   0000000000000000         0     0     0
  [ 1] .hash              HASH              00000000000000e8  000000e8
       000000000000002c   0000000000000004  A      2     0     8
  [ 2] .dynsym            DYNSYM            0000000000000118  00000118
       0000000000000090   0000000000000018  A      3     2     8
  [ 3] .dynstr            STRTAB            00000000000001a8  000001a8
       000000000000001e   0000000000000000  A      0     0     1
  [ 4] .rela.dyn          RELA              00000000000001c8  000001c8
       0000000000000018   0000000000000018  A      2     0     8
  [ 5] .text              PROGBITS          00000000000001e0  000001e0
       000000000000001c   0000000000000000  AX     0     0     16
  [ 6] .rodata            PROGBITS          00000000000001fc  000001fc
       000000000000001a   0000000000000000  A      0     0     4
  [ 7] .eh_frame          PROGBITS          0000000000000218  00000218
       0000000000000000   0000000000000000  A      0     0     8
  [ 8] .dynamic           DYNAMIC           0000000000200218  00000218
       00000000000000f0   0000000000000010  WA     3     0     8
  [ 9] .got.plt           PROGBITS          0000000000200308  00000308
       0000000000000018   0000000000000008  WA     0     0     8
  [10] .shstrtab          STRTAB            0000000000000000  00000320
       0000000000000065   0000000000000000         0     0     1
  [11] .symtab            SYMTAB            0000000000000000  00000388
       00000000000001c8   0000000000000018        12    15     8
  [12] .strtab            STRTAB            0000000000000000  00000550
       000000000000004f   0000000000000000         0     0     1
Key to Flags:
  W (write), A (alloc), X (execute), M (merge), S (strings), l (large)
  I (info), L (link order), G (group), T (TLS), E (exclude), x (unknown)
  O (extra OS processing required) o (OS specific), p (processor specific)


> readelf -S main
There are 14 section headers, starting at offset 0x650:

Section Headers:
  [Nr] Name               Type              Address           Offset
       Size               EntSize           Flags  Link  Info  Align
  [ 0]                    NULL              0000000000000000  00000000
       0000000000000000   0000000000000000         0     0     0
  [ 1] .interp            PROGBITS          0000000000400158  00000158
       000000000000000f   0000000000000000  A      0     0     1
  [ 2] .hash              HASH              0000000000400168  00000168
       0000000000000028   0000000000000004  A      3     0     8
  [ 3] .dynsym            DYNSYM            0000000000400190  00000190
       0000000000000078   0000000000000018  A      4     1     8
  [ 4] .dynstr            STRTAB            0000000000400208  00000208
       0000000000000027   0000000000000000  A      0     0     1
  [ 5] .rela.plt          RELA              0000000000400230  00000230
       0000000000000018   0000000000000018  AI     3     6     8
```

[6] .plt	PROGBITS	0000000000400250	00000250	
0000000000000020	0000000000000010	AX	0 0	16
[7] .text	PROGBITS	0000000000400270	00000270	
0000000000000014	0000000000000000	AX	0 0	16
[8] .eh_frame	PROGBITS	0000000000400288	00000288	
0000000000000000	0000000000000000	A	0 0	8
[9] .dynamic	DYNAMIC	0000000000600288	00000288	
0000000000000110	0000000000000010	WA	4 0	8
[10] .got.plt	PROGBITS	0000000000600398	00000398	
0000000000000020	0000000000000008	WA	0 0	8
[11] .shstrtab	STRTAB	0000000000000000	000003b8	
0000000000000065	0000000000000000		0 0	1
[12] .symtab	SYMTAB	0000000000000000	00000420	
00000000000001e0	0000000000000018		13 15	8
[13] .strtab	STRTAB	0000000000000000	00000600	
000000000000004d	0000000000000000		0 0	1

■ **Question 73** Study the symbol tables for an obtained shared object using `readelf --dyn-syms` and `objdump -ft`.

■ **Question 74** What is the meaning behind the environment variable `LD_LIBRARY_PATH`?

■ **Question 75** Separate the first assignment into two modules. The first module will store all functions defined in `lib.inc`. The second will have the entry point and will call some of these functions.

■ **Question 76** Take one of the standard Linux utilities (from coreutils). Study its object file structure using `readelf` and `objdump`.

The things we observed in this section apply in most situations. However, there is a bigger picture of different **code models** that affect the addressing. We will dive into those details in Chapter 15 after getting more familiar with assembly and C. There we will also revise the dynamic libraries again and introduce the notions of Global Offset Table and Procedure Linkage Table.

5.3.5   Loader

Loader is a part of the operating system that prepares executable file for execution. It includes mapping its relevant sections into memory, initializing **.bss**, and sometimes mapping other files from disk.

The program headers for a file `symbols.asm`, shown in Listing 5-22, are shown in Listing 5-32.

Listing 5-32. symbols_pht

```
> nasm -f elf64 symbols.asm
> nasm -f elf64 executable_object.asm
> ld symbols.o executable_object.o -o main
> readelf -l main
Elf file type is EXEC (Executable file)
Entry point 0x4000d8
There are 2 program headers, starting at offset 64
```

```
Program Headers:
  Type           Offset              VirtAddr             PhysAddr
                 FileSiz             MemSiz                Flags  Align
  LOAD           0x0000000000000000  0x0000000000400000   0x0000000000400000
                 0x00000000000000e3  0x00000000000000e3   R E    200000
  LOAD           0x00000000000000e4  0x00000000006000e4   0x00000000006000e4
                 0x0000000000000010  0x000000000200001c   RW     200000

Section to Segment mapping:
  Segment Sections...
   00     .text
   01     .data .bss
```

The table tells us that two segments are present.

1. 00 segment

   - Is loaded at 0x400000 aligned at 0x200000.

   - Contains section .text.

   - Can be executed and can be read. Cannot be written to (so you cannot overwrite code).

2. 01 segment

   - Is loaded at 0x6000e4 aligned to 0x200000.

   - Can be read and written to.

Alignment means that the actual address will be the closest one to the start, divisible by 0x200000. Thanks to virtual memory, you can load all programs at the same starting address. Usually it is 0x400000.

There are some important observations to be made:

- Assembly sections with similar names, defined in different files, are merged.

- A relocation table is not needed in a pure executable file. Relocations partially remain for shared objects.

Let's launch the resulting file and see its /proc/<pid>/maps file as we did in Chapter 4. Listing 5-33 shows its sample contents. The executable is crafted to loop infinitely.

Listing 5-33. symbols_maps

```
00400000-00401000 r-xp 00000000 08:01 1176842
                       /home/sayon/repos/spbook/en/listings/chap5/main

00600000-00601000 rwxp 00000000 08:01 1176842
                       /home/sayon/repos/spbook/en/listings/chap5/main

00601000-02601000 rwxp 00000000 00:00 0

7ffe19cf2000-7ffe19d13000 rwxp 00000000 00:00 0
                       [stack]
7ffe19d3e000-7ffe19d40000 r-xp 00000000 00:00 0
                       [vdso]
```

```
7ffe19d40000-7ffe19d42000 r--p 00000000 00:00 0
                          [vvar]
ffffffffff600000-ffffffffff601000 r-xp 00000000 00:00 0
                          [vsyscall]
```

As we see, the program header is telling us the truth about section placement.

■ **Note**   In some cases, you will find that the linker needs to be finely tuned. The section loading addresses and relative placement can be adjusted by using **linker scripts**, which describe the resulting file. Such cases usually occur when you are programming an operating system or a microcontroller firmware. This topic is beyond the scope of this book, but we recommend that you look at [4] in case you encounter such a need.

5.4   Assignment: Dictionary

This assignment will further advance us to a working Forth interpreter. Some things about it might seem forced, like the macro design, but it will make a good foundation for an interpreter we are going to do later.

Our task is to implement a dictionary. It will provide a correspondence between keys and values. Each entry contains the address of the next entry, a key, and a value. Keys and values in our case are null-terminated strings.

The dictionary entries form a data structure are called a **linked list**. An empty list is represented by a null pointer, equal to zero. A non-empty list is a pointer to its first element. Each element holds some kind of value and a pointer to the next element (or zero, if it is the last element).

Listing 5-34 shows an exemplary linked list, holding elements 100, 200, and 300. It can be referred to by a pointer to its first element, that is, x1.

Listing 5-34. linked_list_ex.asm

```
section .data

x1:
dq x2
dq 100

x2:
dq x3
dq 200

x3:
dq 0
dq 300
```

Linked lists are often useful in situations that have numerous insertions and removals in the middle of the list. Accessing elements by index, however, is hard because it does not boil down to simple pointer addition. Linked list elements' mutual positions in flat memory are usually not predictable.

In this assignment the dictionary will be constructed statically as a list and each newly defined element will be prepended to it. You have to use macros with local labels and symbol redefinition to automatize the linked list creation. We explicitly instruct you to make a macro colon with two arguments, where the first will hold a dictionary key string and the second will hold the internal element representation name. This differentiation is needed because key strings can sometimes contain characters which are not parts of valid label names (space, punctuation, arithmetic signs, etc.). Listing 5-35 shows an example of such a dictionary.

Listing 5-35. `linked_list_ex_macro.asm`

```
section .data

colon "third word", third_word
db "third word explanation", 0

colon "second word", second_word
db "second word explanation", 0

colon "first word", first_word
db "first word explanation", 0
```

The assignment will contain the following files:

1. `main.asm`

2. `lib.asm`

3. `dict.asm`

4. `colon.inc`

Follow these steps to complete the assignment:

1. Make a separate assembly file containing functions that you have already written in the first assignment. We will call it `lib.o`.

   Do not forget to mark all necessary labels `global`, otherwise they won't be visible outside of this object file!

2. Create a file `colon.inc` and define a `colon` macro there to create dictionary words.

   This macro will take two arguments:

   - Dictionary key (inside quotes).

   - Assembly label name. Keys can contain spaces and other characters, which are not allowed in label names.

   Each entry should start with a pointer to the next entry, then hold a key as a null-terminated string. The content is then directly described by a programmer—for example, using db directives, as in the example shown in Listing 5-35.

3. Create a function `find_word` inside a new file `dict.asm`. It accepts two arguments:

   (a) A pointer to a null terminated key string.

   (b) A pointer to the last word in the dictionary. Having a pointer to the last word defined, we can follow the consecutive links to enumerate all words in the dictionary.

   `find_word` will loop through the whole dictionary, comparing a given key with each key in dictionary. If the record is not found, it returns zero; otherwise it returns record address.

4. A separate include file `words.inc` to define dictionary words using the `colon` macro. Include it in `main.asm`.

5. A simple _start function. It should perform the following actions:

- Read the input string in a buffer of maximum 255 characters long.

- Try to find this key in dictionary. If found, print the corresponding value. If not, print an error message.

Do not forget: all error messages should be written in stderr rather than stdout!

We ship a set of stub files (see Section 2.1 "Setting Up the Environment"); you are free to use them. An additional Makefile describes the building process; type make in the assignment directory to build an executable file main. A quick tutorial to the GNU Make system is available in Appendix B.

As in the first assignment, there is a test.py file to perform automated tests.

5.5 Summary

In this chapter we have looked at the different compilation stages. We have studied the NASM macroprocessor in detail and learned conditionals and loops. Then we talked about three object file types: relocatable, executable, and shared. We elaborated the ELF file structure and observed the relocation process performed by the linker. We have touched on the shared object files, and we will revisit them again in the Chapter 15.

Question 77 What is the linked list?

Question 78 What are the compilation stages?

Question 79 What is preprocessing?

Question 80 What is a macro instantiation?

Question 81 What is the %define directive?

Question 82 What is the %macro directive?

Question 83 What is the difference between %define, %xdefine, and %assign?

Question 84 Why do we need the %% operator inside macro?

Question 85 What types of conditions are supported by NASM macroprocessor? Which directives are used for it?

Question 86 What are the three types of ELF object files?

Question 87 What kinds of headers are present in an ELF file?

Question 88 What is relocation?

Question 89 What sections can be present in ELF files?

Question 90 What is a symbol table? What kind of information does it store?

Question 91 Is there a connection between sections and segments?

Question 92 Is there a connection between assembly sections and ELF sections?

Question 93   What symbol marks the program entry point?

Question 94   Which are the two different kind of libraries?

Question 95   Is there a difference between a static library and a relocatable object file?

CHAPTER 6

■ ■ ■

Interrupts and System Calls

In this chapter we are going to discuss two topics.

First, as von Neumann architecture lacks interactivity, the interrupts were introduced to change that. Although we are not diving into the hardware part of interrupts, we are going to learn exactly how programmer views the interrupts. Additionally, we will speak about input and output ports used to communicate with external devices.

Second, the operating system (OS) usually provides an interface to interact with the resources it controls: memory, files, CPU (central processing unit), etc. This is implemented via system calls mechanism. Transferring control to the operating system routines requires a well defined mechanism of privilege escalation, and we are going to see how it works in Intel 64 architecture.

6.1   Input and Output

When we were extending the von Neumann architecture to work with external devices, we mentioned interrupts only as a way to communicate with them. In fact, there is a second feature, input/output (I/O) ports, which complements it and allows data exchange between CPU and devices.

The applications can access I/O ports in two ways:

1. Through a separate I/O address space.

   There are 2^{16} 1-byte addressable I/O ports, from 0 through FFFFH. The commands in and out are used to exchange data between ports and eax register (or its parts).

   The permissions to perform writes and reads from ports are controlled by checking:

   - IOPL (I/O privilege level) field of rflags registers

   - I/O Permission bit map of a **Task State Segment**. We will speak about it in section 6.1.1.

2. Through memory-mapped I/O.

   A part of address space is specifically mapped to provide interaction with such external devices that respond like memory components. Consecutively, any memory addressing instructions (mov, movsb, etc.) can be used to perform I/O with these devices.

   Standard segmentation and paging protection mechanisms are applied to such I/O tasks.

© Igor Zhirkov 2017
I. Zhirkov, *Low-Level Programming*, DOI 10.1007/978-1-4842-2403-8_6

The IOPL field in `rflags` register works as follows: if the current privilege level is less or equal to the IOPL, the following instructions are allowed to be executed:

- `in` and `out` (normal input/output).
- `ins` and `outs` (string input/output).
- `cli` and `sti` (clear/set interrupt flag).

Thus, setting IOPL in an application individually allows us to forbid it from writing even if it is working at a higher privilege level than the user applications.

Additionally, Intel 64 allows an even finer permission control through an I/O permission bit map. If the IOPL check has passed, the processor checks the bit corresponding to the used port. The operation proceeds only if this bit is not set.

The I/O permission bit map is a part of **Task State Segment** (TSS), which was created to be an entity unique to a process. However, as the hardware task-switching mechanism is considered obsolete, only one TSS (and I/O permission bit map) can exist in long mode.

6.1.1   TR register and Task State Segment

There are some artifacts from the protected mode that are still somehow used in long mode. A segmentation is an example, now mostly used to implement protection rings. Another is a pair of a `tr` register and **Task State Segment** control structure.

The `tr` register holds the segment selector to the TSS descriptor. The latter resides in the GDT (Global Descriptor Table) and has a format similar to segment descriptors.

Likewise for segment registers, there is a **shadow register**, which is updated from **GDT** when `tr` is updated via `ltr` (load task register) instruction.

The TSS is a memory region used to hold information about a task in the presence of a hardware task-switching mechanism. Since no popular OS has used it in protected mode, this mechanism was removed from long mode. However, TSS in long mode is still used, albeit with a completely different structure and purpose.

These days there is only one TSS used by an operating system, with the structure described in Figure 6-1.

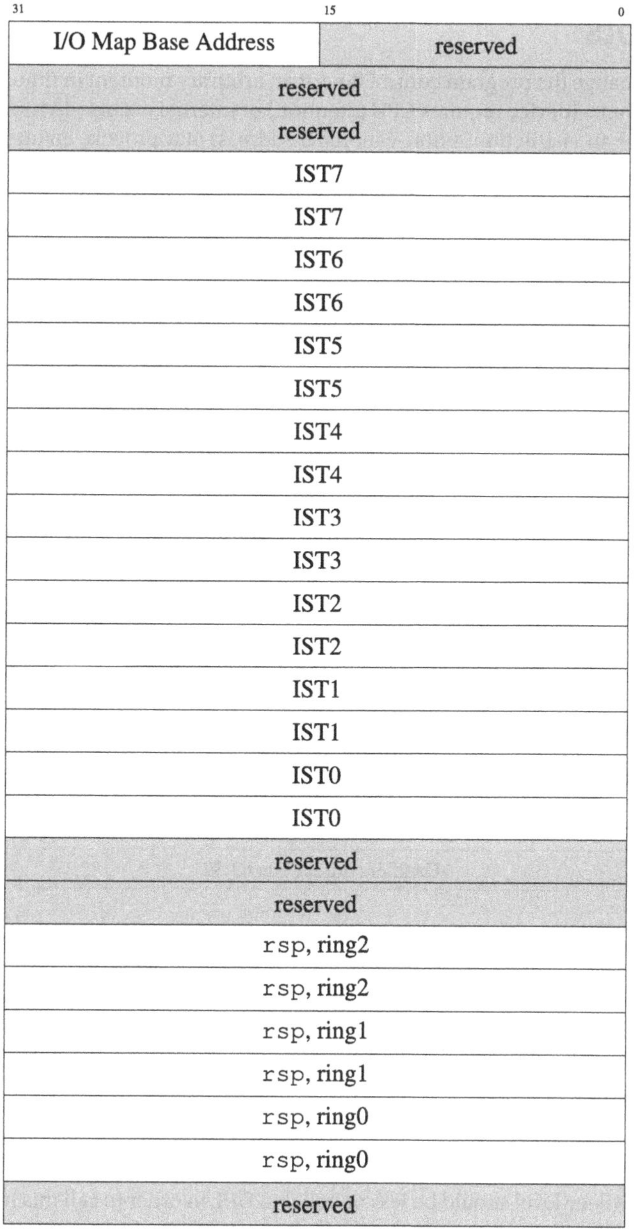

31	15	0
I/O Map Base Address	reserved	
reserved		
reserved		
IST7		
IST7		
IST6		
IST6		
IST5		
IST5		
IST4		
IST4		
IST3		
IST3		
IST2		
IST2		
IST1		
IST1		
IST0		
IST0		
reserved		
reserved		
rsp, ring2		
rsp, ring2		
rsp, ring1		
rsp, ring1		
rsp, ring0		
rsp, ring0		
reserved		

Figure 6-1. *Task State Segment in long mode*

The first 16 bits store an offset to an Input/Output Port Permission Map, which we already discussed in section 6.1. The TSS then holds eight pointers to special **interrupt stack tables** (ISTs) and stack pointers for different rings. Each time a privilege level changes, the stack is automatically changed accordingly. Usually, the new rsp value will be taken from the TSS field corresponding to the new protection ring. The meaning of ISTs is explained in section 6.2.

6.2 Interrupts

Interrupts allow us to change the program control flow at an arbitrary moment in time. While the program is executing, external events (device requires CPU attention) or internal events (division by zero, insufficient privilege level to execute an instruction, a non-canonical address) may provoke an interrupt, which results in some other code being executed. This code is called an **interrupt handler** and is a part of an operating system or driver software.

In [15], Intel separates external asynchronous interrupts from internal synchronous exceptions, but both are handled alike.

Each interrupt is labeled with a fixed number, which serves as its identifier. For us it is not important exactly how the processor acquires the interrupt number from the interrupt controller.

When the n-th interrupt occurs, the CPU checks the **Interrupt Descriptor Table** (IDT), which resides in memory. Analogously to **GDT**, its address and size are stored in idtr. Figure 6-2 describes the idtr.

79	. . .	16	15	. . .	0
IDT address			IDT size		

Figure 6-2. idtr *register*

Each entry in IDT takes 16 bytes, and the n-th entry corresponds to the n-th interrupt. The entry incorporates some utility information as well as an address of the interrupt handler. Figure 6-3 describes the interrupt descriptor format.

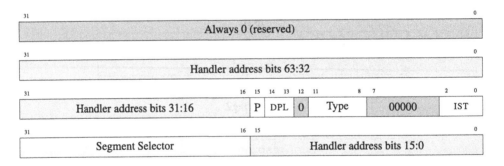

Figure 6-3. *Interrupt descriptor*

DPL Descriptor Privilege Level

> Current privilege level should be less or equal to DPL in order to call this handler using int instruction. Otherwise the check does not occur.

Type 1110 (interrupt gate, IF is automatically cleared in the handler) or 1111 (trap gate, IF is not cleared).

The first 30 interrupts are reserved. It means that you can provide interrupt handlers for them, but the CPU will use them for its internal events such as invalid instruction encoding. Other interrupts can be used by the system programmer.

When the IF flag is set, the interrupts are handled; otherwise they are ignored.

▒ **Question 96** What are non-maskable interrupts? What is their connection with the interrupt with code 2 and `IF` flag?

The application code is executed with low privileges (in ring3). Direct device control is only possible on higher privilege levels. When a device requires attention by sending an interrupt to the CPU, the handler should be executed in a higher privilege ring, thus requiring altering the segment selector.

What about the stack? The stack should also be switched. Here we have several options based on how we set up the IST field of interrupt descriptor.

- If the IST is 0, the standard mechanism is used. When an interrupt occurs, `ss` is loaded with 0, and the new `rsp` is loaded from TSS. The RPL field of `ss` then is set to an appropriate privilege level. Then *old* `ss` and `rsp` are saved in this new stack.

- If an IST is set, one of seven ISTs defined in TSS is used. The reason ISTs are created is that some serious faults (non-maskable interrupts, double fault, etc.) might profit from being executed on a known good stack. So, a system programmer might create several stacks even for ring0 and use some of them to handle specific interrupts.

There is a special `int` instruction, which accepts the interrupt number. It invokes an interrupt handler manually with respect to its descriptor contents. It ignores the `IF` flag: whether it is set or cleared, the handler will be invoked. To control execution of privileged code using `int` instruction, a DPL field exists.

Before an interrupt handler starts its execution, some registers are automatically saved into stack. These are `ss`, `rsp`, `rflags`, `cs`, and `rip`. See a stack diagram in Figure 6-4. Note how segment selectors are padded to 64 bit with zeros.

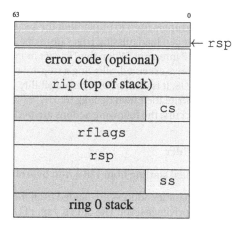

Figure 6-4. *Stack when an interrupt handler starts*

Sometimes an interrupt handler needs additional information about the event. An **interrupt error code** is then pushed into stack. This code contains various information specific for this type of interrupt.

Many interrupts are described using special mnemonics in Intel documentation. For example, the 13-th interrupt is referred to as #**GP** (general protection).[1] You will find the short description of the some interesting interrupts in the Table 6-1.

Table 6-1. *Some Important Interrupts*

VECTOR	MNEMONIC	DESCRIPTION
0	#DE	Divide error
2		Non-maskable external interrupt
3	#BP	Breakpoint
6	#UD	Invalid instruction opcode
8	#DF	A fault while handling interrupt
13	#GP	General protection
14	#PF	Page fault

Not all binary code corresponds to correctly encoded machine instructions. When rip is not addressing a valid instruction, the CPU generates the #UD interrupt.

The #GP interrupt is very common. It is generated when you try to dereference a forbidden address (which does not correspond to any allocated page), when trying to perform an action, requiring a higher privilege level, and so on.

The #PF interrupt is generated when addressing a page which has its present flag cleared in the corresponding page table entry. This interrupt is used to implement the swapping mechanism and file mapping in general. The interrupt handler can load missing pages from disk.

The debuggers rely heavily on the #BP interrupt. When the TF is set in rflags, the interrupt with this code is generated after *each* instruction is executed, allowing a step-by-step program execution. Evidently, this interrupt is handled by an OS. It is thus an OS's responsibility to provide an interface for user applications that allows programmers to write their own debuggers.

To sum up, when an n-th interrupt occurs, the following actions are performed from a programmer's point of view:

1. The **IDT** address is taken from idtr.

2. The interrupt descriptor is located starting from $128 \times n$-th byte of IDT.

3. The segment selector and the handler address are loaded from the IDT entry into cs and rip, possibly changing privilege level. The old ss, rsp, rflags, cs, and rip are stored into stack as shown in Figure 6-4.

4. For some interrupts, an error code is pushed on top of handler's stack. It provides additional information about interrupt cause.

5. If the descriptor's type field defines it as an Interrupt Gate, the interrupt flag IF is cleared. The Trap Gate, however, does not clear it automatically, allowing nested interrupt handling.

---

[1]See section 6.3.1 of the third volume of [15]

If the interrupt flag is not cleared immediately after the interrupt handler start, we cannot have any kind of guarantees that we will execute even its first instruction without another interrupt appearing asynchronously and requiring our attention.

■ **Question 97**   Is the TF flag cleared automatically when entering interrupt handlers? Refer to [15].

The interrupt handler is ended by a `iretq` instruction, which restores all registers saved in the stack, as shown in Figure 6-4, compared to the simple `call` instruction, which restores only `rip`.

6.3   System Calls

System calls are, as you already know, functions that an OS provides for user applications. This section describes the mechanism that allows their secure execution with higher privilege level.

The mechanisms used to implement system calls vary in different architectures. Overall, any instruction resulting in an interrupt will do, for example, division by zero or any incorrectly encoded instruction. The interrupt handler will be called and then the CPU will handle the rest. In protected mode on Intel architecture, the interrupt with code 0x80 was used by *nix operating systems. Each time a user executed `int` 0x80, the interrupt handler checked the register contents for system call number and arguments.

System calls are quite frequent, and you cannot perform any interaction with the outside world without them. Interrupts, however, can be slow, especially in Intel 64, since they require memory accesses to **IDT**.

So in Intel 64 there is a new mechanism to perform system calls, which uses `syscall` and `sysret` instructions to implement them.

Compared to interrupts, this mechanism has some key differences:

- The transition can only happen between ring0 and ring3.As pretty much no one uses ring1 and ring2, this limitation is not considered important.

- Interrupt handlers differ, but all system calls are handled by the same code with only one entry point.

- Some general purpose registers are now implicitly used during system call.

    - `rcx` is used to store old `rip`

    - `r11` is used to store old `rflags`

6.3.1   Model-Specific Registers

Sometimes when a new CPU appears it has additional registers, which other, more ancient ones, do not have. Quite often these are so-called **Model-Specific Registers**. When these registers are rarely modified, their manipulation is performed via two commands: `rdmsr` to read them and `wrmsr` to change them. These two commands operate on the register *identifying number*.

`rdmsr` accepts the MSR number in `ecx`, returns the register value in `edx:eax`.
`wrmsr` accepts the MSR number in `ecx` and stores the value taken from `edx:eax` in it.

6.3.2   syscall and sysret

The `syscall` instruction depends on several **MSRs**.

- STAR (MSR number 0xC0000081), which holds two pairs of cs and ss values: for system call handler and for sysret instruction. Figure 6-5 shows its structure.

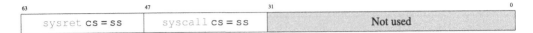

63	47	31	0
sysret cs = ss	syscall cs = ss	Not used	

Figure 6-5. MSR STAR

- LSTAR (MSR number 0xC0000082) holds the system call handler address (new rip).

- SFMASK (MSR number 0xC0000084) shows which bits in rflags should be cleared in the system call handler.

The syscall performs the following actions:

- Loads cs from STAR;

- Changes rflags with regards to SFMASK;

- Saves rip into rcx; and

- Initializes rip with LSTAR value and takes new cs and ss from STAR.

Note that now we can explain why system calls and procedures accept arguments in slightly different sets of registers. The procedures accept their fourth argument in rcx, which, as we know, is used to store the old rip value.

Contrary to the interrupts, even if the privilege level changes, the stack pointer should be changed by the handler itself.

System call handling ends with sysret instruction, which loads cs and ss from STAR and rip from rcx.

As we know, the segment selector change leads to a read from **GDT** to update its paired **shadow register**. However, when executing syscall, these shadow registers are loaded with fixed values and no reads from GDT are performed.

Here are these two fixed values in deciphered form:

- Code Segment shadow register:

  - Base = 0

  - Limit = FFFFFH

  - Type = 11_2 (can be executed, was accessed)

  - S = 1 (System)

  - DPL = 0

  - P = 1

  - L = 1 (Long mode)

  - D = 0

  - G = 1 (always the case in long mode)

Additionally, CPL (current privilege level) is set to 0

- Stack Segment shadow register:
  - Base = 0
  - Limit = FFFFFH
  - Type = 11_2 (can be executed, was accessed)
  - S = 1 (System)
  - DPL = 0
  - P = 1
  - L = 1 (Long mode)
  - D = 1
  - G = 1

However, the system programmer is responsible for fulfilling a requirement: GDT should have the descriptors corresponding to these fixed values.

So, GDT should store two particular descriptors for code and data specifically for `syscall` support.

6.4 Summary

In this chapter we have provided an overview of interrupts and system call mechanisms. We have studied their implementation down to the system data structures residing in memory. In the next chapter we are going to review different models of computation, including stack machines akin to Forth and finite automatons, and finally work on a Forth interpreter and compiler in assembly language.

Question 98 What is an interrupt?

Question 99 What is IDT?

Question 100 What does setting IF change?

Question 101 In which situation does the #GP error occur?

Question 102 In which situations does the #PF error occur?

Question 103 How is #PF error related to the swapping? How does the operating system use it?

Question 104 Can we implement system calls using interrupts?

Question 105 Why do we need a separate instruction to implement system calls?

Question 106 Why does the interrupt handler need a DPL field?

Question 107 What is the purpose of interrupt stack tables?

Question 108   Does a single thread application have only one stack?

Question 109   What kinds of input/output mechanisms does Intel 64 provide?

Question 110   What is a model-specific register?

Question 111   What are the shadow registers?

Question 112   How are the model-specific registers used in the system call mechanism?

Question 113   Which registers are used by `syscall` instruction?

■ ■ ■

## CHAPTER 7

Models of Computation

In this chapter we are going to study two models of computations: finite state machines and stack machines.

Model of computation is akin to the language you are using to describe the solution to a problem. Typically, a problem that is really hard to solve correctly in one model of computation can be close to trivial in another. This is the reason programmers who are knowledgeable about many different models of computations can be more productive. They solve problems in the model of computation that is most suitable and then they implement the solution with the tools they have at their disposal.

When you are trying to learn a new model of computation, do not think about it from the "old" point of view, like trying to think about finite state machines in terms of variables and assignments. Try to start fresh and logically build the new system of notions.

We already know much about Intel 64 and its model of computation, derived from von Neumann's. This chapter will introduce finite state machines (used to implement regular expressions) and stack machines akin to the Forth machine.

7.1 Finite State Machines

7.1.1 Definition

Deterministic finite state machine (deterministic finite automaton) is an abstract machine that acts on input string, following some rules.

We will use "Finite automatons" and "state machines" interchangeably. To define a finite automaton, the following parts should be provided:

1. A set of states.

2. Alphabet—a set of symbols that can appear in the input string.

3. A selected start state.

4. One or multiple selected end states

5. Rules of transition between states. Each rule consumes a symbol from input string. Its action can be described as: "if automaton is in state S and an input symbol C occurs, the next current state will be Z."

If the current state has no rule for the current input symbol, we consider the automaton behavior undefined.

The **undefined behavior** is a concept known more to mathematicians than to engineers. For the sake of brevity we are describing only the "good" cases. The "bad" cases are of no interest to us, so we are not defining the machine behavior in them. However, when implementing such machines, we will consider all undefined cases as erroneous and leading to a special error state.

© Igor Zhirkov 2017
I. Zhirkov, *Low-Level Programming*, DOI 10.1007/978-1-4842-2403-8_7

Why bother with automatons? Some tasks are particularly easy to solve when applying such paradigm of thinking. Such tasks include controlling embedded devices and searching substrings that match a certain pattern.

For example, we are checking, whether a string can be interpreted as an integer number. Let's draw a diagram, shown in Figure 7-1. It defines several states and shows possible transitions between them.

- The alphabet consists of letters, spaces, digits, and punctuation signs.

- The set of states is {A, B, C}.

- The initial state is A.

- The final state is C.

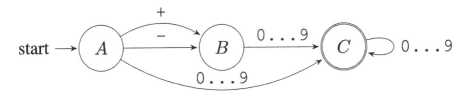

Figure 7-1. *Number recognition*

We start execution from the state A. Each input symbol causes us to change current state based on available transitions.

■ **Note**   Arrows labeled with symbol ranges like 0. . . 9 actually denote multiple rules. Each of these rules describes a transition for a single input character.

Table 7-1 shows what will happen when this machine is being executed with an input string +34. This is called **a trace of execution**.

Table 7-1. *Tracing a finite state machine shown in Figure 7-1, input is: +34*

OLD STATE	RULE	NEW STATE
A	+	B
B	3	C
C	4	C

The machine has arrived into the final state C. However, given an input idkfa, we could not have arrived into any state, because there are no rules to react to such input symbols. This is where the automaton's behavior is undefined. To make it total and always arrive in either *yes*- state or *no*-state, we have to add one more final state and add rules in all existing states. These rules should direct the execution into the new state in case no old rules match the input symbol.

7.1.2   Example: Bits Parity

We are given a string of *zeros* and *ones*. We want to find out whether there is an even or an odd number of *ones*. Figure 7-2 shows the solver in the form of a finite state machine.

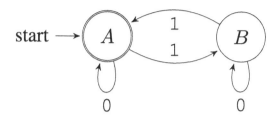

Figure 7-2. *Is the number of ones even in the input string?*

The empty string has zero *ones*; zero is an even number. Because of this, the state *A* is both the starting and the final state.

All *zeros* are ignored no matter the state. However, each *one* occurring in input changes the state to the opposite one. If, given an input string, we arrive into the finite state *A*, then the number of *ones* is even. If we arrive into the finite state *B*, then it is odd.

■ **Confusion**   In finite state machines, there is no memory, no assignments, no if-then-else constructions. This is thus a completely different abstract machine comparing to the von Neumann's. There is really nothing but states and transitions between them. In the von Neumann model, the state is the state of memory and register values.

7.1.3   Implementation in Assembly Language

After designing a finite state machine to solve a specific problem, it is trivial to implement this machine in an imperative programming language such as assembly or C.

Following is a straightforward way to implement such machines in assembly:

1. Make the designed automaton total: every state should possess transition rules for *any* possible input symbol. If this is not the case, add a separate state to design an error or an answer "no" to the problem being solved.

   For simplicity we will call it the **else-rule**.

2. Implement a routine to get an input symbol. Keep in mind that a symbol is not necessarily a character: it can be a network packet, a user action, and other kinds of global events.

3. For each state we should

   • Create a label.

   • Call the input reading routine.

   • Match input symbol with the ones described in transition rules and jump to corresponding states if they are equal.

   • Handle all other symbols by the **else-rule**.

To implement the exemplary automaton in assembly, we will make it total first, as shown in Figure 7-3

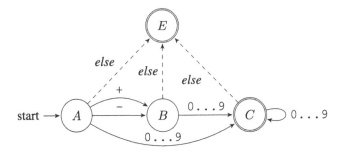

Figure 7-3. *Check if the string is a number: a total automaton*

We will modify this automaton a bit to force the input string to be null-terminated, as shown in Figure 7-4. Listing 7-1 shows a sample implementation.

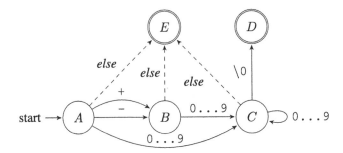

Figure 7-4. *Check if the string is a number: a total automaton for a null-terminated string*

Listing 7-1. `automaton_example_bits.asm`

```
section .text
; getsymbol is a routine to
; read a symbol (e.g. from stdin)
; into al

_A:
    call getsymbol
    cmp al, '+'
    je _B
    cmp al, '-'
    je _B
; The indices of the digit characters in ASCII
; tables fill a range from '0' = 0x30 to '9' = 0x39
; This logic implements the transitions to labels
; _E and _C
    cmp al, '0'
    jb _E
```

```
    cmp al, '9'
    ja _E
    jmp _C

_B:
    call getsymbol
    cmp al, '0'
    jb _E
    cmp al, '9'
    ja _E
    jmp _C

_C:
    call getsymbol
    cmp al, '0'
    jb _E
    cmp al, '9'
    ja _E
    test al, al
    jz _D
    jmp _C

_D:
; code to notify about success

_E:
; code to notify about failure
```

This automaton is arriving into states D or E; the control will be passed to the instructions on either the _D or _E label.

The code can be isolated inside a function returning either 1 (true) in state _D or 0 (false) in state _E.

7.1.4   Practical Value

First of all, there is an important limitation: not all programs can be encoded as finite state machines. This model of computation is not Turing complete, it cannot analyze complex recursively constructed texts, such as XML-code.

C and assembly language are Turing complete, which means that they are more expressive and can be used to solve a wider range of problems.

For example, if the string length is not limited, we cannot count its length or the words in it. Each result would have been a state, and there is only a limited number of states in finite state machines, while the word count can be arbitrary large as well as the strings themselves.

■ **Question 114**   Draw a finite state machine to count the words in the input string. The input length is no more than eight symbols.

The finite state machines are often used to describe embedded systems, such as coffee machines. The alphabet consists of events (buttons pressed); the input is a sequence of user actions.

The network protocols can often also be described as finite state machines. Every rule can be annotated with an optional output action: "if a symbol X is read, change state to Y and output a symbol Z." The input consists of packets received and global events such as timeouts; the output is a sequence of packets sent.

There are also several verification techniques, such as model checking, that allow one to prove certain properties of finite automatons—for example, "if the automaton has reached the state B, he will never reach the state C." Such proofs can be of a great value when building systems required to be highly reliable.

___

■ **Question 115** Draw a finite state machine to check whether there is an even or an odd number of words in the input string.

■ **Question 116** Draw and implement a finite state machine to answer whether a string should be trimmed from left, right, or both or should not be trimmed at all. A string should be trimmed if it starts or ends with consecutive spaces.

___

7.1.5 Regular Expressions

Regular expressions are a way to encode finite automatons. They are often used to define textual patterns to match against. It can be used to search for occurences of a specific pattern or to replace them. Your favorite text editor probably implements them already.

There are a number of regular expressions dialects. We will take as an example a dialect akin to one used in the egrep utility.

A regular expression R can be:

1. A letter.

2. A sequence of two regular expressions: R Q.

3. Metasymbols ^ and $, matching against the beginning and the end of the line.

4. A pair of grouping parentheses with a regular expression inside: (R).

5. An OR expression: R | Q.

6. R* denotes zero or more repetitions of R.

7. R+ denotes one or more repetitions of R.

8. R? denotes zero or one repetitions of R.

9. A dot matches against any character.

10. Brackets denote a range of symbols, for example [0-9] is an equivalent of (0|1|2|3|4|5|6|7|8|9).

You can test regular expressions using the egrep utility. It process its standard input and filters only those lines that match a given pattern. To prevent the from being processed by the shell, enclose it in single quotes like this: egrep 'expression'.

Following are some examples of simple regular expressions:

- `hello .+` matches against `hello Frank` or hello 12; does not match against `hello`.

- `[0-9]+` matches against an unsigned integer, possibly starting with zeros.

- `-?[0-9]+` matches against a possibly negative integer, possibly starting with zeros.

- `0|(-?[1-9][0-9]*)` matches against any integer that does not start with zero (unless it is zero).

These rules allow us to define a complex search pattern. The regular expressions engine will try to match the pattern starting with every position in text.

The regular expression engines usually follow one of these two approaches:

- Using a straightforward approach, trying to match all described symbol sequences. For example, matching a string ab against regular expression aa?a?b may result in such sequence of events:

  1. Trying to match against aaab — failure.

  2. Trying to match against aab — failure.

  3. Trying to match against ab — success.

  So, we are trying out different branches of decisions until we hit a successful one or until we see definitively that all options lead to a failure.

  This approach is usually quite fast and also simple to implement. However, there is a worst-case scenario in which the complexity starts growing exponentially. Imagine matching a string:

  aaa...a (repeat a n times)

  against a regular expression:

  a?a?a?...a?aaa...a (repeat a? n times, then repeat a n times)

  The given string will surely match the regular expression. However, when applying a straightforward approach the engine will have to go through all possible strings that do match this regular expression. To do it, it will consider two possible options for each a? expression, namely, those containing a and those not containing it. There will be 2^n such strings. It is as many as there are subsets in a set of n elements. You do not need more symbols than there are in this line of text to write a regular expression, which a modern computer will evaluate for days or even years. Even for a length $n = 50$ the number of options will hit $2^{50} = 1125899906842624$ options.

  Such regular expressions are called "pathological" because due to the matching algorithm nature they are handled extremely slowly.

- Constructing a finite state machine based on a regular expression.

  It is usually a **NFA (Non-deterministic Finite Automaton)**. As opposed to DFA (Deterministic Finite Automaton), they can have multiple rules for the same state and input symbol. When such a situation occurs, the automaton performs both transitions and now has several states simultaneously. In other words, there is no single state but a set of states an automaton is in.

  This approach is a bit slower in general but has no worst-case scenario with exponential working time. Standard Unix utilities such as grep are using this approach.

  How to build a NFA from a regular expression? The rules are pretty straightforward:

  - A character corresponds to an automaton, which accepts a string of one such character, as shown in Figure 7-5.

  - We can enlarge the alphabet with additional symbols, which we put in the beginning and end of each line.

Figure 7-5. *NFA for one character*

- – This way we handle ˆ and $ just as any other symbol.

- – Grouping parentheses allow one to apply rules to the symbol groups. They are only used for correct regular expression parsing. In other words, they provide the structural information needed for a correct automaton construction.

- – OR corresponds to combining two NFAs by merging their starting state. Figure 7-5 illustrates the idea.

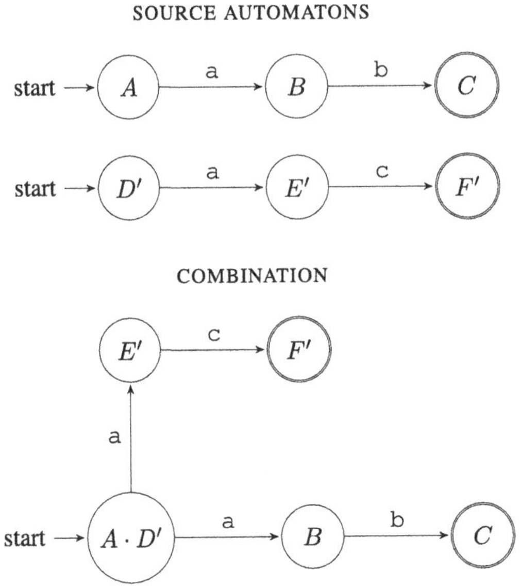

SOURCE AUTOMATONS

COMBINATION

Figure 7-6. *Combining NFAs via OR*

- – An asterisk has a transition to itself and a special thing called ε-rule. This rule occurs always. Figure 7-7 shows the automaton for an expression a*b.

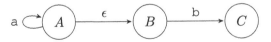

Figure 7-7. *NFA: implementing asterisk*

- – ? is implemented in a similar fashion to `*`. R+ is encoded as RR*.

■ **Question 117**   Using any language you know, implement a `grep` analogue based on **NFA** construction. You can refer to [11] for additional information.

■ **Question 118**   Study this regular expression: `^1?$|^(11+?)\1+$`. What might be its purpose? Imagine that the input is a string consisting of characters `1` uniquely. How does the result of this regular expression matching correlate with the string length?

7.2   Forth Machine

Forth is a language created by Charles Moore in 1971 for the 11-meter radio telescope operated by the National Radio Astronomy Observatory (NRAO) at Kitt Peak, Arizona. This system ran on two early minicomputers joined by a serial link. Both a multiprogrammed system and a multiprocessor system (in that both computers shared responsibility for controlling the telescope and its scientific instruments), it was controlling the telescope, collecting data, and supporting an interactive graphics terminal to interact with the telescope and analyze recorded data.

Today, Forth rests a unique and interesting language, both entertaining to learn and a great thing to change the perspective. It is still used, mostly in embedded software, due to an amazing level of interactivity. Forth can also be quite efficient.

Forth interpreters can be seen in such places as

- FreeBSD loader.

- Robot firmwares.

- Embedded software (printers).

- Space ships software.

It is thus safe to call Forth a system programming language.

It is not hard to implement Forth interpreter *and compiler* for Intel 64 in assembly language. The rest of this chapter will explain the details. There are almost as many Forth dialects as Forth programmers; we will use our own simple dialect.

7.2.1   Architecture

Let's start by studying a Forth abstract machine. It consists of a processor, two separate stacks for data and return addresses, and linear memory, as shown in Figure 7-8.

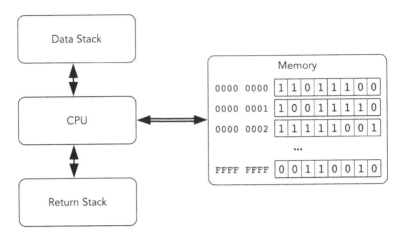

Figure 7-8. *Forth machine: architecture*

Stacks should not necessarily be part of the same memory address space.

The Forth machine has a parameter called cell size. Typically, it is equal to the machine word size of the target architecture. In our case, the cell size is 8 bytes. The stack consists of elements of the same size.

Programs consist of *words* separated by spaces or newlines. Words are executed consecutively. The integer words denote pushing into the data stack. For example, to push numbers 42, 13, and 9 into the data stack you can write simply 42 13 9.

There are three types of words:

1. Integer words, described previously.

2. Native words, written in assembly.

3. Colon words, written in Forth as a sequence of other Forth words.

The return stack is necessary to be able to return from the colon words, as we will see later.

Most words manipulate the data stack. From now on when speaking about the stack in Forth we will implicitly consider the data stack unless specified otherwise.

The words take their arguments from the stack and push the result there. All instructions operating on the stack consume their operands. For example, words +, -, *, and / consume two operands from the stack, perform an arithmetic operation, and push its result back in the stack. A program 1 4 8 8 + * + computes the expression $(8 + 8) * 4 + 1$.

We will follow the convention that the second operand is popped from the stack first. It means that the program '1 2 -' evaluates to –1, not 1.

The word : is used to define new words. It is followed by the new word's name and a list of other words terminated by the word ; . Both semicolon and colon are words on their own and thus should be separated by spaces.

A word sq, which takes an argument from the stack and pushes its square back, will look as follows:

```
: sq dup * ;
```

Each time we use sq in the program, two words will be executed: dup (duplicate cell in top of the stack) and * (multiply two words on top of the stack).

To describe the word's actions in Forth it is common to use **stack diagrams**:

```
swap (a b -- b a)
```

110

In parentheses you see the stack state before and after word execution. The stack cells are names to highlight the changes in stack contents. So, the swap word swaps two topmost elements in stack.

The topmost element is on the right, so the diagram 1 2 corresponds to Forth pushing first 1, then 2 as a result of execution of some words.

rot places on top the third number from stack:

```
rot    (a b c -- b c a)
```

7.2.2   Tracing an Exemplary Forth Program

Listing 7-2 shows a simple program to calculate the discriminant of a quadratic equation $1x^2 + 2x + 3 = 0$.

Listing 7-2. forth_discr

```
: sq dup * ;
: discr rot 4 * * swap sq swap - ;
1 2 3 discr
```

Now we are going to execute discr a b c step by step for some numbers *a*, *b*, and *c*. The stack state at the end of each step is shown on the right.

```
a     ( a )
b     ( a b )
c     ( a b c )
```

Then the discr word is executed. We are stepping into it.

```
rot  ( b c a )
4    ( b c a 4 )
*    ( b c (a*4) )
*    ( b (c*a*4) )
swap ( (c*a*4) b )
sq   ( (c*a*4) (b*b) )
swap ( (b*b) (c*a*4) )
-    ( (b*b - c*a*4) )
```

Now we do the same from the start, but for *a* = 1, *b* = 2, and *c* = 3.

```
1    ( 1 )
2    ( 1 2 )
3    ( 1 2 3 )
rot  ( 2 3 1 )
4    ( 2 3 1 4 )
*    ( 2 3 4 )
*    ( 2 12 )
swap ( 12 2 )
sq   ( 12 4 )
swap ( 4 12 )
-    ( -8 )
```

7.2.3 Dictionary

A dictionary is a part of a Forth machine that stores word definitions. Each word is a header followed by a sequence of other words.

The header stores the link to the previous word (as in linked lists), the word name itself as a null-terminated string, and some flags. We have already studied a similar data structure in the assignment, described in section 5.4. You can reuse a great part of its code to facilitate defining new Forth words. See Figure 7-9 for the word header generated for the discr word described in section 7.2.2

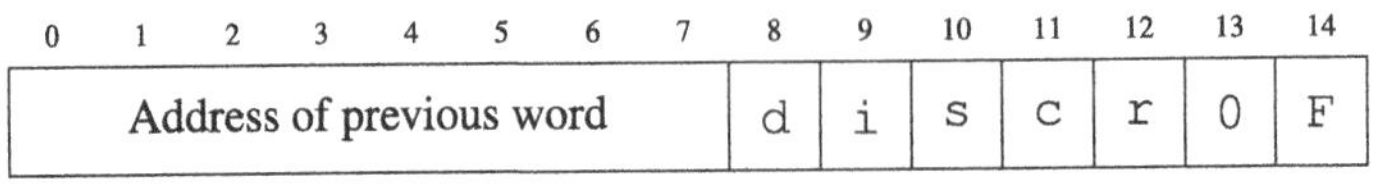

0	1	2	3	4	5	6	7	8	9	10	11	12	13	14
			Address of previous word					d	i	s	c	r	0	F

Figure 7-9. *Word header for* discr

7.2.4 How Words Are Implemented

There are three ways to implement words.

- Indirect threaded code

- Direct threaded code

- Subroutine threaded code

We are using a classic indirect threaded code way. This type of code needs two special cells (which we can call Forth registers):

> **PC** points at the next Forth command. We will see soon that the Forth command is an address of an address of the respective word's assembly implementation code. In other words, this is a pointer to an executable assembly code with two levels of indirection.

> **W** is used in non-native words. When the word starts its execution, this register points at its first word.

These two registers can be implemented through a real register usage. Alternatively, their contents can be stored in memory.

Figure 7-10 shows how words are structured when using the indirect threaded code technique. It incorporates two words: a native word dup and a colon word square.

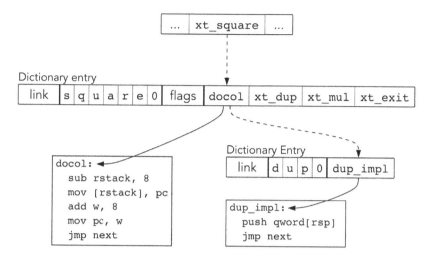

Figure 7-10. *Indirect threaded code*

Each word stores the address of its native implementation (assembly code) immediately after the header. For colon words the implementation is always the same: docol. The implementation is called using the jmp instruction.

Execution token is the address of this cell, pointing to an implementation. So, an execution token is an address of an address of the word implementation. In other words, given the address *A* of a word entry in the dictionary, you can obtain its execution token by simply adding the total header size to *A*.

Listing 7-3 provides us with a sample dictionary. It contains two native words (starting at w_plus and w_dup) and a colon word (w_sq).

Listing 7-3. forth_dict_sample.asm

```
section .data
w_plus:
    dq 0        ; The first word's pointer to the previous word is zero
    db '+',0
    db 0        ; No flags
xt_plus:        ; Execution token for `plus`, equal to
                ; the address of its implementation
    dq plus_impl
w_dup:
    dq w_plus
    db 'dup', 0
    db 0
xt_dup:
    dq dup_impl
w_double:
    dq w_dup
    db 'double', 0
    db 0
    dq docol    ; The `docol` address -- one level of indirection
    dq xt_dup   ; The words consisting `dup` start here.
```

```
    dq xt_plus
    dq xt_exit

last_word: dq w_double
section .text
    plus_impl:
        pop rax
        add rax, [rsp]
        mov [rsp], rax
        jmp next
    dup_impl:
        push qword [rsp]
        jmp next
```

The core of the Forth engine is the **inner interpreter**. It is a simple assembly routine fetching code from memory. It is shown in Listing 7-4.

Listing 7-4. forth_next.asm

```
next:
    mov w, pc
    add pc, 8 ; the cell size is 8 bytes
    mov w, [w]
    jmp [w]
```

It does two things:

1. It reads memory starting at **PC** and sets up **PC** to the next instruction. Remember, that PC points to a memory cell, which stores execution token of a word.

2. It sets up **W** to the execution token value. In other words, after next is executed, **W** stores the address of a pointer to assembly implementation of the word.

3. Finally, it jumps to the implementation code.

Every native word implementation ends with the instruction jmp next. It ensures that the next instruction will be fetched.

To implement colon words we need to use a return stack in order to save and restore PC before and after a call.

While **W** is not useful when executing native words, it is quite important for the colon words. Let us take a look at docol, the implementation of all colon words, shown in Listing 7-5 It also features exit, another word designed to end all colon words.

Listing 7-5. forth_docol.asm

```
docol:
    sub rstack, 8
    mov [rstack], pc
    add w, 8      ;    8
    mov pc, w
    jmp next
```

```
exit:
    mov pc, [rstack]
    add rstack, 8
    jmp next
```

docol saves **PC** in the return stack and sets up new **PC** to the first execution token stored inside the current word. The return is performed by exit, which restores **PC** from the stack.

This mechanism is akin to a pair of instructions call/ret.

▓ **Question 119**   Read [32]. What is the difference between our approach (indirect threaded code) and direct threaded code and subroutine threaded code? What advantages and disadvantages can you name?

To better grasp the concept of an indirect threaded code and the innards of Forth, we prepared a minimal example shown in Listing 7-6. It uses routines developed in the first assignment from section 2.7.

Take your time to launch it (the source code is shipped with the book) and check that it really reads a word from input and outputs it back.

Listing 7-6. itc.asm

```
%include "lib.inc"

global _start

%define pc r15
%define w r14
%define rstack r13

section .bss
resq 1023
rstack_start: resq 1
input_buf: resb 1024

section .text

; this one cell is the program
main_stub: dq xt_main

; The dictionary starts here
; The first word is shown in full
; Then we omit flags and links between nodes for brevity
; Each word stores an address of its assembly implementation

; Drops the topmost element from the stack
dq 0 ; There is no previous node
db "drop", 0
db 0 ; Flags = 0
xt_drop: dq i_drop
i_drop:
    add rsp, 8
    jmp next
```

```
; Initializes registers
xt_init: dq i_init
i_init:
    mov rstack, rstack_start
    mov pc, main_stub
    jmp next

; Saves PC when the colon word starts
xt_docol: dq i_docol
i_docol:
    sub rstack, 8
    mov [rstack], pc
    add w, 8
    mov pc, w
    jmp next

; Returns from the colon word
xt_exit: dq i_exit
i_exit:
    mov pc, [rstack]
    add rstack, 8
    jmp next

; Takes a buffer pointer from stack
; Reads a word from input and stores it
; starting in the given buffer
xt_word: dq i_word
i_word:
    pop rdi
    call read_word
    push rdx
    jmp next
; Takes a pointer to a string from the stack
; and prints it
xt_prints: dq i_prints
i_prints:
    pop rdi
    call print_string
    jmp next

; Exits program
xt_bye: dq i_bye
i_bye:
    mov rax, 60
    xor rdi, rdi
    syscall

; Loads the predefined buffer address
xt_inbuf: dq i_inbuf
i_inbuf:
    push qword input_buf
    jmp next
```

```
; This is a colon word, it stores
; execution tokens. Each token
; corresponds to a Forth word to be
; executed
xt_main: dq i_docol
    dq xt_inbuf
    dq xt_word
    dq xt_drop
    dq xt_inbuf
    dq xt_prints
    dq xt_bye

; The inner interpreter. These three lines
; fetch the next instruction and start its
; execution
next:
    mov w, [pc]
    add pc, 8
    jmp [w]

; The program starts execution from the init word
_start: jmp i_init
```

7.2.5   Compiler

Forth can work in either interpreter or compiler mode. Interpreter just reads commands and executes them.

When executing the colon : word, Forth switches into compiler mode. Additionally, the colon : reads one next word and uses it to create a new entry in the dictionary with docol as implementation. Then Forth reads words, locates them in dictionary, and adds them to the current word being defined.

So, we have to add another variable here, which stores the address of the current position to write words in compile mode. Each write will advance here by one cell.

To quit compiler mode we need special **immediate words**. They are executed no matter which mode we are in. Without them we would never be able to exit compiler mode. The immediate words are marked with an **immediate flag**.

The interpreter puts numbers in the stack. The compiler cannot embed them in words directly, because otherwise they will be treated as execution tokens. Trying to launch a command by an execution token 42 will most certainly result in a segmentation fault. However, the solution is to use a special word lit followed by the number itself. The lit's purpose is to read the next integer that **PC** points at and advance **PC** by one cell further, so that **PC** will never point at the embedded operand.

7.2.5.1   Forth Conditionals

We will make two words stand out in our Forth dialect: branch n and 0branch n. They are only allowed in compilation mode!

They are similar to lit n because the offset is stored immediately after their execution token.

7.3 Assignment: Forth Compiler and Interpreter

This section will describe a big assignment: writing your own Forth interpreter.

Before we start, make sure you have understood the Forth language basics. If you are not certain of it, you can play around with any free Forth interpreter, such as gForth.

■ **Question 120** Look the documentation for commands `sete`, `setl`, and their counterparts.

■ **Question 121** What does `cqo` instruction do? Refer to [15].

It is convenient to store **PC** and **W** in some general purpose registers, especially the ones that are guaranteed to survive function calls unchanged (**caller-saved**): r13, r14, or r15.

7.3.1 Static Dictionary, Interpreter

We are going to start with a static dictionary of native words. Adapt the knowledge you received in section 5.4. From now on we cannot define new words in runtime.

For this assignment we will use the following macro definitions:

- `native`, which accepts three arguments:

  - Word name;

  - A part of word identifier; and

  - Flags.

It creates and fills in the header in `.data` and a label in `.text`. This label will denote the assembly code following the macro instance.

As most words will not use flags, we can overload `native` to accept either two or three arguments. To do it, we create a similar macro definition which accepts two arguments and launches `native` with three arguments, the third being substituted by zero and the first two passed as-is, as shown in Listing 7-7.

Listing 7-7. `native_overloading.asm`

```
%macro native 2
native %1, %2, 0
%endmacro
```

Compare two ways of defining Forth dictionary: without macros (shown in Listing 7-8) and with them (shown in Listing 7-9).

Listing 7-8. `forth_dict_example_nomacro.asm`

```
section .data
w_plus:
    dq w_mul ; previous
    db '+',0
    db 0
xt_plus:
    dq plus_impl
```

```
section .text
   plus_impl:
      pop rax
      add [rsp], rax
      jmp next
```

Listing 7-9. forth_dict_example_macro.asm

```
native '+', plus
      pop rax
      add [rsp], rax
      jmp next
```

Then define a macro `colon`, analogous to the previous one. Listing 7-10 shows its usage.

Listing 7-10. forth_colon_usage.asm

```
colon '>', greater
   dq xt_swap
   dq xt_less
   dq exit
```

Do not forget about `docol` address in every colon word! Then create and test the following assembly routines:

- `find_word`, which accepts a pointer to a null-terminated string and returns the address of the word header start. If there is no word with such name, zero is returned.

- `cfa` (code from address), which takes the word header start and skips the whole header till it reaches the **XT** value.

Using these two functions and the ones you have already written in section 2.7, you can write an interpreter loop. The interpreter will either push a number into the stack or fill the special stub, consisting of two cells, shown in Listing 7-11.

It should write the freshly found execution token to `program_stub`. Then it should point **PC** at the stub start and jump to `next`. It will execute the word we have just parsed, and then pass control back to interpreter.

Remember, that an execution token is just an address of an address of an assembly code. This is why the second cell of the stub points at the third, and the third stores the interpreter address—we simply feed this data to the existing Forth machinery.

Listing 7-11. forth_program_stub.asm

```
program_stub: dq 0
xt_interpreter: dq .interpreter
.interpreter: dq interpreter_loop
```

Figure 7-11 shows the pseudo code illustrating interpreter logic.

1: **interpreter_loop:**
2: $word \leftarrow$ word from `stdin`
3: **if** $word$ is empty **then**
4:     exit
5: **if** $word$ is present in dictionary, its address is $addr$ **then**
6:     $xt \leftarrow cfa(addr)$
7:     $[program\_stub] \leftarrow xt$
8:     $PC \leftarrow program\_stub$
9:     goto $next$
10: **else**
11:     **if** $word$ is a number n **then**
12:       push n
13:     **else**
14:       Error: unknown word

Figure 7-11. *Forth interpreter: pseudocode*

Remember that the Forth machine also has memory. We are going to pre-allocate 65536 Forth cells for it.

■ **Question 122** Should we allocate these cells in `.data` section, or are there better options?

To let Forth know where the memory is, we are going to create the word mem, which will simply push the memory starting address on top of the stack.

7.3.1.1   Word list

You should first make an interpreter that supports the following words:

- .S – prints all stack contents; does not change it. To implement it, save rsp before interpreter start.

- Arithmetic: + - * /, = <. The comparison operations push either 1 or 0 on top of the stack.

- Logic: and, not. All non-zero values are considered true; zero value is considered false. In case of success these instructions push 1, otherwise 0. They also destruct their operands.

- Simple stack manipulations:

```
rot (a b c -- b c a)
swap (a b -- b a)
dup (a -- a a)
drop (a -- )
```

- . (a --) pops the number from the stack and outputs it.

- Input/output:

  key (-- c)—reads one character from stdin; The top cell in stack stores 8 bytes, it is a zero extended character code.

  emit (c --)—writes one symbol into stdout.

  number (-- n)—reads a signed integer number from stdin (guaranteed to fit into one cell).

- mem—stores the user memory starting address on top of the stack.

- Working with memory:

  ! (address data --)—stores data from stack starting at address.

  c! (address char --)—stores a single byte by address.

  @ (address -- value)—reads one cell starting from address

  c@ (address -- charvalue)—reads a single byte starting from address Then test the resulting interpreter.

Then create a memory region for the return stack and implement docol and exit. We recommend allocating a register to point at the return stack's top.

Implement colon-words or and greater using macro colon and test them.

7.3.2 Compilation

Now we are going to implement compilation. It is easy!

1. We need to allocate other 65536 Forth cells for the extensible part of the dictionary.

2. Add a variable state, which is equal to 1 when in compilation mode, 0 for interpretation mode.

3. Add a variable here, which points at the first free cell in the preallocated dictionary space.

4. Add a variable last_word, which stores the address of the last word defined.

5. Add two new colon words, namely, : and ;.

   Colon:

   1: *word* ← stdin

   2: Fill the new word's header starting at here. Do not forget to update it!

   3: Add docol address immediately at here; update here.

   4: Update last_word.

   5: *state* ← 1;

   6: Jump to next.

Semicolon should be marked as **Immediate**!

1: here ← XT of the word exit ; update here.

2: *state* ← 0;

3: Jump to next.

6. Here is what the compiler loop looks like. You can implement it separately, or mix with interpreter loop you already implemented.

1: **compiler loop:**

2: *word* ← word from stdin

3: **if** *word* is empty **then**

4: exit

5: **if** *word* is present and has address *addr* **then**

6: *xt* ← *cf a(addr)*

7: **if** *word* is marked Immediate **then**

8: interpret *word*

9: **else**

10: [here] ← xt

11: here ← here + 8

12: **else**

13: **if** *word* is a number *n* **then**

14: **if** previous word was branch or 0branch **then**

15: [here] ← *n*

16: here ← here + 8

17: **else**

18: [here] ← xt lit

19: here ← here + 8

20: [here] ← *n*

21: here ← here + 8

22: **else**

23: Error: unknown word

Implement 0branch and branch and test them (refer to section 7.3.3 for a complete list of Forth words with their meanings).

■ **Question 123**   Why do we need a separate case for branch and 0branch?

7.3.3 Forth with Bootstrap

We can divide the Forth interpreter into two parts. The very necessary one is called **inner interpreter**; it is written in assembly. Its purpose is to fetch the next **XT** from memory. This is the next routine, shown in Listing 7-4.

The other part is the outer interpreter, which accepts user input and either compiles the word to the current definition or executes it right away. The exciting thing about it is that this interpreter can be defined as a colon word. In order to accomplish that we have to define some additional Forth words.

We have created Forthress, a Forth dialect described in this chapter. The interpreter and compiler are shipped with this book as well. Here is the full set of words known to Forthress.

- drop(a --)
- swap(a b -- b a)
- dup(a -- a a)
- rot(a b c -- b c a)
- Arithmetic:
  - + (y x -- [x + y])
  - * (y x -- [x * y])
  - / (y x -- [x / y])
  - % (y x -- [x mod y])
  - - (y x -- [x - y])
- Logic:
  - not(a -- a') a' = 0 if a != 0 a' = 1 if a == 0
  - =(a b -- c) c = 1 if a == b c = 0 if a != b
- count(str -- len) Accepts a null-terminated string, calculates its length.
- . Drops element from stack and sends it to **stdout**.
- .S Shows stack contents. Does not pop elements.
- init Stores the data stack base. It is useful for **.S**.
- docol This is the implementation of any colon word. The XT itself is not used, but the implementation (known as **docol**) is.
- exit Exit from colon word.
- >r Push from return stack into data stack.
- r> Pop from data stack into return stack.
- r@ Non-destructive copy from the top of return stack to the top of data stack.
- find(str -- header addr) Accepts a pointer to a string, returns pointer to the word header in dictionary.
- cfa(word addr -- xt) Converts word header start address to the execution token.
- emit(c --) Outputs a single character to stdout.

- `word( addr -- len )` Reads word from **stdin** and stores it starting at address `addr`. Word length is pushed into stack.

- `number ( str -- num len)` Parses an integer from string.

- `prints ( addr -- )` Prints a null-terminated string.

- bye Exits Forthress

- `syscall ( call num a1 a2 a3 a4 a5 a6 -- new rax )` Executes syscall The following regis- ters store arguments (according to ABI) rdi, rsi, rdx, r10, r8, and r9.

- `branch <offset>` Jump to a location. Location is an offset relative to the argument end For example:

  ```
  |branch|    24 | <next command>
                 ^ branch adds 24 to this address and stores it in PC
  ```

- `0branch <offset>` Branch is a compile-only word. Jump to a location if TOS = 0. Location is calculated in a similar way. 0branch is a compile-only word.

- `lit <value>` Pushes a value immediately following this XT.

- inbuf Address of the input buffer (is used by interpreter/compiler).

- mem Address of user memory.

- `last word` Header of last word address.

- state State cell address. The state cell stores either 1 (compilation mode) or 0 (interpretation mode).

- here Points to the last cell of the word currently being defined.

- `execute ( xt -- )` Execute word with this execution token on TOS.

- `@   ( addr  -- value  )` Fetch value from memory.

- `!  ( addr val -- )` Store value by address.

- `@c ( addr -- char )` Read one byte starting at addr.

- `,  ( x -- )` Add x to the word being defined.

- `c, ( c -- )` Add a single byte to the word being defined.

- `create ( flags name -- )` Create an entry in the dictionary whose name is the new name. Only immediate flag is implemented ATM.

- : Read word from stdin and start defining it.

- ; End the current word definition

- interpreter Forthress interpreter/compiler.

We encourage you to try to build your own bootstrapped Forth. You can start with a working interpreter loop written in Forth. Modify the file itc.asm, shown in Listing 7-6, by introducing the word interpreter and writing it using Forth words only.

7.4 Summary

This chapter has introduced us to two new models of computation: finite state machines (also known as finite automatons) and stack machines akin to the Forth machine. We have seen the connection between finite state machines and regular expressions, used in multiple text editors and other text processing utilities. We have completed the first part of our journey by building a Forth interpreter and compiler, which we consider a wonderful summary of our introduction to assembly language. In the next chapter we are going to switch to the C language to write higher-level code. Your knowledge of assembly will serve as a foundation for your understanding of C because of how close its model of computation is to the classical von Neumann model of computation.

Question 124   What is a model of computation?

Question 125   Which models of computation do you know?

Question 126   What is a finite state machine?

Question 127   When are the finite state machines useful?

Question 128   What is a finite automaton?

Question 129   What is a regular expression?

Question 130   How are regular expressions and finite automatons connected?

Question 131   What is the structure of the Forth abstract machine?

Question 132   What is the structure of the dictionary in Forth?

Question 133   What is an execution token?

Question 134   What is the implementation difference between embedded and colon words?

Question 135   Why are two stacks used in Forth?

Question 136   Which are the two distinct modes that Forth is operating in?

Question 137   Why does the immediate flag exist?

Question 138   Describe the colon word and the semicolon word.

Question 139   What is the purpose of PC and W registers?

Question 140   What is the purpose of next?

Question 141   What is the purpose of docol?

Question 142   What is the purpose of exit?

Question 143   When an integer literal is encountered, do interpreter and compiler behave alike?

Question 144   Add an embedded word to check the remainder of a division of two numbers. Write a word to check that one number is divisible by another.

■ **Question 145** Add an embedded word to check the remainder of a division of two numbers. Write a word to check the number for primarity.

■ **Question 146** Write a Forth word to output the first *n* number of the Fibonacci sequence.

■ **Question 147** Write a Forth word to perform system calls (it will take the register contents from stack). Write a word that will print "Hello, world!" in stdout.

PART II

The C Programming Language

CHAPTER 8

Basics

In this chapter we are going to start exploring another language called C. It is a low-level language with quite minimal abstractions over assembly. At the same time it is expressive enough so we could illustrate some very general concepts and ideas applicable to all programming languages (such as type system or polymorphism).

C provides almost no abstraction over memory, so the memory management task is the programmer's responsibility. Unlike in higher-level languages, such as C# or Java, the programmer must allocate and free the reserved memory himself, instead of relying on an automated system of garbage collection.

C is a portable language, so if you write correctly, your code can often be executed on other architectures after a simple recompilation. The reason is that the model of computation in C is practically the same old von Neumann model, which makes it close to the programming models of most processors.

When learning C remember that despite the illusion of being a higher-level language, it does not tolerate errors, nor will the system be kind enough to always notify you about things in your program that were broken. An error can show itself much later, on another input, in a completely irrelevant part of the program.

Language standard described   The very important document about the language is the C language standard. You can acquire a PDF file of the standard draft online for free [7]. This document is just as important for us as the Intel Software Developer's Manual [15].

8.1   Introduction

Before we start, we need to state several important points.

- C is *always* case sensitive.

- C does not care about spacing as long as the parser can separate lexemes from one another. The programs shown in Listing 8-1 and Listing 8-2 are equivalent.

Listing 8-1. spacing_1.c

```c
int main     (int argc ,   char * * argv)
{
    return 0;
}
```

© Igor Zhirkov 2017
I. Zhirkov, *Low-Level Programming*, DOI 10.1007/978-1-4842-2403-8_8

Listing 8-2. spacing_2.c

```c
int main(int argc, char** argv)
{
    return 0;
}
```

- There are different C language standards. We do not study the GNU C (a version possessing various extensions), which is supported mostly by GCC. Instead, we concentrate on C89 (also known as ANSI C or C90) and C99, which are supported by many different compilers. We will also mention several new features of C11, some of which are not mandatory to implement in compilers.

  Unfortunately C89 still remains the most pervasive standard, so there are compilers that support C89 for virtually every existing platform. This is why we will focus on this specific revision first and then extend it with the newer features.

  To force the compiler to use only those features supported by a certain standard we use the following set of flags:

  - -std=c89 or -std=c99 to select either the C89 or C99 standard.
  - -pedantic-errors to disable non-standard language extensions.
  - -Wall to show all warnings no matter how important they are.
  - -Werror to transform warnings into errors so you would not be able to compile code with warnings.

■ **Warnings are errors**   It is a very bad practice to ship code that does not compile without warnings. Warnings are emitted for a reason.

Sometimes there are very specific cases in which people are forced to do non-standard things, such as calling a function with more arguments than it accepts, but such cases are extremely rare. In these cases it is much better to turn off one specific warning type for one specific file via a corresponding compiler key. Sometimes compiler directives can make the compiler omit a certain warning for a selected code region, which is even better.

For example, to compile an executable file main from source files file1.c and file2.c you could use the following command:

```
> gcc -o main -ansi -pedantic-errors -Wall -Werror file1.c file2.c
```

This command will make a full compilation pass including object file generation and linking.

8.2 Program Structure

Any program in C consists of

- Data types definitions (structures, new types, etc.) which are based on other existing types. For example, we can create a new name new_int_type_name_t for an integer type int.

  ```c
  typedef int new_int_type_name_t;
  ```

- Global variables (declared outside functions). For example, we can create a global variable i_am_global of type int initialized to 42 outside all function scopes. Note that global variables can only be initialized with constant values.

```
int i_am_global = 42;
```

- Functions. For example, a function named square, which accepts an argument x of type int and returns its square.

```
int square( int x ) { return x * x; }
```

- Comments between /* and */.

```
/* this is a rather complex comment
which span over multiple lines */
```

- Comments starting at // until the end of the line (in C99 and more recent).

```
int x; // this is a one line comment, which ends at the end of the line
```

- Preprocessor and compiler directives. They often start with #.

```
#define CATS_COUNT 42
#define ADD(x, y) (x) + (y)
```

Inside functions, we can define variables or data types local to this function, or perform actions. Each action is a **statement;** these are usually separated by a semicolon. The actions are performed sequentially. You cannot define functions inside other functions.

Statements will declare variables, perform computations and assignments, and execute different branches of code depending on conditions. A special case is a **block** between curly braces {}, which is used to group statements.

Listing 8-3 shows an exemplary C program. It outputs Hello, world! y=42 x=43. It defines a function main, which declares two variables x and y, the first is equal to 43, and the second is computed as the value of x minus one. Then a call to function printf is performed.

The function printf is used to output strings into **stdout**. The string has some parts (so-called **format specifiers**) replaced by the following arguments. The format specifier, as its name suggests, provides information about the argument nature, which usually includes its size and a presence of sign. For now, we will use very few format specifiers.

- %d for int arguments, as in the example.

- %f for float arguments.

Variable declarations, assignment, and a function call all ended by semicolons are statements.

■ **Spare printf for format output**   Whenever possible, use puts instead of printf. This function can only output a single string (and ends it with a newline); no format specifiers are taken into account. Not only is it faster but it works uniformly with all strings and lacks security flaws described in section 14.7.3.

For now, we will always start our programs with line #include <stdio.h>. It allows us to access a part of standard C library. However, we state firmly that this is *not* a library import of any sort and should *never* be treated as one.

Listing 8-3. hello.c

```
/* This is a comment. The next line has a preprocessor directive */
#include <stdio.h>

/* `main` is the entry point for the program, like _start in assembly
 * Actually, the hidden function _start is calling `main`.
 * `main` returns the `return code` which is then given to the `exit` system
 * call.
 * The `void` keyword instead of argument list means that `main` accepts no

 * arguments */
int main(void) {
    /* A  variable local to `main`. Will be destructed as soon as `main` ends*/
    int x = 43;
    int y;
    y = x - 1;
    /* Calling a standard function `printf` with three arguments.
     * It will print 'Hello, world! y=42 x=43
     * All %d  will be replaced by the consecutive arguments */
    printf( "Hello, world! y=%d  x=%d\n", y, x);

    return 0;
}
```

Literal is a sequence of characters in the source code which represents an immediate value. In C, literals exist for

- Integers, for example, 42.

- Floating point numbers, for example, 42.0.

- ASCII-code of characters, written in single quotes, for example, 'a'.

- Pointers to null-terminated strings, for example, "abcde".

The execution of any C program is essentially a data manipulation.

The C **abstract machine** has a von Neumann architecture. It is done on purpose, because C is a language that should be as close to the hardware as possible. The variables are stored in the linear memory and each of them has a starting address.

You can think of variables like labels in assembly.

8.2.1   Data Types

As pretty much everything that happens is a manipulation on data, the nature of the said data is of a particular interest to us. All kinds of data in C has a **type**, which means that it falls into one of (usually) distinct categories. The typing in C is weak and static.

Static typing means that all types are known in compile time. There can be absolutely incertitude about data types. Whether you are using a variable, a literal, or a more complex expression, which evaluates to some data, its type will be known.

Weak typing means that sometimes a data element can be implicitly converted to another type when appropriate.

For example, when evaluating `1 + 3.0` it is apparent that these two numbers have different types. One of them is integer; the other is a real number. You cannot directly add one to another, because their binary representation differs. You need to convert them both to the same type (probably, floating point number). Only then will you be able to perform an addition. In strongly typed languages, such, as OCaml, this operation is not permitted; instead, there are two separate operations to add numbers: one acts on integers (and is written +), the other on real numbers (is written +. in OCaml).

Weak typing is in C for a reason: in assembly, it is absolutely possible to take virtually any data and interpret it as data of another type (pointer as an integer, part of the string as an integer, etc.)

Let's see what happens when we try to output a floating point value as an integer (see Listing 8-4). The result will be the floating point value *reinterpreted* as an integer, which does not make much sense.

Listing 8-4. `float_reinterpret.c`

```
#include <stdio.h>

int main(void) {
    printf("42.0 as an integer %d  \n", 42.0);
    return 0;
}
```

This program's output depends on the target architecture. In our case, the output was

```
42.0 as an integer -266654968
```

For this brief introductory section, we will consider that all types in C fall into one of these categories:

- Integer numbers (`int`, `char`, …).

- Floating point numbers (`double` and `float`).

- Pointer types.

- Composite types: structures and unions.

- Enumerations.

In Chapter 9 we are going to explore the type system in more detail. If you come with a background in a higher-level language, you might find some commonly known items missing from this block. Unfortunately, *there are no string and Boolean types in C89*. An integer value equal to zero is considered false; any non-zero value is considered truth.

8.3   Control Flow

According to von Neumann principles, the program execution is sequential. Each statement is executed one after another. There are several statements to change control flow.

8.3.1   if

Listing 8-5 shows an if statement with an optional else part. If the condition is satisfied, the first block is executed. If the condition is not satisfied, the second block is executed, but the second block is not mandatory.

Listing 8-5. if_example.c

```
int x  =  100;
if (42) {
    puts("42 is not equal to zero and thus considered truth");
}

if (x > 3) {
    puts("X is greater than 3");
}
else
{
    puts("X is less than 3");
}
```

The braces are optional. Without braces, only one statement will be considered part of each branch, as shown in Listing 8-6.

Listing 8-6. if_no_braces.c

```
if (x == 0)
    puts("X is zero");
else
    puts("X is not zero");
```

Notice that there is a syntax fault, called **dangling else**. Check Listing 8-7 and see if you can certainly attribute the else branch to the first or the second if. To solve this disambiguation in case of nested ifs, use braces.

Listing 8-7. dangling_else.c

```
if (x == 0)   if (y == 0) { puts("A"); }  else { puts("B"); }

/* You might have considered one of the following interpretations.
 * The compiler can issue a warning to prevent you */

if (x == 0) {
    if (y == 0) { printf("A"); }
    else { puts("B"); }
}

if (x == 0) {
    if (y == 0) { puts("A"); }
} else { puts("B"); }
```

8.3.2   while

A while statement is used to make cycles.

Listing 8-8. while_example.c

```
int x = 10;
while ( x != 0 ) {
    puts("Hello");
    x = x - 1;
}
```

If the condition is satisfied, then the body is executed. Then the condition is checked once again, and if it is satisfied, then the body is executed again, and so on.

An alternative form do ... while (condition); allows you to check conditions after executing the loop body, thus guaranteeing at least one iteration. Listing 8-9 shows an example.

Notice that a body can be empty, as follows: while (x == 0);. The semicolon after the parentheses ends this statement.

Listing 8-9. do_while_example.c

```
int x = 10;
do {
    printf("Hello\n");      x = x - 1;
}
while ( x != 0 );
```

8.3.3   for

A for statement is ideal to iterate over finite collections, such as linked lists or arrays. It has the following form: for (initializer ; condition; step) body. Listing 8-10 shows an example.

Listing 8-10. for_example.c

```
int a[] = {1, 2, 3, 4}; /* an array of 4 elements */
int i = 0;
for ( i = 0; i < 4; i++ ) {
    printf( "%d",  a[i])
}
```

First, the initializer is executed. Then there is a condition check, and if it holds, the loop body is executed, and then the step statement.

In this case, the step statement is an increment operator ++, which modifies a variable by increasing its value by one. After that, the loop begins again by checking the condition, and so on. Listing 8-11 shows two equivalent loops.

Listing 8-11. while_for_equiv.c

```
int i;

/* as a `while` loop */
i = 0;
while ( i < 10 ) {
    puts("Hello!");
    i = i + 1;
}

/* as a `for` loop */
for( i = 0; i < 10; i = i + 1 ) {
    puts("Hello!");
}
```

The break statement is used to end the cycle prematurely and fall to the next statement in the code. continue ends the current iteration and starts the next iteration right away. Listing 8-12 shows an example.

Listing 8-12. loop_cont.c

```
int n = 0;
for( n = 0; n < 20; n++ ) {
    if (n % 2) continue;
    printf("%d is odd", n );
}
```

Note also that in the for loop, the initializer, step, or condition expressions can be left empty. Listing 8-13 shows an example.

Listing 8-13. infinite_for.c

```
for( ; ; ) {
    /* this cycle will loop forever, unless `break` is issued in its body */
    break; /* `break` is here, so we stop iterating */
}
```

8.3.4   goto

A goto statement allows you to make jumps to a label inside the same function. As in assembly, labels can mark any statement, and the syntax is the same: label: statement. This is often described a bad codestyle; however, it might be quite handy when encoding **finite state machines**. What you should not do is to abandon well-thought-out conditionals and loops for goto-spaghetti.

The goto statement is sometimes used as a way to break from several nested cycles. However, this is often a symptom of a bad design, because the inner loops can be abstracted away inside a function (thanks to the compiler optimizations, probably for no runtime cost at all). Listing 8-14 shows how to use goto to break out of all inner loops.

Listing 8-14. goto.c

```
int i;
int j;
for (i = 0; i < 100; i++ )
```

```
for( j = 0; j < 100; j++ ) {
    if (i * j == 432)
        goto end;
    else
        printf("%d * %d != 432\n", i, j );
}
end:
```

The goto statement mixed with the imperative style makes analyzing the program behavior harder for both humans *and* machines (compilers), so the cheesy optimizations the modern compilers are capable of become less likely, and the code becomes harder to maintain. We advocate restricting goto usage to the pieces of code that perform *no assignments*, like the implementations of finite state machines. This way you won't have to trace all the possible program execution routes and how the values of certain variables change when the program executes one way or another.

8.3.5 switch

A switch statement is used like multiple nested if's when the condition is some integer variable being equal to one or another value. Listing 8-15 shows an example.

Listing 8-15. case_example.c

```
int i = 10;
switch ( i ) {
    case 1: /* if i is equal to 1...*/
        puts( "It is one" );
        break; /* Break is mandatory */

    case 2: /* if i is equal to 2...*/
        puts( "It is two" );
        break;

    default: /* otherwise... */
        puts( "It is not one nor two" );
        break;
}
```

Every case is, in fact, a label. The cases are not limited by anything but an optional break statement to leave the switch block. It allows for some interesting hacks.[1] However, a forgotten break is usually a source of bugs. Listing 8-16 shows these two behaviors: first, several labels are attributed to the same case, meaning no matter whether x is 0, 1 or 10, the code executed will be the same. Then, as the break is not ending this case, after executing the first printf the control will fall to the next instruction labeled case 15, another printf.

Listing 8-16. case_magic.c

```
switch ( x ) {
    case 0:
    case 1:
    case 10:
        puts( "First case: x = 0, 1 or 10" );
```

---

[1]One of the most known hacks is called Duff's device and incorporates a cycle which is defined inside a switch and contains several cases.

```
        /* Notice the absence of `break`! */
    case 15:
        puts( "Second case: x = 0, 1, 10 or 15" );
        break;
}
```

8.3.6 Example: Divisor

Listing 8-17 showcases a program that searches for the first divisor, which is then printed to stdout. The function first_divisor accepts an argument *n* and searches for an integer *r* from 1 exclusive to *n* inclusive, such that *n* is a multiple of *r*. If *r* = *n*, we have obviously found a **prime number**.

Notice how the statement after for was not put between curly braces because it is the only statement inside the loop. The same happened with the if body, which consists of a sole return i. You can of course put it inside braces, and some programmers actually encourage it.

Listing 8-17. divisor.c

```c
#include <stdio.h>

int first_divisor( int n ) {
    int i;
    if ( n == 1 ) return 1;
    for( i = 2; i <= n; i++ )
        if ( n % i == 0 ) return i;
    return 0;
}

int main(void) {
    int i;
    for( i = 1; i < 11; i++ )
        printf( "%d \n", first_divisor( i ) );

    return 0;
}
```

8.3.7 Example: Is It a Fibonacci Number?

Listing 8-18 shows a program that checks whether a number is a Fibonacci number or not. The Fibonacci series is defined recursively as follows:

$$f_1 = 1$$
$$f_2 = 1$$
$$f_n = f_{n-1} + f_{n-2}$$

This series has a large number of applications, notably in combinatorics. Fibonacci sequences appear even in biological settings, such as branching in trees, arrangement of the leaves on a stem, etc.

The first Fibonacci numbers are 1, 1, 2, 3, 5, 8, etc. As you see, each number is the sum of two previous numbers.

In order to check whether a given number *n* is contained in a Fibonacci sequence, we adopt a straightforward (not necessarily optimal) approach of calculating all sequence members prior to *n*. The nature of a Fibonacci sequence implies that it is ascending, so if we found a member greater than n and still have not enumerated n, we conclude, that n is not in the sequence. The function is_fib accepts an integer n and calculates all elements less or equal to n. If the last element of this sequence is n, then n is a Fibonacci number and it returns 1; otherwise, it returns 0.

Listing 8-18. is_fib.c

```
#include <stdio.h>

int is_fib( int n ) {

    int a = 1;
    int b = 1;
    if ( n == 1 ) return 1;

    while ( a <= n && b <= n ) {
        int t = b;

        if (n == a || n == b) return 1;
        b = a;
        a = t + a;
    }
    return 0;

}

void check(int n) { printf( "%d -> %d\n", n, is_fib( n ) ); }

int main(void) {
    int i;
    for( i = 1; i < 11; i = i + 1 ) {
        check( i );
    }
    return 0;
}
```

8.4   Statements and Expressions

The C language is based on notions of statements and **expressions**. Expressions correspond to data entities.

All literals and variable names are expressions. Additionally, complex expressions can be constructed using operations (+, -, and other logical, arithmetic, and bit operations) and function calls (with the exception of routines returning void). Listing 8-19 shows some exemplary expressions.

Listing 8-19. expr_example.c

```
1
13  +  37
17 + 89 * square( 1 )
x
```

Expressions are data, so they can be used at the right side of the assignment operator =. Some of the expressions can be also used at the left side of the assignment. They should correspond to data entities having an address in memory.[2]

Such expressions are called **lvalue**; all other expressions, which have no address, are called **rvalue**. This difference is actually very intuitive as long as you think in terms of abstract machine. Expressions such as shown in Listing 8-20 bear no meaning, because an assignment means memory change.

Listing 8-20. `rvalue_example.c`

```
4 = 2;
"abc"="bcd";
square(3)   =   9;
```

8.4.1 Statement Types

Statements are commands to the C abstract machine. Each command is an imperative: do something! Thus the name"imperative programming": it is a sequence of commands.

There are three types of statements:

1. Expressions terminated by a semicolon.

   ```
   1 + 3;
   42;
   square(3);
   ```

   The purpose of these statements is the computation of the given expressions. If these invoke no assignments (directly as a part of the expression itself or inside one of invoked functions) or input/output operations, their impact on the program state is not observable.

2. A block delimited by { and }. It contains an arbitrary number of sentences. A block should not be ended by a semicolon itself (but the statements inside it likely should). Listing 8-21 shows a typical block.

Listing 8-21. `block_example.c`

```
int y = 1 + 3;
{
    int x;
    x = square( 2 ) + y;
    printf( "%d\n", x );
}
```

3. Control flow statements: `if`, `while`, `for`, `switch`. They do not require a semicolon.

---

[2]We are talking about abstract C machine memory here. Of course, the compiler has the right to optimize variables and never allocate real memory for them on the assembly level. The programmer, however, is not constrained by it and can think that every variable is an address of a memory cell.

We have already talked about assignments; the evil truth is that assignments are expressions themselves, which means that they can be chained. For example, a = b = c means

- Assign c to b;

- Assign the new b value to a.

A typical assignment is thus a statement from the first category: expression ended by a semicolon. Assignment is a right-associative operation. It means that when being parsed by a compiler (or your eye) the parentheses are implicitly put from right to left, the rightmost part becoming the most deeply nested. Listing 8-22 provides an example of two equivalent ways to write a complex assignment.

Listing 8-22. `assignment_assoc.c`

```
x = y = z;
(x = (y = z));
```

On the other hand, the left-associative operations consider the opposite nesting order, as shown in Listing 8-23

Listing 8-23. `div_assoc.c`

```
40 / 2 / 4
((40 / 2) / 4)
```

8.4.2 Building Expressions

An expression is built using other expressions connected with operators and function calls. The operators can be classified

- Based on arity (operand count)

  - Unary (like unary minus: `- expr`)

  - Binary (like binary multiplication: `expr1 * expr2`)

  - Ternary. There is only one ternary operator: `cond ? expr1 : expr2`. If the condition holds, the value is equal to `expr1`, otherwise `expr2`

- Based on meaning

  - Arithmetic Operators: `* / + - % ++ --`

  - Relational Operators: `== != > < >= <=`

  - Logical Operators: `! && || << >>`

  - Bitwise Operators: `~ ^ & |`

  - Assignment Operators `= += -= *= /= %= <<= >>= &= ^= |=`

  - Misc Operators:

    1. `sizeof(var)` as "replace this with the size of `var` in bytes"

    2. `&` as "take address of an operand"

    3. as "dereference this pointer"

    4. `?:` which is the ternary operator we have spoken about before.

    5. `->`, which is used to refer to a field of a structural or union type.

Most operators have an evident meaning. We will mention some of the less used and more obscure ones.

- The increment and decrement operators can be used in either prefix or postfix form: either for a variable i it is i++ or ++i. Both expressions will have an immediate effect on i, meaning it is incremented by 1. However, the value of i++ is the "old" i, while the value of ++i is the "new," incremented i.

- There is a difference between logical and bit-wise operators. For logical operators, any non-zero number is essentially the same in its meaning, while the bit-wise operations are applied to each bit separately. For example, 2 & 4 is equal to zero, because no bits are set in both 2 and 4. However, 2 && 4 will return 1, because both 2 and 4 are non-zero numbers (truth values).

- Logical operators are evaluated in a lazy way. Consider the logical and operator &&. When applied to two expressions, the first expression will be computed. If its value is zero, the computation ends immediately, because of the nature of AND operation. If any of its operands is zero, the result of the big conjunction will be zero as well, so there is no need to evaluate it further. It is important for us because this behavior is noticeable. Listing 8-24 shows an example where the program will output F and will never execute the function g.

Listing 8-24. logic_lazy.c

```c
#include <stdio.h>

int f(void) { puts( "F" ); return 0; }
int g(void) { puts( "G" ); return 1; }

int main(void) {
    f() && g();
    return  0;
}
```

- Tilde (~) is a bit-wise unary negation, hat (^) is a bitwise binary xor.

In the following chapters we will revisit some of these, such as address manipulation operands and sizeof.

8.5 Functions

We can draw a line between procedures (which do not return a value) and functions (which return a value of a certain type). The procedure call cannot be embedded into a more complex expression, unlike the function call.

Listing 8-25 shows an exemplary procedure. Its name is myproc; it returns void, so it does not return anything. It accepts two integer parameters named a and b.

Listing 8-25. proc_example.c

```c
void myproc ( int a, int b )
{
    printf("%d",  a+b);
}
```

Listing 8-26 shows an exemplary function. It accepts two arguments and returns a value of type int. A call to this function is used as a part of a more complex expression later.

Listing 8-26. `function_example.c`

```
int myfunc ( int a, int b )
{
    return a + b;
}

int other( int x ) {
    return 1 + myfunc( 4, 5 );
}
```

Every function's execution is ended with `return` statement; otherwise which value it will return is undefined. Procedures can have the `return` keyword omitted; it might be still used without an operand to immediately return from the procedure.

When there are no arguments, a keyword `void` should be used in function declaration, as shown in Listing 8-27.

Listing 8-27. `no_arguments_ex.c`

```
int always_return_0( void ) { return 0; }
```

The body of function is a block statement, so it is enclosed in braces and is not ended with a semicolon. Each block defines a lexical scope for variables.

All variables should be declared in the block start, before any statements. That restriction is present in C89 but not in C99. We will adhere to it to make the code more portable.

Additionally, it forces a certain self-discipline. If you have a large amount of local variables declared at the scope start, it will look cluttered. At the same time it is usually sign of bad program decomposition and/ or poor choice of data structures.

Listing 8-28 shows examples of good and bad variable declarations.

Listing 8-28. `block_variables.c`

```
/* Good */
void f(void) {
    int x;
    ...
}

/* Bad: `x` is declared after `printf` call */

void f(void) {
    int y = 12;
    printf( "%d", y);
    int x = 10;
    ...
}

/* Bad: `i` can not be declared in `for` initializer */
for( int i = 0; i < 10; i++ ) {
    ...
}
```

```
/* Good: `i` is declared before `for` */
int f(void) {
    int i;
    for( i = 0; i < 10; i++ ) {
        ...
    }
}

/* Good: any block can have additional variables declared in its beginning */
/* `x` is local to one `for` iteration and is always reinitialized to 10 */
for( i = 0; i < 10; i++ ) {
    int x = 10;
}
```

If a variable in a certain scope has the same name as the variable already declared in a higher scope, the more recent variable hides the ancient one. There is no way to address the hidden variable syntactically (by not storing its address somewhere and using the address).

The local variables in different functions can of course have the same names.

■ **Note**   The variables are visible until the end of their respective blocks. So a commonly used notion of 'local' variables is in fact block-local, not function-local. The rule of thumb is: make variables as local as you can (including variables local to loop bodies, for example. It greatly reduces program complexity, especially in large projects.

8.6   Preprocessor

The C preprocessor is acting similar to the NASM preprocessor. Its power, though, is much more limited. The most important **preprocessor directives** you are going to see are

- #define
- #include
- #ifndef
- #endif

The #define directive is very similar to its NASM %define counterpart. It has three main usages.

- Defining global constants (see Listing 8-29 for an example).

Listing 8-29. define_example1.c

```
#define MY_CONST_VALUE 42
```

- Defining parameterized macro substitutions (as shown in Listing 8-30).

Listing 8-30. `define_example2.c`

```
#define MACRO_SQUARE( x ) ((x) * (x))
```

- Defining flags; depending on which, some additional code can be included or excluded from sources.

It is important to enclose in parentheses all argument occurrences inside macro definitions. The reason behind it is that C macros are not syntactic, which means that the preprocessor is not aware of the code structure. Sometimes this results in an unexpected behavior, as shown in Listing 8-31. Listing 8-32 shows the preprocessed code.

Listing 8-31. `define_parentheses.c`

```
#define SQUARE( x ) (x * x)

int x = SQUARE( 4+1 )
```

As you see, the value of x will not be 25 but 4+(1*4)+1 because of multiplication having a higher priority comparing to addition.

Listing 8-32. `define_parentheses_preprocessed.c`

```
int x = 4+1 * 4+1
```

The `#include` directive pastes the given file contents in place of itself. The file name is enclosed in either quotes (`#include "file.h"`) or angle brackets (`#include <stdio.h>`).

- In case of angle brackets, the file is searched in a set of predefined directories. For GCC it is usually:

    - `/usr/local/include`

    - `<libdir>/gcc/target/version/include`

      Here `<libdir>` stands for the directory that holds libraries (a GCC setting) and is usually `/usr/lib` or `/usr/local/lib` by default.

    - `/usr/target/include`

    - `/usr/include`

      Using the `-I` key one can add directories to this list. You can make a special `include/` directory in your project root and add it to the GCC include search list.

- In case of quotes, the files are also searched in the current directory.

You can get the preprocessor output by evaluating a file `filename.c` in the same way as when working with NASM: `gcc -E filename.c`. This will execute all preprocessor directives and flush the results into `stdout` without doing anything.

8.7 Summary

In this chapter we have elaborated the C basics. All variables are labels in memory of the C language abstract machine, whose architecture greatly resembles the von Neumann architecture. After describing a universal program structure (functions, data types, global variables, . . .), we have defined two syntactical categories: statements and expressions. We have seen that expressions are either `lvalues` or `rvalues` and learned to control the program execution using function calls and control statements such as `if` and `while`. We are already able to write simple programs which perform computations on integers. In the next chapter we are going to discuss the type system in C and the types in general to get a bigger picture of how types are used in different programming languages. Thanks to the notion of arrays our possible input and output data will become much more diverse.

Question 148 What is a literal?

Question 149 What are `lvalue` and `rvalue`?

Question 150 What is the difference between the statements and expressions?

Question 151 What is a block of statements?

Question 152 How do you define a preprocessor symbol?

Question 153 Why is `break` necessary at the end of each `switch` case?

Question 154 How are truth and false values encoded in C89?

Question 155 What is the first argument of `printf` function?

Question 156 Is `printf` checking the types of its arguments?

Question 157 Where can you declare variables in C89?

CHAPTER 9

Type System

The notion of type is one of the key ones. A type is essentially a tag assigned to a data entity. Every data transformation is defined for specific data types, which ensures their correctness (you would not want to add the amount of active Reddit users to the average temperature at noon in Sahara, because it makes no sense).

This chapter will study the C type system in depth.

9.1 Basic Type System of C

All types in C fall into one of these categories:

- Predefined numeric types (`int`, `char`, `float`, etc.).

- Arrays, multiple elements of the same type occupying consequent memory cells.

- Pointers, which are essentially the cells storing other cells' addresses. The pointer type encodes the type of cell it is pointing to. A particular case of pointers are function pointers.

- Structures, which are packs of data of different types. For example, a structure can store an integer and a floating point number. Each of the data elements has its own name.

- Enumerations, which are essentially integers, take one of explicitly defined values. Each of these values has a symbolic name to refer to.

- Functional types.

- Constant types, built on top of some other type and making the data immutable.

- Type aliases for other types.

9.1.1 Numeric Types

The most basic C types are the numeric ones. They have different sizes and are either signed or unsigned. Because of a long and loosely controlled language evolution, their description may seem sometimes arcane and quite often very ad hoc. Following is a list of the basic types:

1. `char`

    - Can be `signed` and `unsigned`. By default it is usually signed number, but it is not required by the language standard.

    - Its size is always 1 byte;

© Igor Zhirkov 2017
I. Zhirkov, *Low-Level Programming*, DOI 10.1007/978-1-4842-2403-8_9

- Despite the name making a direct reference to the word "character," this is an integer type and should be treated as such. It is often used to store the ASCII code of a character, but it can be used to store any 1-byte number.

- A literal 'x' and corresponds to an ASCII code of the character "x." Its type is int but it is safe to assign it to a variable of type char.[1]

Listing 9-1 shows an example.

Listing 9-1. char_example.c

```
char number = 5;
char symbol_code = 'x';
char null_terminator = '\0';
```

2. int

- An integer number.

- Can be signed and unsigned. It is signed by default.

- It can be aliased simply as: signed, signed int (similar for unsigned).

- Can be short (2 bytes), long (4 bytes on 32-bit architectures, 8 bytes in Intel 64). Most compilers also support long long, but up to C99 it was not part of standard.

- Other aliases: short, short int, signed short, signed short int.

- The size of int without modifiers varies depending on architecture. It was designed to be equal to the machine word size. In the 16-bit era the int size was obviously 2 bytes, in 32-bit machines it is 4 bytes. Unfortunately, this did not prevent programmers from relying on an int of size 4 in the era of 32-bit computing. Because of the large pool of software that would break if we change the size of int, its size is left untouched and remains 4 bytes.

- It is important to note that all integer literals have the int format by default. If we add suffixes L or UL we will explicitly state that these numbers are of type long int or unsigned int. Sometimes it is of utter importance not to forget these suffixes.

  Consider an expression 1 << 48. Its value is not 2^{48} as you might have thought, but 0. Why? The reason is that 1 is a literal of the type int, which occupies 4 bytes and thus can vary from -2^{31} to $2^{31} - 1$. By shifting 1 to the left 48 times, we are moving the only bit set outside of integer format. Thus the result is zero. However, if we do add a correct suffix, the answer will be more evident. An expression 1L << 48 is evaluated to 2^{48}, because 1L is now 8 bytes long.

3. long long

- In x64 architecture it is the same as a long (except for Windows, where long is 4 bytes).

- Its size is 8 bytes.

- Its range is : $-2^{63} \ldots 2^{63} - 1$ for signed and $0 \ldots 2^{64} - 1$ for unsigned.

---

[1]This language design flaw is corrected in C++, where 'x' has type char.

4. `float`

   - Floating point number.

   - Its size is 4 bytes.

   - Its range is : $\pm 1, 17549 \times 10^{-38} \dots \pm 3, 40282 \times 10^{38}$ (approximately six digits precision).

5. `double`

   - Floating point number.

   - Its size is 8 bytes.

   - Its range is: $\pm 2, 22507 \times 10^{-308} \dots \pm 1, 79769 \times 10^{308}$ (approximately 15 digits precision).

6. `long double`

   - Floating point number.

   - Its size is usually 80 bits.

   - It was only introduced in C99 standard.

■ **Note**   On floating point arithmetic

First of all, remember, that floating point types are a very rough approximation of the real numbers. For example, they are more precise near 0 and less precise for big values. This is exactly the reason their range is so great compared even to `long`s.

As a consequence, doing floating point arithmetic with values closer to zero yields more precise results.

Finally, in certain contexts (e.g., kernel programming) the floating point arithmetic is not available. As a rule of thumb, avoid it when you do not need it. For example, if your computations can be performed by manipulating a quotient and a remainder, calculated by using / and % operators, you should stick with them.

9.1.2 Type Casting

The language allows you to relatively freely convert data between types. To do it you have to write the new type name in parentheses before the expression you want to convert.

Listing 9-2 shows an example.

Listing 9-2. `type_cast.c`

```
int a = 4;

double b = 10.5 * (double)a; /* now a is a double */

int b = 129;
char k = (char)b; //???
```

Surely, this wonderful open world of possibilities is better controlled by your benevolent dictatorship because these implicit conversions often lead to subtle bugs when an expression is not evaluated to what it "should" be evaluated.

For example, as char is a (usually) signed number in range -128 . . . 127, the number 129 is too big to fit into this range. The result of an action, shown in Listing 9-2, is not described in the language standard, but given how typical processors and compilers function, the result will be probably a negative number, consisting of the same bits as an unsigned representation of 129.

■ **Question 158**   What will be the value of *k*? Try to compile and see in your own computer.

9.1.3   Boolean Type

We have already stated that the C89 lacks Booleans. However, C99 introduced Booleans as a type _Bool. If you include stdbool.h, you will have access to the values true / false and the type bool, which is an alias of _Bool. The reasoning behind this is simple. Many existing projects already have Boolean type defined for themselves, usually as bool. To prevent naming conflicts, the C99 type name for Booleans is _Bool. Including the file stdbool.h signifies that your code is free from any custom bool definition, and you are picking the one conforming to the standard, but with a more humane name. We encourage you to use the aliased type bool whenever possible. In the future, the _Bool type name will be probably declared deprecated, and after several standard versions it will not be used anymore.

9.1.4   Implicit Conversions

As a weakly typed language, C allows one to omit casts sometimes even when using data of different type than intended.

When the required numeric type is not equal as the actual type, an implicit conversion is performed, which is called **integer promotion**. If the type is lesser than an int, it gets promoted to signed int or unsigned int, depending on its initial signed or unsigned nature.[2] Then if they are still different, we climb up the ladder, shown in Figure 9-1

```
int → unsigned int → long → unsigned long → long long →
   unsigned long long → float → double → long double
```

Figure 9-1. *Integer conversions*

■ **Note**   Remember that long long and long double have appeared only in C99. They are, however, supported as a language extension by many compilers that do not support C99 yet.

The "convert to int first" rule means that the overflows in lesser types can be handled *differently* than in int type itself. The example shown in Listing 9-3 assumes that sizeof(int) == 4.

Listing 9-3. int_promotion_pitfall.c

```
/* The lesser types */
unsigned char  x = 100, y = 100, z = 100;
unsigned char r = x + y + z; /* will give you 300 % 256 = 44 */
```

---

[2]The keyword is *usual arithmetic conversions*.

```
unsigned int r_int = x + y + z; /* equals to 300, because the promotion to
                                   integers is performed first */

/* Now with the greater types */

unsigned int x = 1e9, y = 2e9, z = 3e9;

unsigned int r_int = x + y + z;    /* 1705032704 equals 6000000000 % (2^32) */

unsigned long r_long = x + y + z;    /*  the same result: 1705032704 */
```

In the last line, neither x, y, nor z is promoted to long, because it is not required by standard. The arithmetic will be performed within the int type and then the result will be converted to long.

■ **Be understood**   As a rule of thumb, when uncertain, always provide the types explicitly! For example, you can write long x = (long)a + (long)b + (long)c.

While the code might seem more verbose after that, it will at least work as intended.

Let's look at an example shown in Listing 9-4. The expression in the third line will be computed as follows:

1. The value of i will be converted to float (of course, the variable itself will not change);

2. This value is added to the value of f, the resulting type is float again; and

3. This result is converted to double to be stored in d.

Listing 9-4. int_float_conv.c

```
int i;
float f;
double d = f + i;
```

All these operations are not free and are encoded as assembly instructions. It means that whenever you are acting on numbers of different formats, it probably has runtime costs. Try to avoid it especially in cycles.

9.1.5   Pointers

Given a type T, one can always construct a type T*. This new type corresponds to data units which hold address of another entity of type T.

As all addresses have the same size, all pointer types have the same size as well. It is specific for architecture and, in our case, is 8 bytes wide.

Using operands & and * one can take an address of a variable or dereference a pointer (look into the memory by the address this pointer stores). Listing 9-5 shows an example.

In section 2.5.4 we discussed a subtle problem: if a pointer is just an address, how do we know, the size of a data entity we are trying to read starting from this address? In assembly, it was straightforward: either the size could have been deduced based on the fact that two mov operands should have the same size or the size should have been explicitly given, for example, mov qword [rax], 0xABCDE. Here the type system takes care of it: if a pointer is of a type int*, we surely know that dereferencing it produces a value of size sizeof(int).

Listing 9-5. ptr_deref.c

```
int x = 10;
int* px = &x; /* Took address of `x` and assigned it to `px` */

*px = 42; /* We modified `x` here! */
printf( "*px = %d\n", *px ); /* outputs: '*px = 42' */
printf( "x = %d\n", x ); /* outputs: 'x = 42' */
```

When you program in C, pointers are your bread and butter. As long as you do not introduce a pointer to non-existing data, the pointers will serve you right.

A special pointer value is 0. When used in pointer context (specifically, comparison with 0), 0 signifies "a special value for a pointer to nowhere." In place of 0 you can also write NULL, and you are advised to do so. It is a common practice to assign NULL to the pointers which are not yet initialized with a valid object address, or return NULL from functions returning an address of something to make the caller aware of an error.

■ **Is zero a zero?**   There are two contexts in which you might use the 0 expression in C. The first context expects just a normal integer number. The second one is a pointer context, when you assign a pointer to 0 or compare it with 0. In the second context 0 does not always mean an integer value with all bits cleared, but will always be equal to this "invalid pointer" value. In some architectures it can be, for example, a value with all bits set. But this code will work no matter the architecture because of this rule:

```
int* px = ... ;

if ( px ) /* if `px` is not NULL */

if ( px == 0 ) /* same thing as the following: */
if (!px ) /* if `px` is NULL */
```

There is a special kind of pointer type: void*. This is the pointer to any kind of data. C allows us to assign any type of pointer to a variable of type void*; however, this variable cannot be dereferenced. Before we do it, we need to take its value and convert to a legit pointer type (e.g., int*). A simple cast is used to do it (see section 9.1.2). Listing 9-6 shows an example.

Listing 9-6. void_deref.c

```
int a = 10;
void* pa = &a;

printf("%d\n", *( (int*) pa) );
```

You can also pass a pointer of type void* to any function that accepts a pointer to some other type. Pointers have many purposes, and we are going to list a couple of them.

- Changing a variable created outside a function.

- Creating and navigating complex data structures (e.g., linked lists).

- Calling functions by pointers means that by changing pointer we switch between different functions being called. This allows for pretty elegant architectural solutions.

Pointers are closely tied with arrays, which are discussed in the next section.

9.1.6 Arrays

In C, an array is a data structure that holds a fixed amount of data of the same type. So, to work with an array we need to know its start, size of a single element and the amount of elements that it can store. Refer to Listing 9-7 to see several variations of array declaration.

Listing 9-7. array_decl.c

```
/* This array's size is computed by compiler */
int arr[] = {1,2,3,4,5};

/* This array is initialized with zeros, its size is 256 bytes */
long array[32] = {0};
```

As the amount of elements should be fixed, it cannot be read from a variable.[3] To allocate memory for such arrays whose dimensions we do not know in advance, memory allocators are used (which are even not always at your disposal, for example, when programming kernels). We will learn to use the standard C memory allocator (malloc / free) and will even write our own.

You can address elements by index. Indices start from 0. The origins of this solution is in the nature of address space. The zero-th element is located at an array's starting address plus 0 times the element size.

Listing 9-8 shows an array declaration, two reads and one write.

Listing 9-8. array_example_rw.c

```
int myarray[1024];
int y = myarray[64];

int first = myarray[0];

myarray[10] = 42;
```

If we think for a bit about the C abstract machine, the arrays are just continuous memory regions holding the data of the same type. There is no information about type itself or about the array length. It is fully a programmer's responsibility to never address an element outside an allocated array.

Whenever you write the allocated array's name, you are actually referring to its address. You can think about it as a constant pointer *value*. Here is the place where the analogy between assembly labels and variables is the strongest. So, in Listing 9-8, an expression myarray has actually a type int*, because it is a pointer to the first array element!

It also means that an expression *myarray will be evaluated to its first element, just as myarray[0].

9.1.7 Arrays as Function Arguments

Let's talk about functions accepting arrays as arguments. Listing 9-9 shows a function returning a first array element (or -1 if the array is empty).

---

[3] Until C99; but even nowadays variable length arrays are discouraged by many because if the array size is big enough, the stack will not be able to hold it and the program will be terminated.

Listing 9-9. fun_array1.c

```c
int first (int array[], size_t sz ) {
    if ( sz == 0 ) return -1;
    return array[0];
}
```

Unsurprisingly, the same function can be rewritten keeping the same behavior, as shown in Listing 9-10.

Listing 9-10. fun_array2.c

```c
int first (int* array, size_t sz ) {
    if ( sz == 0 ) return -1;
    return *array;
}
```

But that's not all. You can actually mix these and use the indexing notation with pointers, as shown in Listing 9-11.

Listing 9-11. fun_array3.c

```c
int first (int* array, size_t sz ) {
    if ( sz == 0 ) return -1;
    return array[0];
}
```

The compiler immediately demotes constructions such as int array[] in the arguments list to a pointer int* array, and then works with it as such. Syntactically, however, you can still specify the array length, as shown in Listing 9-12. This number indicates that the given array should have at least that many elements. However, the compiler *treats it as a commentary and performs no runtime or compile-time checks.*

Listing 9-12. array_param_size.c

```c
int first( int array[10], size_t sz ) { ... }
```

C99 introduced a special syntax, which corresponds essentially to your promise given to a compiler, that the corresponding array will have at least that many elements. It allows the compiler to perform some specific optimizations based on this assumption. Listing 9-13 shows an example.

Listing 9-13. array_param_size_static.c

```c
int fun(int array[static 10] ) {...}
```

9.1.8   Designated Initializers in Arrays

C99 introduces an interesting way to initialize the arrays. It is possible to implicitly initialize an array to default values except for those on several designated positions, for which other values are provided. For example, to initialize an array of eight int elements to all zeros, except for the indices 1 and 5 which will hold values 15 and 29, respectively, the following code might be used:

```c
int a[8] = { [5] = 29, [1] = 15 };
```

The initialization order is irrelevant. It is often useful to use enum values or character values as indices. Listing 9-14 shows an example.

Listing 9-14. `designated_initializers_arrays.c`

```
int whitespace[256] = {
    [' ' ] = 1,
    ['\t'] = 1,
    ['\f'] = 1,
    ['\n'] = 1,
    ['\r'] = 1 };

enum colors {
    RED,
    GREEN,
    BLUE,
    MAGENTA,
    YELLOW
};

int good[5] = { [ RED ] = 1, [ MAGENTA ] = 1 };
```

9.1.9   Type Aliases

You can define your own types using existing types via the `typedef` keyword.

The code shown in Listing 9-15 is creating a new type `mytype_t.` It is absolutely equivalent to `unsigned short int` except for its name. These two types become fully interchangeable (unless later someone changes the `typedef`).

Listing 9-15. `typedef_example.c`

```
typedef unsigned short int mytype_t;
```

You can see the suffix `_t` in type names quite often. All names ending with `_t` are reserved by POSIX standard.[4]

This way newer standards will be able to introduce new types without the fear of colliding with types in existing projects. So, using these type names is discouraged. We will speak about practical naming conventions later.

What are these new types for?

1. Sometimes they improve the ease of reading code.

2. They may enhance portability, because to change the format of all variables of your custom type you should only change the `typedef`.

3. Types are essentially another way of documenting program.

4. Type aliases are extremely useful when dealing with function pointer types because of their cumbersome syntax.

---

[4]POSIX is a family of standards specified by the IEEE Computer Society. It includes the description of utilities, application programming interface (API), etc. Its purpose is to ease the portability of software, mostly between different branches of UNIX-derived systems.

A very important example of a type alias is `size_t`. This is a type defined in the language standard (it requires including one of the standard library headers, for example, `#include <stddef.h>`). Its purpose is to hold array lengths and array indices. It is usually an alias for `unsigned long`; thus, in Intel 64 it typically is an unsigned 8-byte integer.

■ **Never use `int` for array indices** Unless you are dealing with a poorly designed library which forces you to use `int` as an index, always favor `size_t`.

Always use types appropriately. Most standard library functions that deal with sizes return a value of type `size_t` (even the `sizeof()` operator returns `size_t`!). Let's take a look at the example shown in Listing 9-16. An expression `s` of type `size_t` could have been obtained from one of library calls such as `strlen`. There are several problems that arise because of `int` usage:

- `int` is 4 bytes long and signed, so its maximal value is $2^{31} - 1$. What if `i` is used as an array index? It is more than possible to create a bigger array on modern systems, so all elements may not be indexed. The standard says that arrays are limited in size by an amount of elements encodable using a `size_t` variable (unsigned 64-bit integer).

- Every iteration is only performed if the current `i` value is less than `s`. Thus a comparison is needed, but these two variables have a different format! Because of it, a special number conversion code will be executed by each iteration, which can be quite significant for small loops with a lot of iterations.

- When dealing with bit arrays (not so uncommon) a programmer is likely to compute `i/8` for a byte offset in a byte array and `i%8` to see which specific bit we are referring to. These operations can be optimized into shifts instead of actual division, but only for unsigned integers. The performance difference between shifts and "fair" division is radical.

Listing 9-16. `size_int_difference.c`

```
size_t s;
int i;
...
for( i = 0; i < s; i++ ) {
    ...
}
```

9.1.10   The Main Function Revisited

We are already used to writing the `main` function, which serves as an entry point, as a parameterless function. However, it should in fact accept two parameters: the command-line argument count and an array of arguments themselves. What are command-line arguments? Well, every time you launch a program (like `ls`) you might specify additional arguments, for example, `ls -l -a`. The `ls` application will be launched and it will have access to these arguments in its `main` function. In this case

- `argv` will contain three pointers to `char` sequences:

```
INDEX STRING

  0   "ls"
  1   "-l"
  2   "-a"
```

The shell will split the whole calling string into pieces by spaces, tabs, and newline symbols and the loader and C standard library will ensure that main gets this information.

- argc will be equal to 3 as it is a number of elements in argv.

Listing 9-17 shows an example. This program prints all given arguments, each in a separate line.

Listing 9-17. main_revisited.c

```
#include <stdio.h>

int main( int argc, char* argv[] ) {
    int i;
    for( i = 0; i < argc; i++ )
        puts( argv[i] );
    return 0;
}
```

9.1.11   Operator sizeof

We already mentioned the operator sizeof in section 8.4.2. It returns a value of type size_t which holds the operand size in bytes. For example, sizeof(long) will return 8 on x64 computers.

sizeof is *not* a function because it has to be computed in compile time.

sizeof has an interesting usage: you can compute the total size of an array *but only* if the argument is in this exact array. Listing 9-18 shows an example.

Listing 9-18. sizeof_array.c

```
#include <stdio.h>

long array[] = { 1, 2, 3 };

int main(void) {
    printf( "%zu \n", sizeof( array    ) ); /* output: 24 */
    printf( "%zu \n", sizeof( array[0] ) ); /* output: 8 */
    return 0;
}
```

Notice, how you cannot use sizeof to get the size of an array accepted by a function as an argument. Listing 9-19 shows an example. This program will output 8 in our architecture

Listing 9-19. sizeof_array_fun.c

```
#include <stdio.h>
const int arr[] = {1, 2, 3, 4};
void f(int const arr[]) {
    printf("%zu\n", sizeof( arr ) );
}
int main( void ) {
    f(arr);
    return 0;
}
```

■ **Which format specifier?**   Starting at C99 you can use a format specifier %zu for size_t. In earlier versions you should use %lu which stands for unsigned long.

■ **Question 159**   Create sample programs to study the values of these expressions:

- sizeof(void)
- sizeof(0)
- sizeof('x')
- sizeof("hello")

■ **Question 160**   What will be the value of x?

```
int x = 10;
size_t t = sizeof(x=90);
```

■ **Question 161**   How do you compute how many elements an array stores using sizeof?

9.1.12   Const Types

For every type T we can also use a type T const (or, equivalently, const T). Variables of such type cannot be changed directly, so they are **immutable**. It means that such data should be initialized simultaneously with a declaration. Listing 9-20 shows an example of initializing and working with constant variables.

Listing 9-20. const_def.c

```
int a;
a = 42 ;       /* ok */

...

const int a; /* compilation error */

...

const int a = 42; /* ok */
a = 99;   /* compilation error, should not change constant value */

int const a = 42;   /* ok */
const int b = 99;   /* ok, const int === int const */
```

It is interesting to note how the `const` modifier interacts with the asterisk * modifier. The type is read from right to left and so the `const` modifiers as well as the asterisk are applied in this order. Following are the options:

- `int const* x` means "a mutable pointer to an immutable `int`." Thus, `*x = 10` is not allowed, but modifying x itself is allowed.

  An alternate syntax is `const int* x`.

- `int* const x = &y;` means "an immutable pointer to a mutable `int` y." In other words, x will never be pointing at anything but y.

- A superposition of the two cases: `int const* const x = &y;` is "an immutable pointer to an immutable `int` y."

■ **Simple rule**   The `const` modifier on the left of the asterisk protects the data we point at; the `const` modifier on the right protects the pointer itself.

Making a variable constant is not foolproof. There is still a way to modify it. Let's demonstrate it for a variable `const int x` (see Listing 9-21).

- Take a pointer to it. It will have type `const int*`.
- Cast this pointer to `int*`.
- Dereference this new pointer. Now you can assign a new value to x.

Listing 9-21. `const_cast.c`

```
#include <stdio.h>

int main(void) {
    const int x = 10;
    *( (int*)&x ) = 30;

    printf( "%d\n", x );
    return 0;
}
```

This technique is strongly discouraged but you might need it when dealing with poorly designed legacy code. `const` modifiers are made for a reason, and if your code does not compile it, it is by no means a justification for such hacks.

Note that you cannot assign a `int const*` pointer to `int*` (this is true for all types). The first pointer guarantees that its contents will never be changed, while the second one does not. Listing 9-22 shows an example.

Listing 9-22. `const_discard.c`

```
int x;
int y;

int const* px = &x;
int * py = &y;

py = px; /* Error, const qualifier is discarded */
px = py; /* OK   */
```

■ **Should I use const at all? It is cumbersome.**   Absolutely. In large projects it can save you a lifetime of debugging. I myself recall several very subtle bugs that were caught by the compiler and resulted in compilation error. Without the variables being protected by const, the compiler would have accepted the program which would have resulted in the wrong behavior.

Additionally, the compiler may use this information to perform useful optimizations.

9.1.13   Strings

In C, strings are null-terminated. A single character is represented by its ASCII code of type char. A string is defined by a pointer to its start, which means that the equivalent of a string type would be char*. Strings can also be thought of as character arrays, whose last element is always equal to zero.

The type of string literals is char*. Modifying them, however, while being syntactically possible (e.g., "hello"[1] = 32), yields an undefined result. It is one of the cases of **undefined behavior** in C. This usually results in a runtime error, which we will explain in the next chapter.

When two string literals are written one after another, they are concatenated (even if they are separated with line breaks). Listing 9-23 shows an example.

Listing 9-23. string_literal_breaks.c

```
char const* hello = "Hel" "lo"
"world!";
```

■ **Note**   The C++ language (unlike C) forces the string literal type to char const*, so if you want your code to be portable, consider it. Additionally, it forces the immutability of the strings (which is what you will often want) on the syntax level. So whenever you can, assign string literals to const char* variables.

9.1.14   Functional Types

A rather obscure part of C are the functional types. Unlike most types, they cannot be instantiated as variables, but in a way functions themselves are literals of these types. However, you can declare function arguments of functional types, which will be automatically converted to function pointers.

Listing 9-24 shows an example of a function argument f of a functional type.

Listing 9-24. fun_type_example.c

```
#include <stdio.h>

double g( int number ) { return 0.5 + number; }

double apply( double (f)(int), int x ) {
    return f( x ) ;
}
```

```
int main( void ) {
    printf( "%f\n",  apply( g, 10 ) );
    return 0;
}
```

The syntax, as you see, is quite particular. The type declaration is mixed with the argument name itself, so the general pattern is:

```
return_type (pointer_name) ( arg1, arg2, ... )
```

You see an equivalent program in Listing 9-25.

Listing 9-25. fun_type_example_alt.c

```
#include <stdio.h>

double g( int number ) { return 0.5 + number; }

double apply( double (*f)(int), int x ) {
    return f( x ) ;
}

int main( void ) {
    printf( "%f\n",  apply( g, 10 ) );
    return 0;
}
```

What are these types useful for? As the function pointer types are rather difficult to write and read, they are often hidden in a typedef. The bad (but very common) practice is to add an asterisk *inside* the type alias declaration. Listing 9-26 shows an example where a type to a procedure returning nothing is created.

Listing 9-26. typedef_bad_fun_ptr.c

```
Typedef  void(*proc)(void);
```

In this case you can write directly proc my_pointer = &some_proc. However, this hides an information about proc being a pointer: you can deduce it but you do not see it right away, which is bad. The nature of the C language is, of course, to abstract things as much as you can, but pointers are such a fundamental concept and so pervasive in C that you should not abstract them, especially in the presence of **weak typing**.

So, a better solution would be to write down what is shown in Listing 9-27.

Listing 9-27. typedef_good_fun_ptr.c

```
typedef void(proc)(void);

...

proc*  my_ptr  =  &some_proc;
```

Additionally, these types can be used to write function declarations. Listing 9-28 shows an example.

Listing 9-28. fun_types_decl.c

```c
typedef double (proc)(int);

/* declaration */
proc myproc;

/* ... */

/* definition */
double myproc( int x ) { return 42.0 + x; }
```

9.1.15 Coding Well

9.1.15.1 General Considerations

In this book we are going to provide several assignments to be written in C. But first we want to state several rules that you should follow, not only here and now but virtually every time you are writing a program.

1. Always separate program logic from input and output operations. This will allow for a better code reuse. If a function performs actions on data and outputs messages at the same time, you won't be able to reuse its logic in another situation (e.g., it can output messages to an application with a graphical user interface, and in another case you might want to use it on a remote server).

2. Always comment your code in plain English.

3. Name your variables based on their meaning for the program. It is very hard to deduce what variables with meaningless names like aaa mean.

4. Remember to put const wherever you can.

5. Use appropriate types for indexing.

9.1.15.2 Example: Array Summation

This section is an *absolute must read* if you are a beginner with C and even more so if you are a self-taught programmer.

We are going to write a simple program in "beginner style," see what's wrong with it, and modify it appropriately to make it better.

Here is the task: implement an array summation functionality. As simple as it is, there is a huge difference between a solution written by a beginner or one written by a more experienced programmer.

The beginner will come up with a program similar to the one shown in Listing 9-29.

Listing 9-29. beg1.c

```c
#include <stdio.h>
int array[] = {1,2,3,4,5};

int main( int argc, char** argv ) {
    int i;
    int sum;
    for( i = 0; i < 5; i++ )
```

```
        sum = sum + array[i];
    printf("The sum is: %d\n", sum );
    return 0;
}
```

Before we start polishing the code, we can immediately spot a bug: the starting value of sum is not defined and can be random. Local variables in C are not initialized by default, so you have to do it by hand. Check Listing 9-30.

Listing 9-30. beg2.c

```
#include <stdio.h>
int array[] = {1,2,3,4,5};

int main( int argc, char** argv ) {
    int i;
    int sum = 0;
    for( i = 0; i < 5; i++ )
        sum = sum + array[i];
    printf("The sum is: %d\n", sum );
    return 0;
}
```

First of all, this code is totally not reusable. Let's extract a piece of logic into an array_sum procedure, shown in Listing 9-31.

Listing 9-31. beg3.c

```
#include <stdio.h>
int array[] = {1,2,3,4,5};

void array_sum( void ) {
    int i;
    int sum = 0;
    for( i = 0; i < 5; i++ )
        sum = sum + array[i];
    printf("The sum is: %d\n", sum );

}

int main( int argc, char** argv ) {
    array_sum();
    return 0;
}
```

What is this magic number 5? Every time we change an array we have to change this number as well, so we probably want to calculate it dynamically, as shown in Listing 9-32.

Listing 9-32. beg4.c

```
#include <stdio.h>
int array[] = {1,2,3,4,5};
```

```c
void array_sum( void ) {
    int i;
    int sum = 0;
    for( i = 0; i < sizeof(array) / 4; i++ )
        sum = sum + array[i];
    printf("The sum is: %d\n", sum );

}

int main( int argc, char** argv ) {
    array_sum();
    return 0;
}
```

But why are we dividing the array size by 4? The size of int varies depending on the architecture, so we have to calculate it too (in compile time) as shown in Listing 9-33.

Listing 9-33. beg5.c

```c
#include <stdio.h>
int array[] = {1,2,3,4,5};

void array_sum( void ) {
    int i;
    int sum = 0;
    for( i = 0; i < sizeof(array) / sizeof(int); i++ )
        sum = sum + array[i];
    printf("The sum is: %d\n", sum );
}

int main( int argc, char** argv ) {
    array_sum();
    return 0;
}
```

We immediately face a problem: sizeof returns a number of type size_t, not int. So, we have to change the type of i and are doing it for a good reason (see section 9.1.9). Listing 9-34 shows the result.

Listing 9-34. beg6.c

```c
#include <stdio.h>

int array[] = {1,2,3,4,5};

void array_sum( void ) {
    size_t i;
    int sum = 0;
    for( i = 0; i < sizeof(array) / sizeof(int); i++ )
        sum = sum + array[i];
    printf("The sum is: %d\n", sum );
}
```

```
int main( int argc, char** argv ) {
    array_sum();
    return 0;
}
```

Right now, array_sum works only on statically defined arrays, because they are the only ones whose size can be calculated by sizeof. Next we want to add enough parameters to array_sum so it would be able to sum any array. You cannot add only a pointer to an array, because the array size is unknown by default, so you give it two parameters: the array itself and the amount of elements in the array, as shown in Listing 9-35.

Listing 9-35. beg7.c

```
#include <stdio.h>

int array[] = {1,2,3,4,5};

void array_sum( int* array, size_t count ) {
    size_t i;
    int sum = 0;
    for( i = 0; i < count; i++ )
        sum = sum + array[i];
    printf("The sum is: %d\n", sum );
}

int main( int argc, char** argv ) {
    array_sum(array, sizeof(array) / sizeof(int));
    return 0;
}
```

This code is much better but it still breaks the rule of not mixing input/output and logic. You cannot use array_sum anywhere in graphical programs, you also can do nothing with its result. We are going to get rid of the output in the summation function and make it return its result. Check Listing 9-36.

Listing 9-36. beg8.c

```
#include <stdio.h>

int g_array[] = {1,2,3,4,5};

int array_sum( int* array, size_t count ) {
    size_t i;
    int sum = 0;
    for( i = 0; i < count; i++ )
        sum = sum + array[i];
    return sum;
}

int main( int argc, char** argv ) {
    printf(
            "The sum is: %d\n",
            array_sum(g_array, sizeof(g_array) / sizeof(int))
        );
    return 0;
}
```

For convenience, we renamed the global array variable g_array, but it is not necessary.

Finally, we have to think about adding const qualifiers. The most important place is function arguments of pointer types. We really want to declare that array_sum will never change the array that its argument is pointing at. We can also like the idea of protecting the global array itself from being changed by adding a const qualifier.

Remember that if we make g_array itself constant but will not mark array in the argument list as such, we would not be able to pass g_array to array_sum, because there are no guarantees that array_sum will not change data that its argument is pointing at. Listing 9-37 shows the final result.

Listing 9-37. beg9.c

```c
#include <stdio.h>

const int g_array[] = {1,2,3,4,5};

int array_sum( const int* array, size_t count ) {
    size_t i;
    int sum = 0;
    for( i = 0; i < count; i++ )
        sum = sum + array[i];
    return sum;
}

int main( int argc, char** argv ) {
    printf(
            "The sum is: %d\n",
            array_sum(g_array, sizeof(g_array) / sizeof(int))
        );
    return 0;
}
```

When you write a solution for an assignment in this book, remember all the points stated previously and check whether your program conforms to them, and if not, how it can be improved.

Can this program be improved further? Of course, and we are going to give you some hints about how.

- Can the pointer array be NULL? If so, how do we signalize it without dereferencing a NULL pointer, which will probably result in crash?

- Can sum overflow?

9.1.16   Assignment: Scalar Product

A scalar product of two vectors $(a_1, a_2, \ldots, a_n)$ and $(b_1, b_2, \ldots, b_n)$ is the sum

$$\sum_{i=1}^{n} a_i b_i = a_1 b_1 + a_2 b_2 + \cdots + a_n b_n$$

For example, the scalar product of vectors $(1, 2, 3)$ and $(4, 5, 6)$ is

$$1 \cdot 4 + 2 \cdot 5 + 3 \cdot 6 = 4 + 10 + 18 = 32$$

The solution should consist of

- Two global arrays of int of the same size.

- A function to compute the scalar product of two given arrays.

- A main function which calls the product computations and outputs its results.

9.1.17   Assignment: Prime Number Checker

You have to write a function to test the number for primarity. The interesting thing is that the number will be of the type unsigned long and that it will be read from stdin.

- You have to write a function int is_prime(unsigned long n), which checks whether n is a prime number or not. If it is the case, the function will return 1; otherwise 0.

- The main function will read an unsigned long number and call is_prime function on it. Then, depending on its result, it will output either yes or no.

Read man scanf and use scanf function with the format specifier %lu.
Remember, is_prime accepts unsigned long, which is not the same thing as unsigned int!

9.2   Tagged Types

There are three "tagged" kinds of types in C: structures, unions, and enumerations. We call them that because their names consist of a keyword struct, union, or enum followed by a mnemonic tag, like struct pair or union pixel.

9.2.1   Structures

Abstraction is absolutely key to all programming. It replaces the lower-level, more verbose concepts with those closer to our thinking: higher-level, less verbose. When you are thinking about visiting your favorite pizzeria and plan an optimal route, you do not think about "moving your right foot X centimeters forward," but rather about "crossing the road" or "turning to the right." While for program logic the abstraction mechanism is implemented using functions, the data abstraction is implemented using complex data types.

A structure is a data type which packs several fields. Each field is a variable of its own type. Mathematics would probably be happy calling structures "tuples with named fields."

To create a variable of a structural type we can refer to the example shown in Listing 9-38. There we define a variable d which has two fields: a and b of types int and char, respectively. Then d.a and d.b become valid expressions that you can use just as you are using variable names.

Listing 9-38. struct_anon.c

```
struct { int a; char b; } d;
d.a = 0;
d.b = 'k';
```

This way, however, you only create a one-time structure. In fact, you are describing a type of d but you are not creating a new named structural type. The latter can be done using a syntax shown in Listing 9-39.

Listing 9-39. `struct_named.c`

```c
struct pair {
    int a;
    int b;
};

...

struct pair d;
d.a = 0;

d.b = 1;
```

Be very aware that the type name is *not* pair but `struct pair`, and you can*not* omit the `struct` keyword without confusing the compiler. The C language has a concept of **namespaces** quite different from the namespaces in other languages (including C++). There is a global type namespace, and then there is a tag-namespace, shared between `struct, union,` and `enum` datatypes. The name following the `struct` keyword is a tag. You can define a structural type whose name is the same as other type, and the compiler will distinguish them based on the `struct` keyword presence.

An example shown in Listing 9-40 demonstrates two variables of types `struct type` and `type`, which are perfectly accepted by the compiler.

Listing 9-40. `struct_namespace.c`

```c
typedef unsigned int type;
struct type {
    char c;
};

int main( int argc, char** argv ) {
    struct type st;
    type t;
    return 0;
}
```

It does not mean, though, that you really should make types with similar names.

However, as `struct type` is a perfectly fine type name, it can be aliased as `type` using the `typedef` keyword, as shown in Listing 9-41. Then the `type` and `struct type` names will be completely interchangeable.

Listing 9-41. `typedef_struct_simple.c`

```c
typedef struct type type;
```

▪ **Please, do not do it**   It is *not* a good practice to alias structural types using `typedef`, because it hides information about the type nature.

Structures can be initialized similarly to arrays (see Listing 9-42).

Listing 9-42. `struct_init.c`

```
struct S {char const* name; int value; };
...
struct S new_s = { "myname", 4 };
```

You can also assign 0 to all fields of a structure, as shown in Listing 9-43.

Listing 9-43. `struct_zero.c`

```
struct pair { int a; int b; };

...
struct pair p = { 0 };
```

In C99, there is a better syntax for structure initialization, which allows you to name the fields to initialize. The unmentioned fields will be initialized to zeros. Listing 9-44 shows an example.

Listing 9-44. `struct_c99_init.c`

```
struct pair {
    char a;
    char b;
};

struct pair st = { .a = 'a',.b = 'b' };
```

The fields of the structures are guaranteed to not overlap; however, unlike arrays, structures are not continuous in a sense that there can be free space between their fields. Thus, `sizeof` of a structural type can be greater than the sum of element sizes because of these gaps. We will talk about it in Chapter 12.

9.2.2 Unions

Unions are very much like structures, but their fields are always overlapping. In other words, all union fields start at the same address. The unions share their namespace with structures and enumerations.

Listing 9-45 shows an example.

Listing 9-45. `union_example.c`

```
union dword {
    int integer;
    short shorts[2];
};

...
dword test;
test.integer = 0xAABBCCDD;
```

We have just defined a union which stores a number of size 4 bytes (on x86 or x64 architectures). At the same time it stores an array of two numbers, each of which is 2 bytes wide. These two fields (a 4-byte number and a pair of 2-byte numbers) overlap. By changing the `.integer` field we are also modifying `.shorts` array. If we assign `.integer = 0xAABBCCDD` and then try to output `shorts[0]` and `shorts[1]`, we will see `ccdd aabb`.

■ **Question 162** Why do these shorts seem reversed? Will it always be the case, or is it architecture dependent?

By mixing structures and unions we can achieve interesting results. An example shown in Listing 13-17 demonstrates, how one can address parts of a 3-byte structure using indices.[5]

Listing 9-46. `pixel.c`

```
union pixel {
    struct {
        char a,b,c;
    };
    char at[3];
};
```

Remember that if you assigned a union field to a value, the standard does not guarantee you anything about the values of other fields. An exception is made for the structures that have the same initial sequence of fields.

Listing 9-47 shows an example.

Listing 9-47. `union_guarantee.c`

```
struct sa {
    int x;
    char y;
    char z;
};

struct sb {
    int x;
    char y;
    int notz;
};

union test {
    struct sa as_sa;
    struct sb as_sb;
};
```

9.2.3 Anonymous Structures and Unions

Starting from C11, the unions and structures can be anonymous when inside other structures or unions. It allows for a less verbose syntax when accessing inner fields.

In the example shown in Listing 9-48, to access the x field of vec, you need to write `vec.named.x`. You cannot omit `named`.

---

[5]Note that this might not work out of the box for wider types due to possible gaps between `struct` fields.

Listing 9-48. anon_no.c

```
union vec3d {
    struct {
        double x;
        double y;
        double z;
    } named ;
    double raw[3];
};

union vec3d vec;
```

Now, in the next example, shown in Listing 9-49, we got rid of the name of the first field (named). This is an anonymous structure, and now we can access its fields as if they were the fields of vec itself: vec.x.

Listing 9-49. anon_struct.c

```
union vec3d {
    struct {
        double x;
        double y;

        double z;
    };
    double raw[3];
};

union vec3d vec;
```

9.2.4 Enumerations

Enumerations are a simple data type based on int type. It fixes certain values and gives them names, similar to how DEFINE works.

For example, the traffic light can be in one of the following states (based on which lights are turned on):

- Red.
- Red and yellow.
- Yellow.
- Green.
- No lights.

This can be encoded in C as shown in Listing 9-50.

Listing 9-50. enum_example.c

```
enum light {
    RED,
    RED_AND_YELLOW,
    YELLOW,
    GREEN,
```

```
    NOTHING
};

...
enum light l = nothing;
...
```

When is it useful? It is often used to encode a state of an entity, for example, as a part of a finite automaton; it can serve as a bag of error codes or code mnemonics.

The constant value 0 was named `RED`, `RED_AND_YELLOW` stands for 1, etc.

9.3   Data Types in Programming Languages

We have given an overview of data types in C; now let's take a step back from C and look at the bigger picture and the types of systems in programming languages.

In many areas of computer science and programming the evolution went from untyped universe to typing. For example, the following entities are untyped:

1. Lambda terms in untyped lambda calculus;

2. Sets in many set theories, for example, ZF;

3. S expressions in LISP language; and

4. Bit strings.

We are mostly interested in bit strings right now. For the computer, everything is a bit string of some fixed size. Those can be interpreted as numbers (integer or real), sequences of character codes, or something else. We can say that the assembly is an untyped language.

However, when we start working in an untyped environment we are trying to divide objects into several categories. We are working with objects from one category in a similar way. So, we establish a convention: these bit strings are integer numbers, those are floating point numbers, etc.

Is this it, the typing? Not quite yet. We are still not limited in our capabilities and can add a floating point number to a string pointer, because the programming language does not enforce any type control. This type checking can be performed in compile time (**static typing**) or in runtime (**dynamic typing**).

So, not only we are dividing all kinds of possible objects into categories, we are also declaring which operations can be performed on each type. The data of different types is also often encoded in a different way.

9.3.1   Kinds of Typing

Besides static and dynamic typing, there are also other, orthogonal classifications.

Strong typing means that all operations require exactly the argument they need. No implicit conversions from other types into the needed ones are allowed.

Weak typing means that there are implicit conversions between types which make possible the operations on data which is not of exactly the required type (but a conversion to a required type exists).

This division is not strictly binary; in the real world the languages tend to be closer to one of these two poles. We have quite extreme cases, such as Ada for strong typing and JavaScript for the weak one.

Sometimes we also divide languages based on verbosity.

With **explicit typing** we always annotate data with types.

With **implicit typing** we allow the compiler to infer the type whenever it is possible.

Now we are going to give real-world examples of all combinations of static/dynamic and strong/weak typing.

9.3.1.1   Static Strong Typing

Types are checked in compile time and the compiler is pedantic about them.

In OCaml language there are two different addition operators: + for integer numbers and +. for reals. So, this code will raise an error at compile time:

```
4 +. 1.0
```

We used the data of type int when the compiler expected a float and, unlike in C, where a conversion would have occurred, has thrown an error. This is the essence of very strong typing.

9.3.1.2   Static Weak Typing

The C language has exactly this kind of typing. All types are known in compile time, but the implicit conversions occur quite often.

The almost identical line double x = 4 + 3.0; causes no compiler errors, because 4 gets automatically promoted to double and then added to 3.0. The weakness expresses itself in the fact that programmer does not specify conversion operations explicitly.

9.3.1.3   Strong Dynamic Typing

This is the kind of typing used in Python. Python does not allow implicit conversions between types as much as JavaScript does. However, the type errors will not be reported until you launch the program and actually try to execute the erroneous statement.

Python has an interpreter where you can type expressions and statements and immediately execute them. If you try to evaluate an expression "3" + 2 and see its result in an interactive Python interpreter, you will get an error because the first object is a string, and the second is a number. Even though this string contains a number (so a conversion could have been written), the addition is not allowed. Listing 9-51 shows the dump.

Listing 9-51. Python Typing Error

```
>>> "3" + 2
Traceback (most recent call last):
  File "<stdin>", line 1, in <module>
TypeError: cannot concatenate 'str' and 'int' objects
```

Now let's try to evaluate an expression 1 if True else "3" + 2. This expression is evaluated to 1 if True is true (which obviously holds); otherwise its value is a result of the same invalid operation "3" + 2. However, as we are never reaching into the else branch, there will be no error raised even in runtime. Listing 9-52 shows the terminal dump. When applied to two strings, the plus acts as a concatenation operator.

Listing 9-52. Python Typing: No Error Because the Statement Is Not Executed

```
>>> 1 if True else "3" + 2
1
>>> "1" + "2"
'12'
```

9.3.1.4 Weak Dynamic Typing

Probably the most used language with such typing is JavaScript.

In the example we provided for Python we tried to add a number to a string. Despite the fact that the string contained a valid decimal number, an error was reported, because a string is a string, whatever it might hold. Its type won't be automatically changed.

However, JavaScript is much less strict about what you are allowed to do. We are going to use the interactive JavaScript console (which you can access in virtually any modern web browser) and type some expressions. Listing 9-53 shows the result.

Listing 9-53. JavaScript Implicit Conversions

```
>>> 3 == '3'
true
>>> 3 == '4'
false
>>> "7.0" == 7

true
```

By studying this example only we can deduce that when a number and a string are compared, both sides are apparently converted to a number and then compared. It is not clear whether the numbers are integers or reals, but the amount of implicit operations in action here is quite astonishing.

9.3.2 Polymorphism

Now that we have a general understanding of typing, let's go after one of the most important concepts related to the type systems, namely, polymorphism.

Polymorphism (from Greek: polys, "many, much" and morph, "form, shape") is the possibility of calling different actions for different types in a uniform way. You can also think about it in another way: the data entities can take different types.

There are four different kinds of polymorphism [8], which we can also divide into two categories:

1. Universal polymorphism, when a function accepts an argument of an infinite number of types (including maybe even those who are not defined yet) and behaves in a similar way for each of them.

    • Parametric polymorphism, where a function accepts an additional argument, defining the type of another argument.

        In languages such as Java or C#, the generic functions are an example of parametric compile-time polymorphism.

    • Inclusion, where some types are subtypes of other types. So, when given an argument of a child type, the function will behave in the same way as when the parent type is provided.

2. Ad hoc, where functions accept a parameter from a fixed set of types and these functions may operate differently on each type.

    • Overloading, several functions exist with the same name and one of them is called based on an argument type.

    • Coercion, where a conversion exists from type X to type Y and a function accepting an argument of type Y is called with an argument of type X.

The popular object-oriented programming paradigm has popularized the notion of polymorphism, but in a very particular way. The object-oriented programming usually refers to only one kind of polymorphism, namely, **subtyping**, which is essentially the same as inclusion, because the objects of the child type form a subset of objects of the parent type.

Sometimes it is hard to say which type of polymorphism is used in a certain place. Consider the following four lines:

```
3 + 4
3 + 4.0
3.0 + 4
3.0 + 4.0
```

The "plus" operation here is obviously polymorphic, because it is used in the same way with all kinds of int and double operands. But how is it really implemented? We can think of different options, for example,

- This operator has four overloads for all combinations.

- This operator has two overloads for int + int and double + double cases. Additionally, a coercion from int to double is defined.

- This operator can only add up two reals, and all ints are coerced to double.

9.4 Polymorphism in C

The C language allows for different types of polymorphisms, and some can be emulated through little tricks.

9.4.1 Parametric Polymorphism

Can we make a function which will behave differently for different types of arguments based on an explicitly given type? We can do it to some extent, even in C89. However, we will need some rather heavy macro machinery in order to achieve a smooth result.

First, we have to know what this fancy # symbol does in a macro context. When used inside a macro, the # symbol will quote the symbol contents. Listing 9-54 shows an example.

Listing 9-54. `macro_str.c`

```
#define mystr hello
#define res #mystr

puts( res );   /* will be replaced with `puts("hello")` */
```

The ## operator is even more interesting. It allows us to form symbol names dynamically. Listing 9-55 shows an example.

Listing 9-55. `macro_concat.c`

```
#define x1 "Hello"
#define x2 " World"

#define str(i) x##i

puts( str(1) ); /* str(1) -> x1 -> "Hello" */
puts( str(2) ); /* str(2) -> x2 -> " World" */
```

Some higher-level language features can be boiled down to compiler logic performing a program analysis and making a call to one or another function, using one or another data structure, etc. In C we can imitate it by relying on a preprocessor.

Listing 9-56 shows an example.

Listing 9-56. c_parametric_polymorphism.c

```
#include <stdio.h>
#include <stdbool.h>

#define pair(T) pair_##T
#define DEFINE_PAIR(T) struct pair(T) {\
    T fst;\
    T snd;\
};\
bool pair_##T##_any(struct pair(T) pair, bool (*predicate)(T)) {\
    return predicate(pair.fst) || predicate(pair.snd); \
}

#define any(T) pair_##T##_any

DEFINE_PAIR(int)

bool is_positive( int x ) { return x > 0; }
int main( int argc, char** argv ) {
    struct pair(int) obj;
    obj.fst = 1;
    obj.snd = -1;
    printf("%d\n", any(int)(obj, is_positive) );
    return 0;
}
```

First, we included stdbool.h file to get access to the bool type, as we said in section 9.1.3.

- pair(T) when called like that: pair(int) will be replaced by the string pair_int.

- DEFINE_PAIR is a macro which, when called like that: DEFINE_PAIR(int), will be replaced by the code shown in Listing 9-57.

  Notice the backslashes at the end of each line: they are used to escape the newline character, thus making this macro span across multiple lines. The last line of the macro is not ended by the backslash.

  This code defines a new structural type called struct pair_int, which essentially contains two integers as fields. If we instantiated this macro with a parameter other than T, we would have had a pair of elements of a different type.

  Then a function is defined, which will have a specific name for each macro instantiation, since the parameter name T is encoded into its name. In our case it is pair_int_any, whose purpose is to check whether any of two elements in the pair satisfies the condition. It accepts the pair itself as the first argument and the condition as the second. The condition is essentially a pointer to a function accepting T and returning bool, a predicate, as its name suggests.

pair_int_any launches the condition function on the first element and then on the second element.

When used, DEFINE_PAIR defines the structure that holds two elements of a given type, and functions to work with it. We can have only one copy of these functions and structure definition for each type, but we need them, so we want to instantiate DEFINE_PAIR once for every type we want to work with.

Listing 9-57. macro_define_pair.c

```
struct pair_int {
    int fst;
    int snd;
};
bool pair_int_any(struct pair_int pair, bool (*predicate)(int)) {
    return predicate(pair.fst) || predicate(pair.snd);
}
```

- Then a macro #define any(T) pair_##T##_any is defined. Notice that its sole purpose is apparently just to form a valid function name depending on type. It allows us to call pair_##T##_any in a rather elegant way: any(int), as if it was a function returning a pointer to a function.

So, syntactically we got very close to a concept of parametric polymorphism: we are providing an additional argument (int) which serves to determine the type of other argument (struct pair_int). Of course, it is not as good as the type arguments in functional languages or even generic type parameters in C# or Scala, but it is something.

9.4.2   Inclusion

The inclusion is fairly easy to achieve in C for pointer types. The idea is that every struct's address is the same as the address of its first member.

Take a look at the example shown in Listing 9-58.

Listing 9-58. c_inclusion.c

```
#include <stdio.h>

struct parent {
    const char* field_parent;
};

struct child {
    struct parent base;
    const char* field_child;
};

void parent_print( struct parent* this ) {
    printf( "%s\n", this->field_parent );
}
```

```
int main( int argc, char** argv ) {
    struct child c;
    c.base.field_parent = "parent";
    c.field_child = "child";
    parent_print( (struct parent*) &c );

    return 0;
}
```

The function parent_print accepts an argument of a type parent*. As the definition of child suggests, its first field has a type parent. So, every time we have a valid pointer child*, there exists a pointer to an instance of parent which is equal to the former. Thus it is safe to pass a pointer to a child when a pointer to the parent is expected.

The type system, however, is not aware of this; thus you have to convert the pointer child* to parent*, as seen in the call parent_print((struct parent*) &c);. We could replace the type struct parent* with void* in this case, because any pointer type can be converted to void* (see section 9.1.5).

9.4.3 Overloading

Automated overloading was not possible in C until C11. Until recently, people included the argument type names in the function names to provide different "overloadings" given some base name. Now the newer standard has included a special macro which expands based on the argument type: _Generic. It has a wide range of usages.

The _Generic macro accepts an expression E and then many association clauses, separated by a comma. Each clause is of the form type name: string. When instantiated, the type of E is checked against all types in the associations list, and the corresponding string to the right of colon will be the instantiation result.

In the example shown in Listing 9-59, we are going to define a macro print_fmt, which can choose an appropriate printf format specifier based on argument type, and a macro print, which forms a valid call to printf and then outputs newline.

print_fmt matches the type of the expression x with one of two types: int and double. In case the type of x is not in this list, the default case is executed, providing a fairly generic %x specifier. However, in absence of the default case, the program would not compile should you provide print_fmt with an expression of the type, say, long double. So in this case it would be probably wise to just omit default case, forcing the compilation to abort when we don't really know what to do.

Listing 9-59. c_overload_11.c

```
#include <stdio.h>

#define print_fmt(x) (_Generic( (x), \
            int: "%d",\
            double: "%f",\
            default: "%x"))

#define print(x) printf( print_fmt(x), x ); puts("");

int main(void) {
    int x = 101;
    double y = 42.42;
    print(x);
    print(y);
    return 0;
}
```

178

We can use _Generic to write a macro that will wrap a function call and select one of *differently named* functions based on an argument type.

9.4.4 Coercions

C has several coercions embedded into the language itself. We are speaking essentially about pointer conversions to void* and back and integer conversions, described in section 9.1.4. To our knowledge, there is no way to add user-defined coercions or anything that looks at least remotely similar, akin to Scala's implicit functions or C++ implicit conversions.

As you see, in some form, C allows for all four types of polymorphism.

9.5 Summary

In this chapter we have made an extensive study of the C type system: arrays, pointers, constant types. We learned to make simple function pointers, seen the caveats of sizeof, revised strings, and started to get used to better code practices. Then we learned about structures, unions, and enumerations. At the end we talked briefly about type systems in mainstream programming languages and polymorphism and provided some advanced code samples to demonstrate how to achieve similar results using plain C. In the next chapter we are going to take a closer look at the ways of organizing your code into a project and the language properties that are important in this context.

Question 163   What is the purpose of & and * operators?

Question 164   How do we read an integer from an address 0x12345?

Question 165   What type does the literal 42 have?

Question 166   How do we create a literal of types unsigned long, long, and long long?

Question 167   Why do we need size_t type?

Question 168   How do we convert values from one type to another?

Question 169   Is there a Boolean type in C89?

Question 170   What is a pointer type?

Question 171   What is NULL?

Question 172   What is the purpose of the void* type?

Question 173   What is an array?

Question 174   Can any consecutive memory cells be interpreted as an array?

Question 175   What happens when trying to access an element outside the array's bounds?

Question 176   What is the connection between arrays and pointers?

Question 177   Is it possible to declare a pointer to a function?

Question 178   How do we create an alias for a certain type?

Question 179   How are the arguments passed to the main function?

Question 180   What is the purpose of the `sizeof` operator?

Question 181   Is `sizeof` evaluated during the program execution?

Question 182   Why is the `const` keyword important?

Question 183   What are structure types and why do we need them?

Question 184   What are union types? How do they differ from the structure types?

Question 185   What are enumeration types? How do they differ from the structure types?

Question 186   What kinds of typing exist?

Question 187   What kinds of polymorphism exist and what is the difference between them?

## CHAPTER 10

Code Structure

In this chapter we are going to study how to better split your code into multiple files and which relevant language features exist. Having a single file with a mess of functions and type definitions is far from convenient for large projects. Most programs are split into multiple modules. We are going to study which benefits it brings and how each module looks before linkage.

10.1 Declarations and Definitions

The C compilers historically were written as single-pass programs. It means that they should have traversed the file once and translated it right away. However, it does mean a lot to us. When a function is called, and it is not yet defined, the compiler will reject such a program because it does not know what this name stands for. While we are aware of our intention of calling a function in this place, for it, this is just an undefined identifier, and due to the single-pass translation, the compiler can't look ahead and try to find the definition.

In simple cases of linear dependency we can just define all functions before they are used. However, there are cases of circular dependencies, when this schema is not working, namely, the mutual recursive definitions, be they structures or functions.

In the case of functions, there are two functions calling each other. Apparently, in whatever order we define them, we cannot define both of them before the call to it is seen by the compiler. Listing 10-1 shows an example.

Listing 10-1. `fun_mutual_recursive_bad.c`

```c
void f(void) {
    g();    /* What is `g`, asks mr. Compiler? */
}

void g(void) {
    f();
}
```

In case of structures, we are talking about two structural types. Each of them has a field of pointer type, pointing to an instance of the other structure. Listing 10-2 shows an example.

Listing 10-2. `struct_mutual_recursive_bad.c`

```c
struct a {
    struct b* foo;
};
struct b {
    struct a* bar;
};
```

© Igor Zhirkov 2017
I. Zhirkov, *Low-Level Programming*, DOI 10.1007/978-1-4842-2403-8_10

The solution is in using split declarations and definitions. When a declaration precedes the definition, it is called **forward declaration.**

10.1.1   Function Declarations

For functions, the declaration looks like bodyless definition, ended by a semicolon. Listing 10-3 shows an example.

Listing 10-3. `fun_decl_def.c`

```
/* This is declaration */
void f( int x );

/* This is definition */
void f( int x )    {
    puts( "Hello!" );
}
```

Such declarations are sometimes called **function prototypes**. Every time you are using a function whose body is not yet defined OR is defined in another file, you should write its prototype first.

In function prototype the argument names can be omitted, as shown in Listing 10-4.

Listing 10-4. `fun_proto_omit_arguments.c`

```
int square( int x );
/* same as */
int square( int );
```

To sum up, two scenarios are considered correct for functions.

1. Function is defined first, then called (see Listing 10-5).

Listing 10-5. `fun_sc_1.c`

```
int square( int x ) { return x * x; }

...
int z = square(5);
```

2. Prototype first, then call, then the function is defined (see Listing 10-6).

Listing 10-6. `fun_sc_2.c`

```
int square( int x );

...
int z = square(5);

...

int square( int x ) { return x * x; }
```

Listing 10-7 shows a typical error situation, where the function body is declared after the call, but no declaration precedes the call.

Listing 10-7. `fun_sc_3.c`

```
int z = square( 5 );
...

int square( int x ) { return x * x; }
```

10.1.2   Structure Declarations

It is quite common to define a recursive data structure such as **linked list**. Each element stores a value and a link to the next element. The last element stores NULL instead of a valid pointer to mark the end of list. Listing 10-8 shows the linked list definition.

Listing 10-8. `list_definition.c`

```
struct list {
    int value;
    struct list* next;
};
```

However, in case of two mutually recursive structures, you have to add a forward declaration for at least one of them. Listing 10-9 shows an example.

Listing 10-9. `mutually_recursive_structures.c`

```
struct b; /* forward declaration */
struct a {
    int value;
    struct b* next;
};

/* no need to forward declare struct a because it is already defined */
struct b {
    struct a* other;
};
```

If there is no definition of a tagged type but only a declaration, it is called an **incomplete type**. In this case we can work freely with pointers to it, but we can never create a variable of such type, dereference it, or work with arrays of such type. The functions must not return an instance of such type, but, similarly, they can return a pointer. Listing 10-10 shows an example.

Listing 10-10. `incomplete_type_example.c`

```
struct llist_t;

struct llist_t* f() { ... }    /* ok  */
struct llist_t g();            /* ok  */
struct llist_t g()  { ... }    /* bad */
```

These types have a very specific use case which we will elaborate in Chapter 13.

10.2 Accessing Code from Other Files

10.2.1 Functions from Other Files

It is, of course, possible to call functions or reference global variables from other files. To perform a call, you have to add the called function's prototype to the current file. For example, you have two files: square.c, which contains a function square, and main_square.c, which contains the main function. Listing 10-11 and Listing 10-12 show these files.

Listing 10-11. square.c

```
int square( int x ) { return x * x; }
```

Listing 10-12. main_square.c

```
#include <stdio.h>
int square( int x );

int main(void) {
    printf( "%d\n", square( 5 ) );
    return 0;
}
```

Each code file is a separate module and thus is compiled independently, just as in assembly. A .c file is translated into an object file. As for our educational purposes we stick with ELF (Executable and Linkable Format) files; let's crack the resulting object files open and see what's inside. Refer to Listing 10-13 to see the symbol table inside the main_square.o object file, and to Listing 10-14 for the file square.o. Refer to section 5.3.2 for the symbol table format explanation.

Listing 10-13. main_square

```
> gcc -c -std=c89 -pedantic -Wall main_square.c
> objdump -t main_square.o

main.o:     file format elf64-x86-64

SYMBOL TABLE:
0000000000000000 l    df *ABS*  0000000000000000 main.c
0000000000000000 l    d  .text  0000000000000000 .text
0000000000000000 l    d  .data  0000000000000000 .data
0000000000000000 l    d  .bss   0000000000000000 .bss
0000000000000000 l    d  .note.GNU-stack
0000000000000000 .note.GNU-stack
0000000000000000 l    d  .eh_frame
0000000000000000 .eh_frame
0000000000000000 l    d  .comment
0000000000000000 .comment
0000000000000000 g    F .text  000000000000001c main
0000000000000000        *UND*  0000000000000000 square
```

Listing 10-14. square

```
> gcc  -c -std=c89 -pedantic -Wall square.c
> objdump -t square.o
square.o:      file format elf64-x86-64

SYMBOL TABLE:
0000000000000000 l    df *ABS*  0000000000000000 square.c
0000000000000000 l    d  .text  0000000000000000 .text
0000000000000000 l    d  .data  0000000000000000 .data
0000000000000000 l    d  .bss   0000000000000000 .bss
0000000000000000 l    d  .note.GNU-stack
0000000000000000 .note.GNU-stack
0000000000000000 l    d  .eh_frame
0000000000000000 .eh_frame
0000000000000000 l    d  .comment
0000000000000000 .comment
0000000000000000 g      F .text  0000000000000010 square
```

As you see, all functions (namely, square and main) have become global symbols, as the letter g in the second column suggests, despite not being marked in some special way. It means that all functions are like labels marked with global keyword in assembly—in other words, visible to other modules.

The function prototype for square, located in main_square.c, is attributed to an undefined section.

```
0000000000000000       *UND*    0000000000000000    square
```

GCC is providing you an access to the whole compiler toolchain, which means that it is not only translating files but calling linker with appropriate arguments. It also links files against standard C library.

After linking, the symbol table becomes more populated due to standard library and utility symbols, such as .gnu.version.

■ **Question 188**   Compile the file main by using gcc -o main main_square.o square.o line. Study its object table using objdump -t main. What can you tell about functions main and square?

10.2.2   Data in Other Files

If there is a global variable defined in other .c file that we want to address, it should be declared, preferably, but not necessarily, with extern keyword. You should not initialize extern variables; otherwise, compiler issues a warning.

Listing 10-15 and Listing 10-16 show the first example of a global variable usage from another file.

Listing 10-15. square_ext.c

```
extern int z;
int square( int x ) { return x * x + z; }
```

Listing 10-16. `main_ext.c`

```
int z = 0;
int square( int x );

int main(void) {
    printf( "%d\n", square( 5 ) );
    return 0;
}
```

The C standard marks the keyword `extern` as optional. We recommend that you never omit `extern` keyword so that you might easily distinguish in which file exactly you want to create a variable.

However, in case you do omit `extern` keyword, how does the compiler distinguish between variable definition and declaration, when no initializing is provided? It is especially interesting given that the files are compiled separately.

In order to study this question, we are going to take a look at the symbol tables for object files using the `nm` utility.

We write down files `main.c` and `other.c`, and then we compile them into `.o` files by using `-c` flag and then link them. Listing 10-17 shows the command sequence.

Listing 10-17. `glob_build`

```
> gcc -c -std=c89 -pedantic -Wall -o main.o main.c
> gcc -c -std=c89 -pedantic -Wall -o other.o other.c
> gcc -o main main.o other.o
```

There is one global variable called `x`. It is not assigned with a value in `main.c`, but it is initialized in `other.c`.

Using `nm` we can quickly view the symbol table, as shown in Listing 10-18. We have shortened the table for the `main` executable file on purpose to avoid cluttering the listing with service symbols.

Listing 10-18. `glob_nm`

```
> nm main.o
0000000000000000 T main
                 U printf
0000000000000004 C x

> nm other.o
0000000000000000 D x

> nm main
0000000000400526 T main
                 U printf@@GLIBC_2.2.5
0000000000601038 D x
```

As we see, in `main.o` the symbol `x`, corresponding to the variable `int x`, is marked with the flag `C` (global common), while in the other object file `main.o` it is marked `D` (global data). There can be as many similar global common **symbols** as you like, and in the resulting executable file they will all be squashed into one.

However, you cannot have multiple declarations of the same symbol in the same source file; you are limited to a maximum of one declaration and one definition.

10.2.3   Header Files

So, we know how to split the code into multiple files now. Every file that uses an external definition should have its declaration written before the actual usage. However, when the amount of files grows, maintaining consistency becomes hard. A common practice is to use header files in order to ease maintenance.

Let's say there are two files: `main_printer.c` and `printer.c`. Listings 10-19 and 10-20 show them.

Listing 10-19. `main_printer.c`

```
void print_one(void);
void print_two(void);
int main(void) {
    print_one();

    print_two();
    return 0;
}
```

Listing 10-20. `printer.c`

```
#include <stdio.h>

void print_one(void) {
    puts( "One" );
}
void print_two(void) {
    puts( "Two" );
}
```

Here is the real-world scenario. In order to use a function from the file `printer.c` in some file `other.c`, you have to write down prototypes of the functions defined in `printer.c` somewhere in the beginning of `other.c`. To use them in the third file, you will have to write their prototypes in the third file too. So, why do it by hand when we can create a separate file that will only contain functions and global variables declarations, but not definitions, and then include it with the help of a preprocessor?

We are going to modify this example by introducing a new **header file** `printer.h`, containing all declarations from `printer.c`. Listing 10-21 shows the header file.

Listing 10-21. `printer.h`

```
void print_one( void );
void print_two( void );
```

Now, every time you want to use functions defined in `printer.c` you just have to put the following line in the beginning of current code file:

```
#include "printer.h"
```

The preprocessor will replace this line with the contents of `printer.h`. Listing 10-22 shows the new main file.

Listing 10-22. `main_printer_new.c`

```
#include "printer.h"

int main(void) {
    print_one();
    print_two();
    return 0;
}
```

■ **Note**   The header files are not compiled themselves. The compiler only sees them as parts of `.c` files.

This mechanism, which looks similar to the modules or libraries importing from such languages as Java or C#, is by its nature very different. So, telling that the line `#include "some.h"` means "importing a library called `some`" is very wrong. Including a text file is not importing a library! Static libraries, as we know, are essentially the same object files as the ones produced by compiling `.c` files. So, the picture for an exemplary file `f.c` looks as follows:

- Compilation of `f.c` starts.

- The preprocessor encounters the `#include` directives and includes corresponding `.h` files "as is."

- Each `.h` file contains function prototypes, which will become entries in the symbol table after the code translation.

- For each such import-like entry, the linker will search through all object files in its input for a defined symbol (in section **.data, .bss**, or **.text**). In one place, it will find such a symbol and link the import-like entry with it.

This symbol might be found in the C standard library.

But wait, are we giving to the linker the standard library as input? We are going to discuss it in the next section.

10.3   Standard Library

We have already used the headers, corresponding to parts of the standard library, such as `stdio.h`. They contain not the standard functions themselves but their prototypes. You don't have to believe it, because you can check it for yourself.

In order to do it, create a file `p.c` which contains only one line: `#include <stdio.h>`. Then launch GCC on it, providing `-E` flag to stop after preprocessing and output the results into `stdout`. Use `grep` utility to search for `printf` occurrence, and you will find its prototype, as shown in Listing 10-23.

Listing 10-23. `printf_check_header`

```
> cat p.c
#include <stdio.h>

> gcc -E -pedantic -ansi p.c | grep " printf"
extern int printf (const char *__restrict__ format, ...);
```

We won't speak about the restrict keyword yet, so let's pretend it is not here. The file stdio.h, included in our test file p.c, obviously contains the function prototype of printf (pay attention to the semicolon at the end of the line!), which has no body. Three dots in place of the last argument mean an arbitrary arguments count. This feature will be discussed in Chapter 14. The same experiment can be conducted for any function that you gain access to by including stdio.h.

GCC is a universal interface of sort: you can use it to compile single files separately without linkage (-c flag), you can perform the whole compilation cycle including linkage on several files, but you can also call the linker indirectly by providing GCC with .o files as input:

```
gcc -o executable_file obj1.o obj2.o ...
```

When performing linkage, GCC does not just call ld blindly. It also provides it with the correct version of the C library, or libraries. Additional libraries can be specified with help of the -l flag.

In the most common scenario, C library consists of two parts:

- Static part (usually called crt0 – C RunTime, zero stands for "the very beginning") contains _start routine, which performs initialization of the standard utility structures, required by this specific library implementation. Then it calls the main function. In Intel 64, the command-line arguments are passed onto the stack. It means that _start should copy argc and argv from the stack to rdi and rsi in order to respect the function calling convention.

  If you link a single file and check its symbol table before and after linkage, you will see quite a lot of new symbols, which originate in crt0, for example, a familiar _start, which is the real entry point.

- Dynamic part, which contains the functions and global variables themselves. As these are used by a vast majority of running applications, it is wise not to copy it but to share between them for the sake of an overall smaller memory consumption and better locality. We are going to prove its existence by using the ldd utility on a compiled sample file main_ldd.c, shown in Listing 10-24. It will help us to locate the standard C library. Listing 10-25 shows the ldd output.

Listing 10-24. main_ldd.c

```
#include <stdio.h>

int main( void )
{
    printf("Hello World!\n");
    return 0;
}
```

Listing 10-25. ldd_locating_libc

```
>  gcc main.c -o main
   > ldd main
   linux-vdso.so.1 (0x00007fff4e7fc000)
   libc.so.6 => /lib/x86_64-linux-gnu/libc.so.6 (0x00007f2b7f6bf000)
/lib64/ld-linux-x86-64.so.2 (0x00007f2b7fa76000)
```

This file is linked against three dynamic libraries.

1. The ld-linux is the dynamic library loader itself, which is searching and loading all dynamic libraries, required by the executable.

2. vdso, which stands for "virtual dynamic shared object," is a small utility library used by the C standard library to speed up the communication with the kernel in some situations.

3. Finally, libc itself, contains the executable code for standard functions.

Then, as the standard library is just another ELF file, we will launch readelf to print its symbol table and see the printf entry for ourselves. Listing 10-26 shows the result. The first entry is indeed the printf we are using; the tag after @@ marks the symbol version and is used to provide different versions of the same function. The old software, which uses older function versions, will continue using them, while the new software may switch to a better written, more recent variant without breaking compatibility.

Listing 10-26. printf_lib_entry

```
> readelf -s /lib/x86_64-linux-gnu/libc.so.6  | grep " printf"
596: 0000000000050d50   161 FUNC    GLOBAL DEFAULT   12
printf@@GLIBC_2.2.5
1482: 0000000000050ca0    31 FUNC    GLOBAL DEFAULT   12
printf_size_info@@GLIBC_2.2.5
1890: 0000000000050480  2070 FUNC    GLOBAL DEFAULT   12
printf_size@@GLIBC_2.2.5
```

■ **Question 189**   Try to find the same symbols using nm utility instead of readelf.

10.4   Preprocessor

Apart from defining global constants with #define, the preprocessor is also used as a workaround to solve a multiple inclusion problem. First, we are going to briefly review the relevant preprocessor features.

The #define directive is used in the following typical forms:

- #define FLAG means that the preprocessor symbol FLAG is defined, but its value is an empty string (or, you could say it has no value). This symbol is mostly useless in substitutions, but we can check whether a definition exists at all and include some code based on it.

- #define MY_CONST 42 is a familiar way to define global constants. Every time MY_CONST occurs in the program text, it is substituted with 42.

- #define MAX(a, b) ((a)>(b))?(a):(b) is a macrosubstitution with parameters.

A line int x = MAX(4+3, 9) will be then replaced with: int x = ((4+3)>(9))?(4+3):(9).

■ **Macro parameters in parentheses**   Note that all parameters in a macro body should be surrounded by parentheses. It ensures that the complex expressions, given to the macro as parameters, are parsed correctly. Imagine a simple macro SQ.

```
#define SQ(x) x*x
```

A line `int z = SQ(4+3)` will be then replaced with

```
int z = 4 + 3 * 4 + 3
```

which, due to multiplication having a higher priority than addition, will be parsed as `4 + (3*4) + 3`, which is not quite an expression we intended to form.

If you want additional preprocessor symbols to be defined, you can also provide them when launching GCC with the -D key. For example, instead of writing `#define SYM VALUE`, you can launch `gcc -DSYM=VALUE`, or just `gcc -DSYM` for a simple `#define SYM`.

Finally, we need a macro conditional: `#ifdef`. This directive allows us to either include or exclude some text fragment from the preprocessed file, based on whether a symbol is defined or not.

You can include the lines between `#ifdef SYMBOL` and `#endif` if the SYMBOL is defined, as shown in Listing 10-27.

Listing 10-27. `ifdef_ex.c`

```
#ifdef SYMBOL
/*code*/
#endif
```

You can include the lines between `#ifdef SYMBOL` and `#endif` if the SYMBOL is defined, OR ELSE include other code, as shown in Listing 10-28.

Listing 10-28. `ifdef_else_ex.c`

```
#ifdef SYMBOL
/*code*/
#else
/*other code*/

#endif
```

You can also state that some code will only be included if a certain symbol is not defined, as shown in Listing 10-29.

Listing 10-29. `ifndef_ex.c`

```
#ifndef MYFLAG
/*code*/
#else
/*other code*/
#endif
```

10.4.1   Include Guard

One file can contain a maximum of one declaration and one definition for any given symbol. While you will not write duplicate declarations, you will most probably use header files, which might include other header files, and so on. Knowing which declarations will be present in the current file is not easy: you have to navigate through each header file, and each header file that they include, and so on.

For example, there are three files: a.h, b.h, and main.c, shown in Listing 10-30.

Listing 10-30. inc_guard_motivation.c

```
/* a.h */
void a(void);

/* b.h */
#include "a.h"
void b(void);

/* main.c */
#include "a.h"
#include "b.h"
```

What will the preprocessed main.c file look like? We are going to launch gcc -E main.c. Listing 10-31 shows the result.

Listing 10-31. multiple_inner_includes.c

```
# 1 "main.c"
# 1 "<built-in>"
# 1 "<command-line>"
# 1 "/usr/include/stdc-predef.h" 1 3 4
# 1 "<command-line>" 2
# 1 "main.c"
# 1 "a.h" 1
void a(void);
# 2 "main.c" 2
# 1 "b.h" 1
# 1 "a.h" 1
void a(void);
# 2 "b.h" 2

void b(void);
# 2 "main.c" 2
```

Now main.c contains a duplicate function declaration void a(void), which results in a compilation error. The first declaration comes from the a.h file directly; the second one comes from file b.h which includes a.h on its own.

There are two common techniques to prevent that.

- Using a directive #pragma once in the header start. This is a non-standard way of forbidding the multiple inclusion of a header file. Many compilers support it, but because it is not a part of the C standard, its usage is discouraged.

- Using so-called **Include guards.**

Listing 10-32 shows an include guard for some file `file.h`.

Listing 10-32. `file.h`

```
#ifndef _FILE_H_
#define _FILE_H_

void a(void);

#endif
```

The text between directives `#ifndef _FILE_H_` and `#endif` will only be included if the symbol X is not defined. As we see, the very first line in this text is: `#define _FILE_H_`. It means that the next time all this text will be included as a result of `#include` directive execution; the same `#ifndef _FILE_H_` directive will prevent the file contents from being included for the second time.

Usually, people name such preprocessor symbols based on the file name, one such convention was shown and consists of

- Capitalizing file name.

- Replacing dots with underscores.

- Prepending and appending one or more underscores.

We crafted a typical include file for you to observe its structure. Listing 10-33 shows this example.

Listing 10-33. `pair.h`

```
#ifndef _PAIR_H_
#define _PAIR_H_

#include <stdio.h>

struct pair {
    int x;
    int y;
};

void pair_apply( struct pair* pair, void (*f)(struct pair) );
void pair_tofile( struct pair* pair, FILE* file );

#endif
```

The include guard is the first thing we observe in this file. Then come other includes. Why do you need to include files in header files? Sometimes, your functions or structures rely on external types, defined elsewhere. In this example, the function `pair_tofile` accepts an argument of type `FILE*`, which is defined in the `stdio.h` standard header file (or in one of the headers it includes on its own). The type definition comes after that, and then the function prototypes.

10.4.2   Why Is Preprocessor Evil?

Extensive preprocessor usage is considered bad for a number of reasons:

- It often makes code smaller, but also much less readable.

- It introduces unnecessary abstractions.

- In most cases it makes debugging harder.

- Macros often confuse IDEs (integrated development environments) and their autocompletion engines, as well as different static analyzers. Do not be snobbish about these because in larger projects they are of a great help.

The preprocessor knows nothing about language structure, so every preprocessor structure in isolation can be an invalid language statement. For example, a macro `#define OR else {` can become a part of a valid statement after all substitutions, but it is not a valid statement alone. When macros mix and the statement limits are not well defined, understanding such code is hard.

Some tasks can be close to impossible to solve because of the preprocessor. It limits the amount of intelligence that can be put into the programming environment or static analysis tools. Let's explore several pitfalls:

1. How clever should the static code analyzer be to understand what `foo` returns (see Listing 10-34)?

Listing 10-34. ifdef_pitfall_sig.c

```
#ifdef SOMEFLAG
int foo() {
#else
    void  foo()  {
#endif
/* ... */
}
```

2. You have to find all occurrences of the `min` macro, which is defined as

    `#define min(x,y) ((x) < (y) ? (x) : (y)).`

    As you have seen in the previous example, to parse the program you have to first perform preprocessing passes, otherwise the tool might not even understand the functions boundaries. Once you perform preprocessing, all `min` macros are substituted and thus become untraceable and indistinguishable from such lines as

    `int z = ((10) < (y) ? (5) : (3)).`

3. Static analysis (and even your own program understanding) will suffer because of macro usage. Syntactically, macro instantiations with parameters are indistinguishable from function calls. However, while function arguments are evaluated *before* a function call is performed, macro arguments are substituted and then the resulting lines of code are executed.

    For example, take the same macro `#define min(x,y) ((x) < (y) ? (x) : (y))`. The instantiation with arguments a and b-- will look like: `((a) < (b--) ? (a) : (b--))`. As you see, if a `>=` b, then the variable b will be decremented *twice*. If `min` was a function, b-- would have been executed only once.

10.5   Example: Sum of a Dynamic Array

10.5.1   Sneak Peek into Dynamic Memory Allocation

In order to complete the next assignment, you have to learn to use the `malloc` and `free` functions. We will discuss them in greater detail later, but for now, we will do a quick introduction.

The local variables as well as the global ones allow you to allocate a fixed amount of bytes. However, when the allocated memory size depends on input, you can either allocate as much memory as you think will suffice in all cases or use `malloc` function, which allocates as much memory as you ask it to.

`void* malloc(size_t sz)` returns the start of an allocated memory buffer of size `sz` (in bytes) or `NULL` in case of failure. This buffer holds random values on start. As it returns `void*`, this pointer can be assigned to a pointer of any other type.

All these allocated regions of memory should be freed when they are no longer used by calling `free` on them.

In order to use these two functions, you have to include `malloc.h`. Listing 10-35 shows a minimal example of `malloc` and `free` usage.

Listing 10-35. simple_malloc.c

```
#include <malloc.h>

int main( void ) {
    int* array;

    /* malloc returns the allocated memory starting address
     * Notice that its argument is the byte size, elements count multiplied
     * by element size */
array = malloc( 10 * sizeof( int ));

    /* actions on array are performed here */

    free( array ); /* now the related memory region is deallocated */
    return 0;
}
```

10.5.2   Example

Listing 10-36 shows the example. It contains three functions of interest:

- `array_read` to read an array from `stdin`. The memory allocation happens here.

Notice the usage of `scanf` function to read from `stdin`. Do not forget that it accepts not the variable values but their addresses, so it could perform an actual writing into them.

- `array_print` to print a given array to `stdout`.

- `array_sum` to sum all elements in an array.

Notice that the array allocated somewhere using `malloc` persists until the moment `free` is called on its starting address. Freeing an already freed array is an error.

Listing 10-36. sum_malloc.c

```c
#include <stdio.h>

#include <malloc.h>

int* array_read( size_t* out_count ) {
    int* array;
    size_t i;
    size_t cnt;
    scanf( "%zu", &cnt );
    array = malloc( cnt * sizeof( int ) );

    for( i = 0; i < cnt; i++ )
        scanf( "%d", & array[i] );

    *out_count = cnt;
    return array;
}

void array_print( int const* array, size_t count ) {
    size_t i;

    for( i = 0; i < count; i++ )
        printf( "%d  ", array[i] );
    puts("");
}

int array_sum( int const* array, size_t count ) {
    size_t i;
    int sum = 0;
    for( i = 0; i < count; i++ )
        sum = sum + array[i];
    return sum;
}

int main( void ) {
    int* array;
    size_t count;

    array = array_read( &count );
    array_print( array, count );
    printf( "Sum is: %d\n", array_sum( array, count ) );
    free( array );
    return 0;
}
```

10.6   Assignment: Linked List

10.6.1   Assignment

The program accepts an arbitrary number of integers through `stdin`. What you have to do is

1. Save them all in a **linked list** *in reverse order*.

2. Write a function to compute the sum of elements in a linked list.

3. Use this function to compute the sum of elements in the saved list.

4. Write a function to output the *n*-th element of the list. If the list is too short, signal about it.

5. Free the memory allocated for the linked list.

You need to learn to use

-   Structural types to encode the linked list itself.

-   The `EOF` constant. Read the section "Return value" of the `man scanf`.

You can be sure that

-   The input does not contain anything but integers separated by whitespaces.

-   All input numbers can be contained into `int` variables.

Following is the recommended list of functions to implement:

-   `list_create` – accepts a number, returns a pointer to the new linked list node.

-   `list_add_front` – accepts a number and a pointer to a pointer to the linked list. Prepends the new node with a number to the list.

For example: a list (1,2,3), a number 5, and the new list is (5,1,2,3).

-   `list_add_back`, adds an element to the end of the list. The signature is the same as `list_add_front`.

-   `list_get` gets an element by index, or returns 0 if the index is outside the list bounds.

-   `list_free` frees the memory allocated to all elements of list.

-   `list_length` accepts a list and computes its length.

-   `list_node_at` accepts a list and an index, returns a pointer to `struct list`, corresponding to the node at this index. If the index is too big, returns `NULL`.

-   `list_sum` accepts a list, returns the sum of elements.

These are some additional requirements:

-   All pieces of logic that are used more than once (or those which can be conceptually isolated) should be abstracted into functions and reused.

-   The exception to the previous requirement is when the performance drop is becoming crucial because code reusage is changing the algorithm in a radically ineffective way. For example, you can use the function `list_at` to get the *n*-th element of a list in a loop to calculate the sum of all elements. However, the former needs to pass through the whole list to get to the element. As you increase *n*, you will pass the same elements again and again.

In fact, for a list of length N, we can calculate the number of times elements will be addressed to compute a sum.

$$1 + 2 + 3 + \ldots + N = \frac{N(N+1)}{2}$$

We start with a sum equal to 0. Then we add the first element, for that we need to address it alone (1). Then we add the second element, addressing the first and the second (2). Then we add the third element, addressing the first, the second, and the third as we look through the list from its beginning. In the end what we get is something like $O(N^2)$ for those familiar with the O-notation. Essentially it means that by increasing the list size by 1, the time to sum such a list will have N added to it.

In such case it is indeed wiser to just pass through the list, adding a current element to the accumulator.

- Writing small functions is very good most of the time.

- Consider writing separate functions to: add an element to the front, add to the back, create a new linked list node.

- Do not forget to extensively use const, especially in functions accepting pointers as arguments!

10.7   The Static Keyword

In C, the keyword static has several meanings depending on context.

1. Applying static to global variables or functions we make them available only in the current module (.c file).

To illustrate it, we are going to compile a simple program shown in Listing 10-37, and launch nm to look into the symbol table. Remember, that nm marks global symbols with capital letters.

Listing 10-37. static_example.c

```c
int global_int;
static int module_int;

static int module_function() {
    static  int  static_local_var;
    int  local_var;
    return 0;
}
int main( int argc, char** argv ) {
    return 0;
}
```

What we see is that all symbol names are marked global *except* for those marked static in C. In assembly level it means that most labels are marked global, and to prevent it we have to be explicit and use the static keyword.

```
> gcc  -c  --ansi  --pedantic  -o  static_example.o  static_example.c
>  nm  static_example.o
0000000000000004  C  global_int
000000000000000b  T  main
```

```
0000000000000000 t module_function
0000000000000000  b  module_int
0000000000000004  b  static_local_var.1464
```

    2. By applying `static` to the local variable we make it global-like, but no other function can access it directly. In other words, it persists between function calls after being initialized once. Next time the same function is called the value of a local static variable will be the same as when this function terminated last time.

Listing 10-38 shows an example.

Listing 10-38. static_loc_var_example.c

```
int demo (void)
{
    static int a = 42;
    printf("%d\n", a++);
}

...

demo(); //outputs  42
demo(); //outputs  43
demo(); //outputs  44
```

10.8   Linkage

The concept of linkage is defined in the C standard and systematizes what we have studied in this chapter so far. According to it, "an identifier declared in different scopes or in the same scope more than once can be made to refer to the same object or function by a process called linkage" [7].

So, each identifier (variable or a function name) has an attribute called linkage. There are three types of linkage:

- No linkage, which corresponds to local (to a **block**) variables.

- External linkage, which makes an identifier available to all modules that might want to touch it. This is the case for global variables and any functions.

  - All instances of a particular name with external linkage refer to the same object in the program.

  - All objects with external linkage must have one and only one definition. However, the number of declarations in different files is not limited.

- Internal linkage, which restricts the visibility of the identifier to the `.c` file where it was defined.

It's easy for us to map the kinds of language entities we know to the linkage types:

- Regular functions and global variables—external linkage.

- Static functions and global variables—internal linkage.

- Local variables (static or not)—internal linkage.

While being important to grasp in order to read the standard freely, this concept is rarely encountered in everyday programming activities.

10.9 Summary

In this chapter we learned how to split code into separate files. We have reviewed the concepts of header files and studied include guards and learned to isolate functions and variables inside a file. We have also seen what the symbol tables look like for the basic C programs and the effects the keyword static produces on object files. We have completed an assignment and implemented linked lists (one of the most fundamental data structures). In the next chapter we are going to study the memory from the C perspective in greater details.

Question 190   What is the difference between a declaration and a definition?

Question 191   What is a forward declaration?

Question 192   When are function declarations needed?

Question 193   When are structure declarations needed?

Question 194   How can the functions defined in other files be called?

Question 195   What effect does a function declaration make on the symbol table?

Question 196   How do we access data defined in other files?

Question 197   What is the concept of header files? What are they typically used for?

Question 198   Which parts does the standard C library consist of?

Question 199   How does the program accept command-line arguments?

Question 200   Write a program in assembly that will display all command-line arguments, each on a separate line.

Question 201   How can we use the functions from the standard C library?

Question 202   Describe the machinery that allows the programmer to use external functions by including relevant headers.

Question 203   Read about ld-linux.

Question 204   What are the main directives of the C preprocessor?

Question 205   What is the include guard used for and how do we write it?

Question 206   What is the effect of static global variables and functions on the symbol table?

Question 207   What are static local variables?

Question 208   Where are static local variables created?

Question 209   What is linkage? Which types of linkage exist?

CHAPTER 11

Memory

Memory is a core part of the model of computation used in C. It stores all types of variables as well as functions. This chapter will study the C memory model and related language features closely.

11.1 Pointers Revisited

11.1.1 Why Do We Need Pointers?

As the C language has a von Neumann model of computations, the program execution is essentially a sequence of data manipulation commands. The data resides in addressable memory, and the addressability of data is the propriety that allows for a more refined and effective data manipulation. Many higher-level languages lack this property because direct address manipulations are forbidden.

However, that advantage comes at a price: it becomes easier to produce subtle and usually irrecoverable errors in the code.

The necessity of storing and manipulating addresses is why we need pointers. Performing a typical case study for Listing 11-1, we observe, that in terms of the abstract C machine:

- a - is the name of data cells of abstract machine, containing the number 4 of type int.

- p_a - is the name of data cells of abstract machine, which contain the address of a variable of type int.

- p_a stores the address of a.

- *p_a is the same as a;

- &a equals p_a, but these two entities are not the same. While p_a is the name for some consecutive data cells, &a is the contents of p_a, a bit string representing an address.

© Igor Zhirkov 2017
I. Zhirkov, *Low-Level Programming*, DOI 10.1007/978-1-4842-2403-8_11

Listing 11-1. pointers_ex.c

```
int a = 4;
int* p_a = &a;
*p_a = 10; /* a = 10*/
```

■ **Note** You can only apply & once, because for any x the expression &x will already not be an **lvalue**.

11.1.2 Pointer Arithmetic

Following are the *only* actions you can perform on pointers:

- Add or subtract integers (also negatives);

    So, we have pointers, and they contain addresses. For a computer, there is no difference between an address of an integer and an address of a string. In assembly language, as we have seen, all addresses are of the same type. Why do we need to keep the type information about what the pointer points to? What is the difference between int* and char*?

    The size of the element we are pointing at matters. By adding or subtracting an integer value *X* from the pointer of type *T* *, we, in fact, change it by *X* * sizeof(T). Let's see an example shown in Listing 11-2.

Listing 11-2. ptr_change_ex.c

```
int a = 42;            /* Assume this integer's address is 1000 */
int* p_a = &a;
p_a += 42;             /* 1000 + 42 * sizeof( int ) */
p_a = p_a + 1;         /* 1168 + 1 * sizeof( int ) */
p_a --;                /* 1172 - 1 * sizeof( int ) */
```

- Take its own address. If the pointer is a variable, it is located somewhere in memory too. So, it has an address on its own! Use the & operator to take it.

- Dereference, which is a basic operation that we have also seen. We are taking a data entry from memory starting at the address, stored in the given pointer. The * operator does it. Listing 11-3 shows an example.

Listing 11-3. deref_ex.c

```
int catsAreCool = 0;
int* ptr = &catsAreCool;
*ptr = 1; /* catsAreCool = 1 */
```

- Compare (with <, >, == and alike).

    We can compare two pointers. The result is only defined if they both point to the same memory block (e.g., at different elements of the same array). Otherwise the result is random, undefined by the language standard.

- Subtract another pointer.

  If and only if we have two pointers, which are certainly pointing at the contiguous memory block, then by subtracting a smaller valued one from a greater valued one we get the amount of elements between them. For pointers x and y, we are talking about a range of elements from *x inclusive to *y exclusive (so x – x = 0).

  Starting from C99, the type of the expression `ptr2 - ptr1` is a special type `ptrdiff_t`. It is a *signed* type of the same size as `size_t`.

  Note, that the result is different from the amount of bytes between *x and *y! The naively calculated difference would be the amount of bytes, while the result of subtraction is the amount of bytes divided by an element size. Listing 11-4 shows an example.

Listing 11-4. ptr_diff_calc.c

```
int arr[128];
int* ptr1 = &arr[50]; /* `array` address + 50 int sizes */
int* ptr2 = &arr[90]; /* `array` address + 90 int sizes */
ptrdiff_t d = ptr2 - ptr1; /* exactly 40 */
```

In all other cases (subtracting greater pointer from lesser one, subtracting pointers pointing into different areas, etc.) the result can be absolutely random.

Addition, multiplication, and division of two pointers are syntactically incorrect; thus, they trigger an immediate compilation error.

11.1.3   The `void*` Type

Apart from regular pointer types, a type `void*` exists, which is kind of special. It forgets all information about the entity it points to, apart from its address. The pointer arithmetic is forbidden for `void*` pointers, because the size of the entity we are pointing at is unknown and thus cannot be added or subtracted.

Before you can work with such a pointer, you should cast it to another type explicitly. Alternatively, C allows you to assign this pointer to any other pointer (and assign to `void*` a pointer of any type) without any warnings. In other words, while assigning `short*` to `long` is a clear error, assignments treats `void*` as equal to any pointer type.

Listing 11-5 shows an example.

Listing 11-5. void_ptr_ex.c

```
void* a = (void*)4;
short* b = (short*) a;
b ++; /* correct, b = 6 */
b = a; /* correct */
a = b; /* correct */
```

11.1.4   NULL

C defines a special preprocessor constant NULL equal to 0. It means a pointer "pointing to nowhere," an invalid pointer. By writing this value to a pointer, we can be sure that it is not yet initialized to a valid address. Otherwise, we would not be able to distinguish initialized pointers.

In most architectures people reserve a special value for invalid pointers, assuming no program will actually hold a useful value by this address.

As we already know, 0 in pointer context does not always mean a binary number with all bits cleared. Pointer-0 can be equal to 0, but this is not enforced by standard. The history knows architectures where the null-pointer was chosen in a rather exotic way. For example, some Prime 50 series computers used segment 07777, offset 0 for the null pointer; some Honeywell-Bull mainframes use the bit pattern 06000 for a kind of null pointers.

Listing 11-6 shows the correct ways to check whether the pointer is NULL or not.

Listing 11-6. null_check.c

```
if( x ) { ... }
if( NULL != x ) { ... }
if( 0 != x ) { ... }

if( x != NULL ) { ... }
if( x != 0 ) { ... }
```

11.1.5   A Word on ptrdiff_t

Take a look at the example shown in Listing 11-7. Can you spot a bug?

Listing 11-7. ptrdiff_bug.c

```
int* max;
int* cur;

int f( unsigned int e )
{
    if ( max - cur > e )
        return 1;
    else
        return 0;
}
```

What happens if cur > max? It implies, that the difference between cur and max is negative. Its type is ptrdiff_t. Comparing it with a value of type unsigned int is an interesting case to study.

ptrdiff_t has as many bits as the address on the target architecture. Let's study two cases:

- 32-bit system, where sizeof(unsigned int) == 4 and sizeof(ptrdiff_t) == 4. In this case, the types in our comparison will pass through these conversions.

  ```
  int < unsigned int
  (unsigned int)int < unsigned int
  ```

  The compiler will issue a warning, because the cast from int to unsigned int is not always preserving values. You cannot freely map values in range -2^{31} ... $2^{31} - 1$ to the range $0 ... 2^{32} - 1$.

  For example, in case the left-hand side was equal to -1, after the conversion to unsigned int type it will become the maximal value representable in unsigned int type ($2^{32} - 1$). Apparently, the result of this comparison will be almost always equal to 0, which is wrong, because -1 is smaller than *any* unsigned integer.

- 64-bit system, where sizeof(unsigned int) == 4 and sizeof(ptrdiff_t) == 8. In this situation, ptrdiff_t will be probably aliased to the signed long.

```
signed long < unsigned int
long < (signed long)unsigned int
```

Here the right-hand side is going to be cast. This cast preserves information, so the compiler will issue no warning.

As you see, the behavior of this code depends on target architecture, which is a big no. To avoid it, ptrdiff_t should always go in par with size_t, because only then their sizes are guaranteed to be the same.

11.1.6   Function Pointers

The von Neumann model of computations implies that the code and data reside in the same addressable memory. So, functions have addresses on their own. We can take the starting addresses of functions, pass them to other functions, call functions by pointers, store them in variables or arrays, etc. Why, however, would we do all that? It allows us for better abstractions. We can write a function that launches another function and measures its working time, or transforms an array by applying the function to all its elements. This technique allows the code to be reused on a whole new level.

The function pointer stores information about the function type just as the data pointers do. The function type includes the argument types and the return value type. A syntax that mimics the function declaration is used to declare a function pointer:

```
<return_value_type> (*name) (arg1, arg2, ...);
```

Listing 11-8 shows an example.

Listing 11-8. fun_ptr_example.c

```
double doubler (int a) { return a * 2.5; }
...
double (*fptr)( int );
double a;
fptr = &doubler;
a = fptr(10); /* a = 25.0 */
```

We have described the pointer fptr of type "a pointer to a function, that accepts int and returns double." Then we assigned the doubler function address to it and performed a call by this pointer with an argument 10, storing the returned value in the variable a.

typedef works, and is sometimes a great help. The previous example can be rewritten as shown in Listing 11-9.

Listing 11-9. fun_ptr_example_typedef.c

```
double doubler (int a) { return a * 2.5; }
typedef double (megapointer_type)( int );

...
double a;
megapointer_type* variable  = &doubler;
a = variable(10);  /*  a  =  25.0  */
```

Now by means of typedef we have created a function type that cannot be instantiated directly. However, we can create variables of the said pointer type. We cannot create variables of the function types directly, so we add an asterisk.

First-class objects in programming languages are the entities that can be passed as a parameter, returned from functions, or assigned to a variable.

As we see, functions are not first-class objects in C. Sometimes they are called "second-class objects" because the pointers to them are first-class objects.

11.2 Memory Model

The memory of the C abstract machine, while being uniform, has several regions. Pragmatically, each such region is mapped to a different **memory region**, consisting of consecutive pages.

Figure 11-1 shows this model.

Figure 11-1. *C memory model*

The regions that almost every C program has are

- Code, which holds machine instructions.

- Data, which stores regular global variables.

- Constant data, which stores all immutable data, such as string literals and global variables, marked const. The operating system is usually protecting the corresponding pages through the virtual memory mechanism, by allowing or not allowing the reads/writes.

- Heap, which stores dynamically allocated data (by means of malloc, as we will show in section 11.2.1).

- Stack, which stores all local variables, return addresses, and other utility information. If the program is executed in multiple threads, each one gets its own stack.

11.2.1   Memory Allocation

Before you can use memory cells, you have to allocate memory. There are three types of memory allocation in C.

- **Automatic memory allocation** occurs when we are entering a routine. When we enter the function, a part of the stack is dedicated to its local variables. When we leave the function, all information about these variables is lost. The lifetime of this data is limited by the lifetime of a function instance. Once the function terminates, the memory becomes unavailable.

- In assembly level, we have already done it in the very first assignment. The functions that performed integer printing allocated a buffer on the stack to store the resulting string. It was achieved by simply decreasing rsp by the buffer size.

■ **Note**   Never return pointers to local variables from functions! They point to the data that no longer exists.

- **Static memory allocation** happens during compilation in the data or constant data region. These variables exist until the program terminates. By default, the variables are initialized with zeros, and thus end up in **.bss** section. The constant data is allocated in **.rodata**; the mutable data is allocated in **.data**.

- **Dynamic memory allocation** is needed when we do not know the size of the memory we need to allocate until some external events happen. This type of allocation relies on an implementation in the standard C library. It means that when the C standard library is not available (e.g., bare metal programming), this type of memory allocation is also unavailable.

    This type of memory allocation uses the heap.

    A part of the standard library keeps track of the reserved and available memory addresses. This part's interface consists of the following functions, whose prototypes are located in malloc.h header file.

    - void* malloc(size_t size) allocates size bytes in heap and returns an address of the first one. Returns NULL if it fails.

This memory is not initialized and thus holds random values.

- void* calloc(size_t size, size_t count) allocates size * count bytes in heap and initializes them to zero. Returns the address of the first one or NULL if it fails.

- void free(void* p) frees memory, allocated in heap.

- void* realloc(void* ptr, size_t newsize) changes the size of a memory block starting at ptr to newsize bytes. The added memory will not be initialized. The contents are copied into the new block, and the old block is freed. Returns a pointer to the new memory block or NULL on failure.

When we no longer need a memory block we have to free it, otherwise it will stay in a "reserved" state forever, never to be reused. This situation is called **memory leak**. When you are using a heavy piece of software, which contains bugs related to memory management, its memory footprint can grow significantly over time without the program actually needing that much memory.

Usually, the operating system provides the program with a number of pages in advance. These pages are used until the program needs more dynamic memory to allocate. When it happens, the malloc call can internally trigger a system call (such as mmap) to request more pages.

As the void* pointer type can be assigned to any pointer type, the following code will issue no warning (see Listing 11-10) when compiling it as a C code.

Listing 11-10. malloc_no_cast.c

```
#include <malloc.h>


...
int* a =  malloc(200);
a[4]  =  2;
```

However, in C++, a popular language that was originally derived from C (and which tries to maintain backward compatibility), the void* pointer should be explicitly cast to the type of the pointer you are assigning it to. Listing 11-11 shows the difference.

Listing 11-11. malloc_cast_explicit.c

```
int* arr = (int*)malloc( sizeof(int) * 42 );
```

■ **Why some programmers recommend omitting the cast**   The older C standards had an "implicit int" rule about function declarations. Lacking a valid function declaration, its first usage was considered a declaration. If a name that has not been previously declared occurs in an expression and is followed by a left parenthesis, it declares a function name. This function is also assumed to return an int value. The compiler can even create a stub function returning 0 for it (if it does not find an implementation).

In case you do not include a valid header file, containing a malloc declaration, this line will trigger an error, because a pointer is assigned an integer value, returned by malloc:

```
int* x = malloc( 40 );
```

However, the explicit cast will hide this error, because in C we can cast whatever we want to whatever type we want.

```
int* x  =  (int*)malloc( 40  );
```

The modern versions of the C standard (starting at C99) drop this rule and the declarations become mandatory, so this reasoning becomes invalid.

A benefit in explicit casting is a better compatibility with C++.

11.3   Arrays and Pointers

Arrays in C are particular, because any bunch of values residing consecutively in memory can be thought of as an array.

An abstract machine considers that the array name is the address of the first element, thus, a pointer value!

The *i*-th element of an array can be obtained by one of the following equivalent constructions:

```
a[i] = 2;
*(a+i)  =   2
```

The address of the *i*-th element can be obtained by one of these following constructions:

```
&a[i];
a+i;
```

As we see, every operation with pointers can be rewritten using the array syntax! And it even goes further. In fact, the braces syntax a[i] gets immediately translated into a + i, which is the same thing as i+a. Because of this, exotic constructions such as 4[a] are also possible (because 4+a is legitimate).

Arrays can be initialized with zeros using the following syntax:

```
int a[10] = {0};
```

Arrays have a fixed size. However, there are two notable exceptions to this rule, which are valid in C99 and newer versions.

- Stack allocated arrays can be of a size determined in runtime. These are called **variable length arrays**. It is evident that these cannot be marked static because the latter implies allocation in **.data** section.

- Starting from C99, you can add a **flexible array member** as the *last* member of a structure, as shown in Listing 11-12.

Listing 11-12. flex_array_def.c

```
struct char_array {
    size_t length; char  data[];
};
```

In this case, the `sizeof` operator, applied to a structure instance, will return the structure size without the array. The array will refer to the memory immediately following the structure instance. So, in the example given in Listing 11-12, `sizeof(struct char_array)` == `sizeof(size_t)`. Assuming it's equal to 8, `data[0]` refers to the 8-th byte (counting from 0) from the structure instance starting address.

Listing 11-13 shows an example.

Listing 11-13. `flex_array.c`

```c
#include <string.h>
#include <malloc.h>

struct int_array {
    size_t size;
    int  array[];
};

struct int_array* array_create( size_t size ) {
    struct int_array* array = malloc(
                sizeof( *array )
            + sizeof( int ) * size );
    array-> size = size;
    memset( array->array, 0, size );
    return array;
}
```

11.3.1 Syntax Details

C allows us to define several variables in a row.

```c
int a,b = 4, c;
```

To declare several pointers, however, you have to add an asterisk before every pointer. Listing 11-14 shows an example: a and b are pointers, but the type of c is `int`.

Listing 11-14. `ptr_mult_decl.c`

```c
int* a, *b, c;
```

This rule can be worked around by creating a type alias for `int*` using `typedef`, hiding an asterisk.

Defining multiple variables in a row is a generally discouraged practice as in most cases it makes the code harder to read.

It is possible to create rather complex type definitions by mixing function pointers, arrays, pointers, etc. You can use the following algorithm to decipher them:

1. Find an identifier, and start from it.

2. Go to the right until the first closing parenthesis. Find its pair on the left. Interpret an expression between these parentheses.

3. Go "up" one level, relative to the expression we have parsed during the previous step. Find outer parentheses and repeat step 2.

We will illustrate this algorithm in an example shown in Listing 11-15. Table 11-1 describes the parsing process.

Listing 11-15. complex_decl_1.c

```
int* (* (*fp) (int) ) [10];
```

Table 11-1. *Parsing Complex Definition*

Expression	Interpretation
fp	First identifier.
(*fp)	Is a pointer.
(* (*fp) (int))	A function accepting int and returning a pointer...
int* (* (*fp) (int)) [10]	... to an array of ten pointers to int

As you see, the process of deciphering complex declarations is not a breeze. It can be made simpler by using typedefs for parts of the declarations.

11.4   String Literals

Any sequence of char elements ended by a null-terminator can be viewed as a string in C. Here, however, we want to speak about the immediately encoded strings, so, string literals. Most string literals are stored in **.rodata** if they are big enough.

Listing 11-16 shows an example of a string literal.

Listing 11-16. str_lit_example.c

```
char* str = "when the music is over, turn out the lights";
```

str is just a pointer to the string's first character.

According to the language standard, string literals (or pointers to strings created in such a way) cannot be changed.[1] Listing 11-17 shows an example.

Listing 11-17. string_literal_mut.c

```
char* str = "hello world abcdefghijkl";
/* the following line produces a runtime error */
str[15] = '\'';
```

In C++, the string literals have the type char const* by default, which reflects their immutable nature. Consider using variables of type char const* whenever you can when the strings you are dealing with are not intended to be mutated.

The constructions shown in Listing 11-18, are also correct, albeit you are most probably never going to use the second one.

---

[1]To be precise, the result of such an operation is not well defined.

Listing 11-18. `str_lit_ptr_ex.c`

```
char will_be_o = "hello, world!"[4];  /* is 'o' */
char const* tail = "abcde"+3 ; /* is "de", skipping 3 symbols */
```

When manipulating strings, there are several common scenarios based on where the string is allocated.

1. We can create a string among global variables. It will be mutable, and under no circumstances will it be doubled in constant data region. Listing 11-19 shows an example.

Listing 11-19. `str_glob.c`

```
char str[] = "something_global";
void f (void) { ... }
```

In other words, it is just a global array initialized in place with character codes.

2. We can create a string in a stack, in a local variable. Listing 11-20 shows an example.

Listing 11-20. `str_loc.c`

```
void func(void) {
    char str[] = "something_local";
}
```

The string "something_local" itself, however, should be kept somewhere because the local variables are initialized every time the function is launched, and we have to know the values with which they should be initialized.

In case of relatively short strings, the compiler will try to inline them into the instructions stream. Apparently, for smaller strings, it is wiser to just split them into 8-byte chunks and perform mov instructions with each chunk as an immediate operand.

The long strings, however, are better kept in **.rodata**. The statement, shown in Listing 11-20, will allocate enough bytes in stack and then perform a copy from read-only data to this local stack buffer.

3. We can allocate a string dynamically via malloc. The header file string.h contains some very useful functions such as memcpy, used to perform fast copying.

Listing 11-21 shows an example.

Listing 11-21. `str_malloc.c`

```
#include <malloc.h>
#include <string.h>

int main( int argc, char** argv )
{
    char* str = (char*)malloc( 25 );
    strcpy( str, "wow, such a nice string!" );

    free( str );
}
```

■ **Question 210**   Why did we allocate 25 bytes for a 24-character string?

■ **Question 211**   Read man for the functions: memcpy, memset, strcpy.

11.4.1   String Interning

"String interning" is a term more accustomed to Java or C# programmers. However, in reality, a similar thing is happening in C (but only in compile time). The compiler tries to avoid duplicating strings in the read-only data region. It means that usually the equal addresses will be assigned to all three variables in the code shown in Listing 11-22.

Listing 11-22. str_intern.c

```
char* best_guitar_solo  = "Firth of fifth";
char* good_genesis_song = "Firth of fifth";
char* best_1973_live = "Firth of fifth";
```

String interning would be impossible if string literals were not protected from rewriting. Otherwise, by changing such strings in one place of a program we are introducing an unpredictable change in data used in another place, as both share the same copy of string.

11.5   Data Models

We have spoken about the sizes of different integer types. The language standard is enforcing a set of rules like "the size of long is no less than the size of short" or "the size of signed short should be such that it could contain values in range $-2^{16} \dots 2^{16} - 1$." The last rule, however, does not provide us with a fixed size, because short could have been 8 bytes wide and still satisfy this constraint. So, these requirements are far from setting the exact sizes in stone. In order to systematize different sets of sizes, the conventions called **data model** were created. Each of them defines sizes for basic types. Figure 11-2 shows some remarkable data models that could be of interest to us.

short	int	long	ptr	long long	Name	Examples
-	16	-	16	-	IP16	PDP-11 Unix
16	16	32	32	-	I16LP32	Apple Macintosh 68K; early Microsoft Windows
16	32	32	32	-	ILP32	IBM 370; VAX Unix
16	32	32	32	64	ILP32LL	Amdahl; Microsoft Win32
16	32	32	64	64	LLP64 or IL32LLP64	Microsoft Win64
16	32	64	64	64	LP64	Most Unix systems (Linux, Solaris, HP UX 11, Mac OS…)
64	64	64	64	64	SILP64	UNICOS (Unix for Cray supercomputers)

Figure 11-2. Data models

As we have chosen the GNU/Linux 64-bit system for studying purposes, it our data model is LP64. When you develop for 64-bit Windows system, the size of `long` will differ.

Everyone wants to write portable code that can be reused across different platforms, and fortunately there is a standard-conforming way to never run into data model changes.

Before C99, it was a common practice to make a set of type aliases of form `int32` or `uint64` and use them exclusively across the program in lieu of ever-changing `int`s or `long`s. Should the target architecture change, the type aliases were easy to fix. However, it created a chaos because everyone created their own set of types.

C99 introduced **platform independent types**. To use them, you should just include a header `stdint.h`. It gives access to the different integer types of fixed size. Each of them has a form:

- u, if the type is unsigned;

- int;

- Size in bits: 8, 16, 32 or 64; and

- _t.

  For example, `uint8_t`, `int64_t`, `int16_t`.

  The `printf` function (and similar format input/output) functions have been given a similar treatment by introducing special macros to select the correct format specifiers. These are defined in the file `inttypes.h`.

  In the common cases, you want to read or write integer numbers or pointers. Then the macro name will be formed as follows:

- PRI for output (`printf`, `fprintf` etc.) or SCN for input (`scanf`, `fscanf` etc.).

- Format specifier:

  - d for decimal formatting.

  - x for hexadecimal formatting.

  - o for octal formatting.

  - u for unsigned int formatting.

  - i for integer formatting.

- Additional information includes one of the following:

  - N for *N* bit integers.

  - PTR for pointers.

  - MAX for maximum supported bit size.

  - FAST is implementation defined.

We have to use the fact that several string literals, delimited by spaces, are concatenated automatically. The macro will produce a string containing a correct format specifier, which will be concatenated with whatever is around it.

Listing 11-23 shows an example.

Listing 11-23. inttypes.c

```
#include <inttypes.h>
#include <stdio.h>

void f( void ) {
    int64_t i64 = -10;
    uint64_t u64 = 100;
    printf( "Signed 64-bit integer:   %" PRIi64 "\n", i64 );
    printf( "Unsigned 64-bit integer: %" PRIu64 "\n", u64 );
}
```

Refer to section 7.8.1 of [7] for a full list of such macros.

11.6   Data Streams

The C standard library provides us with a way to work with files in a platform-independent way. It abstracts files as **data streams**, from which we can read and to which we can write.

We have seen how the files are handled in Linux on the system calls level: the open system call opens a file and returns its **descriptor**, an integer number, the write and read system calls are used to perform writing and reading, respectively, and the close system call ensures that the file is properly closed. As the C language was created in par with the Unix operating system, they bear the same approach to file interactions. The library counterparts of these functions are called fopen, fwrite, fread, and fclose. On Unix-like systems, they act like an adapter for system calls, providing similar functionality, except that they also work on other platform in the same way. The main differences are as follows:

1. In place of file descriptors, we use a special type FILE, which stores all information about a certain stream. Its implementation is hidden and you should never change its internal state manually. So, instead of working with numeric file descriptors (which is platform-dependent), we use FILE as a black box.

   The FILE instance is allocated in heap internally by the C library itself, so at anytime we will work with a pointer to it, not with the instance itself directly.

2. While file operations in Unix are more or less uniform, there are two types of data streams in C.

   - Binary streams consist of raw bytes that are handled "as is."

   - Text streams include symbols grouped into lines; each line is ended by an end-of-line character (implementation dependent).

Text streams are limited in a number of ways *on some systems*.

   - The line length might be limited.

   - They might only be able to work with printing characters, newlines, spaces, and tabs.

   - Spaces before the newline may disappear.

   On some operating systems, text and binary streams use different file formats, and thus to work with a text file in a way compatible between all its programs, the use of text streams is mandatory.

   While GNU C library, usually associated with GCC, makes no difference between binary and text streams, on other platforms this is not the case, so distinguishing these is crucial.

For example, I have seen a situation in which reading a large block from a picture file on Windows (the compiler was MSVC) ended prematurely because the picture was obviously binary, while the associated stream was created in text mode.

The standard library provides machinery to create and work with streams. Some functions it defines should only be used on text streams (like fscanf). The relevant header file is called stdio.h.

Let's analyze the example shown in Listing 11-24.

Listing 11-24. file_example.c

```
int smth[]={1,2,3,4,5};
FILE* f = fopen( "hello.img", "rwb" );

fread( smth, sizeof(int), 1, f);

/* This line is optional. By means of `fseek` function we can navigate the file */
fseek( f, 0, SEEK_SET );

fwrite(smth, 5 * sizeof( int ), 1, f);
fclose( f );
```

- The instance of FILE is created via a call to fopen function. The latter accepts the path to file and a set of flags, squashed into a string.

The important flags of fopen are listed here.

- b - open file in a binary mode. That is what makes a real distinction between text and binary streams. By default, files are opened in text mode.

- w - open a stream with a possibility to write into it.

- r - open a stream with a possibility to read from it.

- + - if you write simply w, the file will be overwritten. When + is present, the writes will append data to the end of file.

If the file does not exist, it will be created.

The file hello.img is opened in binary mode for both reading and writing. The file contents will be overwritten.

- After being created, the FILE holds a kind of a pointer to a position inside the file, a cursor of sorts. Reads and writes move this cursor further.

- The fseek function is used to move cursor without performing reads or writes. It allows moving cursor relatively to either its current position or the file start.

- fwrite and fread functions are used to write and read data from the opened FILE instance.

Taking fread, for example, it accepts the memory buffer to read from. The two integer parameters are the size of an individual block and the amount of blocks read. The returning value is the amount of blocks successfully read from the file. Every block's read is atomic: either it is completely read, or not read at all. In this example, the block size equals sizeof(int), and the amount of blocks is one.

The fwrite usage is symmetrical.

- fclose should be called when the work with file is complete.

There exist a special constant EOF. When it is returned by a function that works with a file, it means that the end of file is reached.

Another constant BUFSIZ stores the buffer size that works best in the current environment for input and output operations.

Streams can use buffering. It means that they have an internal buffer that proxies all reads and writes. It allows for rarer system calls (which are expensive performance-wise due to context switching). Sometimes when the buffer is full the writing will actually trigger a write system call. A buffer can be manually flushed using fflush command. Any delayed writes will be executed and the buffer will be reset.

When the program starts, three FILE* instances are created and attached to the streams with descriptors 0, 1, and 2. They can be referred to as stdin, stdout, and stderr. All three are usually using a buffer, but the stderr is automatically flushing the buffer after every writing. It is necessary to not delay or lose error messages.

Note Again, descriptors are integers, FILE instances are not. The int fileno(FILE* stream) function is used to get the underlying descriptor for the file stream.

Question 212 Read man for functions: fread, fread, fwrite, fprintf, fscanf, fopen, fclose, fflush.

Question 213 Do research and find out what will happen if the fflush function is applied to a bidirectional stream (opened for both reading and writing) when the last action on the stream before it was reading.

11.7   Assignment: Higher-Order Functions and Lists

11.7.1   Common Higher-Order Functions

In this assignment, we are going to implement several higher-order functions on linked lists, which should be familiar to those used to functional programming paradigm.

These functions are known under the names foreach, map, map_mut, and foldl.

- foreach accepts a pointer to the list start and a function (which returns void and accepts an int). It launches the function on each element of the list.

- map accepts a function f and a list. It returns a new list containing the results of the f applied to all elements of the source list. The source list is not affected.

For example, $f(x) = x + 1$ will map the list $(1, 2, 3)$ into $(2, 3, 4)$.

- map_mut does the same but changes the source list.

- foldl is a bit more complicated. It accepts:

  - The accumulator starting value.

  - A function $f(x, a)$.

  - A list of elements.

It returns a value of the same type as the accumulator, computed in the following way:

1. We launch f on accumulator and the first element of the list. The result is the new accumulator value a'.

2. We launch f on a' and the second element in list. The result is again the new accumulator value a''.

3. We repeat the process until the list is consumed. In the end the final accumulator value is the final result.

For example, let's take $f(x, a) = x * a$. By launching `foldl` with the accumulator value 1 and this function we will compute the product of all elements in the list.

- `iterate` accepts the initial value s, list length n, and function f. It then generates a list of length n as follows:

$$\left[s, f(s), f(f(s)), f(f(f(s)))\ldots \right]$$

The functions described above are called **higher-order functions**, because they do accept other functions as arguments. Another example of such a function is the array sorting function `qsort`.

```
void qsort( void *base,
            size_t nmemb,
            size_t size,
            int (*compar)(const void *, const void *));
```

It accepts the array starting address base, elements count nmemb, size of individual elements size, and the comparator function compar. This function is the decision maker which tells which one of the given elements should be closer to the beginning of the array.

■ **Question 214**   Read man qsort.

11.7.2   Assignment

The input contains an arbitrary number of integers.

1. Save these integers in a linked list.

2. Transfer all functions written in previous assignment into separate .h and c files. Do not forget to put an include guard!

3. Implement foreach; using it, output the initial list to stdout twice: the first time, separate elements with spaces, the second time output each element on the new line.

4. Implement map; using it, output the squares and the cubes of the numbers from list.

5. Implement foldl; using it, output the sum and the minimal and maximal element in the list.

6. Implement map_mut; using it, output the modules of the input numbers.

7. Implement iterate; using it, create and output the list of the powers of two (first 10 values: 1, 2, 4, 8, …).

8. Implement a function bool save(struct list* lst, const char* filename);, which will write all elements of the list into a text file filename. It should return true in case the write is successful, false otherwise.

9. Implement a function bool load(struct list** lst, const char* filename);, which will read all integers from a text file filename and write the saved list into *lst. It should return true in case the write is successful, false otherwise.

10. Save the list into a text file and load it back using the two functions above. Verify that the save and load are correct.

11. Implement a function `bool serialize(struct list* lst, const char* filename);`, which will write all elements of the list into a *binary* file filename. It should return `true` in case the write is successful, `false` otherwise.

12. Implement a function `bool deserialize(struct list** lst, const char* filename);`, which will read all integers from a *binary* file filename and write the saved list into *lst. It should return `true` in case the write is successful, `false` otherwise.

13. Serialize the list into a binary file and load it back using two functions above. Verify that the serialization and deserialization are correct.

14. Free all allocated memory.

You will have to learn to use

- Function pointers.

- `limits.h` and constants from it. For example, in order to find the minimal element in an array, you have to use `foldl` with the maximal possible `int` value as an accumulator and a function that returns a minimum of two elements.

- The `static` keyword for functions that you only want to use in one module.

You are guaranteed, that

- Input stream contains only integer numbers separated by whitespace characters.

- All numbers from input can be contained as `int`.

It is probably wise to write a separate function to read a list from `FILE`.
The solution takes about 150 lines of code, not counting the functions, defined in the previous assignment.

Question 215 In languages such as C#, code like the following is possible:

```
var count = 0;

mylist.Foreach(  x  =>  count  +=  1  );
```

Here we launch an anonymous function (i.e., a function which has no name, but whose address can be manipulated, for example, passed to other function) for each element of a list. The function is written as `x => count += 1` and is the equivalent of

```
void no_name( int x ) { count += 1; }
```

The interesting thing about it is that this function is aware of some of the local variables of the caller and thus can modify them.

Can you rewrite the function `forall` so that it accepts a pointer to a "context" of sorts, which can hold an arbitrary number of variables addresses and then pass the context to the function called for each element?

11.8 Summary

In this chapter we have studied the memory model. We have gotten a better understanding of the type dimensions and the data models, studied pointer arithmetic, and learned to decipher complex type declarations. Additionally, we have seen how to use the standard library functions to perform the input and output. We have practiced it by implementing several higher-order functions and doing a little file input and output.

We will further deepen our understanding of memory layout in the next chapter, where we will elaborate the difference between three "facets" of a language (syntax, semantics, and pragmatics), study the notions of undefined and unspecified behavior, and show why the data alignment is important.

Question 216 What arithmetic operations can you perform with pointers, and on what conditions?

Question 217 What is the purpose of `void*`?

Question 218 What is the purpose of `NULL`?

Question 219 What is the difference between 0 in pointer context and 0 as an integer value?

Question 220 What is `ptrdiff_t` and how is it used?

Question 221 What is the difference between `size_t` and `ptrdiff_t`?

Question 222 What are first-class objects?

Question 223 Are functions first-class objects in C?

Question 224 What data regions does the C abstract machine contain?

Question 225 Is the constant data region usually write-protected by hardware?

Question 226 What is the connection between pointers and arrays?

Question 227 What is the dynamic memory allocation?

Question 228 What is the `sizeof` operator? When is it computed?

Question 229 When are the string literals stored in **.rodata**?

Question 230 What is string interning?

Question 231 Which data model are we using?

Question 232 Which header contains platform-independent types?

Question 233 How do we concatenate string literals in compile time?

Question 234 What is the data stream?

Question 235 Is there a difference between a data stream and a descriptor?

Question 236 How do we get the descriptor from stream?

Question 237 Are there any streams opened when the program starts?

Question 238 What is the difference between binary and text streams?

Question 239 How do we open a binary stream? A text stream?

## CHAPTER 12

Syntax, Semantics, and Pragmatics

In this chapter we are going to revise the very essence of what the programming language is. These foundations will allow us to better understand the language structure, the program behavior, and the details of translation that you should be aware of.

12.1   What Is a Programming Language?

A programming language is a formal computer language designed to describe algorithms in a way understandable by a machine. Each program is a sequence of characters. But how do we tell the programs from all other strings? We need to define the language somehow.

The brute way is to say that the compiler itself is the language definition, since it parses programs and translates them into executable code. This approach is bad for a number of reasons. What do we do with compiler bugs? Are they really bugs, or do they affect the language definition? How do we write other compilers? Why should we mix the language definition and the implementation details?

Another way is to provide a cleaner and implementation-independent way of describing language. It is quite common to view three facets of a single language.

- The rules of statement constructions. Often the description of correctly structured programs is made using formal grammars. These rules form the language **syntax**.

- The effects of each language construction on the abstract machine. This is the language **semantics**.

- In any language there is also a third aspect, called **pragmatics**. It describes the influence of the real-world implementation on the program behavior.

  – In some situations, the language standard does not provide enough information about the program behavior. Then it is entirely up to compiler to decide how it will translate this program, so it is often assigning some specific behavior to such programs.

    For example, in the call f(g(x), h(x)) the order of evaluation of g(x) and h(x) is not defined by standard. We can either compute g(x) and then h(x), or vice versa. But the compiler will pick a certain order and generate instructions that will perform calls in exactly this order.

  – Sometimes there are different ways to translate the language constructions into the target code. For example, do we want to prohibit the compiler from inlining certain functions, or do we stick with laissez-faire strategy?

In this chapter we are going to explore these three facets of languages and apply them to C.

© Igor Zhirkov 2017
I. Zhirkov, *Low-Level Programming*, DOI 10.1007/978-1-4842-2403-8_12

12.2 Syntax and Formal Grammars

First of all, a language is a subset of all possible strings that we can construct from a certain alphabet. For example, a language of arithmetic expressions has an alphabet $\Sigma = \{0, 1, 2, 3, 4, 5, 6, 7, 8, 9, +, -, \times, /, .\}$, assuming only these four arithmetic operations are used and the dot separates an integer part. Not all combinations of these symbols form a valid string—for example, +++-+ is not a valid sentence of this language.

Formal grammars were first formalized by Noam Chomsky. They were created in attempt to formalize natural languages, such as English. According to them, sentences have a tree-like structure, where the leaves are kind of "basic blocks" and more complex parts are built from them (and other complex parts) according to some rules.

All those primitive and composite parts are usually called **symbols**. The atomic symbols are called **terminals**, and the complex ones are **nonterminals**.

This approach was adopted to construct synthetic languages with very simple (in comparison to natural languages) grammars.

Formally, a grammar consists of

- A finite set of terminal symbols.

- A finite set of nonterminal symbols.

- A finite set of production rules, which hold information about language structure.

- A starting symbol, a nonterminal which will correspond to any correctly constructed language statement. It is a starting point for us to parse any statement.

The class of grammars that we are interested in has a very particular form of production rules. Each of them looks like

```
<nonterminal> ::= sequence of terminals and nonterminals
```

As we see, this is exactly the description of a nonterminal complex structure. We can write multiple possible rules for the same nonterminal and the convenient one will be applied. To make it less verbose, we will use the notation with the symbol | to denote "or," just as in regular expressions.

This way of describing grammar rules is called **BNF (Backus-Naur form)**: the terminals are denoted using quoted strings, the production rules are written using ::= characters, and the nonterminal names are written inside brackets.

Sometimes it is also quite convenient to introduce a terminal ϵ, which, during parsing, will be matched with an empty (sub)string.

So, grammars are a way to describe language structure. They allow you to perform the following kinds of tasks:

- Test a language statement for syntactical correctness.

- Generate correct language statements.

- Parse language statements into hierarchical structures where, for example, the if condition is separated from the code around it and unfolded into a tree-like structure ready to be evaluated.

12.2.1   Example: Natural Numbers

The language of natural numbers can be represented using a grammar.

We will take this set of characters as the alphabet: $\Sigma = \{0, 1, 2, 3, 4, 5, 6, 7, 8, 9\}$. However, we want a more decent representation than just all possible strings built of the characters from Σ, because the numbers with leading zeros (000124) do not look nice.

We define several nonterminal symbols: first, <notzero> for any digit except zero, <digit> for any digit, and <raw> for any sequence of <digit>s.

As we know, several rules are possible for one nonterminal. So, to define <notzero>, we can write as many rules as there are different options:

```
<notzero> ::= '1'
<notzero> ::= '2'
<notzero> ::= '3'
<notzero> ::= '4'
<notzero> ::= '5'
<notzero> ::= '6'
<notzero> ::= '7'
<notzero> ::= '8'
<notzero> ::= '9'
```

However, as it is very cumbersome and not so easy to read, we will use the different notation to describe exactly the same rules:

```
<notzero> ::= '1' | '2' | '3' | '4' | '5' | '6' | '7' | '8' | '9'
```

This notation is a part of canonical **BNF**.

After adding a zero, we get a rule for nonterminal <digit>, that encodes any digit.

```
<digit> ::= '0' | <notzero>
```

Then we define the nonterminal <raw> to encode all digit sequences. A sequence of digits is defined in a recursive way as either one digit or a digit followed by another sequence of digits.

```
<raw> ::= <digit> | <digit> <raw>
```

The <number> will serve us as a starting symbol. Either we deal with a one-digit number, which has no constraints on itself, or we have multiple digits, and then the first one should not be zero (otherwise it is a leading zero we do not want to see); the rest can be arbitrary.

Listing 12-1 shows the final result.

Listing 12-1. grammar_naturals

```
<notzero> ::= '1' | '2' | '3' | '4' | '5' | '6' | '7' | '8' | '9'
<digit> ::= '0' | <notzero>
<raw> ::= <digit> | <digit> <raw>
<number> ::=    <digit> | <notzero> <raw>
```

12.2.2   Example: Simple Arithmetics

Let's add a couple of simple binary operations. For a start, we will limit ourselves to addition and multiplication. We will base it on an example shown in Listing 12-1.

Let's add a nonterminal <expr> that will serve as a new starting symbol. An expression is either a number or a number followed by a binary operation symbol and another expression (so, an expression is also defined recursively).

Listing 12-2 shows an example.

Listing 12-2. grammar_nat_pm

```
<notzero> ::= '1' | '2' | '3' | '4' | '5' | '6' | '7' | '8' | '9'
<digit> ::= '0' | <notzero>
<raw> ::= <digit> | <digit> <raw>
<number> ::=    <digit> | <notzero> <raw>

<expr> ::= <number> | <number> '+' <expr> | <number> '-' <expr>
```

The grammar allows us to build a tree-like structure on top of the text, where each leaf is a terminal, and each other node is a nonterminal. For example, let's apply the current set of rules to a string 1+42 and see how it is deconstructed. Figure 12-1 shows the result.

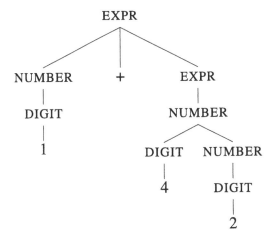

Figure 12-1. *Parse tree for the expression 1+42*

The first expansion is performed according to the rule <expr> ::= number '+' <expr>. The latter expression is just a number, which in turn is a sequence of digit and a number.

12.2.3   Recursive Descent

Writing parsers by hand is not hard. To illustrate it, we are going to show a parser that applies our new knowledge about grammars to literally translate the grammar description into the parsing code.

Let's take a grammar for natural numbers that we have already described in section 12.2.1 and add just one more rule to it. The new starting symbol will be str, which corresponds to "a number ended by a null-terminator." Listing 12-3 shows the revised grammar definition.

Listing 12-3. grammar_naturals_nullterm

```
<notzero> ::= '1' | '2' | '3' | '4' | '5' | '6' | '7' | '8' | '9'
<digit> ::= '0' | <notzero>
<raw> ::= <digit> | <digit> <raw>
<number> ::= <digit> | <notzero> <raw>

<str> ::= <number> '\0'
```

People usually operate with a notion of stream when performing parsing with grammar rules. A stream is a sequence of whatever is considered symbols. Its interface consists of two functions:

- `bool expect(symbol)` accepts a single terminal and returns true if the stream contains exactly this kind of terminal in the current position.

- `bool accept(symbol)` does the same and then advances the stream position by one in case of success.

Up to now, we operated with abstractions such as symbols and streams. We can map all the abstract notions to the concrete instances. In our case, the symbol will correspond to a single char.[1]

Listing 12-4 shows an example text processor built based on grammar rules definitions. This is a syntactic checker, which verifies whether the string is holding a natural number without leading zeroes and nothing else (like spaces around the number).

Listing 12-4. rec_desc_nat.c

```c
#include <stdio.h>
#include  <stdbool.h>

char const* stream = NULL ;

bool accept(char c) {
    if (*stream == c) {
        stream++;
        return  true;
    }
    else return false;
}
bool notzero( void ) {
    return accept( '1' ) || accept( '2' ) || accept( '3' )
    || accept( '4' )     || accept( '5' ) || accept( '6' )
    || accept( '7' )     || accept( '8' ) || accept( '9' );

}
bool digit( void ) {
    return accept('0') || notzero();
}
```

---

[1]For parsers of programming languages it is much simpler to pick keywords and word classes (such as identifiers or literals) as terminal symbols. Breaking them into single characters introduces unnecessary complexity.

```
bool raw( void ) {
    if ( digit() ) { raw(); return true; }
    return false;
}
bool number( void ) {
    if ( notzero() ) {
        raw();
        return true;
    } else return accept('0');
}
bool str( void ) {
    return number() && accept( 0 );
}
void check( const char* string ) {
    stream = string;
    printf("%s -> %d\n", string, str() );
}
int main(void) {
    check("12345");
    check("hello12");
    check("0002");
    check("10dbd");
    check("0");
    return 0;
}
```

This example shows how each nonterminal is mapped to a function with the same name that tries to apply the relevant grammar rules. The parsing occurs in a top-down manner: we start with the most general starting symbol and try to break it into parts and parse them.

When the rules start alike we **factorize** them by applying the common part first and then trying to consume the rest, as in number function. The two branches start with overlapping nonterminals: <digit> and <notzero>. Each of them contains the range 1...9, the only difference being <digit>'s range including zero. So, if we found a terminal in range 1...9 we try to consume as many digits after that as we can and we succeed anyway. If not, we check for the first digit being 0 and stop if it is so, consuming no more terminals.

The <notzero> function succeeds if at least one of the symbols in range 1-9 is found. Due to the lazy application of ||, not all accept calls will be performed. The first of them that succeeds will end the expression evaluation, so only one advancement in stream will occur.

The <digit> function succeeds if a zero is found or if <notzero> succeeded, which is a literal translation of a rule:

<digit> ::= '0' | <notzero>

The other functions are performing in the same manner. Should we not limit ourselves with a null-terminator, the parsing would answer us a question: "does this sequence of symbols start with a valid language sentence?"

In Listing 12-4 we have used a global variable on purpose in order to facilitate understanding. We still strongly advise against their usage in real programs.

The parsers for real programming languages are usually quite complex. In order to write them programmers use a special toolset that can generate parsers from the declarative description close to BNF. In case you need to write a parser for a complex language we recommend you taking a look at ANTLR or yacc parser generators.

Another popular technique of handwriting parsers is called **parser combinators**. It encourages creating parsers for the most basic generic text elements (a single character, a number, a name of a variable, etc.). Then these small parsers are combined (OR, AND, sequence...) and transformed (one or many occurences, zero or more occurences...) to produce more complex parsers. This technique, however, is easy to apply when the language supports a functional style of programming, because it often relies on higher-order functions.

■ **On recursion in grammars**   The grammar rules can be recursive, as we see. However, depending on the parsing technique using certain types of recursion might be ill-advised. For example, a rule `expr ::= expr '+' expr`, while being valid, will not permit us to construct a parser easily. To write a grammar well in this sense, you should avoid left-recursive rules such as the one listed previously, because, encoded naively, it will only produce an infinite recursion, when the `expr()` function will start its execution with another call to `expr()`. The rules that refine the first nonterminal on the right-hand side of the production avoid this problem.

■ **Question 240**   Write a recursive descent parser for floating point arithmetic with multiplication, subtraction, and addition. For this assignment, we consider no negative literals exist (so instead of writing -1.20 we will write 0-1.20).

12.2.4   Example: Arithmetics with Priorities

The interesting part of expressions is that different operations have different priorities. For example, the addition operation has a lower priority than the multiplication operation, so all multiplications are done prior to addition.

Let's see the naive grammar for natural numbers with addition and multiplication in Listing 12-5.

Listing 12-5. grammar_nat_pm_mult

```
<notzero> ::= '1' | '2' | '3' | '4' | '5' | '6' | '7' | '8' | '9'
<digit> ::= '0' | <notzero>
<raw> ::= <digit> | <digit> <raw>
<number> ::= <digit> | <notzero> <raw>

<expr> ::= <number> | <number> '+' <expr>
        | <number> '-' <expr> | <number> '*' <expr>
```

Without taking the multiplication priority into account, the parse tree for the expression 1*2+3 will look as shown in Figure 12-2.

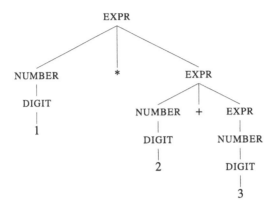

Figure 12-2. *Parse trees without priorities for the expression 1*2+3*

However, as we notice, the multiplication and addition are equals here: they are expanded in order of appearance. Because of this, the expression 1*2+3 is parsed as 1*(2+3), breaking the common evaluation order, tied to the tree structure.

From a parser's point of view, the priority means that in the parse tree the "add" nodes should be closer to the root than the "multiply" nodes, since addition is performed on the bigger parts of the expression. The evaluation of the arithmetical expressions is performed, informally, starting from leaves and ending in the root.

How do we prioritize some operations over others? It is acquired by splitting one syntactical category ⟨expr⟩ into several classes. Each class is a refinement of the previous class of sorts. Listing 12-6 shows an example.

Listing 12-6. grammar_priorities

```
<expr> ::= <expr0> "<" <expr> | <expr0> "<=" <expr>
| <expr0> "==" <expr> | <expr0> ">" <expr> | <expr0> ">=" <expr> | <expr0>

<expr0> = <expr1> "+" <expr> | <expr1> "-" <expr> | <expr1>
<expr1> ::= <atom> "*" <expr1> | <atom> "/" <expr1> | <atom>
<atom> ::= "(" <expr> ")" | <NUMBER>
```

We can understand this example in the following way:

- ⟨expr⟩ is really any expression.

- ⟨expr0⟩ is an expression without <, >, == and other terminals, which are present in the first rule.

- ⟨expr1⟩ is also free of addition and subtraction.

12.2.5   Example: Simple Imperative Language

To illustrate that this knowledge can be applied to programming languages, we are giving an example of one's syntax. This syntax description provides definitions for the statements, comprising typical imperative constructs: if, while, print and assignments. The keywords can be treated as atomic terminals. Listing 12-7 shows the grammar.

Listing 12-7. imp

```
<statements> ::= <statement> | <statement> ";" <statements>
<statement> ::= "{" <statements> "}" | <assignment> | <if> | <while> | <print>
<print> ::= "print" "(" <expr> ")"
<assignment> ::= IDENT "=" <expr>
<if> ::= "<if>" "(" <expr> ")" <statement> "<else>" <statement>
<while> ::= "<while>" "(" <expr> ")" <statement>

<expr> ::= <expr0> "<" <expr> | <expr0> "<=" <expr>
| <expr0> "==" <expr> | <expr0> ">" <expr> | <expr0> ">=" <expr> | <expr0>
<expr0> = <expr1> "+" <expr> | <expr1> "-" <expr> | <expr1>
<expr1> ::= <atom> "*" <expr1> | <atom> "/" <expr1> | <atom>
<atom> ::= "(" <expr> ")" | NUMBER
```

12.2.6   Chomsky Hierarchy

The formal grammars as we have studied them are actually but a subclass of formal grammars as Chomsky viewed them. This class is called **context-free grammars** for reasons that will soon be apparent.

The hierarchy consists of four levels ranging from 3 to 0, lower levels being more expressive and powerful.

3. The regular grammars are surprisingly described by our old friends **regular expressions**. The finite automatons are the weakest type of parsers because they cannot handle the fractal structures such as arithmetical expressions.

   Even in the simplest case, <expr> ::= number '+' <expr>, the part of the expression on the right-hand side of '+' is similar to the whole expression. This rule can be applied recursively an arbitrary amount of time.

2. The context-free grammars, which we have studied already, have rules that are of the form

   ```
   nonterminal ::=
           <sequence of terminal and nonterminal symbols>
   ```

   Any regular expression can be also described in terms of context-free grammars.

1. The **context-sensitive grammars** have rules of form:

   ```
   a A  b ::= a y b
   ```

   a and b denote an arbitrary (possibly empty) sequence of terminals and/or nonterminals, y denotes a *non-empty* sequence of terminals and/or nonterminals, and A is the nonterminal being expanded.

The difference between levels 2 and 1 is that the nonterminal on the left side is substituted for y only when it occurs between a and b (which are left untouched). Remember, both a and b can be rather complex.

0. The **unrestricted grammars** have rules of form:

```
sequence of terminal and nonterminal symbols ::=
    sequence of terminal and nonterminal symbols
```

As there are absolutely no restrictions on the left- and right-hand sides of the rules, these grammars are most powerful. It can be shown that these types of grammars can be used to encode any computer program, so these grammars are Turing-complete.

The real programming languages are almost never truly context-free. For example, a usage of a variable declared earlier is apparently a context-sensitive construction, because it is only valid when following a corresponding variable declaration. However, for simplicity, they are often approximated with context-free grammars and then additional passes on the parsing tree transform are done to check whether such context-sensitive conditions are satisfied.

12.2.7 Abstract Syntax Tree

There exists a notion of **abstract syntax**. It describes the trees that are constructed from the source code. The **concrete syntax** describes the exact mapping between keywords and the tree node types they are mapped to. For example, imagine that we have rewritten the C compiler so that the while keyword is replaced by _while_. Then imagine that we have rewritten all programs so that this new keyword is used instead of while. The concrete syntax did change indeed, but the abstract syntax is the same, because the language constructions stayed the same. On the contrary, if we add a finally clause to if, it incorporates a statement to be executed no matter the condition value, and we will change the abstract syntax as well.

The abstract syntax tree is usually also much more minimalistic in comparison to the parse trees. The parse tree would hold information that was only relevant for parsing (see Figure 12-3).

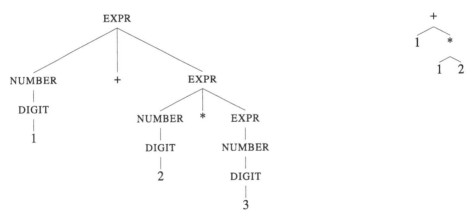

Figure 12-3. *Parse tree and abstract syntax tree of the expression 1 + 2*3*

As we see, the tree on the right is much more concise and to the point. This tree can be directly evaluated by an interpreter or some executable code to calculate what might be generated.

12.2.8   Lexical Analysis

In reality, applying grammar rules directly to the individual characters is overkill. It can be convenient to add a prepass called **lexical analysis**. The raw text is first transformed into a sequence of lexemes (also called **tokens**). Each token is described with a regular expression and extracted from the character stream. For example, a number can be described with a regular expression [0-9]+, and an identifier can be [a-zA-Z_] [0-9a-zA-Z_]*. After performing such processing, the text will no longer be a flat sequence of characters but rather a linked list of tokens. Each token will be marked with its type and for the parser, the token types will be mapped to terminals.

It is easy to ignore all formatting details (such as line breaks and other whitespace symbols) during this step.

12.2.9   Summary on Parsing

The compiler parses the source code in several steps. Two important steps are lexical and syntactic analysis.

During the lexical analysis, the program text is broken into lexemes, such as integer literals or keywords. The text formatting is no more relevant after this step. Each lexeme type is best described using a regular expression.

During the syntactic analysis, a tree structure is built on top of the stream of tokens. This structure is called an abstract syntax tree. Each node corresponds to a language construct.

12.3   Semantics

The language semantics is a correspondence between the sentences as syntactical constructions and their meaning. Each sentence is usually described as a type of node in the program **abstract syntax tree**. This description is performed in one of the following ways:

- **Axiomatically.** The current program state can be described with a set of logical formulas. Then each step of the abstract machine will transform these formulas in a certain way.

- **Denotationally.** Each language sentence is mapped into a mathematical object of a certain theory (e.g., domain theory). Then the program effects can be described in terms of this theory. It is of a particular interest when reasoning about program behavior of different programs written in different languages.

- **Operationally.** Each sentence produces a certain change of state in the abstract machine, which is subject to description. The descriptions in the C standard are informal but resemble the operational semantic description more than the other two.

The language standard is the language description in human-readable form. However, while being more comprehensible for an unprepared one, it is more verbose and sometimes less unambiguous. In order to write concise descriptions, a language of mathematical logic and lambda calculus is usually used. We will not dive into details in this book, because this topic demands a pedantic approach on its own. We refer you to the books [29] and [35] for an immaculate study of type theory and language semantics.

12.3.1   Undefined Behavior

The completeness of the semantics description is not enforced. It means that some language constructions are only defined for a subset of all possible situations. For example, a pointer dereference *x is only guaranteed to behave in a consistent way when x points to a "valid" memory location. When x is NULL or points to deallocated memory, the **undefined behavior** occurs. However, such expression is absolutely correct syntactically.

The standard intentionally introduces cases of undefined behavior. Why?

First of all, it is easier to write compilers that produce code with less guarantees. Second, all defined behavior has to be implemented. If we want that dereferencing null pointer triggers an error, the compiler has two do two things each time *any* pointer is dereferenced:

- Try to deduce that in this exact place the pointer can never have NULL as its value.

- If the compiler can not deduce, that this pointer is never NULL, it emits assembly code to check it. If the pointer is NULL, this code will execute a handler to it. Otherwise, it will proceed with dereferencing the pointer.

Listing 12-8 shows an example.

Listing 12-8. ptr_analysis1.c

```
int x = 0;
int* p = &x;
...
/* there are no writes to `p` in these lines */
...
*p =  10; /* this pointer can not be NULL  */
```

However, this is much trickier than it might appear. In the example in Listing 12-8, we could have assumed, that as no writes to variable p are performed, it is always holding the address of x. However, this is not always true, as illustrated by the example shown in Listing 12-9.

Listing 12-9. ptr_analysis2.c

```
int x = 0;
int* p = &x;
...
/* there are no writes to `p` in these lines */
int**  z  =  &p;
*z = NULL; /* Still not a direct write to `p` */
...
*p =  10; /* this pointer can not be NULL -- not true anymore */
```

So, solving this problem actually requires a *very* complex analysis in presence of pointer arithmetic. Once the variable's address is taken, or worse still, its address is passed to a function, you have to analyze the entire function calling sequence, take function pointers into account, pointers to the pointers, etc.

The analysis will not always yield correct results (in the most general case this problem is even theoretically undecidable), and the performance can suffer because of it. So, in accordance with the C laissez-faire spirit, the correctness of pointer dereferencing is left to the responsibility of the programmer himself.

In managed languages such as Java or C#, the defined behavior of pointer dereferencing is much easier to achieve. First, they are usually run inside a framework, which provides code for exception raising and handling. Second, the nullability analysis is much simpler in the absence of address arithmetic. Finally, they are usually compiled just-in-time, which means that the compiler has access to runtime information and can use it to perform some optimizations unavailable to an ahead-of-time compiler. For example, after the program has launched and given the user input, a compiler deduced that the pointer x is never NULL if a certain condition P holds. Then it can generate two versions of the function f containing this dereference: one with a check and the other without check. Then every time f is called, only one of two versions is called. If the compiler can prove that P holds in a calling situation, the non-checked version is called; otherwise the checked one is called.

The undefined behavior can be dangerous (and usually is). It leads to subtle bugs, because it does *not* guarantee an error in compile or in runtime. The program can encounter a situation with undefined behavior and continue execution silently; however, its behavior will randomly change after a certain amount of instructions are executed.

A typical situation is the heap corruption. The heap is in fact structured; each block is delimited with utility information, used by the standard library. Writing out of block bounds (but close to them) is likely to corrupt this information, which will result in a crash during one of *future* calls to malloc of free, making this bug a time-bomb.

Here are some cases of undefined behavior, explicitly specified by the C99 standard. We are not providing the full list, because there are at least 190 cases.

- Signed integer overflow.

- Dereferencing an invalid pointer.

- Comparing the pointers to elements of two different memory blocks.

- Calling function with arguments that do not match its initial signature (possible by taking a pointer to it and casting to other function type).

- Reading from an uninitialized local variable.

- Division by 0.

- Accessing an array element out of its bounds.

- Attempting to change a string literal.

- The return value of a function, which does not have an executed return statement.

12.3.2   Unspecified Behavior

It is important to distinguish between undefined behavior and unspecified behavior. Unspecified behavior defines a set of behaviors that might happen but does not specify which one exactly will be selected. The selection will depend on the compiler.

For example,

- The function argument's evaluation order is not specified. It means that while evaluating f(g(), h()) we have no guarantees that g() will be evaluated first and h() second. However, it is guaranteed that both g() and h() will be evaluated before f().

- The order of subexpression evaluation in general, f(x) + g(x), does not enforce f to be executed before g. Unspecified behavior describes the cases of nondeterminism in the abstract C machine.

12.3.3   Implementation-Defined Behavior

The standard also defines the implementation-defined behavior, such as the size of int (which, as we told you, is architecture-dependent). We can think about such choices as the abstract machine parameters: before we start it, we have to choose these parameters.

Another example of such behavior is the modulo operation x % y. The result in case of negative y is implementation-defined.

What is the difference between implementation-defined and unspecified behavior? The answer is that the implementation (compiler) has to explicitly document the choices it makes, while in cases of unspecified behavior anything from a set of possible behaviors can occur.

12.3.4   Sequence Points

Sequence points are the places in the program where the state of the abstract machine is coherent to the state of the target machine. We can think about them this way: when we debug a program, we can execute it in a step-by-step fashion, where each step is roughly equivalent to a C statement. We usually stop on semicolon, function calls, || operator, etc. However, we can switch to the assembly view, where each statement will be encoded by possibly many instructions, and execute these instructions in the same manner. It allows us to execute only a part of statement, pausing in a halfway. In this moment, the state of the abstract C machine is not well defined. Once we finish executing instructions that implement one single statement, the machines' states "synchronize," allowing us to explore not only the state of assembly level but also the state of the C program itself. This is the sequence point.

The second, equivalent definition of sequence point is the place in the program where the side effects of previous expressions are already applied, but the side effects of the following ones are not yet applied.

The sequence points are

- Semicolon.

- Comma (which in C can act the same way as a semicolon, but also groups statements. Its usage is discouraged.).

- Logic AND/OR (not bitwise versions!).

- When the function arguments are evaluated but the function has not started its execution yet.

- Question mark in the ternary operator.

Multiple real-world cases of undefined behavior are tied to the notion of sequence points. Listing 12-10 shows an example.

Listing 12-10. seq_points.c

```
int i = 0;
i = i ++ * 10;
```

What is i equal to? Unfortunately, the best answer we can give is the following: there is an undefined behavior in this code. Apparently, we do not know whether the i will be incremented before assigning i*10 to i or after that. There are two writes in the same memory location before the sequence point and it is undefined in which order will they occur.

The cause of this is as we have seen in section 12.3.2, the subexpression evaluation order is not fixed. As subexpressions might have effects on the memory state (think function calls or pre-or postincrement operators), and there is no enforced order in which these effects occur, even the result of one subexpression may depend on the effects of the other.

12.4   Pragmatics

12.4.1   Alignment

From the point of view of the abstract machine, we are working with bytes of memory. Each byte has its address. The hardware protocols, used on the chip, are, however, quite different. It is quite common that the processor can only read packs of, say, 16 bytes, which start from an address divisible by 16. In other words, it can either read the first 16 byte-chunk from memory or the second one, but not a chunk that starts from an arbitrary address.

We say that the data is **aligned** on N-byte boundary if it starts from an address divisible by N. Apparently, if the data is aligned on kn-byte boundary, it is automatically aligned on n-byte boundary. For example, if the variable is aligned on 16-byte boundary, it is simultaneously aligned on an 8-byte boundary.

```
Aligned data (8-byte boundary):
0x00 00 00 00 00 00 00 00 :    11 22 33 44 55 66 77 88

Unaligned data (8-byte boundary):
0x00 00 00 00 00 00 00 00 :    .. .. .. 11 22 33 44 55
0x00 00 00 00 00 00 00 07 :    66 77 88 .. .. .. .. ..
```

What happens when the programmer requests a read of a multibyte value which spans over two such blocks (e.g., 8-byte value, whose first three bytes lie in one chunk, and the rest is in another one)? Different architectures give different answers to this question.

Some hardware architectures forbid unaligned memory access. It means that an attempt to read any value which is not aligned to, for example, an 8-byte boundary results in an interrupt. An example of such architecture is SPARC. The operating systems can emulate unaligned accesses by intercepting the generated interrupt and placing the complex accessing logic into the handler. Such operations, as you might imagine, are extremely costly because the interrupt handling is relatively slow.

Intel 64 adapts a less strict behavior. The unaligned accesses are allowed but bear an overhead. For example, if we want to read 8 bytes starting from the address 6 and we can only read chunks that are 8 bytes long, the CPU (central processing unit) will perform two reads instead of one and then compose the requested value from the parts of two quad words.

So, aligned accesses are cheaper, because they require less reads. The memory consumption is often a lesser concern for a programmer than the performance; thus compilers automatically adjust variables alignment in memory even if it creates gaps of unused bytes. This is commonly referred to as **data structure padding**.

The alignment is a parameter of the code generation and program execution, so it is usually viewed as a part of language **pragmatics**.

12.4.2   Data Structure Padding

For structures, the alignment exists in two different senses:

- The alignment of the structure instance itself. It affects the address the structure starts at.

- The alignment of the structure fields. Compiler can intentionally introduce gaps between structure fields in order to make accesses to them faster. Data structure padding relates to this.

For example, we have created a structure, shown in Listing 12-11.

Listing 12-11. align_str_ex1

```
struct mystr {
    uint16_t a;
    uint64_t b;
};
```

Assuming an alignment on an 8-byte boundary, the size of such structure, returned by `sizeof`, will be 16 bytes. The a field starts at an address divisible by 8, and then six bytes are wasted to align b on an 8-byte boundary.

There are several instances in which we should be aware of it:

- You might want to change the trade-off between memory consumption and performance to lesser memory consumption. Imagine you are creating a million copies of structures and every structure wastes 30% of its size because of alignment gaps. Forcing the compiler to decrease these gaps will then lead to a memory usage gain of 30% which is nothing to sneeze at. It also brings benefits of better locality which can be far more beneficial than the alignment of individual fields.

- Reading file headers or accepting network data into structures should take possible gaps between structure fields into account. For example, the file header contains a field of 2 bytes and then a field of 8 bytes. There are no gaps between them. Now we are trying to read this header into a structure, as shown in Listing 12-12.

Listing 12-12. align_str_read.c

```
struct str {
    uint16_t a; /* a gap of 4 bytes */
    uint64_t b;
};
struct str mystr;
fread( &mystr, sizeof( str ), 1, f );
```

The problem is that the structure's layout has gaps inside it, while the file stores fields in a contiguous way. Assuming the values in file are a=0x1111 and b=0x 22 22 22 22 22 22 22, Figure 12-4 shows the memory state after reading.

```
In file:
      11  11  22  22  22  22  22  22  22  22  ??  ??  ??  ??  ??  ??

In memory:
      11  11  22  22  22  22  22  22  22  22  ??  ??  ??  ??  ??  ??
      _____
      uint16_t a                                uint64_t b
```

Figure 12-4. *Memory layout structure and the data read from file*

There are ways to control alignment; up until C11 they are compiler-specific. We will study them first.

The #pragma keyword allows us to issue one of the pragmatic commands to the compiler. It is supported in MSVC, Microsoft's C compiler, and is also understood by GCC for compatibility reasons.

Listing 12-13 shows how to use it to locally change the alignment choosing strategy by using the pack pragma.

Listing 12-13. pragma_pack.c

```
#pragma pack(push, 2)
struct mystr {
    short a;
    long b;
};
#pragma pack(pop)
```

The second argument of pack is a presumed size of the chunk that the machine is able to read from memory on the hardware level.

The first argument of pack is either push or pop. During the translation process, the compiler keeps track of the current padding value by checking the top of the special internal stack. We can temporarily override the current padding value by pushing a new value into this new stack and restore the old value when we are done. Changing padding value globally is possible by using the following form of this pragma:

```
#pragma pack(2)
```

However, it is very dangerous because it leads to unpredictable subtle changes in other parts of program, which are very difficult to trace.

Let's see how the alignment value affects the individual field's alignment by analyzing an example shown in Listing 12-14.

Listing 12-14. pack_2.c

```
#pragma pack(push, 2)
struct mystr {
    uint16_t a;
    int64_t b;
};
#pragma pack(pop)
```

The padding value tells us how many bytes a hypothetical target computer can fetch from memory in one read. The compiler tries to minimize the amount of reads for each field. There is no reason to skip bytes between a and b here, because it brings no benefits with regard to the padding value. Assuming that a=0x11 11 and b=0x22 22 22 22 22 22 22 22, the memory layout will look like the following:

```
11 11 22 22 22 22 22 22 22 22
```

Listing 12-15 shows another example with the padding value equal to 4.

Listing 12-15. pack_4.c

```
#pragma pack(push, 4)
struct mystr {
    uint16_t a;
    int64_t b;
};
#pragma pack(pop)
```

What if we adapt the same memory layout without gaps? As we can only read 4 bytes at a time, it is not optimal. We have delimited the bounds of memory chunks that are readable atomically.

```
Pack: 2
11 11 | 22 22 | 22 22 | 22 22 | 22 22 | ?? ??
Pack: 4, same memory layout
11 11   22 22 | 22 22   22 22 | 22 22   ?? ??
Pack: 4, memory layout really used
11 11   ?? ?? | 22 22   22 22 | 22 22   22 22
```

As we see, when the padding is set to 4, adapting a gapless memory layout forces the CPU to perform three reads to access b. So, basically, the idea is to minimize the amount of reads while placing struct members as close as possible.

The GCC specific way of doing roughly the same thing is the packed specification of the __attribute__ directive. In general, __attribute__ is describing the additional specification of a code entity such as a type or a function. This packed keyword means that the structure fields are stored consecutively in memory without gaps at all. Listing 12-16 shows an example.

Listing 12-16. str_attribute_packed.c

```c
Struct__attribute__(( packed )) mystr {
    uint8_t first;
    float delta;
    float position;
};
```

Remember that packed structures are not part of the language and are not supported on some architectures (such as SPARC) *even on the hardware level,* which means not only a performance hit but also program crashes or reading invalid values.

12.5   Alignment in C11

C11 introduced a standardized way of alignment control. It consists of

- Two keywords:
    - _Alignas
    - _Alignof
- stdalign.h header file, which defines preprocessor aliases for _Alignas and _Alignof as alignas and alignof
- aligned_alloc function.

Alignment is only possible to the powers of 2: 1, 2, 4, 8, etc.

alignof is used to know an alignment of a certain variable or type. It is computed in compile time, just as sizeof. Listing 12-17 shows an example of its usage. Note the "%zu" format specifier used to print or scan values of type size_t.

Listing 12-17. alignof_ex.c

```c
#include <stdio.h>
#include <stdalign.h>

int  main(void) {
    short x;
    printf("%zu\n", alignof(x));
    return 0;
}
```

In fact, alignof(x) returns the greatest power of two x is aligned at, since aligning anything at, for example, 8 implies alignment on 4, 2, and 1 as well (all its divisors).

Prefer using alignof to _Alignof and alignas to _Alignas.

alignas accepts a constant expression and is used to force an alignment on a certain variable or array. Listing 12-18 shows an example. Once launched, it outputs 8.

Listing 12-18. alignas_ex.c

```c
#include <stdio.h>
#include <stdalign.h>

int main( void ) {
    alignas( 8 ) short x;
    printf( "%zu\n", alignof( x ) );
    return 0;
}
```

By combining alignof and alignas we can align variables at the same boundary as other variables.

You cannot align variables to a value less than their size and alignas cannot be used to produce the same effect as __attribute__((packed)).

12.6   Summary

In this chapter we have structured and expanded our knowledge about what the programming language is. We have seen the basics of writing parsers and studied the notions of undefined and unspecified behavior and why they are important. We then introduced the notion of pragmatics and elaborated one of the most important things

We defer an assignment for this chapter until the next one, where we will elaborate the most important good code practices. Assuming our readers are not yet very familiar with C, we want them to adapt good habits as early as possible in the course of their C journey.

■ **Question 241**   What is the language syntax?

■ **Question 242**   What are grammars used for?

■ **Question 243**   What does a grammar consist of?

■ **Question 244**   What is BNF?

■ **Question 245**   How do we write a recursive descent parser having the grammar description in BNF?

Question 246 How do we incorporate priorities in grammar description?

Question 247 What are the levels of the Chomsky hierarchy?

Question 248 Why are regular languages less expressive than context-free grammars?

Question 249 What is the lexical analysis?

Question 250 What is the language semantic?

Question 251 What is undefined behavior?

Question 252 What is unspecified behavior and how is it different from undefined behavior?

Question 253 What are the cases of undefined behavior in C?

Question 254 What are the cases of unspecified behavior in C?

Question 255 What are sequence points?

Question 256 What is pragmatics?

Question 257 What is data structure padding? Is it portable?

Question 258 What is the alignment? How can it be controlled in C11?

■ ■ ■

## CHAPTER 13

Good Code Practices

In this chapter we want to concentrate on the coding style. When writing code a developer is constantly faced with a decision-making procedure. What kinds of data structures should he use? How should they be named? Where and when should they be allocated? Experienced programmers make these decisions in a different way compared to beginners, and we find it extremely important to speak about this decision making process.

13.1   Making Choices

Decisions often require balancing between two poles that are mutually exclusive. The classical example is that you cannot ship a quality product cheaply and quickly. Fine performance tuning of the code often makes it harder to read and to debug. So, some code characteristics should be prioritized over others based on common sense and the task itself. Because of this, such code guidelines are a good start, but following them blindly is not the way to go.

Our code writing advices are based on the following premises:

1. We want the code to be as reusable as possible. This often requires careful planning and coordination between developers, which does not let you write code really *fast* but pays off very soon because it spares time for debugging and actually allows you to write complex software. Debugging programs is generally considered harder than writing them. So, less code often means less time spent debugging and more robust functions. It is especially important for such languages as C, which are

   - Unsafe in a large sense (allows for pointer arithmetic, does not perform bound checks, etc.)

   - Lack an expressive type system, seen in such languages as Scala, Haskell, or OCaml. Such types impose a number of restrictions on the program that should be satisfied, otherwise the compiler will reject it.

   This rule has a notable exception. If reusing functions results in a drastic performance decrease, the algorithm has an unnecessary large O-complexity. For example, we have done an assignment with linked lists in Chapter 10. There was a function to calculate sum of all integers in a certain list. One way of creating it is roughly shown in Listing 13-1.

© Igor Zhirkov 2017

I. Zhirkov, *Low-Level Programming*, DOI 10.1007/978-1-4842-2403-8_13

Listing 13-1. `list_sum_bad.c`

```
int list_sum( const struct list* l ) {
    size_t i;
    int sum = 0;
    /* We do not want to launch the full computation
     * of size at each cycle iteration */
    size_t sz = list_size( l ) ;
    for( i = 0; i < sz; l = l-> next )
        sum = sum + l->value;
    return sum;
}
```

In this example, for each i in the range from 0 inclusive to the list length exclusive we actually start walking through the list from its very first element. This results in a drastic decrease in performance in comparison with the single summing pass through the list. In the latter case, appending another element to the list results in an additional list access, while in the program shown in Listing 13-1 this leads to `list_length(l)` additional list accesses!

2. The program should be easy to modify. This point is interdependent with the previous one. Smaller functions are often more reusable, and thus the modifications become easier, because more code can be left untouched from the previous version.

3. The code should be as easy to read as possible. The key factors here are

   - Sane naming. Even if you are not a native English speaker, you should not write variable names, function names, or commentary in your native language.

   - Consistency. Use the same naming conventions and uniform ways of performing similar operations.

   - Short and concise functions. If the logic description is overly verbose, it is often a sign of a lack of sane decomposition or you need an abstraction layer. It has also a good effect on maintainability.

4. The code should be easy to test. Testing assures us that at least in some elaborated cases the code behaves as intended.

Sometimes the task demands the opposite. For example, if we are writing the code for a controller in absence of a good optimizing compiler and with very restricted resources, we can be forced to abandon beautiful code structure because the compiler cannot inline functions properly; thus each call will impact the performance, often in an unacceptable way.

13.2 Code Elements

13.2.1 General Naming

The specific naming convention is often imposed by the language itself. In cases in which the project is based on an existing codebase, it might be reasonable to not deviate from it for the sake of consistency. In this book we are using the following naming conventions:

- All names are written in lowercase letters.

- The name parts are separated with an underscore, as follows: `list_count`.

The rest of this section concentrates on different language features and associated naming and usage conventions.

13.2.2   File Structure

Include files should have an include guard.

They should be self-contained, which means that for each header file `thisfile.h` a `.c` file with only the line `#include "thisfile.h"` should compile. The order of includes is often chosen as follows:

- Related header.
- C library.
- Other libraries' `.h`.
- Your project's `.h`.

Then adhere to a consistent order of declaration of macros, types, functions, variables, etc. It greatly simplifies navigating the project. A typical order is

- for headers:
    1. Include files.
    2. Macros.
    3. Types.
    4. Variables (globals).
    5. Functions.
- for `.c` files
    1. Include files.
    2. Macros.
    3. Types.
    4. Variables (globals).
    5. Static variables.
    6. Functions.
    7. Static functions.

13.2.3   Types

- When possible (C99 or newer), prefer the types defined in `stdint.h`, such as `uint64_t` or `uint8_t`.
- If you want to be POSIX-compliant, do not define your own types with `_t` suffix. It is reserved for standard types, so the new types that might be introduced in future revisions of standard will not clash with the custom types defined in some programs.
- Types are often named with a prefix common to the project. For example, you want to write a calculator, then the type tags will be prefixed with `calc_`.

- When you are defining structures and if you can choose the order of fields, define them in the following order:

  – First try to minimize the memory losses from **data structure padding**.

  – Then order fields by size.

  – Finally, sort them alphabetically.

  – Sometimes structures have fields that should not be modified by user directly. For example, a library defines the structure shown in Listing 13-2.

Listing 13-2. struct_private_ex.c

```
struct mypair {
    int x;
    int y;
    int _refcount;
};
```

The fields of such structure can be modified directly using dot or arrow syntax. Our convention, however, implies that only specific library functions should modify the _refcount field, and the library user should never do it by hand.

C lacks a concept of structure private fields, so it is as close as we can get without using more or less dirty hacks.

  – Enumeration members should be written in uppercase, like constants. The common prefix is suggested for the members of one enumeration. An example is shown in Listing 13-3.

Listing 13-3. enum_ex.c

```
Enum exit_code   {
    EX_SUCCESS,
    EX_FAILURE,
    EX_INVALID_ARGUMENTS
};
```

13.2.4   Variables

Choosing the right names for variables and functions is crucial.

- Use nouns for names.

- Boolean variables should have meaningful names too. Prefixing them with is_ is advisable. Then append the exact property that is being checked. is_good is probably too broad to be a good name in most cases, unlike is_prime or is_before_last.

  Prefer positive names to negative ones, as the human brain parses them easily— for example, is_even over is_not_odd.

- It is not advisable to use names that bear no meaning, like a, b, or x4. The notable exception is the code that illustrates an article or a paper, which describes an algorithm in pseudo code using such names. In this case, any naming change is more likely to confuse readers than to bring more clarity. The indices are traditionally named i and j and you will be understood if you stick to them.

- Including the measuring units might be a good idea—for example, `uint32_t delay_msecs`.

- Other suffixes are useful too, such as `cnt`, `max`, etc.

  For example, `attempts_max` (maximum attempts allowed), `attempts_cnt` (attempts made).

- Global constants are named in all capital letters. Global *mutable* variables are prefixed with `g_`.

- The tradition says that the global constants should be defined using `#define` directive. However, the modern approach is to use `const static` or just `const` global variables. Contrary to `#define`s, they are typed and also better seen when debugging. If you have an access to a quality compiler, it will inline them anyway (if it decides that it will be faster).

- Use `const` modifier whenever appropriate. C99 allows you to create variables in arbitrary places inside functions, not just at the block start. Use it to store intermediate results in named constants.

- Do not define global variables in header files! Define them in `.c` files and declare them in `.h` file as `extern`.

13.2.5   On Global Variables

Do not use global mutable variables if you can. We cannot stress this enough. Here are the most important problems they bring:

- In medium scale and more in large projects with a whopping number of lines, all information about the function effects is better localized in its signature. A function f might call another function g, and so on, and somewhere in this chain a global variable will be changed. We cannot see that this change *might* occur by looking at f; we have to study all functions it calls, and the functions they call, and so on.

- They make functions that are not **reenterable**. It means that a function f cannot be called if is already being executed. The latter can happen in two cases:

  – Function f is calling other functions, which after some inner calls might call f again, when the first instance of f has not yet been terminated.

Listing 13-4 shows an example of a function f that is not reenterable.

Listing 13-4. `reenterability.c`

```c
bool flag = true;
int var = 0;
void g(void) {
    f();
    flag = false;
}
void f(void) {
    if (flag) g();
}
```

  – The program is parallelized and the function is being used in multiple threads (which is often the case on modern computers).

In case of a complex call hierarchy, knowing whether the function is reenterable or not requires an additional analysis.

- They introduce security risks, because usually their values have to be checked before being modified or used. Programmers tend to forget these checks. If something can go wrong, it will go wrong.

- They make testing function harder because of the data dependency they are introducing. Writing code without tests, however, is always a practice to avoid.

Global static mutable variables are evil too, but at least they do not pollute the global namespace in other files. Global static immutable variables (const static) are, however, perfectly fine and can be often inlined by compiler.

13.2.6   Functions

- Use verbs to name functions—for example, packet_checksum_calc.

- The prefix is_ is also quite common for functions checking conditions—for example, int is_prime(long num).

- The functions that operate on a struct with a certain tag are often prefixed with the respective tag name—for example, bool list_is_empty(struct list* lst);.

As C does not allow for fine namespace control, this seems to be the simplest form of controlling the chaos that emerges when most functions are accessible from anywhere.

- Use the static modifier for all functions except for those you want to be available for everyone.

- Probably the most important place to use const is for function arguments of type "pointer to immutable data." It ensures that function does not occasionally change them due to a programmer's mistake.

13.3   Files and Documentation

As the project grows, the number of files increases and it becomes more difficult to navigate them. To be able to cope with voluminous projects, you have to structure them from the very beginning.

Following is a common template for the project root directory.

src/	Source files
doc/	Documentation
res/	Resource files (such as images).
lib/	Static libraries that will be linked to the executable file.
build/	The artifacts: an executable file and other generated files.
include/	Include files. This directory is added to the compiler include search path by -I flag.
obj/	Generated object files. They are assembled in the executable files and libraries by the linker and are not needed after the compilation end.
configure	The initial configuration script that should be launched prior to building. It can set up different target architectures or turn on and off features.
Makefile	Contains instructions for the automated build system. The file name and format varies depending on system used.

There are many build systems; some of the most popular ones for C are make, cmake, and automake. Different languages have different ecosystems and often have dedicated build tools (e.g., Gradle or OCamlBuild).

- We recommend you study these projects, which, to our knowledge, are well organized www.gnu.org/software/gsl/

- www.gnu.org/software/gsl/design/gsl-design.html

- www.kylheku.com/kaz/kazlib.html

Doxygen is a de facto standard for creating documentation for C and C++ programs. It allows us to generate a fully structured set of HTML or LATEXpages from the program source code. The descriptions of functions and variables are taken from specifically formatted comments. Listing 13-5 shows an example of a source file which is accepted by Doxygen.

Listing 13-5. doxygen_example.h

```
#pragma once
#include <common.h>
#include <vm.h>

/** @defgroup const_pool Constant pool */

/** Free allocated memory for the pool contents
*/
void const_pool_deinit( struct vm_const_pool* pool );

/** Non-destructive constant pool combination
 * @param a First pool.
 * @param b Second pool.
 * @returns An initialized constant pool combining contents of both arguments
 * */
struct vm_const_pool const_combine(
        struct vm_const_pool const* a,
        struct vm_const_pool const* b );

/** Change the constant pool by adding the other pool's contents in its end.
 * @param[out] src The source pool which will be modified.
 * @param fresh The pool to merge with the `src` pool.
 */
void const_merge(
        struct vm_const_pool* src,
        struct vm_const_pool const* fresh );

/**@} */
```

The specially formatted comments (starting with /** and containing commands such as @defgroup) are processed by Doxygen to generate documentation for the respective code entities. For more information, refer to Doxygen documentation.

13.4 Encapsulation

One of the thinking fundamentals is abstraction. In software engineering, it is a process of hiding implementation details and data.

If we want to implement a certain behavior like an image rotation, we would like to think only about the image rotation. The input file format, the format of its headers, is of little importance to us. What is really important is to be able to work with dots which form the image and know its dimensions. However, you cannot write a program without considering all this information that is actually independent of the rotation algorithm itself.

We are going to split the program into parts; each part will do its purpose and only it. This logic can be used by calling a set of exposed functions and/or a set of exposed global variables. Together they form an **interface** for this program part. To implement them, however, we usually have to write more functions, which are better hidden from the end user.

■ **Working with version control systems**   When working in a team where many people perform changes simultaneously, making smaller functions is very important. If a function performs many actions, and its code is huge, multiple independent changes will be harder to merge automatically.

In programming languages supporting packages or classes, these are used to hide pieces of code and create interfaces for them. Unfortunately, C has none of them; furthermore, there is no concept of "private fields" in structures: all fields are seen by everyone.

The support for separate code files, called translation units, is the only real language feature to help us isolate parts of program code. We use a notion of module as a synonym for a translation unit, a .c file.

The C standard does not define a notion of module. In this book we are using them interchangeably because for the C language they are roughly equivalent.

As we know, functions and global variables become public symbols by default and thus accessible to other files. What is reasonable is to mark all "private" functions and global variables as static in the .c file and declare all "public" functions in the .h file.

As an example, we are going to write a module that implements a stack.

The header file will describe the structure and the functions that can operate its instances. It resembles object-oriented programming without subtyping (no inheritance).

The interface will consist of the following functions:

- Create or destroy a stack;

- Push and pop elements from a stack.

- Check if the stack is empty.

- Launch a function for each element in the stack.

The code file will define all functions and probably some more, which won't be accessible outside of it and are only created for the sake of decomposition and code reusability.

Listings 13-6 and 13-7 show the resulting code. stack.h describes an interface. It has an include guard, enumerates all other headers (first standard headers, then custom ones), and defines custom types.

Listing 13-6. stack.h

```
#ifndef _STACK_H_
#define _STACK_H_

#include <stddef.h>
#include <stdint.h>
#include <stdbool.h>

struct list;

struct stack  {
    struct list* first;
    struct list* last;
    size_t count;
};

struct stack stack_init    ( void );
void stack_deinit( struct stack* st );

void stack_push( struct stack* s, int value );
int  stack_pop ( struct stack* s );
bool stack_is_empty( struct stack const* s );

void stack_foreach( struct stack* s, void (f)(int) );

#endif  /* _STACK_H_  */
```

There are two types defined: list and stack. The first one is only used internally inside the stack, and so we declared it an **incomplete type**. Only pointers to instances of such type are allowed unless its definition is specified later.

For everyone who includes stack.h, the type struct list will remain incomplete. The implementation file stack.c, however, will define the structure, completing the type and allowing to access its fields (but only in stack.c).

Then the struct stack is defined and the functions that work with it are declared (stack_push, stack_pop, etc.) (see Listing 13-7).

Listing 13-7. stack.c

```
#include <malloc.h>
#include "stack.h"

struct list { int value; struct list* next; };

static struct list* list_new( int item, struct list* next ) {
    struct list* lst = malloc( sizeof( *lst ) );
    lst->value = item;
    lst->next  = next;
    return lst;

}
```

```c
void stack_push( struct stack* s, int value ) {
    s->first = list_new( value, s->first );
    if ( s->last ==  NULL  ) s->last =  s-> first;
    s->count++;
}

int stack_pop( struct stack* s ) {
    struct list* const head = s->first;
    int value;
    if ( head ) {
        if ( head->next ) s->first = head->next;
        value = head->value;
        free( head );
        if( -- s->count ) {
            s->first =  s->last =  NULL;
        }
        return value;
    }
    return 0;
}

void stack_foreach( struct stack* s, void (f)(int) ) {
    struct list* cur;
    for( cur = s->first; cur; cur = cur-> next )
        f( cur->value );

}

bool stack_is_empty( struct stack const* s ) {
    return s->count == 0;
}

struct stack stack_init( void ) {
    struct stack empty = { NULL, NULL, 0 };
    return empty;
}

void stack_deinit( struct stack* st ) {
    while( ! stack_is_empty( st ) ) stack_pop( st );
    st-> first = NULL;
    st-> last = NULL;
}
```

This file defines all functions declared in the header. It can be split into multiple .c files, which will sometimes do good for the project structure; what is important is that the compiler should accept them all and then the compiled code should get to the linker.

A static function list_new is defined to isolate the instance initialization of struct list. It is not exposed to the outside world. During optimizations, not only can the compiler inline it, but it can even delete the function itself, effectively eliminating any possible implications on the code performance. Marking function static is necessary (but not sufficient) for this optimization to occur. Additionally, the instructions of static functions might be placed closer to their respective callers, improving locality.

By splitting the program on modules with well-described interfaces you reduce the overall complexity and achieve better reusability.

The need to create header files makes modifications a bit cumbersome because the consistency of headers with the code itself is the programmer's responsibility. However, we can benefit from it as well by specifying a clear interface description, which lacks the implementation details.

13.5   Immutability

It is quite common to have to choose between creating a new modified copy of a structure and performing modifications in place.

Here are some advantages and disadvantages of both choices.

- Creating copy:
    - Easier to write: you won't accidentally pass the wrong instance to a function.
    - Easier to debug, because you don't have to track changes of variable.
    - Can be optimized by the compiler.
    - Friendly to parallelization.
    - Can be slower.

- Mutating existing instance.
    - Faster.
    - Can become very hard to debug, especially in a multithreaded environment.
    - Sometimes simpler because you don't have to carefully and recursively copy structures with multiple pointers to other structures (this process is called deep copying).
    - For objects with a distinct identity, this approach may be more intuitive and is also robust enough.

Our perception of the real world is based on mutable objects, because the objects in the real world often have a distinct identity. When you are turning on your phone, the phone is not replaced by its copy, but the state of the same phone is changed instead. In other words, the identity of the phone is maintained, while its state is changing. Thus, in situations where you only have one instance of a certain type and the consecutive changes are performed on it, it is fine to mutate it instead of making a copy at every change.

13.6   Assertions

There is a mechanism that allows you to test certain conditions during program execution. When such a condition is not being satisfied, an error is produced and the program is terminated abnormally.

To use the assertion mechanism, we have to use #include <assert.h> and then use the assert macro. Listing 13-8 shows an example.

Listing 13-8. assert.c

```
#include <assert.h>
int main() {
    int x = 0;
    assert( x != 0 );
    return 0;
}
```

The condition, given to the assert macro, is obviously false; hence the program will terminate abnormally and inform us about the failed assertion:

```
assert: assert.c:6: main: Assertion `x != 0' failed.
```

If the preprocessor symbol NDEBUG is defined (which can be achieved by using -D NDEBUG compiler option or #define NDEBUG directive), the assert is replaced by an empty string and thus turned off. So, assertions will produce zero overhead and the checks will not be performed.

You should use asserts to check for impossible conditions that signify the inconsistency of the program state. Never use asserts to perform checks on user input.

13.7 Error Handling

While higher-level languages have some kind of error handling mechanism (which does not interfere with the main logic description), C lacks one. There are three principal ways to deal with errors:

1. Use return codes. A function should not return a result as such but a code that shows whether it has processed well or not. In the latter case the code reflects the exact type of error that has occurred. The computation result is assigned by a pointer that is accepted as an additional argument.

Listing 13-9 shows an example.

Listing 13-9. error_code.c

```
enum   div_res   {
    DIV_OK,
    DIV_BYZERO
};

enum div_res div( int x, int y, int* result ) {
    if ( y != 0  ) { *result = x/y; return DIV_OK;  }
    else return DIV_BYZERO;
}
```

Symmetrically, you can return values as you do and set up error code using a pointer to a respective variable.

Error codes can be described using an enum or with several #defines. Then you can use them as indices in a static array of messages or use a switch statement. Listing 13-10 shows an example.

Listing 13-10. err_switch_arr.c

```
enum   error_code   {
    ERROR1,
    ERROR2
};
...
enum  error_code  err;
...
switch (err) {
    case ERROR1: ... break;
    case ERROR2: ... break;
```

```
        default: ... break;
}

/* alternatively */

static const char* const messages[] = {
    "It is the first error\n",
    "The second error it is\n"
};

fprintf( stderr, messages[err] );
```

Never use global variables as error code holders (or to return a value from a function).

According to C standard, a standard variable-like entity errno exists. It should be a modifiable lvalue and must not be explicitly declared. Its usage is akin to a global variable, albeit its value is thread-local. The library functions use it as an error code holder, so after seeing a failure from a function (e.g., fopen returned NULL), one should check the errno value for an error code. The man pages for the respective function enumerate possible errno values (e.g., EEXIST).

Despite this feature having sneaked into the standard library, it is largely considered an anti-pattern and should not be imitated.

    2. Using callbacks.

Callbacks are function pointers that are passed as arguments and called by the function that accepts them. They can be used to isolate the error handling code, but they often look weird to people who are more accustomed to traditional return code usage. Additionally, the execution order becomes less obvious.

Listing 13-11 shows an example.

Listing 13-11. div_cb.c

```
#include <stdio.h>

int div( int x, int y, void (onerror)(int, int)) {
    if ( y != 0 )
        return x/y;
    else  {
        onerror(x,y);
        return 0;
    }
}

static void div_by_zero(int x, int y) {
    fprintf( stderr, "Division by zero: %d / %d\n", x, y );
}

int main(void) {
    printf("%d %d\n",
            div( 10, 2, div_by_zero ),
            div( 10, 0, div_by_zero ) );
    return 0;
}
```

3. Using `longjmp`. This advanced technique will be explained in section 14.3.

There is a classical error recovering technique, which requires the `goto` usage. Listing 13-12 shows an example is shown.

Listing 13-12. `goto_error_recover.c`

```c
void foo(void)

{
    if (!doA()) goto exit;
    if (!doB()) goto revertA;
    if (!doC()) goto revertB;

    /* doA, doB and doC succeeded */
    return;

revertB:
    undoB();
revertA:
    undoA();
exit:
    return;
}
```

In this example, three actions have been performed, and they all can fail. The nature of these actions is such that we have to do a cleanup after. For example, doA might trigger dynamic memory allocation. In case doA succeeded but doB did not, we have to free this memory to prevent memory leak. This is what the code labeled revertA does.

The recoveries are performed in reverse order. If doA and doB succeeded, but doC failed, we have to revert to B, and then to A. So, we label the reverting stages with the labels and let the control fall through them. So, goto revertB will revert to doB first and then fall to the code, reverting to doA. This trick can often be seen in a Linux kernel. However, be wary, gotos usually make verification much harder, which is why they are sometimes banned.

13.8 On Memory Allocation

- Many programmers advise against flexible arrays allocated on a stack. It is an easy way to get a stack overflow if you do not check the length well enough. What's even worse, there is no way to tell whether you *can* safely allocate a said amount of bytes on a stack or not.

- Do not overuse `malloc`! As you will see in the last assignment of this chapter, `malloc` is not cheap at all. Whenever you want to allocate something reasonably small, do it on a stack, as a local variable. If some function needs an address of a structure, you can take the address of a stack allocated structure and pass to it. This prevents memory leaks and improves performance and code readability.

- Global variables pose no threat as long as they are constants. Static local variables are the same. Use them if you want to limit the usage of a certain constant by one function.

13.9   On Flexibility

We advocate code reusability indeed. However, taking this to the extreme results in an absurd amount of abstraction layers and boilerplate code that is only present to support a possible future need for additional features (which might never happen).

There is no silver bullet, in the large sense. Every programming style, every model of computation, is good and concise in some cases and bulky and verbose in other ones. Analogously, the best tool is specialized rather than a jack of all trades. You could transform an image viewer into a powerful editor, capable of playing video and editing IDv3 tags, but the image viewer facet will surely suffer, and so will the user experience.

Writing more abstract code can bring benefits because such code is easier to adapt to new contexts. At the same time, it introduces complexity that might be unnecessary. Only generalize to an extent that does no harm. To know when to stop you need to answer several questions for yourself, such as

- What is the purpose of your program or library?

- What are the limits of functionality that you imagine for your program?

- Will it be easier to write, use, and/or debug this function if it is written in a more general way?

While the first two questions are very subjective, the latter one can be provided with an example. Let's take a look at the code shown in Listing 13-13.

Listing 13-13. dump_1.c

```c
void dump( char const* filename ) {
    FILE* f = fopen( filename, "w" );
    fprintf(f, "this is the dump %d", 42 );
    fclose( f );
}
```

Compare it to another version with the same logic, split in two functions, shown in Listing 13-14.

Listing 13-14. dump_2.c

```c
void dump( FILE* f ) {
    fprintf(f, "this is the dump %d", 42 );
}
void fun( void ) {
    FILE* f = fopen( "dump.txt", "w" );
    dump( f );
    fclose( f );
}
```

The second version is preferable for two reasons:

- The first version requires a filename, which means that you cannot use it to write to stderr or stdout.

- The second version decouples file opening logic and file writing logic. If you want to handle errors that might occur on fprintf, fopen, or fclose calls, you will do it separately for fopen, keeping the functions relatively simple. The dump function will not handle file opening errors: it will not be called at all if the opening failed.

Listing 13-15 shows an example of the same logic with error handling. As you see, there is no error handling for file opening and closing in dump function; it is performed in fun instead.

Listing 13-15. file_open_sep.c

```c
#include <stdio.h>

enum stat {
    STAT_OK,
    STAT_ERR_OPEN,
    STAT_ERR_CLOSE,
    STAT_ERR_WRITE
};

enum stat dump( FILE * f ) {
    if ( fprintf( f, "this is the dump %d", 42 ) ) return STAT_OK;
    return  STAT_ERR_WRITE;
}

enum stat fun( void ) {

    enum stat dump_stat;
    FILE * f;

    f = fopen( "dump.txt", "w" );
    if (!f) return STAT_ERR_OPEN;
    dump_stat = dump( f );
    if ( dump_stat != STAT_OK ) return dump_stat;
    if (! fclose( f ) ) return STAT_ERR_CLOSE;

    return STAT_OK;
}
```

In case of multiple writes in the dump function, the function will become encumbered and thus less readable.

13.10 Assignment: Image Rotation

You have to create a program to rotate a BMP image of any resolution to 90 degrees clockwise.

13.10.1 BMP File Format

BMP (BitMaP) format is a raster graphics format, which means that it stores an image as a table of colored dots (pixels). In this format the color is encoded with numbers of a fixed size (can be 1, 4, 8, 16, or 24 bits). If 1 bit is used per pixel, the image is black and white. If 24 bits are used, the number of different colors possible is roughly 16 million. We only implement the rotation of 24-bit images.

The subset of BMP files that your program should be able to work with is described by the structure shown in Listing 13-16. It represents the file header, followed immediately by the pixel data.

Listing 13-16. bmp_struct.c

```c
#include  <stdint.h>
Struct __attribute__((packed))
    bmp_header {
        uint16_t bfType;
        uint32_t bfileSize;
        uint32_t bfReserved;
        uint32_t bOffBits;
        uint32_t biSize;

        uint32_t biWidth;
        uint32_t biHeight;
        uint16_t biPlanes;
        uint16_t biBitCount;
        uint32_t biCompression;
        uint32_t biSizeImage;
        uint32_t biXPelsPerMeter;
        uint32_t biYPelsPerMeter;
        uint32_t biClrUsed;
        uint32_t biClrImportant;
};
```

■ **Question 259**   Read BMP file specifications to identify what these fields are responsible for.

The file format depends on the bit count per pixel. There are no color palettes when 16 or 24 bits per pixel are used.

Each pixel is encoded by 24 bits or 3 bytes as shown in Listing 13-17. Each component is a number from 0 to 255 (one byte) which shows the presence of blue, green, or red color in this pixel. The resulting color is a superposition of these three base colors.

Listing 13-17. pixel.c

```c
struct  pixel  {
    unsigned char b, g, r;
}
```

Every row of pixels is padded so that its length would be a multiple of 4. For example, the image width is 15 pixels. It corresponds to $15 \times 3 = 45$ bytes. To pad it we skip 3 bytes (to the closest multiple of 4, 48) before starting the new row of pixels. Because of this, the real image size will differ from the product of width, height, and pixel size (3 bytes).

■ **Note**   Remember to open the image in a binary mode!

13.10.2 Architecture

We want to think about program architecture that is extensible and modular.

1. Describe the pixel structure struct pixel to not work with the raster table directly (as with completely structureless data). This should always be avoided.

2. Separate the inner image representation from the input format. The rotation is performed on the inner image format, which is then serialized back to BMP. There can be changes in BMP format, you might want to support other formats, and you do not want to couple the rotation algorithm tightly to BMP.

To achieve that, define a structure structure image to store the pixel array (continuous, now without padding) and some information that should really be kept. For example, there is absolutely no need to store BMP signature here, or any of the never-used header fields. We can get away with the image width and height in pixels.

You will need to create functions to read an image from BMP file and to write it to BMP file (probably also to generate a BMP header from the inner representation).

3. Separate file opening from its reading.

4. Make error handling unified and handle errors in exactly one place (for this very program it is enough).

To achieve that, define the from_bmp function, which will read a file from the stream and will return one of the codes that show whether the operation completed successfully or not.

Remember the flexibility concerns. Your code should be easy to use in applications with graphical user interface (GUI) as well as in those without GUI at all, so throwing prints into stderr all over the place is not a good option: restrict them to the error handling piece of code. Your code should be easily adaptable for different input formats as well.

Listing 13-18 shows several snippets of starting code.

Listing 13-18. image_rot_stub.c

```
#include   <stdint.h>
#include   <stdio.h>

struct pixel { uint8_t b,g,r; };

struct image {
    uint64_t width, height;
    struct pixel_t* data;
};

/*  deserializer    */
enum read_status {
    READ_OK = 0,
    READ_INVALID_SIGNATURE,
    READ_INVALID_BITS,
    READ_INVALID_HEADER
        /* more codes   */
};

enum read_status from_bmp( FILE* in, struct image* const read );
```

```
/*  image_t from_jpg( FILE* );...
 *  and other deserializers are possible
 *  All information needed will be
 *  stored in image structure */

/* makes a rotated copy */
struct image rotate( struct image const source );

/*  serializer    */
enum  write_status  {
    WRITE_OK = 0,
    WRITE_ERROR
        /* more codes */
};

enum write_status to_bmp( FILE* out, struct image const* img );
```

Question 260   Implement blurring. It is done in a very simple way: for each pixel you compute its new components as an average in a 3 × 3 pixels window (called **kernel**). The border pixels are left untouched.

Question 261   Implement rotation to an arbitrary angle (not only 90 or 180 degrees).

Question 262   Implement "dilate" and "erode" transformations. They are similar to the blur, but instead of doing an average in a window, you have to compute the minimal (erode) or maximal (dilate) component values.

13.11   Assignment: Custom Memory Allocator

In this assignment, we are going to implement our own version of malloc and free based on the memory mapping system call mmap and a linked list of chunks of arbitrary sizes. It can be viewed as a simplified version of a memory manager typical for the standard C library and shares most of its weaknesses.

For this assignment, the usage of malloc/calloc, free and realloc is forbidden.

As we know, these functions are used to manipulate the heap. The heap consists of **anonymous pages** and is in fact a linked list of chunks. Each chunk consists of a header and the data itself. The header is described by a structure shown in Listing 13-19.

Listing 13-19. mem_str.c

```
struct mem  {
    struct mem* next;
    size_t capacity;
    bool is_free;
};
```

The header is immediately followed by the usable area.

We need to store both the size and the link to the next block because in our case the heap can have gaps for two reasons.

- The heap start can be placed between two already mapped regions.

- The heap can grow to an arbitrary size.

An allocation in a heap is splitting the first available chunk in two (given its size is enough). It marks the first part as not free and returns its address. If there are no free chunks big enough for the requested size, the allocator attempts to get more memory from OS by calling mmap.

There is no point allocating blocks of 1 or 3 bytes; they are too small. It is usually a waste since the header size is superior anyway. So we are going to introduce a constant BLOCK_MIN_SIZE for the minimal allowed block size (not including header).

Given a request of query bytes, we first change it to BLOCK_MIN_SIZE if it is too small. Then we iterate over the block chain and apply the following logic to each block:

- query <= capacity-sizeof(struct mem) - MINIMAL_BLOCK_SIZE

In this case, we can split the block in two and use the first part as the allocated memory chunk, leaving the second one free.

- Otherwise the block is not large enough to hold a requested amount of bytes.

    - If the block is not last, we continue to the next block.

    - Otherwise we need to map more pages (enough to allocate query bytes).

First we try to do it immediately after the block end (flag MAP_FIXED for mmap), and if we succeed, we enlarge the current block to incorporate new pages. At the end, we split it in two and use the first of the pair.

If we cannot map more pages immediately at the heap end, we try to map them anywhere (enough to store query bytes). Then we split it in two and use the first of the pair.

If all mappings fail, we return NULL, just as malloc does.

The free is easier to implement. Given the block start we have to calculate the respective header start, which changes its status from "allocated" to "free." If it is followed immediately by a free block, they are merged. This is not the case when the block is the last in its memory region and the next one is mapped after a certain gap. You can use the header file shown in Listing 13-20 as a starting point.

Listing 13-20. mem.h

```
#ifndef _MEM_H_
#define _MEM_H_

#define _USE_MISC

#include <stddef.h>
#include  <stdint.h>
#include <stdio.h>

#include <sys/mman.h>

#define  HEAP_START  ((void*)0x04040000)

struct mem;
```

```
#pragma pack(push, 1)
struct mem  {
    struct mem* next;
    size_t capacity;
    bool is_free;
};
#pragma pack(pop)

void* _malloc( size_t query );
void  _free( void* mem );
void* heap_init( size_t initial_size );

#define DEBUG_FIRST_BYTES 4

void memalloc_debug_struct_info( FILE* f,
        struct mem const* const address );

void memalloc_debug_heap( FILE* f,   struct mem  const* ptr );

#endif
```

Remember that complex logic begs for well-thought-out decomposition on smaller functions.

You can use the code shown in Listing 13-21 to debug the heap state. Do not forget that you can also wait for user input and check the /proc/PID/maps file to see the actual mappings of a process with the identifier PID.

Listing 13-21. mem_debug.c

```
#include "mem.h"

void memalloc_debug_struct_info( FILE* f,
        struct mem const* const address ) {

    size_t i;

    fprintf( f,
            "start: %p\nsize: %lu\nis_free: %d\n",
            (void*)address,
            address-> capacity,
            address-> is_free );
    for ( i = 0;
            i <  DEBUG_FIRST_BYTES  && i <  address-> capacity;
            ++i )
        fprintf( f, "%hhX",
                ((char*)address)[ sizeof( struct mem_t ) + i ] );
    putc( '\n', f );
}

void memalloc_debug_heap( FILE* f, struct mem const* ptr ) {
    for( ; ptr; ptr = ptr->next )
        memalloc_debug_struct_info( f, ptr );
}
```

An estimated number of lines of code is 150 to 200. Do not forget to write a Makefile.

13.12 Summary

In this chapter we have extensively studied some of the most important recommendations considering coding style and program architecture. We have seen the naming conventions and the reasons behind the common code guidelines. When we write code, we should adhere to certain restrictions derived from our requirements for the code as well as the development process itself. We have seen such important concepts as encapsulation. Finally, we have provided two more advanced assignments, where you can apply your new knowledge about program architecture. In the next part we are going to dive into the details of translation, review some language features that are easier to understand on the assembly level, and talk about performance and compiler optimizations.

PART III

Between C and Assembly

CHAPTER 14

Translation Details

In this chapter we are going to revisit the notion of calling convention to deepen our understanding and work through translation details. This process requires both understanding program functioning on the assembly level and a certain degree of familiarity with C. We are also going to review some classic low-level security vulnerabilities that might be opened by a careless programmer. Understanding these low-level translation details is sometimes crucial for eradicating very subtle bugs that do not reveal themselves at every execution.

14.1   Function Calling Sequence

In Chapter 2 we studied how to call the procedures, how they return values, and how they accept arguments. The full calling sequence is described in [24] and we highly recommend you to take a look at it. We are going to revisit this process and add valuable details.

14.1.1   XMM Registers

Besides the registers we have already talked about, the modern processors have several sets of special registers that come from processor extensions. An extension provides additional circuitry, expands an instruction set, and sometimes adds usable registers. A notable extension is called **SSE** (Streaming SIMD Extensions) and describes a set of xmm registers: xmm0, xmm1, ..., xmm15. They are 128 bits wide and are usually used for two kinds of tasks:

- Floating point arithmetic; and

- SIMD instructions (such instructions are performing an action on multiple data).

The usual mov command cannot work with xmm registers. The movq command is used instead to copy data between the least significant half of xmm registers (64 bits of 128) on one side and xmm registers, general purpose registers, or memory on the other side (also 64 bits).

To fill the whole xmm register, you have two options: movdqa and movdqu. The first one is deciphered as "move aligned double quad word," the second is the unaligned version.

Most SSE instructions require the memory operands to be properly aligned. The unaligned versions of these instructions often exist with different mnemonic and imply a performance penalty due to an unaligned read. As SSE instructions are often used in performance sensitive places, it is usually wiser to stick to the instructions requiring operand alignment.

We will use the SSE instructions to perform high-performance computations in section 16.4.1.

Question 263   Read about the movq, movdqa, and movdqu instructions in [15].

© Igor Zhirkov 2017
I. Zhirkov, *Low-Level Programming*, DOI 10.1007/978-1-4842-2403-8_14

14.1.2   Calling Convention

Calling convention is a set of rules about function calling sequence a programmer willingly adheres to. If everyone is following the same rules, a smooth interoperability is guaranteed. However, once someone breaks the rules, for example, makes changes, and does not restore rbp in a certain function, anything can happen: nothing, a delayed crash, or an immediate one. The reason is that other functions are written with the implication that these rules are respected and they count on rbp being left untouched.

The calling conventions declare, among other things, the argument passing algorithm. In the case of the typical *nix x86 64 convention we are using (described fully in [24]), the description that follows is an accurate enough approximation of how the function is called.

1. First, the registers that need to be preserved are saved. All registers except for seven callee-saved registers (rbx, rbp, rsp, and r12-r15) can be changed by the called function, so if their value is of any importance, they should be stored (probably in a stack).

2. The registers and stack are populated with arguments.

   The size of each argument gets rounded up to 8 bytes.

   The arguments are split into three lists:

   (a) Integer or pointer arguments.

   (b) Floats and doubles.

   (c) Arguments passed in memory via stack ("memory").

   The first six arguments from the first list are passed in general purpose registers (rdi, rsi, rdx, rcx, r8, and r9). The first eight arguments from the second list are passed in registers xmm0 to xmm7. If there are more arguments from these lists to pass, they are passed on to the stack in reverse order. It means that the last argument will be on top of the stack before the call is performed.

   While integers and floats are quite trivial to handle, structures are a bit trickier.

   If a structure is bigger than 32 bytes, or has unaligned fields, it is passed in memory.

   A smaller structure is decomposed in fields and each field is treated separately and, if in an inner structure, recursively. So, a structure of two elements can be passed the same way as two arguments. If one field of a structure is considered "memory," it propagates to the structure itself.

   The rbp register, as we will see, is used to address the arguments passed in memory and local variables.

   What about return values? Integer and pointer values are returned in rax and rdx. Floating point values are returned in xmm0 and xmm1. Big structures are returned through a pointer, provided as an additional hidden argument, in the spirit of the following example:

```
struct s {
    char vals[100];
};

struct s f( int x ) {
    struct s mys;
    mys.vals[10] = 42;
    return mys;
}

void f( int x, struct s* ret ) {
    ret->vals[10] = 42;
}
```

3. Then the call instruction should be called. Its parameter is the address of the first instruction of a called function. It pushes the return address into the stack.

Each program can have multiple instances of the same function launched at the same time, not only in different threads but also due to recursion. Each such function instance is stored in the stack, because its main principle—"last in, first out"—corresponds to how functions are launched and terminated. If a function f is launched and then invokes a function g, g is terminated first (but was invoked last), and f is terminated last (while being invoked first).

Stack frame is a part of a stack dedicated to a single function instance. It stores the values of the local variables, temporal variables, and saved registers.

The function code is usually enclosed inside a pair of **prologue** and **epilogue**, which are similar for all functions. Prologue helps initialize the stack frame, and epilogue deinitializes it.

During the function execution, rbp stays unchanged and points to the beginning of its stack frame. It is possible to address local variables and stack arguments relatively to rbp. It is reflected in the function prologue shown in Listing 14-1.

Listing 14-1. prologue.asm

```
func:
push rbp
mov rbp, rsp

sub rsp, 24      ; given 24 is total size of local variables
```

The old rbp value is saved to be restored later in epilogue. Then a new rbp is set up to the current top of the stack (which stores the old rbp value now by the way). Then the memory for the local variables is allocated in the stack by subtracting their total size from rsp. This is the automatic memory allocation in C and the technique we have used in the very first assignment to allocate buffers on stack.

The functions end with an epilogue shown in Listing 14-2.

Listing 14-2. epilogue.asm

```
mov rsp, rbp
pop rbp
ret
```

By moving the stack frame the beginning address into `rsp` we can be sure that all memory allocated in the stack is deallocated. Then the old `rbp` value is restored, and now `rbp` points at the start of the previous stack frame. Finally, `ret` pops the return address from stack into `rip`.

A fully equivalent alternative form is sometimes chosen by the compiler. It is shown in Listing 14-3.

Listing 14-3. epilogue_alt.asm

```
Leave
ret
```

The `leave` instruction is made especially for stack frame destruction. Its counterpart, `enter`, is not always used by compilers because it is more functional than the instruction sequence shown in Listing 14-1. It is aimed at languages with inner functions support.

4. After leaving the function, our work is not always done. In case there were arguments that were passed in memory (stack), we have to get rid of them too.

14.1.3   Example: Simple Function and Its Stack

Let's take a look at a simple function that calculates a maximum of two values. We are going to compile it without optimizations and see the assembly listing.

Listing 14-4 shows an example.

Listing 14-4. maximum.c

```
int maximum( int a, int b ) {
    char buffer[4096];
    if (a < b) return b;
    return a;
}

int main(void) {
    int x = maximum( 42, 999 );
    return 0;
}
```

Listing 14-5 shows the disassembly produced by `objdump`.

Listing 14-5. maximum.asm

```
00000000004004b6 <maximum>:
4004b6:     55                      push    rbp
4004b7:     48 89 e5                mov     rbp,rsp
4004ba:     48 81 ec 90 0f 00 00    sub     rsp,0xf90
4004c1:     89 bd fc ef ff ff       mov     DWORD PTR [rbp-0x1004],edi
4004c7:     89 b5 f8 ef ff ff       mov     DWORD PTR [rbp-0x1008],esi
4004cd:     8b 85 fc ef ff ff       mov     eax,DWORD PTR [rbp-0x1004]
4004d3:     3b 85 f8 ef ff ff       cmp     eax,DWORD PTR [rbp-0x1008]
```

```
4004d9:        7d 08                    jge      4004e3 <maximum+0x2d>
4004db:        8b 85 f8 ef ff ff        mov      eax,DWORD PTR [rbp-0x1008]
4004e1:        eb 06                    jmp      4004e9 <maximum+0x33>
4004e3:        8b 85 fc ef ff ff        mov      eax,DWORD PTR [rbp-0x1004]
4004e9:        c9                       leave
4004ea:        c3                       ret

00000000004004eb <main>:
4004eb:        55                       push     rbp
4004ec:        48 89 e5                 mov      rbp,rsp
4004ef:        48 83 ec 10              sub      rsp,0x10
4004f3:        be e7 03 00 00           mov      esi,0x3e7
4004f8:        bf 2a 00 00 00           mov      edi,0x2a
4004fd:        e8 b4 ff ff ff           call     4004b6 <maximum>
400502:        89 45 fc                 mov      DWORD PTR [rbp-0x4],eax
```

After a bit of cleaning, we get a pure and more readable assembly code, which is shown in Listing 14-6.

Listing 14-6. maximum_refined.asm

```
mov rsi, 999
mov rdi, 42
call maximum

...
maximum:
push rbp
mov rbp, rsp
sub rsp, 3984

mov [rbp-0x1004], edi
mov [rbp-0x1008], esi
mov eax, [rbp-0x1004]
...

Leave
ret
```

■ **Register assignment**   Refer to section 3.4.2 for the explanation about why changing esi means a change in the whole rsi.

We are going to trace the function call and its prologue (check Listing 14-6) and show the stack contents immediately after its execution.

`call maximum`

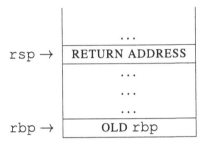

`push rbp`

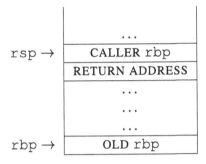

`mov rbp, rsp`

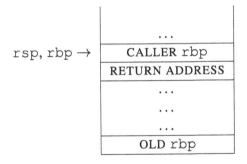

```
sub rsp, 3984
```

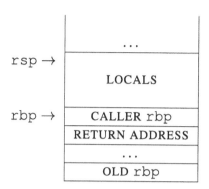

14.1.4   Red Zone

The red zone is an area of 128 bytes that spans from rsp to lower addresses. It relaxes the rule "no data below rsp"; it is safe to allocate data there and it will not be overwritten by system calls or interrupts. We are speaking about direct memory writes relative to rsp without changing rsp. The function calls will, however, still overwrite the red zone.

The red zone was created to allow a specific optimization. If a function never calls other functions, it can omit stack frame creation (rbp changes). Local variables and arguments will then be addressed relative to rsp, not rbp.

- The total size of local variables is less than 128 bytes.

- A function is a leaf function (does not call other functions).

- Function does not change rsp; otherwise it is impossible to address memory relative to it.

By moving rsp ahead you can still get more free space to allocate your data in, than 128 bytes in the stack. See also section 16.1.3.

14.1.5   Variable Number of Arguments

The calling convention that we are using supports the variable arguments count. It means that the function can accept an arbitrary number of arguments. It is possible because arguments passing (and cleaning the stack after the function termination) is the responsibility of the calling function.

The declaration of such functions contains a so-called **ellipsis**—three dots instead of the last argument. The typical function with variable number of arguments is our old friend printf.

```
void printf( char const* format, ... );
```

How does `printf` know the exact number of arguments? It knows for sure that at least one argument is passed (`char const* format`). By analyzing this string and counting the specifiers it will compute the total number of arguments as well as their types (in which registers they should be).

■ **Note** In case of variable number of arguments, `al` should contain the number of xmm registers used by arguments.

As you see, there is absolutely no way to know how many arguments have been exactly passed. The function deduces it from the arguments that are certainly present (`format` in this case). If there are more format specifiers than arguments, `printf` will not know about it and will try to get the contents of the respective registers and memory naively.

Apparently, this functionality cannot be encoded in C by a programmer directly, because the registers cannot be accessed directly. However, there is a portable mechanism of declaring functions with variable argument count that is a part of the standard library. Each platform has its own implementation of this mechanism. It can be used after `stdarg.h` file is included and consists of the following:

- `va_list`-a structure that stores information about arguments.

- `va_start`-a **macro** that initializes `va_list`.

- `va_end`-a **macro** that deinitializes `va_list`.

- `va_arg`-a **macro** that takes a next argument from the argument list when given an instance of `va_list` and an argument type.

Listing 14-7 shows an example. The function `printer` accepts a number of arguments and an arbitrary number of them.

Listing 14-7. `vararg.c`

```c
#include <stdarg.h>
#include <stdio.h>

void printer( unsigned long argcount, ... ) {
    va_list args;
    unsigned long i;
    va_start( args, argcount );
    for (i = 0; i < argcount; i++ )
        printf(" %d\n", va_arg(args, int ) );

    va_end( args );
}

int main () {
    printer(10, 1, 2, 3, 4, 5, 6, 7, 8, 9, 0 );
    return 0;
}
```

First, `va_list` is initialized with the name of the last argument before dots by `va_start`. Then, each call to `va_arg` gets the next argument. The second parameter is the name of the fresh argument's type. In the end, `va_list` is deinitialized using `va_end`.

Since a type name becomes an argument and va_list is used by name, but is mutated, this example can look confusing.

■ **Question 264**   Can you imagine a situation in which a function, not a macro, accepts a variable by name (syntactically) and changes it? What should be the type of such variable?

14.1.6   vprintf and Friends

Functions such as printf, fprintf, etc., have special versions. Those accept va_list as their last arguments. Their names are prefixed with a letter v, for example,

```
int vprintf(const char *format, va_list ap);
```

They are being used inside custom functions which in their turn accept an arbitrary number of arguments.

Listing 14-8 shows an example.

Listing 14-8. vsprintf.c

```
#include <stdarg.h>
#include <stdio.h>

void logmsg( int client_id, const char* const str, ... ) {
    va_list args;
    char buffer[1024];
    char* bufptr = buffer;

va_start( args, str );

bufptr += sprintf(bufptr, "from client %d :", client_id );
vsprintf( bufptr, str, args );
fprintf( stderr, "%s", buffer );

va_end( args );
}
```

14.2   volatile

The volatile keyword affects greatly the way the compiler optimizes the code.

The model of computation for C is a von Neumann one. It does not support parallel program execution and the compiler usually tries to do as many optimizations as it can without changing the observable program behavior. It might include reordering of instructions and caching variables in registers. Reading a value from memory which is not written anywhere is omitted.

However, reading and writing in volatile variables always happen. The order of operations is also preserved.

The main use cases are as follows:

- **memory mapped IO**, when the communication with external devices is performed by interacting with a certain dedicated memory region. Writing a character into video memory (which results in it displayed on screen) really means it.

- Data sharing between threads. If memory is used to communicate with other threads, you do not want the writes or the reads to be optimized out.

Note that `volatile` alone is not enough to perform robust communication between threads.

Just like the `const` qualifier, in case of a pointer, `volatile` can be applied to the data it points to, as well as to the pointer itself. The rule is the same: `volatile` on the left of the asterisk relates to the data it points to, and on the right -- to the pointer itself.

14.2.1   Lazy Memory Allocation

Many operating systems map pages lazily, at the time of the first usage rather than right after `mmap` call (or its equivalent).

If the programmer wants no delays on the first-page usages, he might choose to address each page individually so that the operating system really creates it, as shown in Listing 14-9.

Listing 14-9. `lma_bad.c`

```
char* ptr;
for( ptr = start; ptr < start + size; ptr += pagesize )
*ptr;
```

However, this code has no observable effect from the point of view of the compiler, so it might be optimized away completely. However, when the pointer is marked `volatile`, this will not be the case. Listing 14-10 shows an example.

Listing 14-10. `lma_good.c`

```
volatile char* ptr;
for( ptr = start; ptr < start + size; ptr += pagesize )
*ptr;
```

■ **Volatile pointers in the language standard**   If the volatile pointer is pointing at the non-volatile memory, according to the standard there are no guarantees! They exist only when both the pointer and the memory are volatile. So, according to the standard, the example above is incorrect. However, as programmers are using the volatile pointers with exactly this reasoning, the most used compilers (MSVC, GCC, clang) do not optimize away the dereferencing of volatile pointers. There is no a standard-conforming way of doing this.

14.2.2   Generated Code

We are going to study the example shown in Listing 14-11.

Listing 14-11. volatile_ex.c

```c
#include <stdio.h>

int main( int argc, char** argv ) {
    int ordinary = 0;
    volatile int vol = 4;
    ordinary++;
    vol++;
    printf( "%d\n", ordinary );
    printf( "%d\n", vol );
    return 0;
}
```

There are two variables: one is volatile, the other is not. Both are incremented and given to printf as arguments. GCC will generate the following code (with -02 optimization level), shown in Listing 14-12:

Listing 14-12. volatile_ex.asm

```
; these are two arguments for `printf`
mov    esi,0x1
mov    edi,0x4005d4

; vol = 4
mov    DWORD PTR [rsp+0xc],0x4

; vol ++
mov    eax,DWORD PTR [rsp+0xc]
add    eax,0x1
mov    DWORD  PTR  [rsp+0xc],eax

xor    eax,eax

; printf( "%d\n", ordinary )
; the `ordinary` is not even created in stack frame
; its final precomputed value 1 was placed in `rsi` in the first line!
call   4003e0 <printf@plt>

; the second argument is taken from memory, it is volatile!
mov    esi,DWORD PTR [rsp+0xc]

; First argument is the address of "%d\n"
mov    edi,0x4005d4
xor    eax,eax

; printf( "%d\n", vol )
call   4003e0 <printf@plt>
xor    eax,eax
```

As we see, the contents of a volatile variable are really read and written each time it occurs in C. The ordinary variable will not even be created: the computations will be performed in compile time and the final result is stored in rsi, waiting to be used as the second argument of a call.

14.3 Non-Local jumps–setjmp

The standard C library contains machinery to perform a very tricky kind of hack. It allows storing a computation context and restoring it. The context describes the program execution state *with the exception of* the following:

- Everything related to the external world (e.g., opened descriptors).

- Floating point computations context.

- Stack variables.

It allows saving context and jumping back to it in case we feel like we have to return. We are not limited by the same function scope.

Include the setjmp.h to gain access to the following machinery:

- jmp_buf is a type of a variable which can store the context.

- int setjmp(jmp_buf env) is a function that accepts a jmp_buf instance and stores the current context in it. By default it returns 0.

- void longjmp(jmp_buf env, int val) is used to return to a saved context, stored in a certain variable of type jmp_buf.

When returning from the longjmp, setjmp returns not necessarily 0 but the value val fed to longjmp. Listing 14-13 shows an example. The first setjmp will return 0 by default and so will be the val value. However, the longjmp accepts 1 as its argument, and the program execution will continue from the setjmp call (because they are linked through the usage of the jb). This time setjmp will return 1 and this is the value that will be assigned to val.

Listing 14-13. longjmp.c

```
#include <stdio.h>
#include <setjmp.h>

int main(void) {
    jmp_buf jb;
    int val;
    val = setjmp( jb );
    puts("Hello!");
    if (val == 0) longjmp( jb, 1 );
    else puts("End");
    return 0;
}
```

Local variables that are not marked volatile will all hold undefined values after longjmp. This is the source of bugs as well as memory freeing related issues: it is hard to analyze the control flow in presence of longjmp and ensure that all dynamically allocated memory is freed.

In general, it is allowed to call setjmp as a part of a complex expression, but only in rare cases. In most cases, this is an undefined behavior. So, better not to do it.

It is important to remember that all this machinery is based on stack frames usage. It means that you cannot perform longjmp in a function with a deinitialized stack frame. For example, the code, shown in Listing 14-14, yields an undefined behavior for this very reason.

Listing 14-14. `longjmp_ub.c`

```
jmp_buf jb;
void f(void) {
    setjmp( jb );
}

void g(void) {
    f();
    longjmp(jb);
}
```

The function f has terminated already, but we are performing longjmp into it. The program behavior is undefined because we are trying to restore a context inside a destroyed stack frame.

In other words, you can only jump into the same function or into a function that is launched.

14.3.1   Volatile and setjmp

The compiler thinks that setjmp is just a function. However, this is not really so, because this is the point from which the program might start to execute again. In normal conditions, some local variables might have been cached in registers (or never allocated) before the call to setjmp. When we return to this point due to a longjmp call, they will not be restored.

Turning off optimizations changes this behavior. So optimizations turned off hide bugs related to setjmp usage.

To write correctly, remember that only volatile local variables are holding defined values after longjmp. They are *not* restored to their ancient values, because jmp_buf does not save stack variables but keeps the values from before longjmp.

Listing 14-15 shows an example.

Listing 14-15. `setjmp_volatile.c`

```
#include <stdio.h>
#include <setjmp.h>

jmp_buf buf;

int main( int argc, char** argv ) {
    int var = 0;
    volatile int b = 0;
    setjmp( buf );
    if (b < 3) {
        b++;
        var ++;
        printf( "\n\n%d\n", var );
        longjmp( buf, 1 );
    }

    return 0;
}
```

We are going to compile it without optimizations (gcc -O0, Listing 14-16) and with optimizations (gcc -O2, Listing 14-17).

Without optimizations,

Listing 14-16. volatile_setjmp_oO.asm

```
main:
push      rbp
mov       rbp,rsp
sub       rsp,0x20

; `argc` and `argv` are saved in stack to make `rdi` and `rsi` available
mov    DWORD PTR [rbp-0x14],edi
mov    QWORD PTR [rbp-0x20],rsi

; var = 0
mov    DWORD PTR [rbp-0x4],0x0

; b = 0
mov    DWORD PTR [rbp-0x8],0x0

; 0x600a40 is the address of `buf` (a global variable of type `jmp_buf`)
mov    edi,0x600a40
call   400470 <_setjmp@plt>

; if (b < 3), the good branch is executed
; This is encoded by skipping several instructions to the `.endlabel` if b > 2
mov    eax,DWORD PTR [rbp-0x8]
cmp    eax,0x2
jg     .endlabel

; A fair increment
; b++
mov    eax,DWORD PTR [rbp-0x8]
add    eax,0x1
mov    DWORD PTR [rbp-0x8],eax

; var++
add    DWORD PTR [rbp-0x4],0x1

; `printf` call
mov    eax,DWORD PTR [rbp-0x4]
mov    esi,eax
mov    edi,0x400684
; There are no floating point arguments, thus rax = 0
mov    eax,0x0
call   400450 <printf@plt>

; calling `longjmp`
mov    esi,0x1
mov    edi,0x600a40
call   400490 <longjmp@plt>

.endlabel:
Mov    eax,0x0
Leave
ret
```

The program output will be

```
1
2
3
```

With optimizations,

Listing 14-17. volatile_setjmp_o2.asm

```
main:

; allocating memory in stack
sub    rsp,0x18

; a `setjmp` argument, the address of `buf`

mov    edi,0x600a40

; b = 0
mov    DWORD PTR [rsp+0xc],0x0
; instructions are placed in the order different
; from C statements to make better use of pipeline and other inner
; CPU mechanisms.
call   400470 <_setjmp@plt>

; `b` is read and checked in a fair way
mov    eax,DWORD PTR [rsp+0xc]
cmp    eax,0x2
jle    .branch

; return 0
xor    eax,eax
add    rsp,0x18
ret

.branch:

mov    eax,DWORD PTR [rsp+0xc]

; the second argument of `printf` is var + 1
; It was not even read from memory nor allocated.
; The computations were performed in compile time
mov    esi,0x1

; The first argument of `printf`
mov    edi,0x400674

; b = b + 1
add    eax,0x1
mov    DWORD PTR [rsp+0xc],eax
```

```
xor     eax,eax
call    400450 <printf@plt>

; longjmp( buf, 1 )
mov     esi,0x1
mov     edi,0x600a40
call    400490 <longjmp@plt>
```

The program output will be

```
1
1
1
```

The volatile variable b, as you see, behaved as intended (otherwise, the cycle would have never ended). The variable var was always equal to 1, despite being "incremented" according to the program text.

Question 265 How do you implement "try–catch"-alike constructions using setjmp and longjmp?

14.4 inline

inline is a function qualifier introduced in C99. It mimics the behavior of its C++ counterpart.

Before you read an explanation, please, do *not* assume that this keyword is used to force function inlining!

Before C99, there was a static qualifier, which was often used in the following scenario:

- The header file includes not the function declaration but the full function *definition*, marked as static.

- The header is then included in multiple translation units. Each of them receives a copy of the emitted code, but as the corresponding symbol is object-local, the linker does not see it as a multiple definition conflict.

In a big project, this gives the compiler the access to the function source code, which enables it to really inline the function if needed. Obviously, the compiler might also decide that the function is better left not inlined. In this case we start getting the clones of this function pretty much everywhere. Each file is calling its own copy, which is bad for locality and bloats the memory image as well as the executable itself.

The inline keyword addresses this issue. Its correct usage is as follows:

- Describe an inline function in a relevant header, for example,

  ```
  inline int inc( int x ) { return x+1; }
  ```

- In exactly one translation unit (i.e., a .c file), add the external declaration

  ```
  extern inline int inc( int x ) ;
  ```

This file will contain the function code, which will be referenced by every other file, where the function was not inlined.

■ **Semantics change**   In GCC prior to 4.2.1 the `inline` keyword had a slightly other meaning. See the post [14] for an in-depth analysis.

14.5   restrict

`restrict` is a keyword akin to `volatile` and `const` which first appeared in the C99 standard. It is used to mark pointers and is thus placed to the right of the asterisk, as follows:

```
int x;
int* restrict p_x = &x;
```

If we create a restricted pointer to an object, we make a promise that all accesses to this object will pass through the value of this pointer. A compiler can either ignore this or make use of it for certain optimizations, which is often possible.

In other words, any write by another pointer will not affect the value stored by a restricted pointer.

Breaking this promise leads to subtle bugs and is a clear case of undefined behavior.

Without `restrict`, every pointer is a source of possible memory aliasing, when you can access the same memory cells by using different names for them. Consider a very simple example, shown in Listing 14-18. Is the body of f equal to `*x += 2 * (*add);`?

Listing 14-18. `restrict_motiv.c`

```
void f(int* x, int* add) {
    *x += *add;
    *x += *add;
}
```

The answer is, surprisingly, no, they are not equal. What if add and x are pointing to the same address? In this case, changing *x changes *add as well. So, in case x == add, the function will add *x to *x making it two times the initial value, and then repeat it making it four times the initial value. However, when x != add, even if *x == *add the final *x will be three times the initial value.

The compiler is well aware of it, and even with optimizations turned on it will not optimize away two reads, as shown in Listing 14-19.

Listing 14-19. `restrict_motiv_dump.asm`

```
0000000000000000 <f>:
0:   8b 06               mov     eax,DWORD PTR [rsi]
2:   03 07               add     eax,DWORD PTR [rdi]
4:   89 07               mov     DWORD PTR [rdi],eax
6:   03 06               add     eax,DWORD PTR [rsi]
8:   89 07               mov     DWORD PTR [rdi],eax
a:   c3                  ret
```

However, add restrict, as shown in Listing 14-20, and the disassembly will demonstrate an improvement, as shown in Listing 14-21. The second argument is read exactly once, multiplied by 2, and added to the dereferenced first argument.

Listing 14-20. restrict_motiv1.c

```
void f(int* restrict x, int* restrict add) {
    *x += *add;
    *x += *add;
}
```

Listing 14-21. restrict_motiv_dump1.asm

```
0000000000000000 <f>:
   0:   8b 06                   mov     eax,DWORD PTR [rsi]
   2:   01 c0                   add     eax,eax
   4:   01 07                   add     DWORD PTR [rdi],eax
   6:   c3                      ret
```

Only use restrict if you are sure what you are doing. Writing a slightly ineffective program is much better than writing an incorrect one.

It is important to use restrict also to document code. For example, the signature for memcpy, a function that copies *n* bytes from some starting address s2 to a block starting with s1, has changed in C99:

```
void*
memcpy(void*       restrict s1,
       const void* restrict s2,

       size_t              n );
```

This reflects the fact that these two areas should not overlap; otherwise the correctness is not guaranteed.

Restricted pointers can be copied from one to another to create a hierarchy of pointers. However, the standard limits this by cases when the copy is not residing in the same block with the original pointer. Listing 14-22 shows an example.

Listing 14-22. restrict_hierarchy.c

```
struct s {
    int* x;
} inst;

void f(void) {
    struct s* restrict p_s = &inst;
    int* restrict p_x = p_s->x; /* Bad */
    {
        int* restrict p_x2 = p_s->x; /* Fine, other block scope */
    }
}
```

14.6 Strict Aliasing

Before restrict was introduced, programmers sometimes achieved the same effect by using different structure names. The compiler thinks that different data types imply that the respective pointers cannot point to the same data (which is known as the **strict aliasing rule**).

The assumptions include the following:

- Pointers to different built-in types do not alias.

- Pointers to structures or unions *with different tags* do not alias (so struct foo and struct bar are never used one for another).

- Type aliases, created using typedef, *can* refer to the same data.

- The type char* is exceptional (signed or not). The compiler always assumes that char* can alias other types, but *not* vice versa. It means that we can create a char buffer, use it to get data, and then alias it as an instance of some struct packet.

Breaking these rules can lead to subtle optimization bugs, because it triggers undefined behavior.

The example shown in Listing 14-18, can be rewritten to achieve the same effect without the restrict keyword. The idea is to use the strict aliasing rules to our benefit, packing both parameters into the structures with different tags.

Listing 14-23 shows the modified source.

Listing 14-23. restrict-hack.c

```
struct a {
    int v;
};
struct b {
    int v;
};

void f(struct a* x, struct b* add) {
    x->v += add->v;
    x->v += add->v;
}
```

To our satisfaction, the compiler optimizes the reads away just as we wanted. Listing 14-24 shows the disassembly.

Listing 14-24. restrict-hack-dump

```
0000000000000000 <f>:
   0:   8b 06                mov    eax,DWORD PTR [rsi]
   2:   01 c0                add    eax,eax
   4:   01 07                add    DWORD PTR [rdi],eax
   6:   c3                   ret
```

We discourage using aliasing rules for optimization purposes in code for C99 and newer standards because restrict makes the intention more obvious and does not introduce unnecessary type names.

14.7   Security Issues

C was not created as a language to create robust software. It allows working with memory directly and has no means of controlling the correctness, neither static, like Rust, nor dynamic, like Java. We are going to review some classical security holes, which we now can explain in full detail.

14.7.1   Stack Buffer Overrun

Suppose that the program uses a function f with a local buffer, as shown in Listing 14-25.

Listing 14-25. buffer_overrun.c

```c
#include <stdio.h>

void f( void ) {
    char buffer[16];
    gets( buffer );
}

int main( int argc, char** argv ) {
    f();
    return 0;
}
```

After being initialized, the layout of the stack frame will look as follows:

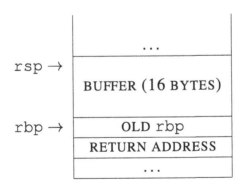

The gets function reads a line from stdin and places it in the buffer, whose address is accepted as an argument. Unfortunately, it does not control the buffer size at all and thus can surpass it.

If the line is too long, it will overwrite the buffer, then the saved rbp value, and then the return address. When the ret instruction is executed, the program will most probably crash. Even worse, if the attacker forms a clever line, it can rewrite the return address with specific bytes forming a valid address.

Should the attacker choose to redirect the return address directly into the buffer being overrun, he can transmit the executable code directly in this buffer. Such code is often called **shellcode**, because it is small and usually only opens a remote shell to work with.

Obviously, this is not only the flaw in `gets` but the feature of the language itself. The moral is never to use `gets` and always to provide a way to check the bounds of the target memory block.

14.7.2   return-to-libc

As we have already elaborated, the malevolent user can rewrite the return address if the program allows him to overrun the stack buffer. The return-to-libc attack is performed when the return address is the address of a function in the standard C library. One function is of a particular interest, `int system(const char* command)`. This function allows you to execute an arbitrary shell command. What's even worse, it will be executed with the same privileges as the attacked program.

When the current function terminates by executing the `ret` command, we will start executing the function from libc. It is yet a question, how do we form a valid argument for it?

In the presence of **ASLR** (address space layout randomization), doing this attack is nontrivial (but still possible).

14.7.3   Format Output Vulnerabilities

Format output functions can be a source of very nasty bugs. There are several such functions in standard library; Table 14-1 shows them.

Table 14-1. *String Format Functions*

Function	Description
printf	Outputs a formatted string.
fprintf	Writes the printf to a file.
sprintf	Prints into a string.
snprintf	Prints into a string checking the length.
vfprintf	Prints the va_arg structure to a file.
vprintf	Prints the va_arg structure to stdout.
vsprintf	Prints the va_arg to a string.
vsnprintf	Prints the va_arg to a string checking the length.

Listing 14-26 shows an example. Suppose that the user inputs less than 100 symbols. Can you crash this program or produce other interesting effects?

Listing 14-26. `printf_vuln.c`

```c
#include <stdio.h>
int main(void) {
    char buffer[1024];
    gets(buffer);
    printf( buffer );
    return 0;

}
```

The vulnerability does not come from `gets` usage but from usage of the format string taken from the user. The user can provide a string that contains format specifiers, which will lead to an interesting behavior. We will mention several potentially unwanted types of behavior.

- The "%x" specifiers and its likes can be used to view the stack contents. First 5 "%x" will take arguments from registers (`rdi` is already occupied with the format string address), then the following ones will show the stack contents. Let's compile the example shown in Listing 14-26 and see its reaction on an input "%x %x %x %x %x %x %x %x %x %x %x".

```
> %x %x %x %x %x %x %x %x %x %x
b1b6701d b19467b0 fbad2088 b1b6701e 0 25207825 20782520 78252078 25207825
```

As we see, it actually gave us four numbers that share a certain informal similarity, a 0 and two more numbers. Our hypothesis is that the last two numbers are taken from the stack already.

Getting into gdb and exploring the memory near the stack top right after `printf` call we are going to get results that prove our point. Listing 14-27 shows the output.

Listing 14-27. gdb_printf

```
(gdb) x/10 $rsp
0x7fffffffdfe0: 0x25207825    0x78252078    0x20782520    0x25207825
0x7fffffffdff0: 0x78252078    0x20782520    0x25207825    0x00000078
0x7fffffffe000: 0x00000000    0x00000000
```

- The "%s" format specifier is used to print strings. As a string is defined by the address of its start, this means addressing memory by a pointer. So, if no valid pointer is given, the invalid pointer will be dereferenced.

Question 266   What will be the result of launching the code shown in Listing 14-26 on input "%s %s %s %s %s"?

- The "%n" format specifier is a bit exotic but still harmful. It allows one to write an integer into memory. The `printf` function accepts a *pointer* to an integer which will be rewritten with an amount of symbols written so far (before "%n" occurs). Listing 14-28 shows an example of its usage.

Listing 14-28. printf_n.c

```c
#include <stdio.h>

int main(void) {
    int count;
    printf( "hello%n world\n", &count);
    printf( "%d\n", count );
    return 0;
}
```

This will output 5, because there were five symbols output before "%n". This is not a trivial string length because there can be other format specifiers before, which will result in an output of variable length (e.g., printing an integer can emit seven or ten symbols). Listing 14-29 shows an example.

Listing 14-29. printf_n_ex.c

```
int x;
printf("%d %n", 10, &x);  /* x = 3 */
printf("%d %n", 200, &x); /* x = 4 */
```

To avoid that, do not use the string accepted from the user as a format string. You can always write `printf("%s", buffer)`, which is safe as long as the buffer is not `NULL` and is a valid null-terminated string. Do not forget about such functions as `puts` of `fputs`, which are not only faster but also safer.

14.8   Protection Mechanisms

Rewriting a return address can lead to one of the following two consequences:

- The program abnormally terminates.

- Attacker executes arbitrary code.

In the first case, we can fall victim to a DoS (Denial of Service) attack, when the program, providing a specific service, becomes unavailable. However, the second option is much worse.

14.8.1   Security Cookie

The **security cookie** (stack guard, canary) is supposed to protect us from arbitrary code execution by forcing abnormal program termination once the return address is changed.

The security cookie is a random value residing in the stack frame near the saved `rbp` and return address.

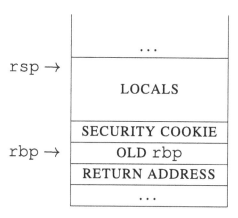

Overrunning the buffer will rewrite the security cookie. Before the `ret` instruction, the compiler emits a special check that verifies the integrity of the security cookie, and if it is changed, it crashes the program. The `ret` instruction does not get to be executed.

Both MSVC and GCC have this mechanism turned on by default.

14.8.2   Address Space Layout Randomization

Loading each program section to a random place in an address space makes it nearly impossible to guess a correct return address to perform an intelligent jump. Most commonly used operating systems support it; however, that feature should be enabled during the compilation. In this case, the information about ASLR support will be stored in the executable file itself, which will force the loader to perform a correct relocation.

14.8.3   DEP

We have already discussed **Data Execution Prevention** in Chapter 4 This technology protects some pages from executing instructions stored on these pages. To enable it, programs should be also compiled with support turned on.

The sad fact is that it does not work well with programs that use just-in-time compilation, which forms executable code during the program execution itself. This is not as rare as it might seem; for example, virtually all browsers are using JavaScript engines which support just-in-time compilation.

14.9   Summary

In this chapter we have revisited the calling convention used in *nix on Intel 64. We have seen the example usages of the more advanced C features, namely, `volatile` and `restrict` type qualifiers and non-local jumps. Finally, we have given a brief overview of several classical vulnerabilities that are possible because of the way stack frames are organized, and the compiler features that were designed to automatically cope with them. The next chapter will explain more low-level details related to the creation and usage of dynamic libraries to strengthen our understanding of them.

■ **Question 267**   What are xmm registers? How many are they?

■ **Question 268**   What are SIMD instructions?

■ **Question 269**   Why do some SSE instructions require the memory operands to be aligned?

■ **Question 270**   What registers are used to pass arguments to functions?

■ **Question 271**   When passing arguments to the function, why is `rax` sometimes used?

■ **Question 272**   How is `rbp` register used?

■ **Question 273**   What is a stack frame?

■ **Question 274**   Why aren't we addressing the local variables relative to `rsp`?

■ **Question 275**   What are prologue and epilogue?

■ **Question 276**   What is the purpose of `enter` and `leave` instructions?

Question 277 Describe in details, how is the stack frame changing during the function execution.

Question 278 What is the red zone?

Question 279 How do we declare and use a function with a variable number of arguments?

Question 280 Which kind of context is `va_list` holding?

Question 281 Why are functions such as `vfprintf` used?

Question 282 What is the purpose of `volatile` variables?

Question 283 Why do only `volatile` stack variables persist after `longjmp`?

Question 284 Are all local variables allocated on stack?

Question 285 What is `setjmp` used for?

Question 286 What is the return value of `setjmp`?

Question 287 What is the use of `restrict`?

Question 288 Can `restrict` be ignored by the compiler?

Question 289 How can we achieve the same result without using the `restrict` keyword?

Question 290 Explain the mechanism of exploiting stack buffer overrun.

Question 291 When is the `printf` usage unsafe?

Question 292 What is a security cookie? Does it solve program crashes on buffer overflow?

CHAPTER 15

Shared Objects and Code Models

Chapter 5 already provided a short overview of dynamic libraries (also known as shared objects). This chapter will revisit dynamic libraries and expand our knowledge by introducing the concepts of the Program Linkage Table and the Global Offset Table. As a result, we will be able to build a shared library in pure assembly and C, compare the results, and study its structure. We will also study a concept of code models, which is rarely discussed but gives a consistent view of several important details of assembly code generation.

15.1 Dynamic Loading

As you might remember, an ELF (Executable and Linkable Format) file contains three headers:

- The main header, located at an offset zero. It defines the general information about the file, including the entry point and offsets to two tables elaborated below.

  You can view it using the `readelf -h` command.

- Section headers table, which contains information about different ELF sections.

  You can view it using the `readelf -S` command.

- Program headers table, which contains information about the file segments. Each segment is a runtime structure, which contains one or more sections, defined in the section headers table.

  You can view it using the `readelf -l` command.

The initial stage of loading an executable is to create an address space and perform memory mappings according to the program headers table with appropriate permissions. This is performed by the operating system kernel. Once the virtual address space is set, the other program has to interfere (i.e., dynamic loader). The latter should be an executable program, and fully relocatable (so it should be able to be loaded at whatever address we want).

The purpose of the dynamic linker is to

- Determine all dependencies and load them.

- Perform **relocation** of the applications and dependencies.

- Initialize the application and its dependencies and pass the control to the application. Now, the program execution will start.

© Igor Zhirkov 2017
I. Zhirkov, *Low-Level Programming*, DOI 10.1007/978-1-4842-2403-8_15

Determining dependencies and loading them is relatively easy: it boils down to searching dependencies recursively and checking whether the object has been already loaded or not. Initializing is also not very mystified. The relocation, however, is of interest to us.

There are two kinds of relocations:

- Links to locations in the same object. The static linker is performing all such relocations since they are known at the link time.

- Symbol dependencies, which are usually in the different object.

The second kind of relocation is more costly and is performed by the dynamic linker.

Before doing relocations, we need to do a lookup first to find the symbols we want to link. There is a notion of **lookup scope** of an object file, which is an ordered list containing some other loaded objects. The lookup scope of an object file is used to resolve symbols necessary for it. The way it is computed is described in [24] and is rather complex, so we refer you to the relevant document in case of need.

The lookup scope consists of three parts, which are listed in reverse order of search—that is, the symbol gets searched in the third part of the scope first.

1. Global lookup scope, which consists of the executable file and all its dependencies, including dependencies of the dependencies, etc. They are enumerated in a breadth-first search fashion, that is:

   - The executable itself.

   - Its dependencies.

   - The dependencies of its first dependency, then of the second, etc. Each object is loaded only once.

2. The part constructed if DF_SYMBOLIC flag is set in the ELF executable file metadata. It is considered legacy; its usage is discouraged, so we are not studying it here.

3. Objects loaded dynamically with all their dependencies by means of dlopen function call. They are not searched for normal lookups.

Each object file contains a hash table which is used for lookup.[1] This table stores the symbol information and is used to quickly find the symbol by its name. The first object in the lookup scope, which contains the needed symbol, is linked, which allows for symbol overloading—for example, using LD_PRELOAD mechanism—which will be explored in section 15.5.

The hash table size and the number of exported symbols are affecting the lookup time. When the -O flag for *linker* is provided,[2] it tries to optimize these parameters for better lookup speed. Remember, that in languages such as C++, not only are the symbol names computed based on, for example, function name, but they have all their namespaces (and classname) encoded, which may easily result in names of several hundred characters. In the case of collisions in hash tables (which are usually frequent), the string comparison should be performed between the symbol name we are looking for and all symbols in the bucket we have chosen by computing its hash.

The modern GNU-style hash tables provide an additional heuristic of using a Bloom filter[3] in order to quickly answer a question: "is this symbol even defined in this object file?" That makes unnecessary lookups much less frequent, which positively impacts performance.

---

[1]We will not provide the details on what the hash tables are or how are they implemented, but if you do not know about them, we highly advise you to read about them! This is an absolutely classic data structure used everywhere. A good explanation can be found in [10]

[2]Do not confuse with -O flag for the compiler!

[3]A probabilistic data structure that is widely used. It allows us to quickly check whether an element is contained in a certain set, but the answer "yes" is subject to an additional check, while "no" is always certain.

15.2   Relocations and PIC

Now, what kind of relocations are performed? We have seen the process of relocations during static linking in Chapter 5. Can we do the same, relocating all code and data elements? The answer is yes, we can, and until common architectures added special features to ease the position-independent code writing, it was extensively used. However, this approach has the following drawbacks:

- Relocations are slow to perform, especially when dependencies are numerous. That can delay the startup of the application.

- The **.text** section cannot be shared, because it has to be patched. While static linking implies patching object file contents when building the final object file, dynamic linking implies patching object files in memory. Not only does it waste memory, it also poses a security risk, because, for example, shellcode can rewrite the program in memory directly to alter its behavior.

Nowadays, PIC is the recommended way, and it allows to keep **.text** read-only (while **.data** cannot be shared anyway).

The number of relocations will be smaller, because no code relocations will be performed. PIC implies using two utility tables: Global Offset Table (GOT) and Program Linkage Table (PLT).

15.3   Example: Dynamic Library in C

Before we start studying GOT and PLT, let us create a minimal working example of a dynamic library in C. It is actually quite easy.

Our program will consist of two files: mainlib.c (shown in Listing 15-1) and dynlib.c (shown in Listing 15-2).

Listing 15-1. mainlib.c

```
extern void libfun( int value );

int global = 100;

int main( void ) {
    libfun( 42 );
    return 0;
}
```

Listing 15-2. dynlib.c

```
#include <stdio.h>

extern int global;
void libfun(int value) {
    printf( "param: %d\n", value );
    printf( "global: %d\n", global );
}
```

As we see, there is a global variable in the main file, which we will want to share with the library; the library explicitly states that it is extern. The main file has the declaration of the library function (which is usually placed in the header file, shipped with the compiled library).

To compile these files, the following commands should be issued:

```
> # creating object file for the main part
> gcc -c  -o mainlib.o mainlib.c
> # creating object file for the library
> gcc -c -fPIC -o dynlib.o  dynlib.c
> gcc -o dynlib.so -shared dynlib.o # creating dynamic library itself
> # creating an executable and linking it with the dynamic library
> gcc -o main  mainlib.o dynlib.so
```

First, we create object files as usual. Then we build the dynamic library using -shared flag. When we build an executable, we provide all dynamic libraries from which it depends, because this information should be included in ELF metadata. Notice the usage of -fPIC flag, which forces to generate position-independent code. We will see the effects of this flag on assembly later.

Let's check the file dependencies using ldd.

```
> ldd main
        linux-vdso.so.1 => (0x00007fffcd428000)
        lib.so => not found
        libc.so.6 => /lib/x86_64-linux-gnu/libc.so.6 (0x00007ff988d60000)
        /lib64/ld-linux-x86-64.so.2 (0x00007ff989200000)
```

Our fresh library is present in the list of dependencies, but ldd cannot find it. An attempt to launch the executable fails with the expected message:

```
./main: error while loading shared libraries:
        lib.so: cannot open shared object file: No such file or directory
```

The libraries are searched in the default locations (such as /lib/). Ours is not there, so we have another option: an environment variable LD_LIBRARY_PATH is parsed to get a list of additional directories where the libraries might be located. As soon as we set it to the current directory, ldd finds the library. Note, that the search starts with the directories defined in LD_LIBRARY_PATH and proceeds to the standard directories.

```
> export LD_LIBRARY_PATH=.
> ldd main
        linux-vdso.so.1 =>  (0x00007ffff1315000)
        lib.so => ./lib.so (0x00007f3a7bc70000)
        libc.so.6 => /lib/x86_64-linux-gnu/libc.so.6 (0x00007f3a7b890000)
        /lib64/ld-linux-x86-64.so.2 (0x00007f3a7c000000)
```

The launch produces expected results.

```
> ./main
  param: 42
  global: 100
```

15.4   GOT and PLT

15.4.1   Accessing External Variables

To keep **.text** read-only and never patch it due to relocations, we add a level of indirection when addressing any symbol that is not guaranteed to be defined in the same object—in other words, for every symbol defined in executable or shared object file after the static linking. This indirection is performed through a special **Global Offset Table**.

Two facts are important to make PIC code work.

- Intel 64 makes it possible to address instruction operands relative to `rip` register. It is possible to get the current `rip` value using a pair of `call` and `pop` instructions, but the hardware support surely helps performance-wise.

- The offset between the **.text** section and **.data** section is known at link time, that is, when the dynamic library is *being created*. It also means that the distance between `rip` and the beginning of the **.data** section is also known. So, we place the Global Offset Table in the **.data** section or near it. It will hold the absolute addresses of global variables.

We address the GOT cell relatively to `rip` and get an absolute address of the global variable from there—see Figure 15-1.

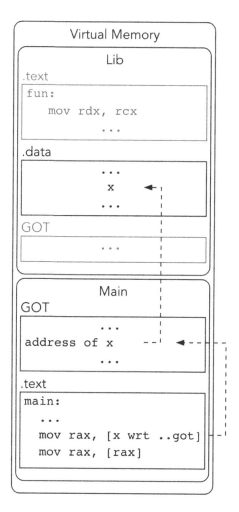

Figure 15-1. *Accessing global variable through GOT*

Let's see, how the variable global, created in the main executable file, is addressed in the dynamic library. To do it, we are going to study a fragment of objdump -D -Mintel-mnemonic output, shown in Listing 15-3.

Listing 15-3. libfun

```
00000000000006d0 <libfun>:

# Function prologue
6d0: 55                      push    rbp
6d1: 48 89 e5                mov     rbp,rsp
6d4: 48 83 ec 10             sub     rsp,0x10

# Second argument for printf( "param: %d\n", value );
6d8: 89 7d fc                mov     DWORD PTR [rbp-0x4],edi
6db: 8b 45 fc                mov     eax,DWORD PTR [rbp-0x4]
6de: 89 c6                   mov     esi,eax

# First argument for printf( "param: %d\n", value );
6e0: 48 8d 3d 32 00 00 00    lea     rdi,[rip+0x32]

# Printf call; no XMM registers used
6e7: b8 00 00 00 00          mov     eax,0x0
6ec: e8 bf fe ff ff          call    5b0 <printf@plt>

# Second argument for printf( "global: %d\n", global );
6f1: 48 8b 05 e0 08 20 00    mov     rax,QWORD PTR [rip+0x2008e0]
6f8: 8b 00                   mov     eax,DWORD PTR [rax]
6fa: 89 c6                   mov     esi,eax

# First argument for printf( "global: %d\n", global );
6fc: 48 8d 3d 21 00 00 00    lea     rdi,[rip+0x21]

# Printf call; no XMM registers used
703: b8 00 00 00 00          mov     eax,0x0
708: e8 a3 fe ff ff          call    5b0 <printf@plt>

# Function epilogue
70d: 90                      nop
70e: c9                      leave
70f: c3                      ret
```

Remember that the source code is shown in Listing 15-2. We are interested in seeing how the global variables are accessed.

First, note that the first argument of printf (which is the address of the format string, residing in **.rodata**) is accessed not in a typical way.

In such cases, we used to have an absolute address value (which would have been filled by linker during the relocation, as explained in section 5.3.2). However, here an address relative to rip is used. As we understand, rdi as the first argument should hold the address of the format string. So, this address is stored *in memory* by the address [rip + 0x32]. This place is a part of GOT.

Now, let's see, how `global` is accessed from the dynamic library code. In fact, the mechanism is absolutely the same, though there is a need in one more memory read. First we read the GOT contents in

```
mov rax,QWORD PTR [rip+0x2008e0]
```

to get the address of `global`, then we read its value by accessing the memory again in

```
mov eax,DWORD PTR [rax].
```

Quite simple for global variables. For functions, however, the implementation is a bit more complicated.

15.4.2 Calling External Functions

While the exact same approach could have worked for functions, an additional feature is implemented to perform the lazy, on-demand function lookup. Let us first discuss the reasons for it.

Looking up symbol definitions is not trivial, as we have seen in this chapter. There are usually many more functions than the global variables exported, and only a small fraction of them are actually called during program execution (e.g., error handling functions). In general, when programmers get a dynamic library to use with their program, they often acquire a third-party library which has much more functions than they actually need to call.

We add another level of indirection through the special Program Linkage Table (PLT). It resides in the **.text** section. Each function called by the shared library has an entry in PLT. Each entry is a small chunk of executable code, which is linked statically and thus can be called directly. Instead of calling a function, whose address would have been stored in GOT, we call the stub entry for it.

To illustrate it, we sketch a PLT in Listing 15-4.

Listing 15-4. plt_sketch.asm

```
; somewhere in the program
call func@plt

; PLT
PLT_0:           ; the common part
call resolver

...

PLT_n:      func@plt:
jmp [GOT_n]
PLT_n_first:
; here the arguments for resolver are prepared
jmp PLT_0

GOT:
...
GOT_n:
dq PLT_n_first
```

Now, what is happening there?

- The function call refers to PLT entry bypassing GOT.

- The zero-th PLT entry defines the "common code" of all entries. They all end up jumping to this entry.

- An *n*-th entry starts with the jump to an address, stored in the *n*-th GOT entry. The default value of this entry is the address of the next instruction after this jump! In our example, it is denoted by the label PLT_n_first. So, the first time the function is called we jump to the next instruction, effectively performing a NOP operation.

- This code prepares arguments for the dynamic loader and jumps to the common code in PLT_0.

- In PLT_0 the loader is called. It performs lookup and resolves the function address, filling GOT_n with the actual function address.

The next function call will involve no dynamic loader: the PLT_n stub will be called, which will immediately jump to the resolved function, whose address now resides in GOT.

Refer to Figures 15-2 and 15-3 for a schematic of changes in PLT due to symbol resolution process.

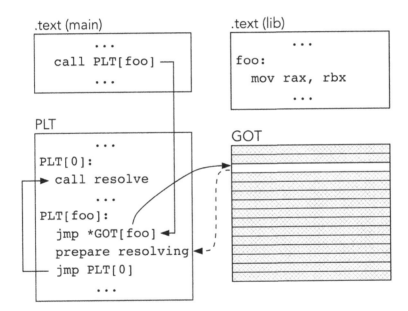

Figure 15-2. *PLT before linking function in runtime*

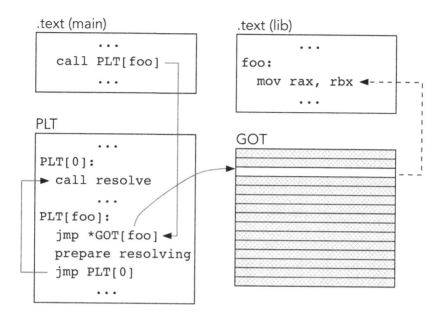

Figure 15-3. *PLT after linking function in runtime*

Question 293 Read in man `ld.so` about environment variables (such as `LD_BIND_NOT`), which can alter the loader behavior.

15.4.3 PLT Example

To be completely fair, we will study the code generated for the example shown in section 15.3.
The main function calls libfun, which is performed through PLT as we expected.

```
Disassembly of section .text:

00000000004006a6 <main>:
  push   rbp
  mov    rbp,rsp
  mov    edi,0x2a
  call   400580 <libfun@plt>
  mov    eax,0x0
  pop    rbp
  ret
```

Next, let's see how PLT looks like. The PLT entry for libfun is called libfun@plt. Find it in Listing 15-5.

Listing 15-5. plt_rw.asm

```
Disassembly of section .init:

0000000000400550 <_init>:
sub     rsp,0x8
mov     rax,QWORD PTR [rip+0x200a9d]        # 600ff8 <_DYNAMIC+0x1e0>
test    rax,rax
je      400565 <_init+0x15>
call    4005a0 <__libc_start_main@plt+0x10>
add     rsp,0x8
ret
Disassembly of section .plt:

0000000000400570 <libfun@plt-0x10>:
push    QWORD PTR [rip+0x200a92]       # 601008 <_GLOBAL_OFFSET_TABLE_+0x8>
jmp     QWORD PTR [rip+0x200a94]       # 601010 <_GLOBAL_OFFSET_TABLE_+0x10>
nop     DWORD PTR [rax+0x0]

0000000000400580 <libfun@plt>:
imp     QWORD PTR [rip+0x200a92]       # 601018 <_GLOBAL_OFFSET_TABLE_+0x18>
push    0x0
jmp     400570 <_init+0x20>

0000000000400590 <__libc_start_main@plt>:
jmp     QWORD PTR [rip+0x200a8a]       # 601020 <_GLOBAL_OFFSET_TABLE_+0x20>
push    0x1
jmp     400570 <_init+0x20>

Disassembly of section .got:
0000000000600ff8 <.got>:

...
Disassembly of section .got.plt:

0000000000601000 <_GLOBAL_OFFSET_TABLE_>:
...
```

The first instruction is a jump into GOT to its third element (because each entry is 8 bytes long and the offset is 0x18). Then the push instruction is issued, whose operand is the function number in PLT. For libfun it is 0x0, for libc_start_main it is 0x1.

The next instruction in libfun@plt is a jump to _init+0x20, which is strange, but if we check the actual _init address, we will see, that

- _init is at 0x400550.

- _init+0x20 is at 0x400570.

- libfun@plt-0x10 is at 0x400570 as well, so they are the same.

- This address is also the start of .plt section and, according to the explanation previously, should correspond to the "common" code shared by all PLT entries. It pushes one more GOT value into the stack and takes an address of the dynamic loader from GOT to jump to it.

The comments issued by objdump show that the last two values refer to addresses 0x601008 and 0x601010. As we see, they should be stored somewhere in .got.plt section, which is the part of GOT related to PLT entries. Listing 16 shows the contents of this section.

Listing 15-6. got_plt_dump_ex.c

```
Contents of section .got.plt:
0x601000    180e6000 00000000 00000000 00000000
0x601010    00000000 00000000 86054000 00000000
0x601020    96054000 00000000
```

By looking carefully we see that starting at the address 0x601018 the following bytes are located:

```
86 05 40 00 00 00 00 00
```

Remembering the fact that Intel 64 uses little endian, we conclude that the actual quad word stored here is 0x400586, which is really the address of libfun@plt + 6, in other words, the address of the push 0x0 instruction. That illustrates the fact that the initial values for functions in GOT point at the second instructions of their respective PLT entries.

15.5 Preloading

Setting up the LD_PRELOAD variable allows you to preload shared objects before any other library (including the C standard library). The functions from this library will have a priority lookup-wise, so they can override the functions defined in the normally loaded shared objects.

The dynamic loader ignores the LD_PRELOAD value if the effective user ID and the real user ID do not match. This is done for security reasons.

We are going to write and compile a simple program, shown in Listing 15-7.

Listing 15-7. preload_launcher.c

```
#include <stdio.h>

int main(void) {
    puts("Hello, world!");
    return 0;
}
```

It does nothing spectacular, but it is important that it uses the puts function, defined in the C standard library. We are going to overwrite it with our version of puts, which ignores its input and simply outputs a fixed string.

When this program is launched, the standard puts function is being executed.

Now let us make a simple dynamic library with the contents shown in Listing 15-8. It proxies the `puts` function with its alternative, which ignores its argument and always outputs a fixed string.

Listing 15-8. `prelib.c`

```
#include <stdio.h>
int puts( const char* str ) {
    return printf("We took control over your C library! \n");
}
```

We compile it using the following commands:

```
> gcc -o preload_launcher preload_launcher.c
> gcc -c -fPIC prelib.c
> gcc -o prelib.so -shared prelib.o
```

Note that the executable was *not* linked against the dynamic library. Listing 15-9 shows the effect of setting the `LD_PRELOAD` variable.

Listing 15-9. `ld_preload_effect`

```
> export LD_PRELOAD=
> ./a.out
Hello, world!
> export LD_PRELOAD=$PWD/prelib.so
> ./a.out
We took control over your C library!
```

As we see, if the `LD_PRELOAD` contains a path to a shared object that defines some functions, they will override other functions that are present in the process address space.

■ **Question 294**   Refer to the assignment. Use this technique to test your `malloc` implementation against some standard utilities from `coreutils`.

■ **Question 295**   Read about `dlopen`, `dlsym`, `dlclose` functions.

15.6   Symbol Addressing Summary

Before we start with assembly and C examples, let us summarize the possible cases considering symbol addressing. The main executable file is usually not relocatable or position independent and loaded by a fixed absolute address, say, 0x40000.[4] The dynamic library is nowadays built using position-independent code and thus its **.text** can be placed anywhere; in other sections the relocations might be needed.

The symbol can be:

1. Defined in executable and used locally there.

    This is trivial, because the symbols will be bound to absolute addresses. The data addressing will be absolute, the code jumps and calls will usually be generated with offsets relative to `rip`.

---

[4]This is not always the case, for example, OS X recommends that all executables are made position independent.

2. Defined in dynamic library and used only there locally (unavailable to external objects).

   In the presence of PIC, it is done by using `rip`-relative addressing (for data) or relative offsets (for function calls). The more general case will be discussed later in section 15.10.

   NASM uses the `rel` keyword to achieve `rip`-relative addressing. This does not involve GOT or PLT.

3. Defined in executable and used globally.

   This requires the GOT usage (and also PLT for functions) if the user is external. For internal usage the rules are the same: we do not need GOT or PLT for addressing inside the same object file.

4. Defined in dynamic library and used globally.

Should be a part of linked list item rather than a paragraph on its own.

15.7 Examples

It is very possible to write a dynamic library in assembly language, which will be position independent and will use GOT and PLT tables.

Linking with gcc   The recommended way of linking libraries is by using GCC. However, for this chapter we will sometimes use more primitive `ld` to show what is really done in greater detail. When the C runtime is involved, never use `ld`.

We will also limit ourselves with Intel 64 as always. The PIC code was a bit harder to write before `rip`-relative addressing was introduced.

15.7.1   Calling a Function

In the first example, the following features will be shown:

- Addressing dynamic library data inside the same library.

- Calling a function of dynamic library from the main executable file.

This example consists of `main.asm` (Listing 15-10) and `lib.asm` (Listing 15-11). The `Makefile` is provided in Listing 15-12 to show the building process. Notice that providing the dynamic linker explicitly is *mandatory* unless you are using the GCC to link files (which will take care of the appropriate dynamic linker path). See section 15.7.2 for more explanations.

Listing 15-10. `ex1-main.asm`

```
extern _GLOBAL_OFFSET_TABLE_
global _start

extern sofun

section .text
_start:
call sofun wrt ..plt

; `exit` system call
mov rdi, 0
mov rax, 60
syscall
```

The first thing that we notice is that extern `_GLOBAL_OFFSET_TABLE_` is usually imported in every file that is dynamically linked.[5]

The main file imports the symbol called sofun. Then, the call contains not only the function name but also the wrt `..plt` qualifier.

Referring to a symbol using wrt `..plt` forces the linker to create a PLT entry. The corresponding expression will be evaluated to an offset to PLT entry relative to the current position in code. Before static linkage, this offset is unknown, but it will be filled by the static linker. The type of this kind of relocation should be a rip-relative relocation (like the one used in call or jmp-like instructions). ELF structure does not provide means to address the PLT entries by their absolute addresses.

Listing 15-11. `ex1-lib.asm`

```
extern _GLOBAL_OFFSET_TABLE_
global sofun:function

section .rodata
msg: db "SO function called", 10
.end:

section .text
sofun:
mov rax, 1
mov rdi, 1
lea rsi, [rel msg]
mov rdx, msg.end - msg
syscall
ret
```

Notice that the global symbol sofun is marked as `:func` (there should be no space before the colon). It is very important to mark exported functions like this in case they should be accessed by other objects dynamically.

The `.end` label allows us to calculate the string length statically to feed it to the write system call. The important change is the rel keyword usage.

---

[5]This name is specific to ELF and should be changed for other systems. See section 9.2.1 of [27].

The code is position independent, so the absolute address of msg can be arbitrary. Its offset relative to this point in code (lea rsi, [rel msg] instruction) is fixed. So, we can use lea to calculate its address as an offset from rip. This line will be compiled to lea rsi, [rip + offset], where offset is a constant that will be filled in by the static linker.

The latter form ([rip + offset]) is syntactically incorrect in NASM.

Listing 15-12 shows the Makefile used to build this example. Before launching, make sure that the environment variable LD_LIBRARY_PATH includes the current directory, otherwise you can simply type

```
export LD_LIBRARY_PATH=.
```

for test purposes and then launch the executable.

Listing 15-12. ex1-makefile

```
main: main.o lib.so
      ld --dynamic-linker=/lib64/ld-linux-x86-64.so.2 main.o lib.so -o main

lib.so: lib.o
    ld -shared lib.o -o lib.so

lib.o:
   nasm -felf64 lib.asm -o lib.o

main.o: main.asm
     nasm -felf64 main.asm -o main.o
```

■ **Question 296**   Perform an experiment. Omit the wrt ..plt construction for the call and recompile everything. Then use objdump -D -Mintel-mnemonic on the resulting main executable to check whether the PLT is still in the game or not. Try to launch it.

15.7.2   On Various Dynamic Linkers

The dynamic linker is not set in stone. It is encoded as part of metadata in the ELF file and can be viewed by means of ldd.

During linkage, you can control, which dynamic linker will be chosen, for example,

```
ld --dynamic-linker=/lib64/ld-linux-x86-64.so.2
```

If you do not specify it, ld will choose the default path, which might lead to a nonexistent file in your case.

If the dynamic linker does not exist, the attempt to load the library will result in a cryptic message which does not make any sense. Suppose that you have built an executable main and it uses a library so_lib, and the LD_LIBRARY_PATH is set correctly.

```
./main
bash: no such file or directory: ./main
> ldd ./main
linux-vdso.so.1 => (0x00007ffcf7f9f000)
so_lib.so => ./so_lib.so (0x00007f0e1cc0a000)
```

The problem is that the linkage was done without an appropriate dynamic linker provided and the ELF metadata does not hold a correct path to it. Relinking the object files with an appropriate dynamic linker path should solve this problem. For example, in the Debian Linux distribution installed on the virtual machine, shipped with this book, the dynamic linker is /lib64/ld-linux-x86-64.so.2.

15.7.3   Accessing an External Variable

For the next example, we will make the message string reside in the main executable file; except for that, the code will stay the same. It will allow us to show how to access the external variable.

The main file is shown in Listing 15-13, while the library source is shown in Listing 15-14.

Listing 15-13. ex2-main.asm

```
extern _GLOBAL_OFFSET_TABLE_
global _start

extern sofun
global msg:data (msg.end - msg)

section .rodata
msg: db "SO function called -- message is stored in 'main'", 10
.end:

section .text
_start:
call sofun  wrt ..plt

mov rdi, 0
mov rax, 60
syscall
```

Listing 15-14. ex2-lib.asm

```
extern _GLOBAL_OFFSET_TABLE_
global sofun:func

extern msg

section  .text
sofun:
mov rax, 1
mov rdi, 1
mov rsi, [rel msg wrt ..got]
mov rdx, 50
syscall
ret
```

It is very important to mark the dynamically shared data declaration with its size. The size is given as an expression, which may include labels and operations on them, such as subtraction. Without the size, the symbol will be treated as global by the static linker (visible to other modules during static linking phase) but will not be exported by the dynamic library.

When the variable is declared as `global` with its size and type (`:data`), it will live in the **.data** section of the executable file rather than the library! Because of this, you will *always have to access it through GOT, even in the same file.*

The GOT, as we know, stores the *addresses* of the variables global to the process. So, if we want to know the address of `msg`, we have to read an entry from GOT. However, as the dynamic library is position independent, we have to address its GOT relatively to `rip` as well. If we want to read its value, we need an additional memory read after fetching its address from GOT.

If the variable is declared in the dynamic library and accessed in the main executable file, it should be done with exactly the same construction: its address can be read from `[rel varname wrt ..got]`. If you need to store an address of the GOT variable, use the following qualifier:

```
othervar: dq global_var wrt ..sym
```

For additional information, refer to section 7.9.3 of [27].

15.7.4   Complete Assembly Example

Listing 15-15 and Listing 15-16 show a complete example with all common features needed from dynamic library.

Listing 15-15. `ex3-main.asm`

```
extern _GLOBAL_OFFSET_TABLE_

extern fun1

global commonmsg:data commonmsg.end - commonmsg
global mainfun:function
global _start

section .rodata
commonmsg: db "fun2", 10, 0
.end:

mainfunmsg: db "mainfun", 10, 0

section .text
_start:
    call fun1 wrt ..plt
    mov rax, 60
    mov rdi, 0
    syscall

mainfun:
    mov rax, 1
    mov rdi, 1
    mov rsi, mainfunmsg
    mov rdx, 8
    syscall
    ret
```

Listing 15-16. `ex3-lib.asm`

```asm
extern _GLOBAL_OFFSET_TABLE_

extern commonmsg
extern mainfun

global fun1:function

section .rodata
msg: db "fun1", 10

section .text
fun1:
    mov rax, 1
    mov rdi, 1
    lea rsi, [rel msg]
    mov rdx, 6
    syscall
    call fun2
    call mainfun wrt ..plt
    ret

fun2:
    mov rax, 1
    mov rdi, 1
    mov rsi, [rel commonmsg wrt ..got]
    mov rdx, 5
    syscall
    ret
```

15.7.5   Mixing C and Assembly

Disclaimer: we are going to provide an example which is compiler and architecture specific, so in your case the process may vary. However, the core ideas will stay more or less the same.

What can complicate mixing C and assembly code is that you have to take into account the C standard library and link everything correctly.

The easiest way is to build the object files separately with GCC and NASM, respectively, and then link them using GCC as well. Other than that, there is not much to fear. Listing 15-17 and Listing 15-8 show an example of calling the assembly library from C.

Listing 15-17. `ex4-main.c`

```c
#include <stdio.h>

extern int sofun( void );
extern const char sostr[];

int main( void ) {
    printf( "%d\n", sofun() );
    puts( sostr );
    return 0;
}
```

In the main file, an external function sofun is called from the dynamic library. Its result is printed to stdout by printf. Then the string, taken from the dynamic library, is output by puts. Note that the global string is the global character buffer, not a pointer!

Listing 15-18. ex4-lib.asm

```
extern _GLOBAL_OFFSET_TABLE_

extern puts

global sostr:data (sostr.end - sostr)
global sofun:function

section .rodata
sostr: db "sostring", 10, 0
.end:

localstr: db "localstr", 10, 0

section .text
sofun:
    lea rdi, [rel localstr]
    call puts wrt ..plt
    mov rax, 42
    ret
```

In the library, the sofun is defined as well as the sostr global string. sofun calls puts, the standard C library function with the localstr address as an argument. As the library is written in a position-independent way, the address should be calculated as an offset from rip; hence the lea command is used. This function always returns 42.

Listing 15-19 shows the relevant Makefile.

Listing 15-19. ex4-Makefile

```
all: main

main: main.o lib.so
    gcc -o main main.o lib.so

lib.so: lib.o
    gcc -shared lib.o -o lib.so

lib.o: lib.asm
    nasm -felf64 lib.asm -o lib.o

main.o: main.asm
    gcc -ansi -c main.c -o main.o

clean:
    rm -rf *.o *.so main
```

15.8   Which Objects Are Linked?

The C standard library is usually implemented as one or many static libraries (which, for example, define _start) and a dynamic library, containing the function we are used to call. The library structure is strictly architecture dependent, but we are going to perform several experiments to investigate it.

The relevant documentation for our specific case can be found in [3].

How do we find which libraries GCC links the executable to? We can make an experiment using GCC with the –v argument.

Following is the list of the additional arguments GCC will implicitly accept during the final linkage according to the Makefile, shown in Listing 15-19:

```
/usr/lib/gcc/x86_64-linux-gnu/4.9/collect2
-plugin
/usr/lib/gcc/x86_64-linux-gnu/4.9/liblto_plugin.so
-plugin-opt=/usr/lib/gcc/x86_64-linux-gnu/4.9/lto-wrapper
-plugin-opt=-fresolution=/tmp/ccqEOGnU.res
-plugin-opt=-pass-through=-lgcc
-plugin-opt=-pass-through=-lgcc_s
-plugin-opt=-pass-through=-lc
-plugin-opt=-pass-through=-lgcc
-plugin-opt=-pass-through=-lgcc_s
--sysroot=/
--build-id
--eh-frame-hdr
-m elf_x86_64
--hash-style=gnu
-dynamic-linker /lib64/ld-linux-x86-64.so.2
-o main
/usr/lib/gcc/x86_64-linux-gnu/4.9/../../../x86_64-linux-gnu/crt1.o
/usr/lib/gcc/x86_64-linux-gnu/4.9/../../../x86_64-linux-gnu/crti.o
/usr/lib/gcc/x86_64-linux-gnu/4.9/crtbegin.o
-L/usr/lib/gcc/x86_64-linux-gnu/4.9
-L/usr/lib/gcc/x86_64-linux-gnu/4.9/../../../x86_64-linux-gnu
-L/usr/lib/gcc/x86_64-linux-gnu/4.9/../../../../lib
-L/lib/x86_64-linux-gnu
-L/lib/../lib
-L/usr/lib/x86_64-linux-gnu
-L/usr/lib/../lib
-L/usr/lib/gcc/x86_64-linux-gnu/4.9/../../..
main.o
lib.so
-lgcc
--as-needed  -lgcc_s
--no-as-needed -lc
-lgcc
--as-needed  -lgcc_s
--no-as-needed /usr/lib/gcc/x86_64-linux-gnu/4.9/crtend.o
/usr/lib/gcc/x86_64-linux-gnu/4.9/../../../x86_64-linux-gnu/crtn.o
```

The lto abbreviation corresponds to "link-time optimizations", which is of no interest to us. The interesting part consists of additional libraries linked. These are:

- crti.o
- crtbegin.o
- crtend.o
- crtn.o
- crt1.o

ELF files support multiple sections, as we know. A separate section **.init** is used to store code that will be executed before main, another section **.fini** is used to store code that is called when the program terminates. These sections' contents are split into multiple files. crti and crto contain the prologue and epilogue of __init function (and likewise for __fini function). These two functions are called before and after the program execution, respectively. crtbegin and crtend contain other utility code included in **.init** and **.fini** sections. They are not always present. We want to repeat that their order is important. crt1.o contains the _start function.

To prove our statements, we are going to disassemble crti.o, crtn.o, and crt1.o files using good old

objdump -D -Mintel-mnemonic.

Listings 15-20, 15-22, and 15-21 show the refined disassembly.

Listing 15-20. da_crti

```
/usr/lib/x86_64-linux-gnu/crti.o:       file format elf64-x86-64

Disassembly of section .init:

0000000000000000 <_init>:
0:   sub    rsp, 0x8
4:   mov    rax, QWORD PTR [rip+0x0]        # b <_init+0xb>
b:   test   rax, rax
e:   je     15 <_init+0x15>
10: call    15 <_init+0x15>

Disassembly of section .fini:

0000000000000000 <_fini>:
0:   sub    rsp, 0x8
```

Listing 15-21. da_crtn

```
/usr/lib/x86_64-linux-gnu/crtn.o:       file format elf64-x86-64

Disassembly of section .init:

0000000000000000 <.init>:
0: add     rsp,0x8
4: ret

Disassembly of section .fini:
```

311

```
0000000000000000 <.fini>:
0: add     rsp,0x8
4: ret
```

Listing 15-22. da_crt1

```
/usr/lib/x86_64-linux-gnu/crt1.o:      file format elf64-x86-64


Disassembly of section .text:
0000000000000000 <_start>:
0:        xor     ebp,ebp
2:        mov     r9,rdx
5:        pop     rsi
6:        mov     rdx,rsp
9:        and     rsp,0xfffffffffffffff0
d:        push    rax
e:        push    rsp
f:        mov     r8,0x0
16:       mov     rcx,0x0
1d:       mov     rdi,0x0
24:       call    29 <_start+0x29>
29:       hlt
```

As we see, these form functions end up in the executable. To see the complete linked and relocated code, we are going to take a part of objdump -D -Mintel-mnemonic output for the resulting file, as shown in Listing 15-23.

Listing 15-23. dasm_init_fini

```
Disassembly of section .init:


00000000004005d8 <_init>:
4005d8: sub     rsp,0x8
4005dc: mov     rax,QWORD PTR [rip+0x200a15]        # 600ff8 <_DYNAMIC+0x1e0>
4005e3: test    rax,rax
4005e6: je      4005ed <_init+0x15>
4005e8: call    400650 <__libc_start_main@plt+0x10>
4005ed: add     rsp,0x8
4005f1: ret


Disassembly of section .text:


0000000000400660 <_start>:
400660: xor     ebp,ebp
400662: mov     r9,rdx
400665: pop     rsi
400666: mov     rdx,rsp
400669: and     rsp,0xfffffffffffffff0
40066d: push    rax
40066e: push    rsp
40066f: mov     r8,0x400800
```

```
400676:   mov     rcx,0x400790
40067d:   mov     rdi,0x400756
400684:   call    400640 <__libc_start_main@plt>
400689:   hlt

Disassembly of section .fini:

0000000000400804 <_fini>:
400804:   sub     rsp,0x8
400808:   add     rsp,0x8
40080c:   ret
```

15.9 Optimizations

What impacts the performance when working with a dynamic library?

First of all, never forget the -fPIC compiler option.[6] Without it, even the **.text** section will be relocated, making dynamic libraries way less attractive to use. It is also crucial to disable some optimizations that might prevent dynamic libraries from working correctly.

As we have seen, when the function is declared static in the dynamic library and thus is not exported, it can be called directly without the PLT overhead. Always use static to limit visibility to a single file.

It is also possible to control visibility of the symbols in a compiler-dependent way. For example, GCC recognizes four types of visibility (default, hidden, internal, protected), of which only the first two are of interest to us. The visibility of all symbols altogether can be controlled using the -fvisibility compiler switch, as follows:

```
> gcc -fvisibility=hidden ... # will hide all symbols from shared object
```

The "default" visibility level implies that all non-static symbols are visible from outside the shared object. By using __attribute__ directive, we can finely control visibility on a per-symbol basis. Listing 15-24 shows an example.

Listing 15-24. visibility_symbol.c

```
int
__attribute__ (( visibility( "default" ) ))
func(int x) { return 42; }
```

The good thing that you can do is to hide all symbols of the shared object and explicitly mark the symbols with default visibility. This way you will fully describe the interface. It is especially good because no other symbols will be exposed and you will be free to change the library internals without breaking binary compatibility of any kind.

The data relocations can slow things down a bit. Every time a variable in **.data** is storing an address of another variable, it should be initialized by dynamic linker once the absolute address of the latter becomes known. Avoid such situations when possible.

Since the access to local symbols bypasses PLT, you might want to reference only "hidden" functions inside your code and make publicly available wrappers for the functions you want to export. Only the calls to the wrappers will use PLT. Listing 15-25 shows an example.

---

[6]The -fpic option implies a limit on GOT size for some architectures, which is often faster.

Listing 15-25. so_adapter.c

```c
static int _function( int x ) { return x + 1; }

void otherfunction( ) {
    printf(" %d \n", _function( 41 ) );
}

int function( int x ) { return _function( x ); }
```

To eliminate possible overhead of the wrapper functions, a technique exists of writing symbol aliases (which is also compiler specific). GCC handles it by using alias attribute. Listing 15-26 shows an example.

Listing 15-26. gcc_alias.c

```c
#include <stdio.h>

int global = 42;

extern int global_alias
__attribute__ ((alias ("global"), visibility ("hidden" ) ));

void fun( void ) {
    puts("1337\n");
}
extern void fun_alias( void )
__attribute__ ((alias ("fun"), visibility ("hidden" ) ));

int tester(void) {
    printf( "%d\n", global );
    printf( "%d\n", global_alias );

    fun();
    fun_alias();
    return 0;
}
```

When we compile it using gcc -shared -O3 -fPIC and disassemble it, we see the code shown in Listing 15-27 (disassembly for tester function).

Listing 15-27. gcc_aliased_gain.asm

```asm
; global -> rsi
787:    mov    rax,QWORD  PTR  [rip+0x20084a]      # 200fd8 <_DYNAMIC+0x1c8>
78e:    mov    eax,DWORD PTR [rax]
790:    mov    esi,eax

792:    lea    rdi,[rip+0x46]         # 7df <_fini+0xf>
799:    mov    eax,0x0
79e:    call   650 <printf@plt>
```

```
; global_alias -> rsi
7a3:    mov     eax,DWORD PTR [rip+0x20088f]        # 201038 <global>
7a9:    mov     esi,eax

7ab:    lea     rdi,[rip+0x2d]      # 7df <_fini+0xf>
7b2:    mov     eax,0x0
7b7:    call    650 <printf@plt>

; calling global `fun`
7bc:    call    640 <fun@plt>

; calling aliased `fun` directly
7c1:    call    770 <fun>
```

The global and global_aliased are handled differently; the latter requires one less memory read. The function call of fun is also handled more efficiently, bypassing PLT and thus sparing an extra jump.

Finally, remember, that the zero-initialized globals are always faster to initialize. However, we strongly advocate against global variables usage.

More information about shared object optimizations can be found in [13].

Note   The common way of linking against libraries is by using -l key, for example, gcc -lhello. The only two differences with specifying the full file path are:

- -lhello will search for a library named libhello.a (so, prefixed with lib and with an extension .a).

- The library is searched in the standard list of directories. It is also searched in custom directories, which can be supplied using -L option. For example, to include the directory /usr/libcustom and the current directory, you can type:

    > gcc -lhello -L. -L/usr/libcustom main.c

Remember, the order in which you supply libraries matters.

15.10   Code Models

The code models are a rarely discussed topic. [24] can be viewed as a reference for this matter, and we are going to discuss code models in this section.

The starting point for the discussion is the fact, that rip-relative addressing is limited. [15] elaborates that the offset should be an immediate value of 32 bits maximum. This leaves us with ± 2 GB offsets. Making it possible to use 64-bit offsets directly is wasteful since most code would never use the extra bits; however, such offsets are directly encoded into the instructions themselves, making the code take up more space, which is not good for instruction cache. The address space size is far greater than 32 bits, so what do we do when 32 bits are not enough?

A code model is a convention to which the programmer and the compiler both adhere; it describes the constraints on the program that will use the object file that is currently being compiled. The code generation depends on it. In short, when the program is relatively small, there is no harm in using 32-bit offsets. However, when it can be large enough, the slower 64-bit offsets, which are handled by multiple instructions, should be used.

The 32-bit offsets correspond to the **small code model**; the 64-bit offsets correspond to the **large code model**. There is also a sort of compromise called the **medium code model**. All these models are treated differently in context of position-dependent and position-independent code, so we are going to review all six possible combinations.

There can be other code models, such as the kernel code model, but we will leave them out of this volume. If you make your own operating system you can invent one for your own pleasure.

The relevant GCC option is -mcmodel, for example, -mcmodel=large. The default model is the small model.[7]

The GCC manual says the following about the -mcmodel option[8]:

-mcmodel=small
    Generate code for the small code model: the program and its symbols must be linked in the lower 2 GB of the address space. Pointers are 64 bits. Programs can be statically or dynamically linked. This is the default code model.

-mcmodel=kernel
    Generate code for the kernel code model. The kernel runs in the negative 2 GB of the address space. This model has to be used for Linux kernel code.

-mcmodel=medium
    Generate code for the medium model: the program is linked in the lower 2 GB of the address space. Small symbols are also placed there. Symbols with sizes larger than -mlarge-data-threshold are put into large data or BSS sections and can be located above 2GB. Programs can be statically or dynamically linked.

-mcmodel=large
    Generate code for the large model. This model makes no assumptions about addresses and sizes of sections.

To illustrate the differences in compiled code when using different code models, we are going to use a simple example shown in Listing 15-28.

Listing 15-28. cm-example.c

```
char glob_small[100] = {1};
char glob_big[10000000] = {1};
static char loc_small[100] = {1};
static char loc_big[10000000] = {1};

int global_f(void) { return 42; }
static int local_f(void) { return 42; }

int main(void) {
    glob_small[0] = 42;
    glob_big[0] = 42;
    loc_small[0] = 42;
```

---

[7]Not all compilers and GCC versions support the large model.

[8]Note that there are different descriptions for different architectures.

```
        loc_big[0] = 42;
        global_f();
        local_f();
        return 0;
}
```

We will use the following line to compile it:

```
gcc -O0 -g cm-example.c
```

The -g flag adds debug information such as **.line** section, which describes the correspondence between assembly instructions and the source code lines.

In this example, there are bigger and smaller arrays. It matters only for medium code model, hence we will omit the big array accesses from other disassembly listings.

15.10.1   Small Code Model (No PIC)

In the small code model the program is limited in size. All objects should be within 4GB of each other to be linked. The linking can be done either statically or dynamically. As this is the default code model, we are not going to see anything interesting here.

By feeding the -S key to objdump we will intersperse the assembly code with the source C lines (if the corresponding file was compiled with -g flag). The full command sequence will look as follows:

```
gcc -O0 -g cm-example.c -o example
objdump -D -Mintel-mnemonic -S example
```

Listing 15-29 shows the compiled assembly.

Listing 15-29. mc-small

```
;       glob_small[0] = 42;
4004f0:  c6 05 49 0b 20 00 2a     mov      BYTE PTR [rip+0x200b49],0x2a

;       loc_small[0] = 42;
4004fe:  c6 05 3b a2 b8 00 2a     mov      BYTE PTR [rip+0xb8a23b],0x2a

;       global_f();
40050c:  e8 c5 ff ff ff           call     4004d6 <global_f>

;       local_f();
400511:  e8 cb ff ff ff           call     4004e1 <local_f>
```

The second column shows us the hex codes of the bytes that correspond to each instruction. The array accesses are performed explicitly relative to rip, and the calls accept the offsets (which are also implicitly relative to rip). We can see that the size of data accessing instructions is 7 bytes of which 1 byte is the value (0x2a) and 4 bytes encode the offset relative to rip. It illustrates the core idea of the small code model: rip-relative addressing.

15.10.2   Large Code Model (No PIC)

Now let us compile the same code using the large code model (-mcmodel=large).

```
;     glob_small[0] = 42;
    4004f0:    48 b8 40 10 60 00 00    mov      rax,0x601040
    4004f7:    00 00 00
    4004fa:    c6 00 2a                mov      BYTE PTR [rax],0x2a

;     loc_small[0] = 42;
    40050a:    48 b8 40 a7 f8 00 00    mov      rax,0xf8a740
    400511:    00 00 00
    400514:    c6 00 2a                mov      BYTE PTR [rax],0x2a

;     global_f();
    400524:    48 b8 d6 04 40 00 00    mov      rax,0x4004d6
    40052b:    00 00 00
    40052e:    ff d0                   call     rax

;     local_f();
    400530:    48 b8 e1 04 40 00 00    mov      rax,0x4004e1
    400537:    00 00 00
    40053a:    ff d0                   call     rax
```

Both data accesses and calls are performed uniformly. We always start by moving an immediate value into one of the general purpose registers and then reference memory using the address stored in this register.[9]

For a cost of a more spacious assembly code (and probably a bit slower one) we take the safest road possible allowing to reference anything in any part of the 64-bit virtual address space.

15.10.3   Medium Code Model (No PIC)

In the medium code model, the arrays of size greater than specified by the -mlarge-data-threshold compiler parameter are placed into a special **.ldata** and **.lbss** section. These sections can be placed above the 2GB mark. Basically, it is a small code model except for big chunks of data, which are placed separately. Performance-wise it is better than accessing everything via 64-bit pointers, because of locality.

The disassembly for the sources compiled with -mcmodel=medium is as follows:.

```
  glob_small[0] = 42;
400530:    c6 05 09 0b 20 00 2a     mov      BYTE PTR [rip+0x200b09],0x2a

  glob_big[0] = 42;
400537:    48 b8 40 11 a0 00 00     movabs   rax,0xa01140
40053e:    00 00 00
400541:    c6 00 2a                 mov      BYTE PTR [rax],0x2a

  loc_small[0]  =  42;
400544:    c6 05 75 0b 20 00 2a     mov      BYTE PTR [rip+0x200b75],0x2a
```

---

[9]If you encounter the movabs instruction, consider it equivalent to the mov instruction.

```
  loc_big[0] = 42;
40054b:   48 b8 c0 a7 38 01 00      movabs    rax,0x138a7c0
400552:   00 00 00
400555:   c6 00 2a                  mov       BYTE PTR [rax],0x2a

  global_f();
400558:   e8 b9 ff ff ff            call      400516 <global_f>

  local_f();
40055d:   e8 bf ff ff ff            call      400521 <local_f>
```

As we see, the generated code is using the large model to access big arrays and the small one for the rest of accesses. It is quite clever and might save you if you only need to work with a big chunk of statically allocated data.

15.10.4   Small PIC Code Model

Now we are going to investigate the position-independent counterparts of these three code models. As before, the small model will not surprise us, because up to now we have only worked with a small code model. For convenience, we provide the example code compiled with gcc -g -O0 -mcmodel=small -fpic.

```
  glob_small[0] = 42;
4004f0:   48 8d 05 49 0b 20 00      lea       rax,[rip+0x200b49]
  # 601040 <glob_small>

4004f7:   c6 00 2a                  mov       BYTE PTR [rax],0x2a

  glob_big[0] = 42;
4004fa:   48 8d 05 bf 0b 20 00      lea       rax,[rip+0x200bbf]
  # 6010c0 <glob_big>

400501:   c6 00 2a                  mov       BYTE PTR [rax],0x2a

  loc_small[0] = 42;
400504:   c6 05 35 a2 b8 00 2a      mov       BYTE PTR [rip+0xb8a235],0x2a
  # f8a740 <loc_small>

  loc_big[0] = 42;
40050b:   c6 05 ae a2 b8 00 2a      mov       BYTE PTR [rip+0xb8a2ae],0x2a
  # f8a7c0 <loc_big>

  global_f();
400512:   e8 bf ff ff ff            call      4004d6 <global_f>
  local_f();
400517:   e8 c5 ff ff ff            call      4004e1 <local_f>
```

The static arrays are accessed easily relative to rip as expected. The globally visible arrays are accessed through GOT, which implies an additional read from the table itself to get its address.

15.10.5   Large PIC Code Model

Interesting things start to emerge when using a large code model with position-independent code. Now we cannot use rip-relative addressing to get to the GOT, because it can be further than 2GB in address space! Because of this, we need to allocate a register to store its address (rbx in our case).

```
# Standard prologue
400594:    55                            push    rbp
400595:    48 89 e5                      mov     rbp,rsp

# What is that?
400598:    41 57                         push    r15
40059a:    53                            push    rbx
40059b:    48 8d 1d f9 ff ff ff          lea     rbx,[rip+0xfffffffffffffff9]
# 40059b <main+0x7>
4005a2:    49 bb 65 0a 20 00 00          movabs  r11,0x200a65
4005a9:    00 00 00
4005ac:    4c 01 db                      add     rbx,r11

# Accessing global symbols
  glob_small[0] = 42;
4005af:    48 b8 e8 ff ff ff ff          movabs  rax,0xffffffffffffffe8
4005b6:    ff ff ff
4005b9:    48 8b 04 03                   mov     rax,QWORD PTR [rbx+rax*1]
4005bd:    c6 00 2a                      mov     BYTE PTR [rax],0x2a

# Accessing local symbols
  loc_small[0] = 42;
4005d1:    48 b8 40 97 98 00 00          movabs  rax,0x989740
4005d8:    00 00 00
4005db:    c6 04 03 2a                   mov     BYTE  PTR  [rbx+rax*1],0x2a

# Calling global function
  global_f();
4005ed:    49 89 df                      mov     r15,rbx
4005f0:    48 b8 56 f5 df ff ff          movabs  rax,0xffffffffffdff556
4005f7:    ff ff ff
4005fa:    48 01 d8                      add     rax,rbx
4005fd:    ff d0                         call    rax

# Calling local function
  local_f();
4005ff:    48 b8 75 f5 df ff ff          movabs  rax,0xffffffffffdff575
400606:    ff ff ff
400609:    48 8d 04 03                   lea     rax,[rbx+rax*1]
40060d:    ff d0                         call    rax

    return 0;
  40060f:    b8 00 00 00 00              mov     eax,0x0
}
```

```
400614:    5b                                 pop      rbx
400615:    41 5f                              pop      r15
400617:    5d                                 pop      rbp
400618:    c3                                 ret
```

This example needs to be studied carefully. First we want to break down the unusual code in the function prologue.

```
400598:    41 57                              push     r15
40059a:    53                                 push     rbx
40059b:    48 8d 1d f9 ff ff ff               lea      rbx,[rip+0xfffffffffffffff9]
# 40059b <main+0x7>
4005a2:    49 bb 65 0a 20 00 00               movabs   r11,0x200a65
4005a9:    00 00 00
4005ac:    4c 01 db                           add      rbx,r11
```

We use rbx and r15 because they are **callee-saved**. They are used here to build up the GOT address out of the following two components:

- The address of the current instruction, calculated in lea rbx,[rip+0xfffffffffffffff9]. The operand is equal to -6, while the instruction itself is 6 bytes long. When it is being executed, the rip value points to the next address after the instruction.

- Then the number 0x200a65 is being added to rbx. It is done through another register, because adding an immediate operand of 64 bits wide is not supported by the add instruction (check the instruction description in [15]!).

- This number is a displacement of GOT relative to the address of lea rbx,[rip+0xfffffffffffffff9], which, as we know, is always known at link time in position-independent code.[10]

The ABI considers that r15 should hold GOT address at all times. rbx is also used by GCC for its convenience.

The GOT absolute address is unknown at link time since the code is written to be position independent.

Now to the data accesses: the global symbol is accessed through GOT the same way as in non-PIC code; however, as the GOT address is stored in rbx, we have to compute the entry address using more instructions.

```
# Accessing global symbols
  glob_small[0] = 42;
4005af:    48 b8 e8 ff ff ff ff               movabs   rax,0xffffffffffffffe8
4005b6:    ff ff  ff
4005b9:    48 8b 04 03                        mov      rax,QWORD PTR [rbx+rax*1]
4005bd:    c6 00 2a                           mov      BYTE PTR [rax],0x2a
```

The entry is located with a negative offset of -24 relatively to the rbx (r15) value. This displacement can be of arbitrary length, so we need to store it in a register to consider cases where it cannot be contained in 32 bits. Then we load the GOT entry to rax and use this address for our purposes (in this case we store a value in the array start).

---

[10]Obviously, here r15 and rbx hold not the beginning of GOT but its end, but it does not matter.

The variables not visible as other objects are accessed using GOT as well. However, we are not reading their addresses from GOT. Rather than that, we use the rbx value as the base (as it points somewhere in the data segment). Every global variable has a fixed offset from this base, so we can just pick this offset and use the base indexed addressing mode.

```
# Accessing local symbols
  loc_small[0] = 42;
4005d1:   48 b8 40 97 98 00 00      movabs    rax,0x989740
4005d8:   00 00 00
4005db:   c6 04 03 2a               mov       BYTE PTR [rbx+rax*1],0x2a
```

This is obviously faster, so whenever you can, you should prefer limiting symbol visibility as explained in section 15.9

The local functions are called in the same manner. Their address is calculated relative to GOT and stored in a register. We cannot simply use the call command, because its immediate operand is limited to 32 bits (in its description given in [15], there are only operand types rel16 and rel32, but no rel64).

```
# Calling local  function
  local_f();
4005ff:   48 b8 75 f5 df ff ff      movabs    rax,0xffffffffffffdff575
400606:   ff ff ff
400609:   48 8d 04 03               lea       rax,[rbx+rax*1]
40060d:   ff d0                     call      rax
```

Calling global functions is done in a more traditional way. Its PLT entry is used, whose address is also calculated as a fixed offset to a known GOT position.

```
# Calling global function
  global_f();
4005ed:   49 89 df                  mov       r15,rbx
4005f0:   48 b8 56 f5 df ff ff      movabs    rax,0xffffffffffffdff556
4005f7:   ff ff ff
4005fa:   48 01 d8                  add       rax,rbx
4005fd:   ff d0                     call      rax
```

15.10.6   Medium PIC Code Model

The medium code model, as in non-PIC code, is a mixture of large and small code models.

We can think of it as a small PIC code model with an addition of big arrays, residing separately.

```
int main(void) {
  40057a:   55                        push    rbp
  40057b:   48 89 e5                  mov     rbp,rsp

# Different from small model: we save GOT address locally.
  40057e:   48 8d 15 7b 0a 20 00      lea     rdx,[rip+0x200a7b]

    glob_small[0] = 42;
  400585:   48 8d 05 b4 0a 20 00      lea     rax,[rip+0x200ab4]
  40058c:   c6 00 2a                  mov     BYTE PTR [rax],0x2a
```

```
  glob_big[0] = 42;
40058f:    48 8b 05 62 0a 20 00     mov     rax,QWORD PTR [rip+0x200a62]
400596:    c6 00 2a                 mov     BYTE PTR [rax],0x2a

  loc_small[0] = 42;
400599:    c6 05 20 0b 20 00 2a     mov     BYTE PTR [rip+0x200b20],0x2a

  loc_big[0] = 42;
4005a0:    48 b8 c0 97 d8 00 00     movabs  rax,0xd897c0
4005a7:    00 00 00
4005aa:    c6 04 02 2a              mov     BYTE PTR [rdx+rax*1],0x2a

  global_f();
4005ae:    e8 a3 ff ff ff           call    400556 <global_f>

  local_f();
4005b3:    e8 b0 ff ff ff           call    400568 <local_f>

  return 0;
4005b8:    b8 00 00 00 00           mov     eax,0x0
}
  4005bd: 5d                        pop     rbp
4005be:    c3                       ret
```

The GOT address is also in reach of rip-relative addressing, so its address is loaded with one instruction.

```
40057e:    48 8d 15 7b 0a 20 00     lea     rdx,[rip+0x200a7b]
```

It is thus not always needed to dedicate a register for it, since this address will not be used everywhere.

The code references are considered to be in reach of 32-bit rip-relative offsets. So, calling any functions is trivial.

```
  global_f();
4005ae:    e8 a3 ff ff ff     call    400556 <global_f>

  local_f();
4005b3:    e8 b0 ff ff ff     call    400568 <local_f>
```

As for the data accesses, the accesses to global variables are performed uniformly no matter the size. The GOT is involved in any case, and it contains 64-bit global variables addresses, so we have the possibility of addressing anything for free.

```
  glob_small[0] = 42;
400585:    48 8d 05 b4 0a 20 00     lea     rax,[rip+0x200ab4]
40058c:    c6 00 2a                 mov     BYTE PTR [rax],0x2a

  glob_big[0] = 42;
40058f:    48 8b 05 62 0a 20 00     mov     rax,QWORD PTR [rip+0x200a62]
400596:    c6 00 2a                 mov     BYTE PTR [rax],0x2a
```

The local variables, however, differ. Small arrays can be accessed relative to rip.

```
loc_small[0] = 42;
400599:    c6 05 20 0b 20 00 2a       mov       BYTE PTR [rip+0x200b20],0x2a
```

Local big arrays are found relative to GOT starting addresses, as in the large model.

```
loc_big[0] = 42;
4005a0:    48 b8 c0 97 d8 00 00       movabs    rax,0xd897c0
4005a7:    00 00 00
4005aa:    c6 04 02 2a                mov       BYTE PTR [rdx+rax*1],0x2a
```

15.11   Summary

In this chapter we have received the knowledge we need to understand the machinery behind dynamic library loading and usage. We have written a library in assembly language and in C and successfully linked it to an executable.

For further reading we address you above all to a classic article [13] and to the ABI description [24].

In the next chapter we are going to speak about compiler optimizations and their effects on performance as well as about specialized instruction set extensions (SSE/AVX), aimed to speed up certain types of computations.

Question 297   What is the difference between static and dynamic linkage?

Question 298   What does the dynamic linker do?

Question 299   Can we resolve all dependencies at the link time? What kind of system should we be working with in order for this to be possible?

Question 300   Should we always relocate the **.data** section?

Question 301   Should we always relocate the **.text** section?

Question 302   What is PIC?

Question 303   Can we share a **.text** section between processes when it is being relocated?

Question 304   Can we share a **.data** section between processes when it is being relocated?

Question 305   Can we share a **.data** section when it is being relocated?

Question 306   Why are we compiling dynamic libraries with an -fPIC flag?

Question 307   Write a simple dynamic library in C from scratch and demonstrate the calling function from it.

Question 308   What is ldd used for?

Question 309   Where are the libraries searched?

Question 310   What is the environment variable LD_LIBRARY_PATH for?

Question 311   What is GOT? Why is it needed?

Question 312   What makes GOT usage effective?

Question 313   How come that position-independent code can address GOT directly but cannot address global variables directly?

Question 314   Is GOT unique for each process?

Question 315   What is PLT?

Question 316   Why don't we use GOT to call functions from different objects (or do we)?

Question 317   What does the initial GOT entry for a function point at?

Question 318   How do we preload a library and what can it be used for?

Question 319   In assembly, how is the symbol addressed if it is defined in the executable and accessed from there?

Question 320   In assembly, how is the symbol addressed if it is defined in the library and accessed from there?

Question 321   In assembly, how is the symbol addressed if it is defined in the executable and accessed from everywhere?

Question 322   In assembly, how is the symbol addressed if it is defined in the library and accessed from everywhere?

Question 323   How do we control the visibility of a symbol in a dynamic library? How do we make it private for the library but accessible from anywhere in it?

Question 324   Why do people sometimes write wrapper functions for those used in library?

Question 325   How do we link against a library that is stored in `libdir`?

Question 326   What is a code model and why do we care about code models?

Question 327   What limitations impose the small code model?

Question 328   Which overhead does the large code model carry?

Question 329   What is the compromise between large and small code models?

Question 330   When is the medium model most useful?

Question 331   How do large code models differ for PIC and non-PIC code?

Question 332   How do medium code models differ for PIC and non-PIC code?

CHAPTER 16

Performance

In this chapter we will study how to write faster code. In order to do that, we will look into SSE (Streaming SIMD Extensions) instructions, study compiler optimizations, and hardware cache functioning.

Note that this chapter is a mere introduction to the topic and will not make you an expert in optimization.

There is no silver bullet technique to magically make everything fast. Hardware has become so complex that even an educated guess about the code that is slowing down program execution might fail. Testing and profiling should always be performed, and the performance should be measured in a reproducible way. It means that everything about the environment should be described in such detail that anyone would be able to replicate the conditions of the experiment and receive similar results.

16.1 Optimizations

In this section we want to discuss the most important optimizations that happen during the translation process. They are crucial to understanding how to write quality code. Why? A common type of decision making in programming is balancing between code readability and performance. Knowing optimizations is necessary in order to make good decisions. Otherwise, when choosing between two versions of code, we might choose a less readable one because it "looks" like it performs fewer actions. In reality, however, both versions will be optimized to exactly the same sequences of assembly instructions. In this case, we just made a less readable code for no benefit at all.

Note In the listings presented in this section we will often use an `__attribute__` `((noinline))` GCC directive. Applying it to a function definition suppresses inlining for the said function. Exemplary functions are often small, which encourages compilers to inline them, which we do not want to better show various optimization effects.

Alternatively, we could have compiled the examples with `-fno-inline` option.

16.1.1 Myth About Fast Languages

There is a common misunderstanding that the language defines the program execution speed. It is not true.

Better and more useful performance tests are usually highly specialized. They measure performance in very specific cases. It prevents us from making bold generalizations. So, when giving statements about the performance it is wise to give the most possibly detailed description of the scenario and test results. The description should be enough to build a similar system and launch similar tests, getting comparable results.

© Igor Zhirkov 2017
I. Zhirkov, *Low-Level Programming*, DOI 10.1007/978-1-4842-2403-8_16

There are cases in which a program written in C can be outperformed by another program performing similar actions but written in, say, Java. It has no connection with the language itself.

For example, a typical `malloc` implementation has a particular property: it is hard to predict its execution time. In general, it is dependent on the current heap state: how many blocks exist, how fragmented the heap is, etc. In any case it is most likely greater than allocating memory on a stack. In a typical Java Virtual Machine implementation, however, allocating memory is fast. It happens because Java has a simpler heap structure. With some simplifications, it is just a memory region and a pointer inside it, which delimits an occupied area from the free one. Allocating memory means moving this pointer further into the free part, which is fast.

However, it has its cost: to get rid of the memory chunks we do not need anymore, garbage collection is performed, which might stop the program for an unknown period of time.

We imagine a situation in which garbage collection never happens, for example, a program allocates memory, performs computations, and exits, destroying all address space without invoking the garbage collector. In this case it is possible that a Java program performs faster just because of the careful allocation overhead imposed by `malloc`. However, if we use a custom memory allocator, fitting our specific needs for a particular task, we might do the same trick in C, changing the outcome drastically.

Additionally, as Java is usually interpreted and compiled in runtime, virtual machine has access to runtime optimizations that are based on how exactly the program is executed. For example, methods that are often executed one after another can be placed near each other in memory, so that they are placed in a cache together. In order to do that, certain information about program execution trace should be collected, which is only possible in runtime.

What really distinguishes C from other languages is a very transparent costs model. Whatever you are writing, it is easy to imagine which assembly instructions will be emitted. Contrary to that, languages destined primarily to work inside a runtime (Java, C#), or providing multiple additional abstractions, such as C++ with its virtual inheritance mechanism, are harder to predict. The only two real abstractions C provides are structures/unions and functions.

Being translated naively in machine instructions, a C program works very slowly. It is no match to a code generated by a good optimizing compiler. Usually, a programmer does not have more knowledge about low-level architecture details than the compiler, which is much needed to perform low-level optimizations, so he will not be able to compete with the compiler. Otherwise, sometimes, for a particular platform and compiler, one might change a program, usually reducing its readability and maintainability, but in a way that will speed up the code. Again, performance tests are mandatory for everyone.

16.1.2   General Advice

When programming we should not usually be concerned with optimizations right away. Premature optimization is evil for numerous reasons.

- Most programs are written in a way that only a fraction of their code is repeatedly executed. This code determines how fast the program will be executing, and it can slow down everything else. Speeding up other parts will in these circumstances have little to no effect.

  Finding such parts of the code is best performed using a **profiler** —a utility program that measures how often and how long different parts of code are executed.

- Optimizing code by hand virtually always makes it less readable and harder to maintain.

- Modern compilers are aware of common patterns in high-level language code. Such patterns get optimized well because the compiler writers put much work into it, since the work is worth it.

The most important part of optimizations is often choosing the right algorithm. Low-level optimizations on the assembly level are rarely so beneficial. For example, accessing elements of a linked list by index is slow, because we have to traverse it from the beginning, jumping from node to node. Arrays are more beneficial when the program logic demands accessing its elements by index. However, insertion in a linked list is easy compared to array, because to insert an element to the *i*-th position in an array we have to move all following elements first (or maybe even reallocate memory for it first and copy everything).

A simple, clean code is often also the most efficient.

Then, if the performance is unsatisfactory, we have to locate the code that gets executed the most using profiler and try to optimize it by hand. Check for duplicated computations and try to memorize and reuse computation results. Study the assembly listings and check if forcing inlining for some of the functions used is doing any good.

General concerns about hardware such as locality and cache usage should be taken into account at this time. We will speak about them in section 16.2.

The compiler optimizations should be considered then. We will study the basic ones later in this section. Turning specific optimizations on *or off* for a dedicated file or a code region can have a positive impact on performance. By default, they are usually all turned on when compiling with -O3 flag.

Only then come lower-level optimizations: manually throwing in SSE or AVX (Advanced Vector Extensions) instructions, inlining assembly code, writing data bypassing hardware cache, prefetching data into caches before using it, etc.

The compiler optimizations are boldly controlled by using compiler flags -O0, -O1, -O2, -O3, -Os (optimize space usage, to produce the smallest executable file possible). The index near -O, increases as the set of enabled optimizations grows.

Specific optimizations can be turned on and off. Each optimization type has two associated compiler options for that, for example, -fforward-propagate and -fno-forward-propagate.

16.1.3   Omit Stack Frame Pointer

Related GCC options: -fomit-frame-pointer

Sometimes we do not really need to store old `rbp` value and initialize it with the new base value. It happens when

- There are no local variables.

- Local variables fit into the red zone AND the function calls no other function.

However, there is a downside: it means that less information about the program state is kept at runtime. We will have trouble unwinding call stack and getting local variable values because we lack information about where the frame starts.

It is most troublesome in situations in which a program crashed and a dump of its state should be analyzed. Such dumps are often heavily optimized and lack debug information.

Performance-wise the effects of this optimizations are often negligible [26].

The code shown in Listing 16-1 demonstrates how to unwind the stack and display frame pointer addresses for all functions launched when `unwind` gets called. Compile it with -O0 to prevent optimizations.

Listing 16-1. stack_unwind.c

```c
void unwind();
void f( int count ) {
    if ( count ) f( count-1 ); else unwind();
}
int main(void) {
    f( 10 ); return 0;
}
```

Listing 16-2 shows an example.

Listing 16-2. stack_unwind.asm

```
extern printf
global unwind

section .rodata
format : db "%x ", 10, 0

section .code
unwind:
push rbx

; while (rbx != 0) {
    ;      print rbx; rbx = [rbx];
    ; }
    mov rbx, rbp
    .loop:
    test rbx, rbx
    jz .end
    mov rdi, format
    mov rsi, rbx
    call printf
    mov rbx, [rbx]
    jmp .loop

    .end:
    pop rbx
    ret
```

How do we use it? Try it as a last resort to improve performance on code involving a huge amount of non-inlineable function calls.

16.1.4   Tail recursion

Related GCC options: -fomit-frame-pointer -foptimize-sibling-calls
    Let us study a function shown in Listing 16-3.

Listing 16-3. factorial_tailrec.c

```
__attribute__ (( noinline ))
    int factorial( int acc, int arg ) {
        if ( arg == 0 ) return acc;
        return factorial( acc * arg, arg-1 );
    }

int main(int argc, char** argv) { return factorial(1, argc); }
```

It calls itself recursively, but this call is particular. Once the call is completed, the function immediately returns.

We say that the function is **tail recursive** if the function either

- Returns a value that does not involve a recursive call, for example, `return 4;`.

- Launches itself recursively with other arguments and returns the result immediately, without performing further computations with it. For example, `return factorial ( acc * arg, arg-1 );`.

A function is not tail recursive when the recursive call result is then used in computations.

Listing 16-4 shows an example of a non-tail-recursive factorial computation. The result of a recursive call is multiplied by arg before being returned, hence no tail recursion.

Listing 16-4. `factorial_nontailrec.c`

```
__attribute__ (( noinline ))
    int factorial( int arg ) {

    if ( arg == 0 ) return acc;
    return arg * factorial( arg-1 );
}

int main(int argc, char** argv) { return factorial(argc); }
```

In Chapter 2, we studied Question 20, which proposes a solution in the spirit of tail recursion. When the last thing a function does is call other function, which is immediately followed by the return, we can perform a jump to the said function start. In other words, the following pattern of instructions can be a subject to optimization:

```
; somewhere else:
    call f

...
...

f:

    ...
    call g
    ret       ; 1
g:

    ...
    ret       ; 2
```

The `ret` instruction in this listing are marked as the first and the second one.

Executing `call g` will place the return address into the stack. This is the address of the first `ret` instruction. When g completes its execution, it executes the second `ret` instruction, which pops the return address, leaving us at the first `ret`. Thus, two `ret` instructions will be executed in a row before the control passes to the function that called f. However, why not return to the caller of f immediately? To do that, we replace `call g` with `jmp g`. Now g we will never return to function f, nor will we push a useless return address into the stack. The second `ret` will pick up the return address from `call f`, which should have happened somewhere, and return us directly there.

```
; somewhere else:
    call f

...
...

f:

    ...
    jmp g
g:

    ...
    ret      ; 2
```

When g and f are the same function, it is exactly the case of tail recursion. When not optimized, factorial(5, 1) will launch itself five times, polluting the stack with five stack frames. The last call will end executing ret five times in a row in order to get rid of all return addresses.

Modern compilers are usually aware of tail recursive calls and know how to optimize tail recursion into a cycle. The assembly listing produced by GCC for the tail recursive factorial (Listing 16-3) is shown in Listing 16-5.

Listing 16-5. factorial_tailrec.asm

```
00000000004004c6 <factorial>:
4004c6:   89 f8              mov     eax,edi
4004c8:   85 f6              test    esi,esi
4004ca:   74 07              je      4004d3 <factorial+0xd>
4004cc:   0f af c6           imul    eax,esi
4004cf:   ff ce              dec     esi
4004d1:   eb f5              jmp     4004c8 <factorial+0x2>
4004d3:   c3                 ret
```

As we see, a tail recursive call consists of two stages.

- Populate registers with new argument values.

- Jump to the function start.

Cycles are faster than recursion because the latter needs additional space in the stack (which might lead to stack overflow as well). Why not always stick with cycles then?

Recursion often allows us to express some algorithms in a more coherent and elegant way. If we can write a function so that it becomes tail recursive as well, that recursion will not impact the performance.

Listing 16-6 shows an exemplary function accessing a linked list element by index.

Listing 16-6. tail_rec_example_list.c

```c
#include <stdio.h>
#include <malloc.h>

struct llist {
    struct llist* next;
    int value;
};
```

```c
struct llist* llist_at(
        struct llist* lst,
        size_t idx ) {
    if ( lst && idx ) return llist_at( lst->next, idx-1 );
    return lst;
}
struct llist* c( int value, struct llist* next) {
    struct llist* lst = malloc( sizeof(struct llist*) );
    lst->next = next;
    lst->value = value;
    return lst;
}

int main( void ) {
    struct llist* lst = c( 1, c( 2, c( 3, NULL )));
    printf("%d\n", llist_at( lst, 2 )->value );
    return 0;
}
```

Compiling with -Os will produce the non-recursive code, shown in Listing 16-7.

Listing 16-7. `tail_rec_example_list.asm`

`0000000000400596 <llist_at>:`

```
400596:     48 89 f8                mov     rax,rdi
400599:     48 85 f6                test    rsi,rsi
40059c:     74 0d                   je      4005ab <llist_at+0x15>
40059e:     48 85 c0                test    rax,rax
4005a1:     74 08                   je      4005ab <llist_at+0x15>
4005a3:     48 ff ce                dec     rsi
4005a6:     48 8b 00                mov     rax,QWORD PTR [rax]
4005a9:     eb ee                   jmp     400599 <llist_at+0x3>
4005ab:     c3                      ret
```

How do we use it? Never be afraid to use tail recursion if it makes the code more readable for it brings no performance penalty.

16.1.5   Common Subexpressions Elimination

Related GCC options: `-fgcse` and others containing `cse` substring.

Computing two expressions with a common part does not result in computing this part twice. It means that it makes no sense performance-wise to compute this part ahead, store its result in a variable, and use it in two expressions.

In an example shown in Listing 16-8 a subexpression $x^2 + 2x$ is computed once, while the naive approach suggests otherwise.

Listing 16-8. `common_subexpression.c`

```
#include <stdio.h>

__attribute__ ((noinline))
    void test(int x) {
        printf("%d %d",
                x*x + 2*x + 1,
                x*x + 2*x - 1 );
    }

int main(int argc, char** argv) {
    test( argc );
    return 0;
}
```

As a proof, Listing 16-9 shows the compiled code, which does not compute $x^2 + 2x$ twice.

Listing 16-9. `common_subexpression.asm`

```
0000000000400516 <test>:
; rsi = x + 2
400516:        8d 77 02              lea        esi,[rdi+0x2]
400519:        31 c0                 xor        eax,eax
40051b:        0f af f7              imul       esi,edi
; rsi = x*(x+2)
40051e:        bf b4 05 40 00        mov        edi,0x4005b4
; rdx = rsi-1 = x*(x+2) - 1
400523:        8d 56 ff              lea        edx,[rsi-0x1]
; rsi = rsi + 1 = x*(x+2) - 1
400526:        ff c6                 inc        esi
400528:        e9 b3 fe ff ff        jmp        4003e0 <printf@plt>
```

How do we use *it?* Do not be afraid to write beautiful formulae with same common subexpressions: they will be computed efficiently. Favor code readability.

16.1.6   Constant Propagation

Related GCC options: `-fipa-cp`, `-fgcse`, `-fipa-cp-clone`, etc.

If compiler can prove that a variable has a specific value in a certain place of the program, it can omit reading its value and put it there directly.

Sometimes it even generates specialized function versions, partially applied to some arguments, if it knows an exact argument value (option `-fipa-cp-clone`). For example, Listing 16-10 shows the typical case when a specialized function version will be created for sum, which has only one argument instead of two, and the other argument's value is fixed and equal to 42.

Listing 16-10. `constant_propagation.c`

```
__attribute__ ((noinline))
static int sum(int x, int y) { return x + y; }

int main( int argc, char** argv ) {
    return sum( 42, argc );
}
```

Listing 16-11 shows the translated assembly code.

Listing 16-11. constant_propagation.asm

```
00000000004004c0 <sum.constprop.0>:
4004c0:      8d 47 2a                        lea      eax,[rdi+0x2a]
4004c3:      c3                              ret
```

It gets better when the compiler computes complex expressions for you (including function calls). Listing 16-2 shows an example.

Listing 16-12. cp_fact.c

```
#include <stdio.h>

int fact( int n ) {
    if (n == 0) return 1;
    else return n * fact( n-1 );
}

int main(void) {
    printf("%d\n", fact( 4 ) );
    return 0;
}
```

Obviously, the factorial function will always compute the same result, because this value does not depend on user input. GCC is smart enough to precompute this value erasing the call and substituting the fact(4) value directly with 24, as shown in Listing 16-13. The instruction mov edx, 0x18 places $24_{10} = 18_{16}$ directly into rdx.

Listing 16-13. cp_fact.asm

```
0000000000400450 <main>:
400450:   48 83 ec 08                      sub      rsp,0x8
400454:   ba 18 00 00 00                   mov      edx,0x18
400459:   be 44 07 40 00                   mov      esi,0x400744
40045e:   bf 01 00 00 00                   mov      edi,0x1
400463:   31 c0                            xor      eax,eax
400465:   e8 c6 ff ff ff                   call     400430 <__printf_chk@plt>
40046a:   31 c0                            xor      eax,eax
40046c:   48 83 c4 08                      add      rsp,0x8
400470:   c3                              ret
```

How do we use it? Named constants are not harmful, nor are constant variables. A compiler can and will precompute as much as it is able to, including functions without side effects launched on known arguments.

Multiple function copies for each distinct argument value can be bad for locality and will make the executable size grow. Take that into account if you face performance issues.

16.1.7   (Named) Return Value Optimization

Copy elision and return value optimization allow us to eliminate unnecessary copy operations.

Recall that naively speaking, local variables are created inside the function stack frame. So, if a function returns an instance of a structural type, it should first create it in its own stack frame and then copy it to the outside world (unless it fits into two general purpose registers rax and rdx).

Listing 16-14 shows an example.

Listing 16-14. nrvo.c

```
struct p  {
    long x;
    long y;
    long z;
};

__attribute__ ((noinline))
    struct p f(void) {
        struct p copy;
        copy.x = 1;
        copy.y = 2;
        copy.z = 3;
        return copy;
    }

int main(int argc, char** argv) {
    volatile struct p inst = f();
    return 0;
}
```

An instance of struct p called copy is created in the stack frame of f. Its fields are populated with values 1, 2, and 3, and then it is copied to the outside world, presumably by the pointer accepted by f as a hidden argument.

Listing 16-15 shows the resulting assembly code.

Listing 16-15. nrvo_off.asm

```
00000000004004b6 <f>:
; prologue
4004b6:   55                              push    rbp
4004b7:   48 89 e5                        mov     rbp,rsp
; A hidden argument is the address of a structure which will hold the  result.
; It is saved into stack.
4004ba:   48 89 7d d8                     mov     QWORD PTR [rbp-0x28],rdi
; Filling the fields of `copy` local variable
4004be:   48 c7 45 e0 01 00 00            mov     QWORD PTR [rbp-0x20],0x1
4004c5:   00
4004c6:   48 c7 45 e8 02 00 00            mov     QWORD PTR [rbp-0x18],0x2
4004cd:   00
4004ce:   48 c7 45 f0 03 00 00            mov     QWORD PTR [rbp-0x10],0x3
4004d5:   00
; rax = address of the destination struct
```

```
4004d6:    48 8b 45 d8                mov      rax,QWORD PTR [rbp-0x28]
; [rax] = 1 (taken from `copy.x`)
4004da:    48 8b 55 e0                mov      rdx,QWORD PTR [rbp-0x20]
4004de:    48 89 10                   mov      QWORD PTR [rax],rdx
; [rax + 8] = 2 (taken from `copy.y`)
4004da:    48 8b 55 e0                mov      rdx,QWORD PTR [rbp-0x20]
4004e1:    48 8b 55 e8                mov      rdx,QWORD PTR [rbp-0x18]
4004e5:    48 89 50 08                mov      QWORD PTR [rax+0x8],rdx
; [rax + 10] = 3 (taken from `copy.z`)
4004e9:    48 8b 55 f0                mov      rdx,QWORD PTR [rbp-0x10]
4004ed:    48 89 50 10                mov      QWORD PTR [rax+0x10],rdx
; rax =  address where we have put the structure contents
; (it was the hidden argument)
4004f1:    48 8b 45 d8                mov      rax,QWORD PTR [rbp-0x28]
4004f5:    5d                         pop      rbp
4004f6:    c3                         ret

00000000004004f7 <main>:
4004f7:    55                         push     rbp
4004f8:    48 89 e5                   mov      rbp,rsp
4004fb:    48 83 ec 30                sub      rsp,0x30
4004ff:    89 7d dc                   mov      DWORD PTR [rbp-0x24],edi
400502:    48 89 75 d0                mov      QWORD PTR [rbp-0x30],rsi
400506:    48 8d 45 e0                lea      rax,[rbp-0x20]
40050a:    48 89 c7                   mov      rdi,rax
40050d:    e8 a4 ff ff ff             call     4004b6 <f>
400512:    b8 00 00 00 00             mov      eax,0x0
400517:    c9                         leave
400518:    c3                         ret
400519:    0f 1f 80 00 00 00 00       nop      DWORD PTR [rax+0x0]
```

The compiler can produce a more efficient code as shown in Listing 16-16.

Listing 16-16. nrvo_on.asm

```
00000000004004b6 <f>:
4004b6:    48 89 f8                   mov      rax,rdi
4004b9:    48 c7 07 01 00 00 00       mov      QWORD PTR [rdi],0x1
4004c0:    48 c7 47 08 02 00 00       mov      QWORD PTR [rdi+0x8],0x2
4004c7:    00
4004c8:    48 c7 47 10 03 00 00       mov QWORD PTR [rdi+0x10],0x3
4004cf:    00
4004d0:    c3                         ret

00000000004004d1 <main>:
4004d1:    48 83 ec 20                sub      rsp,0x20
4004d5:    48 89 e7                   mov      rdi,rsp
4004d8:    e8 d9 ff ff ff             call     4004b6 <f>
4004dd:    b8 00 00 00 00             mov      eax,0x0
4004e2:    48 83 c4 20                add      rsp,0x20
4004e6:    c3                         ret
4004e7:    66 0f 1f 84 00 00 00       nop      WORD PTR [rax+rax*1+0x0]
4004ee:    00 00
```

We do not allocate a place in the stack frame for copy at all! Instead, we are operating directly on the structure passed to us through a hidden argument.

How do we use it? If you want to write a function that fills a certain structure, it is usually not beneficial to pass it a pointer to a preallocated memory area directly (or allocate it via malloc usage, which is also slower).

16.1.8   Influence of Branch Prediction

On the microcode level the actions performed by the CPU (central processing unit) are even more primitive than the machine instructions; they are also reordered to better use all CPU resources.

Branch prediction is a hardware mechanism that is aimed at improving program execution speed. When the CPU sees a conditional branch instruction (such as jg), it can

- Start executing both branches simultaneously; or

- Guess which branch will be executed and start executing it.

It happens when the computation result (e.g., the GF flag value in jg [rax]) on which this jump destination depends is not yet ready, so we start executing code speculatively to avoid wasting time.

The branch prediction unit can fail by issuing a **misprediction**. In this case, once the computation is completed, the CPU will do an additional work of reverting the changes made by instructions from the wrong branch. It is slow and has a real impact on program performance, but mispredictions are relatively rare.

The exact branch prediction logic depends on the CPU model. In general, two types of prediction exist [6]: **static** and **dynamic.**

- If the CPU has no information about a jump (when it is executed for the first time), a static algorithm is used. A possible simple algorithm is as follows:

  - If this is a forward jump, we assume that it happens.

  - If it is a backward jump, we assume that it does not happen.

  It makes sense because the jumps used to implement loops are more likely to happen than not.

- If a jump has already happened in the past, the CPU can use more complex algorithms. For example, we can use a ring buffer, which stores information about whether the jump occurred or not. In other words, it stores the history of jumps. When this approach is used, small loops of length dividing the buffer length are good for prediction.

The best source of relevant information with regard to the exact CPU model can be found in [16]. Unfortunately, most information about the CPU innards is not disclosed to public.

How do we use it? When using if-then-else or switch start with the most likely cases. You can also use special hints such as __builtin_expect GCC directives, which are implemented as special instruction prefixes for jump instructions (see [6]).

16.1.9   Influence of Execution Units

A CPU consists of many parts. Each instruction is executed in multiple stages, and at each stage different parts of the CPU are handling it. For example, the first stage is usually called instruction fetch and consists of loading instruction from memory[1] without thinking about its semantics at all.

---

[1]We omit the talk about instruction cache for brevity.

A part of the CPU that performs the operations and calculations is called the **execution unit**. It is implementing different kinds of operations that the CPU wants to handle: instruction fetching, arithmetic, address translation, instruction decoding, etc. In fact, CPUs can use it in a more or less independent way. Different instructions are executed in a different number of stages, and each of these stages can be performed by a different execution unit. It allows for interesting circuitry usages such as the following:

- Fetching one instruction immediately after the other was fetched (but has not completed its execution).

- Performing multiple arithmetic actions simultaneously despite their being described sequentially in assembly code.

CPUs of the Pentium IV family were already capable of executing four arithmetic instructions simultaneously in the right circumstances.

How do we use the knowledge about execution unit's existence? Let us look at the example shown in Listing 16-17.

Listing 16-17. cycle_nonpar_arith.asm

```
looper:
    mov     rax,[rsi]

    ; The next instruction depends on the previous one.
    ; It means that we can not swap them because
    ; the program behavior will change.
    xor     rax, 0x1

    ; One more dependency here
    add     [rdi],rax
    add     rsi,8
    add     rdi,8
    dec     rcx
    jnz     looper
```

Can we make it faster? We see the dependencies between instructions, which hinder the CPU microcode optimizer. What we are going to do is to unroll the loop so that two iterations of the old loop become one iteration of the new one. Listing 16-18 shows the result.

Listing 16-18. cycle_par_arith.asm

```
looper:
    mov     rax, [rsi]
    mov     rdx, [rsi + 8]
    xor     rax, 0x1
    xor     rdx, 0x1
    add     [rdi], rax
    add     [rdi+8], rdx
    add     rsi, 16

    add     rdi, 16
    sub     rcx, 2
    jnz     looper
```

Now the dependencies are gone, the instructions of two iterations are now mixed. They will be executed faster in this order because it enhances the simultaneous usage of different CPU execution units. Dependent instructions should be placed away from each other to allow other instructions to perform in between.

■ **Question 333** What is the instruction pipeline and superscalar architecture?

We cannot tell you which execution units are in your CPU, because this is highly model dependent. We have to read the optimization manuals for a specific CPU, such as [16]. Additional sources are often helpful; for example, the Haswell processors are well explained in [17].

16.1.10   Grouping Reads and Writes in Code

Hardware operates better with sequences of reads and writes which are not interleaved. For this reason, the code shown in Listing 16-19 is usually slower than its counterpart shown in Listing 16-20. The latter has sequences of sequential reads and writes grouped rather than interleaved.

Listing 16-19. `rwgroup_bad.asm`

```
mov rax,[rsi]
mov [rdi],rax
mov rax,[rsi+8]
mov [edi+4],eax
mov rax,[rsi+16]
mov [rdi+16],rax
mov rax,[esi+24]
mov [rdi+24],eax
```

Listing 16-20. `rwgroup_good.asm`

```
mov rax, [rsi]
mov rbx, [rsi+8]
mov rcx, [rsi+16]
mov rdx, [rsi+24]
mov [rdi], rax
mov [rdi+8], rbx
mov [rdi+16], rcx
mov [rdi+24], rdx
```

16.2   Caching

16.2.1   How Do We use Cache Effectively?

Caching is one of the most important mechanisms of performance boosting. We spoke about the general concepts of caching in Chapter 4. This section will further investigate how to use these concepts effectively.

We want to start by elaborating that contrary to the spirit of von Neumann architecture, the common CPUs have been using separate caches for instructions and data for at least 25 years. Instructions and code inhabit virtually always different memory regions, which explains why separate caches are more effective. We are interested in data cache.

By default, all memory operations involve cache, excluding the pages marked with cache-write-through and cache-disable bits (see Chapter 4).

Cache contains small chunks of memory of 64 bytes called **cache-lines, aligned** on a 64-byte boundary.

Cache memory is different from the main memory on a circuit level. Each cache-line is identified by a **tag**—an address of the respective memory chunk. Using special circuitry it is possible to retrieve the cache line by its address very fast (but only for small caches, like 4MB per processor, otherwise it is too expensive).

When trying to read a value from memory, the CPU will try to read it from the cache first. If it is missing, the relevant memory chunk will be loaded into cache. This situation is called **cache-miss** and often makes a *huge* impact on program performance.

There are usually several levels of cache; each of them is bigger and slower.

The **LL-cache** is the last level of cache closest to main memory.

For programs with good locality, caching works well. However, when the locality is broken for a piece of code, bypassing cache makes sense. For example, writing values into a large chunk of memory which will not be accessed any time soon is better performed without using cache.

The CPU tries to predict what memory addresses will be accessed in the near future and preloads the relevant memory parts into cache. It favors sequential memory accesses.

This gives us two important empirical rules needed to use caches efficiently.

- Try to ensure locality.

- Favor sequential memory access (and design data structures with this point in mind).

16.2.2   Prefetching

It is possible to issue a special hint to the CPU to indicate that a certain memory area will be accessed soon. In Intel 64 it is done using a prefetch instruction. It accepts an address in memory; the CPU will do its best to preload it into cache in the near future. This is used to prevent cache misses.

Using prefetch can be effective enough, but it should be coupled with testing. It should be executed before the data accesses themselves, but not too close. The cache preloading is being executed asynchronously, which means that it is a running at the same time when the following instructions are being executed. If prefetch is too close to data accesses, the CPU will not have enough time to preload data in cache and cache-miss will occur anyway.

Moreover, it is very important to understand that "close" and "far" from the data access mean the instruction position in the execution trace. We should not necessarily place prefetch close with regard to the program structure (in the same function), but we have to choose a place that precedes data access. It can be located in an entirely different module, for example, in the logging module, which just *happens to usually be executed before the data access*. This is of course very bad for code readability, introduces non-obvious dependencies between modules, and is a "last resort" kind of technique.

To use prefetch in C, we can use one of GCC built-ins:

```
Void __builtin_prefetch (const void *addr, ...)
```

It will be replaced with an architecture-specific prefetching instruction.

Besides address, it also accepts two parameters, which should be integer constants.

1. Will we read from that address (0, default) or write (1)?

2. How strong is locality? Three for maximal locality to zero for minimal. Zero indicates that the value can be cleared from cache after usage, 3 means that all levels of caches should continue to hold it.

Prefetching is performed by the CPU itself *if* it can predict where the next memory access is likely to be. While it works well for continuous memory accesses, such as traversing arrays, it starts being ineffective as soon as the memory access pattern starts seeming random for the predictor.

16.2.3   Example: Binary Search with Prefetching

Let us study an example shown in Listing 16-21.

Listing 16-21. prefetch_binsearch.c

```c
#include <time.h>
#include <stdio.h>
#include <stdlib.h>

#define SIZE 1024*512*16

int binarySearch(int *array, size_t number_of_elements, int key) {
    size_t low = 0, high = number_of_elements-1, mid;
    while(low <= high) {
        mid = (low + high)/2;
#ifdef DO_PREFETCH
        // low path
        __builtin_prefetch (&array[(mid + 1 + high)/2], 0, 1);
        // high path
        __builtin_prefetch (&array[(low + mid - 1)/2], 0, 1);
#endif

        if(array[mid] < key)
            low = mid + 1;
        else if(array[mid] == key)
            return mid;
        else if(array[mid] > key)
            high = mid-1;
    }
    return -1;
}

int main() {
    size_t i = 0;
    int NUM_LOOKUPS = SIZE;
    int *array;
    int *lookups;

    srand(time(NULL));
    array =  malloc(SIZE*sizeof(int));

    lookups = malloc(NUM_LOOKUPS * sizeof(int));

    for (i=0;i<SIZE;i++) array[i] = i;
    for (i=0;i<NUM_LOOKUPS;i++) lookups[i] = rand() % SIZE;

    for (i=0;i<NUM_LOOKUPS;i++)
        binarySearch(array, SIZE, lookups[i]);
    free(array);
    free(lookups);
}
```

The memory access pattern of the binary search is hard to predict. It is highly nonsequential, jumping from the start to the end, then to the middle, then to the fourth, etc. Let us see the difference in execution times.

Listing 16-22 shows the results of execution with prefetch off.

Listing 16-22. binsearch_prefetch_off

```
> gcc -O3 prefetch.c -o prefetch_off && /usr/bin/time -v ./prefetch_off

    Command being timed: "./prefetch_off"
    User time (seconds): 7.56
    System time (seconds): 0.02
    Percent of CPU  this job got: 100%
    Elapsed (wall clock) time (h:mm:ss or m:ss): 0:07.58
    Average shared text size (kbytes): 0
    Average unshared data size (kbytes): 0
    Average stack size (kbytes): 0
    Average total size (kbytes): 0
    Maximum resident set size (kbytes): 66432
    Average resident set size (kbytes): 0
    Major (requiring I/O) page faults: 0
    Minor (reclaiming a frame) page faults: 16444
    Voluntary context switches: 1
    Involuntary context switches: 51
    Swaps: 0
    File system inputs: 0
    File system outputs: 0
    Socket messages sent: 0
    Socket messages received: 0
    Signals delivered: 0
    Page size (bytes): 4096
    Exit status: 0
```

Listing 16-23 shows the results of execution with prefetch on.

Listing 16-23. binsearch_prefetch_on

```
> gcc -O3 prefetch.c -o prefetch_off && /usr/bin/time -v ./prefetch_off

    Command being timed: "./prefetch_on"
    User time  (seconds):  6.56
    System time (seconds): 0.01
    Percent of CPU  this job got: 100%
    Elapsed (wall clock) time (h:mm:ss or m:ss): 0:06.57
    Average shared text size (kbytes): 0
    Average unshared data size (kbytes): 0
    Average stack size (kbytes): 0
    Average total size (kbytes): 0
    Maximum resident set size (kbytes): 66512
    Average resident set size (kbytes): 0
    Major (requiring I/O) page faults: 0
    Minor (reclaiming a frame) page faults: 16443
    Voluntary context switches: 1
```

```
Involuntary context switches: 42
Swaps: 0
File system inputs: 0
File system outputs: 0
Socket messages sent: 0
Socket messages received: 0
Signals  delivered: 0
Page size (bytes): 4096
Exit status: 0
```

Using valgrind utility with cachegrind module we can check the amount of cache misses. Listing 16-24 shows the results for no prefetch, while Listing 16-25 shows the results with prefetching.

I corresponds to instruction cache, D to the data cache, LL – **Last Level Cache**). There are almost 100% data cache misses, which is very bad.

Listing 16-24. binsearch_prefetch_off_cachegrind

```
==25479== Cachegrind, a cache and branch-prediction profiler
==25479== Copyright (C) 2002-2015, and GNU GPL'd, by Nicholas Nethercote et al.
==25479== Using Valgrind-3.11.0 and LibVEX; rerun with -h for copyright info
==25479== Command: ./prefetch_off
==25479==
--25479-- warning: L3 cache found, using its data for the LL simulation.
==25479==
==25479== I   refs:       2,529,064,580
==25479== I1  misses:             778
==25479== LLi misses:             774
==25479== I1  miss rate:         0.00%
==25479== LLi miss rate:         0.00%
==25479==
==25479== D   refs:         404,809,999  (335,588,367 rd  + 69,221,632 wr)
==25479== D1  misses:       160,885,105  (159,835,971 rd  +  1,049,134 wr)
==25479== LLd misses:       133,467,980  (132,418,879 rd  +  1,049,101 wr)
==25479== D1  miss rate:          39.7% (      47.6%     +       1.5%  )
==25479== LLd miss rate:          33.0% (      39.5%     +       1.5%  )
==25479==
==25479== LL refs:          160,885,883  (159,836,749 rd  +  1,049,134 wr)
==25479== LL misses:        133,468,754  (132,419,653 rd  +  1,049,101 wr)
==25479== LL miss rate:           4.5% (       4.6%     +       1.5%  )
```

Listing 16-25. binsearch_prefetch_on_cachegrind

```
==26238== Cachegrind, a cache and branch-prediction profiler
==26238== Copyright (C) 2002-2015, and GNU GPL'd, by Nicholas Nethercote et al.
==26238== Using Valgrind-3.11.0 and LibVEX; rerun with -h for copyright info
==26238== Command: ./prefetch_on
==26238==
--26238-- warning: L3 cache found, using its data for the LL simulation.
==26238==
==26238== I   refs:       3,686,688,760
```

```
==26238== I1  misses:              777
==26238== LLi misses:              773
==26238== I1  miss rate:         0.00%
==26238== LLi miss rate:         0.00%
==26238==
==26238== D   refs:        404,810,009  (335,588,374  rd  + 69,221,635 wr)
==26238== D1  misses:      160,887,823  (159,838,690  rd  +  1,049,133 wr)
==26238== LLd misses:      133,488,742  (132,439,642  rd  +  1,049,100 wr)
==26238== D1  miss  rate:        39.7%  (      47.6%      +       1.5%  )
==26238== LLd miss rate:         33.0%  (      39.5%      +       1.5%  )
==26238==
==26238== LL refs:         160,888,600  (159,839,467  rd  +  1,049,133 wr)
==26238== LL misses:       133,489,515  (132,440,415  rd  +  1,049,100 wr)
==26238== LL miss rate:           3.3%  (       3.3%      +       1.5%  )
```

As we see, the amount of cache misses has drastically decreased.

16.2.4 Bypassing Cache

There exists a way to write into memory bypassing cache, which works even in user mode, so in order to use it we should not have access to the page table entries, holding CWT bit. In Intel 64 an instruction `movntps` allows us to do it. The operating system itself usually sets the bit CWT (cache-write-through) in page tables when memory-mapped IO is happening (when virtual memory acts as an interface for external devices). In this case, any memory read or write would lead to cache invalidation, which only hinders performance without giving any benefits.

GCC has intrinsic functions that are translated into machine-specific instructions that perform memory operations without involving cache. Listing 16-26 shows them.

Listing 16-26. `cache_bypass_intrinsics.c`

```c
#include <emmintrin.h>
void _mm_stream_si32(int *p, int a);
void _mm_stream_si128(int *p, __m128i a);
void _mm_stream_pd(double *p, __m128d a);

#include <xmmintrin.h>
void _mm_stream_pi(__m64 *p, __m64 a);
void _mm_stream_ps(float *p, __m128 a);

#include <ammintrin.h>
void _mm_stream_sd(double *p, __m128d a);
void _mm_stream_ss(float *p, __m128 a);
```

Bypassing cache is useful if we are sure that we will not touch the related memory area for quite a long time. For further information refer to [12].

16.2.5   Example: Matrix Initialization

To illustrate a good memory access pattern, we are going to use a huge matrix with values 42. The matrix is stored row after row.

One program, shown in Listing 16-27, initializes each row; the other, shown in Listing 16-28, initializes each column. Which one will be faster?

Listing 16-27. matrix_init_linear.c

```
#include <stdio.h>
#include <malloc.h>
#define DIM (16*1024)

int main( int argc, char** argv ) {
    size_t i, j;
    int* mat = (int*)malloc( DIM * DIM * sizeof( int ) );
    for( i = 0; i < DIM; ++i )
        for( j = 0; j < DIM; ++j )
            mat[i*DIM+j] = 42;
    puts("TEST DONE");
    return 0;
}
```

Listing 16-28. matrix_init_ra.c

```
#include <stdio.h>
#include <malloc.h>
#define DIM (16*1024)

int main( int argc, char** argv ) {
    size_t i, j;
    int* mat = (int*)malloc( DIM * DIM * sizeof( int ) );
    for( i = 0; i < DIM; ++i )
        for( j = 0; j < DIM; ++j )
            mat[j*DIM+i] = 42;
    puts("TEST DONE");
    return 0;
}
```

We will use the time utility (not shell built-in) again to test the execution time.

```
> /usr/bin/time -v ./matrix_init_ra
    Command being timed: "./matrix_init_ra"
    User time (seconds): 2.40
    System time (seconds): 1.01
    Percent of CPU this job got: 86%
    Elapsed (wall clock) time (h:mm:ss or m:ss): 0:03.94
    Average shared text size (kbytes): 0
    Average unshared data size (kbytes): 0
    Average stack size (kbytes): 0
    Average total size (kbytes): 0
    Maximum resident set size (kbytes): 889808
```

```
   Average resident set size (kbytes): 0
   Major (requiring I/O) page faults: 2655
   Minor (reclaiming a frame) page faults: 275963
   Voluntary context switches: 2694
   Involuntary context switches: 548
   Swaps: 0
   File system inputs: 132368
   File system outputs: 0
   Socket messages sent: 0
   Socket messages received: 0
   Signals delivered: 0
   Page size (bytes): 4096
   Exit status: 0

> /usr/bin/time -v ./matrix_init_linear

   Command being timed: "./matrix_init_linear"
   User time (seconds): 0.12
   System time (seconds): 0.83
   Percent of CPU this job got: 92%
   Elapsed (wall clock) time (h:mm:ss or m:ss): 0:01.04
   Average shared text size (kbytes): 0
   Average unshared data size (kbytes): 0
   Average stack size (kbytes): 0
   Average total size (kbytes): 0
   Maximum resident set size (kbytes): 900280
   Average resident set size (kbytes): 0
   Major (requiring I/O) page faults: 4
    Minor (reclaiming a frame) page faults: 262222
   Voluntary context switches: 29
   Involuntary context switches: 449
   Swaps: 0
   File system inputs: 176
   File system outputs: 0
   Socket messages sent: 0
   Socket messages received: 0
   Signals  delivered: 0
   Page size (bytes): 4096
   Exit status: 0
```

The execution is so much slower because of cache misses, which can be checked using valgrind utility with cachegrind module as shown in in Listing 16-29.

Listing 16-29. cachegrind_matrix_bad

```
> valgrind --tool=cachegrind ./matrix_init_ra

==17022== Command: ./matrix_init_ra
==17022==
--17022-- warning: L3 cache found, using its data for the LL simulation.
==17022==
==17022== I   refs:      268,623,230
==17022== I1  misses:            809
```

347

```
==17022== LLi misses:             804
==17022== I1  miss rate:         0.00%
==17022== LLi miss rate:         0.00%
==17022==
==17022== D   refs:       67,163,682  (40,974 rd  + 67,122,708 wr)
==17022== D1  misses:     67,111,793  ( 2,384 rd  + 67,109,409 wr)
==17022== LLd misses:     67,111,408  ( 2,034 rd  + 67,109,374 wr)
==17022== D1  miss rate:       99.9%  (  5.8%    +      100.0%  )
==17022== LLd miss rate:       99.9%  (  5.0%    +      100.0%  )
==17022==
==17022== LL refs:        67,112,602  ( 3,193 rd  + 67,109,409 wr)
==17022== LL misses:      67,112,212  ( 2,838 rd  + 67,109,374 wr)
==17022== LL miss rate:        20.0%  (  0.0%    +      100.0%  )
```

As we see, accessing memory sequentially decreases cache misses radically:

```
==17023== Command: ./matrix_init_linear
==17023==
--17023-- warning: L3 cache found, using its data for the LL simulation.
==17023==
==17023== I   refs:      336,117,093
==17023== I1  misses:            813
==17023== LLi misses:            808
==17023== I1  miss rate:        0.00%
==17023== LLi miss rate:        0.00%
==17023==
==17023== D   refs:       67,163,675  (40,970 rd  + 67,122,705 wr)
==17023== D1  misses:     16,780,146  ( 2,384 rd  + 16,777,762 wr)
==17023== LLd misses:     16,779,760  ( 2,033 rd  + 16,777,727 wr)
==17023== D1  miss rate:       25.0%  (  5.8%    +       25.0%  )
==17023== LLd miss rate:       25.0%  (  5.0%    +       25.0%  )
==17023==
==17023== LL refs:        16,780,959  ( 3,197 rd  + 16,777,762 wr)
==17023== LL misses:      16,780,568  ( 2,841 rd  + 16,777,727 wr)
==17023== LL miss rate:         4.2%  (  0.0%    +       25.0%  )
```

■ **Question 334**   Take a look at the GCC man pages, section "Optimizations."

16.3   SIMD Instruction Class

The von Neumann computational model is sequential by its nature. It does not presume that some operations can be executed in parallel. However, in time it became apparent that executing actions in parallel is necessary to achieve better performance. It is possible when the computations are independent from one another. For example, in order to sum 1 million integers we can calculate the sum of the chunks of 100,000 numbers on ten processors and then sum up the results. It is a typical kind of task that is solved well by the **map-reduce** technique [5].

We can implement parallel execution in two ways.

- Parallel execution of several sequences of instructions. That is achievable by introducing additional processor cores. We will discuss the multithreaded programming that makes use of multiple cores in Chapter 17.

- Parallel execution of actions that are needed to complete a *single instruction*. In this case we can have instructions which invoke multiple independent computations spanning the different parts of processor circuits, which are exploitable in parallel. To implement such instructions, the CPU has to include several ALUs to have actual performance gains, but it does not need to be able to execute multiple instructions truly simultaneously. These instructions are called **SIMD** (Single Instruction, Multiple Data) instructions.

In this section we are going to overview the CPU extensions called **SSE (Streaming SIMD Extensions)** and its newer analogue **AVX (Advanced Vector Extensions).**

Contrary to SIMD instructions, most instructions we have studied yet are of the type SISD (Single Instruction, Single Data).

16.4   SSE and AVX Extensions

The SIMD instructions are the basis for the instruction set extensions SSE and AVX. Most of them are used to perform operations on multiple data pairs; for example, `mulps` can multiply four pairs of 32-bit floats at once. However, their single operand pair counterparts (such as `mulss`) are now a recommended way to perform all floating point arithmetic.

By default, GCC will generate SSE instructions to operate floating point numbers. They accept operands either in `xmm` registers or in memory.

▓ **Consistency**   We omit the description of the legacy floating point dedicated stack for brevity. However, we want to point out that all program parts should be translated using the same method of floating point arithmetic: either floating point stack or SSE instructions.

We will start with an example shown in Listing 16-30.

Listing 16-30. `simd_main.c`

```c
#include <stdlib.h>
#include <stdio.h>

void sse( float[static 4], float[static 4] );

int main() {
    float x[4] = {1.0f, 2.0f, 3.0f, 4.0f };
    float y[4] = {5.0f, 6.0f, 7.0f, 8.0f };

    sse( x, y );

    printf( "%f %f %f %f\n", x[0], x[1], x[2], x[3] );
    return 0;
}
```

In this example there is a function sse defined somewhere else, which accepts two arrays of floats. Each of them should be at least four elements wide. This function performs computations and modifies the first array.

We call the values **packed** if they fill an xmm register of consecutive memory cells of the same size. In Listing 16-30, float x[4] is four packed single precision float values.

We will define the function sse in the assembly file shown in Listing 16-31.

Listing 16-31. simd_asm.asm

```
section .text
global sse

; rdi = x, rsi = y

sse:
    movdqa xmm0, [rdi]
    mulps  xmm0, [rsi]
    addps  xmm0, [rsi]
    movdqa [rdi], xmm0
    ret
```

This file defines the function sse. It performs four SSE instructions:

- movdqa (**MOV**e **D**ouble **Q**word **A**ligned) copies 16 bytes from memory pointed by rdi into register xmm0. We have seen this instruction in section 14.1.1.

- mulps (**MUL**tiply **P**acked **S**ingle precision floating point values) multiplies the contents of xmm0 by four consecutive float values stored in memory at the address taken from rsi.

- addps (**ADD P**acked **S**ingled precision floating point) adds the contents of four consecutive float values stored in memory at the address taken from rsi again.

- movdqa copies xmm0 into the memory pointed by rdi.

In other words, four pair of floats are getting multiplied and then the second float of each pair is added to the first one.

The naming pattern is common: the action semantics (mov, add, mul...) with suffixes. The first suffix is either **P** (packed) or **S** (scalar, for single values). The second one is either **D** for double precision values (double in C) or **S** for single precision values (float in C).

We want to emphasize again that most SSE instructions accept only aligned memory operands.

In order to complete the assignment, you will need to study the documentation for the following instructions using the Intel Software Developer Manual [15]:

- movsd–Move Scalar Double-Precision Floating- Point Value.

- movdqa–Move Aligned Double Quad word.

- movdqu–Move Unaligned Double Quad word.

- mulps–Multiply Packed Single-Precision Floating Point Values.

- mulpd–Multiply Packed Double-Precision Floating Point Values.

- addps–Add Packed Single-Precision Floating Point Values.

- haddps–Packed Single-FP Horizontal Add.

- `shufps`–Shuffle Packed Single-Precision Floating Point Values.

- `unpcklps`–Unpack and Interleave High Packed Double-Precision Floating Point Values.

- `packswb`–Pack with Signed Saturation.

- `cvtdq2pd`–Convert Packed Dword Integers to Packed Double-Precision FP Values.

These instructions are part of the SSE extensions. Intel introduced a new extension called AVX, which has new registers `ymm0, ymm1, ... , ymm15`. They are 256 bits wide, their least significant 128 bits (lesser half) can be accessed as old `xmm` registers.

New instructions are mostly prefixed with v, for example `vbroadcastss`.

It is important to understand that if your CPU supports AVX instructions it does not mean that they are faster than SSE! Different processors of the same family do not differ by the instruction set but by the amount of circuitry. Cheaper processors are likely to have fewer ALUs.

Let us take `mulps` with ymm registers as an example. It is used to multiply 8 pairs of floats.

Better CPUs will have enough ALUs (arithmetic logic units) to multiply all eight pairs simultaneously. Cheaper CPUs will only have, say, four ALUs, and so will have to iterate on the microcode level twice, multiplying first four pairs, then last. The programmer will not notice that when using instruction, the semantic is the same, but performance-wise it will be noticeable. A single AVX version of `mulps` with ymm registers and eight pairs of floats can even be slower than two SSE versions of `mupls` with xmm registers with four pairs each!

16.4.1   Assignment: Sepia Filter

In this assignment, we will create a program to perform a sepia filter on an image. A sepia filter makes an image with vivid colors look like an old, aged photograph. Most graphical editors include a sepia filter.

The filter itself is not hard to code. It recalculates the red, green, and blue components of each pixel based on the old values of red, green, and blue. Mathematically, if we think about a pixel as a three-dimensional vector, the transformation is nothing but a multiplication of a vector by matrix.

Let the new pixel value be $(B\ G\ R)^T$ (where T superscript stands for transposition). B, G, and R stand for blue, green, and red levels. In vector form the transformation can be described as follows:

$$\begin{pmatrix} B \\ G \\ R \end{pmatrix} = \begin{pmatrix} b \\ g \\ r \end{pmatrix} \times \begin{pmatrix} c_{11} & c_{12} & c_{13} \\ c_{21} & c_{22} & c_{23} \\ c_{31} & c_{32} & c_{33} \end{pmatrix}$$

In scalar form, we can rewrite it as

$$B = bc_{11} + gc_{12} + rc_{13}$$
$$G = bc_{21} + gc_{22} + rc_{23}$$
$$R = bc_{31} + gc_{32} + rc_{33}$$

In the assignment given in section 13.10 we coded a program to rotate the image. If you thought out its architecture well, it will be easy to reuse most of its code.

We will have to use saturation arithmetic. It means, that all operations such as addition and multiplication are limited to a fixed range between a minimum and maximum value. Our typical machine arithmetic is modular: if the result is greater than the maximal value, we will come from the different side of the range. For example, for `unsigned char`: 200 + 100 = 300 mod 256 = 44. Saturation arithmetic implies that for the same range between 0 and 255 included 200 + 100 = 255 since it is the maximal value in range.

C does not implement such arithmetic, so we will have to check for overflows manually. SSE contains instructions that convert floating point values to single byte integers with saturation.

Performing the transformation in C is easy. It demands direct encoding of the matrix to vector multiplication and taking saturation into account. Listing 16-32 shows the code.

Listing 16-32. image_sepia_c_example.c

```
#include <inttypes.h>
struct pixel { uint8_t b, g, r; };

struct image {
    uint32_t width, height;
    struct pixel* array;
};

static unsigned char sat( uint64_t x) {
    if (x < 256) return x; return 255;
}
static void sepia_one( struct pixel* const pixel ) {
    static const float c[3][3] =  {
    { .393f, .769f, .189f },
    { .349f, .686f, .168f },
    { .272f, .543f, .131f } };
struct pixel const old = *pixel;

pixel->r = sat(
        old.r * c[0][0] + old.g * c[0][1] + old.b * c[0][2]
        );
pixel->g = sat(
        old.r * c[1][0] + old.g * c[1][1] + old.b  * c[1][2]
        );
pixel->b = sat(
        old.r * c[2][0] + old.g * c[2][1] + old.b * c[2][2]
        );
}

void sepia_c_inplace( struct image* img ) {
    uint32_t x,y;
    for( y = 0; y < img->height; y++ )
        for( x = 0; x < img->width; x++ )
            sepia_one( pixel_of( *img, x, y ) );
}
```

Note that using uint8_t or unsigned char is very important.

In this assignment you have to

- Implement in a separate file a routine to apply a filter to a big part of image (except for the last pixels maybe). It will operate on chunks of multiple pixels at a time using SSE instructions.

The last few pixels that did not fill the last chunk can be processed one by one using the C code provided in Listing 16-32.

- Make sure that both C and assembly versions produce similar results.

- Compile two programs; the first should use a naive C approach and the second one should use SSE instructions.

- Compare the time of execution of C and SSE using a huge image as an input (preferably hundreds of megabytes).

- Repeat the comparison multiple times and calculate the average values for SSE and C.

To make a noticeable difference, we have to have as many operations in parallel as we can. Each pixel consists of 3 bytes; after converting its components into floats it will occupy 12 bytes. Each xmm register is 16 bytes wide. If we want to be effective we will have use the last 4 bytes as well. To achieve that we use a frame of 48 bytes, which corresponds to three xmm registers, to 12-pixel components, and to 4 pixels.

Let the subscript denote the index of a pixel. The image then looks as follows:

$$b_1 g_1 r_1 b_2 g_2 r_2 b_3 g_3 r_3 b_4 g_4 r_4 \dots$$

We would like to compute the first four components. Three of them correspond to the first pixel, the fourth one corresponds to the second one.

To perform necessary transformations it is useful to first put the following values into the registers:

$$xmm_0 = b_1 b_1 b_1 b_2$$

$$xmm_1 = g_1 g_1 g_1 g_2$$

$$xmm_2 = r_1 r_1 r_1 r_2$$

We will store the matrix coefficients in either xmm registers or memory, but it is important to store the *columns*, not the rows.

To demonstrate the algorithm, we will use the following start values:

$$xmm_3 = c_{11} | c_{21} | c_{31} | c_{11}$$

$$xmm_4 = c_{12} | c_{22} | c_{32} | c_{12}$$

$$xmm_5 = c_{13} | c_{23} | c_{33} | c_{13}$$

We use mulps to multiply these packed values with xmm0...xmm2.

$$xmm_3 = b_1 c_{11} | b_1 c_{21} | b_1 c_{31} | b_2 c_{11}$$

$$xmm_4 = g_1 c_{12} | g_1 c_{22} | g_1 c_{32} | g_2 c_{12}$$

$$xmm_5 = r_1 c_{13} | r_1 c_{23} | r_1 c_{33} | r_2 c_{13}$$

The next step is to add them using addps instructions.

The similar actions should be performed with two other two 16-byte-wide parts of the frame, containing

$$g_2 r_2 b_3 g_3 \text{ and } r_3 b_4 g_4 r_4$$

This technique using transposed coefficients matrix allows us to cope without horizontal addition instructions such as haddps. It is described in detail in [19].

To measure time, use getrusage(RUSAGE_SELF, &r) (read man getrusage pages first). It fills a struct r of type struct rusage whose field r.ru_utime contains a field of type struct timeval. It contains, in turn, a pair of values for seconds spent and millise conds spent. By comparing these values before transformation and after it we can deduce the time spent on transformation.

Listing 16-33 shows an example of single time measurement.

Listing 16-33. execution_time.c

```c
#include <sys/time.h>
#include <sys/resource.h>
#include <stdio.h>
#include <unistd.h>
#include <stdint.h>

int main(void) {
    struct rusage r;
    struct timeval start;
    struct timeval end;

    getrusage(RUSAGE_SELF, &r );
    start = r.ru_utime;

    for( uint64_t i = 0; i < 100000000; i++ );

    getrusage(RUSAGE_SELF, &r );
    end = r.ru_utime;

    long res = ((end.tv_sec - start.tv_sec) * 1000000L) +
        end.tv_usec - start.tv_usec;

    printf( "Time elapsed in microseconds: %ld\n", res );
    return 0;
}
```

Use a table to perform a fast conversion from unsigned char into float.

```c
float const byte_to_float[] = {
    0.0f, 1.0f, 2.0f, ..., 255.0f };
```

■ **Question 335** Read about methods of calculating the confidence interval and calculate the 95% confidence interval for a reasonably high number of measurements.

16.5 Summary

In this chapter we have talked about the compiler optimizations and why they are needed. We have seen how far the translated optimized code can go from its initial version. Then we have studied how to get the most benefit from caching and how to parallelize floating point computations on the instruction level using SSE instructions. In the next chapter we will see how to parallelize instruction sequences execution, create multiple threads, and change our vision of memory in the presence of multithreading.

Question 336   What GCC options control the optimization options globally?

Question 337   What kinds of optimizations can potentially bring the most benefits?

Question 338   What kinds of benefits and disadvantages can omitting a frame pointer bring?

Question 339   How is a tail recursive function different from an ordinary recursive function?

Question 340   Can any recursive function be rewritten as a tail recursive without using additional data structures?

Question 341   What is a common subexpression elimination? How does it affect our code writing?

Question 342   What is constant propagation?

Question 343   Why should we mark functions `static` whenever we can to help the compiler optimizations?

Question 344   What benefits does named return value optimization bring?

Question 345   What is a branch prediction?

Question 346   What are Dynamic Branch Prediction, Global and Local History Tables?

Question 347   Check the notes on branch prediction for your CPU in [16].

Question 348   What is an execution unit and why do we care about them?

Question 349   How are AVX instruction speed and the amount of execution units related?

Question 350   What kinds of memory accessing patterns are good?

Question 351   Why do we have many cache levels?

Question 352   In which cases might `prefetch` bring performance gains and why?

Question 353   What are SSE instructions used for?

Question 354   Why do most SSE instructions require aligned operands?

Question 355   How do we copy data from general purpose registers to `xmm` registers?

Question 356   In which cases using SIMD instructions is worth it?

■ ■ ■

## CHAPTER 17

Multithreading

In this chapter we will explore the multithreading capabilities provided by the C language. Multithreading is a topic for a book on its own, so we will concentrate on the language features and relevant properties of the abstract machine rather than good practices and program architecture-related topics.

Until C11, the support of the multithreading was external to the language itself, via libraries and nonstandard tricks. A part of it (atomics) is now implemented in many compilers and provides a standard-compliant way of writing multithreaded applications. Unfortunately, to this day, the support of threading itself is not implemented in most toolchains, so we are going to use the library pthreads to write down code examples. We will still use the standard-compliant atomics.

This chapter is by no means an exhaustive guide to multithreaded programming, which is a beast worth writing a dedicated book about, but it will introduce the most important concepts and relevant language features. If you want to become proficient in it, we recommend lots of practice, specialized articles, books such as [34], and code reviews from your more experienced colleagues.

17.1 Processes and Threads

It is important to understand the difference between two key concepts involved in most talks about multithreading: threads and processes.

A **process** is a resource container that collects all kinds of runtime information and resources a program needs to be executed. A process contains the following:

- An address space, partially filled with executable code, data, shared libraries, other mapped files, etc. Parts of it can be shared with other processes.

- All other kinds of associated state such as open file descriptors, registers, etc.

- Information such as process ID, process group ID, user ID, group ID . . .

- Other resources used for interprocess communication: pipes, semaphores, message queues . . .

thread is a stream of instructions that can be scheduled for execution by the operating system.

The operating system does not schedule processes but threads. Each thread lives as a part of a process and has a piece of process state, which is its own.

- Registers.

- Stack (technically, it is defined by the stack pointer register; however, as all processor's threads share the same address space, one of them can access the stacks of other threads, although this is rarely a good idea).

© Igor Zhirkov 2017
I. Zhirkov, *Low-Level Programming*, DOI 10.1007/978-1-4842-2403-8_17

- Properties of importance to the scheduler such as priority.

- Pending and blocked signals.

- Signal mask.

When the process is closed, all associated resources are freed, including all its threads, open file descriptors, etc.

17.2 What Makes Multithreading Hard?

Multithreading allows you to make use of several processor cores (or several processors) to execute threads at the same time. For example, if one thread is reading file from a disk (which is a very slow operation), the other might use the pause to perform CPU-heavy computations, distributing CPU (central processing unit) load more uniformly in time. So, it can be faster, if your program can benefit from it.

Threads should often work on the same data. As long as the data is not modified by any of them, there are no problems working with it, because reading data has zero effect on other threads execution. However, if the shared data is being modified by one (or multiple) threads, we face several problems, such as the following:

- When does thread *A* see the changes performed by *B*?

- In which order do threads change the data? (As we have seen in the Chapter 16, the instructions can be reordered for optimization purposes.)

- How can we perform operations on the complex pieces of data without other threads interfering?

When these problems are not addressed properly, a very problematic sort of bug appears, which is hard to catch (because it only appears casually, when the instruction of the different threads are executed in a specific, unlucky order). We will try to establish an understanding and study these problems and how they can be solved.

17.3 Execution Order

When we started to study the C abstract machine, we got used to thinking that the sequence of C statements corresponds to the actions performed by the compiled machine instructions—naturally, in the same order. Now it is time to dive into the more pragmatic details of why it is not really the case.

We tend to describe algorithms in a way that is easier to understand, and this is almost always a good thing. However, the order given by the programmer is not always optimal performance-wise.

For example, the compiler might want to improve **locality** without changing the code semantics. Listing 17-1 shows an example.

Listing 17-1. `ex_locality_src.c`

```
char x[1000000], y[1000000];
...
x[4] = y[4];
x[10004] = y[10004];

x[5] = y[5];
x[10005] = y[10005];
```

Listing 17-2 shows a possible translation result.

Listing 17-2. ex_locality_asm1.asm

```
mov al,[rsi + 4]
mov [rdi+4],al

mov al,[rsi + 10004]
mov [rdi+10004],al

mov al,[rsi + 5]
mov [rdi+5],al

mov al,[rsi + 10005]
mov [rdi+10005],al
```

However, it is evident, that this code could be rewritten to ensure better locality; that is, first assign x[4] and x[5], then assign x[10004] and x[10005], as shown in Listing 17-3.

Listing 17-3. ex_locality_asm2.asm

```
mov al,[rsi + 4]
mov [rdi+4],al
mov al,[rsi + 5]
mov [rdi+5],al

mov al,[rsi + 10004]
mov [rdi+10004],al

mov al,[rsi + 10005]
mov [rdi+10005],al
```

The effects of these two instruction sequences are similar *if the abstract machine only considers one CPU*: given any initial machine state, the resulting state after their executions will be the same. The second translation result often performs faster, so the compiler might prefer it. This is the simple case of **memory reordering**, a situation in which the memory accesses are reordered comparing to the source code.

For single thread applications, which are executed "really sequentially," we can often expect the order of operations to be irrelevant as long as the observable behavior will be unchanged. This freedom ends as soon as we start communicating between threads.

Most inexperienced programmers do not think much about it because they limit themselves with single-threaded programming. In these days, we can no longer afford not to think about parallelism because of how pervasive it is and how it is often the only thing that can really boost the program performance. So, in this chapter, we are going to talk about memory reorderings and how to set them up correctly.

17.4   Strong and Weak Memory Models

Memory reorderings can be performed by the compiler (as shown above), or by the processor itself, in the microcode. Usually, both of them are being performed and we will be interested in both of them. A uniform classification can be created for them all.

A **memory model** tells us which kinds of reorderings of load and store instructions can be expected. We are not interested in the exact instructions used to access memory most of the time (mov, movq, etc.), only the fact of reading or writing to memory is of importance to us.

There are two extreme poles: weak and strong memory models. Just like with the strong and weak typing, most existing conventions fall somewhere between, closer to one or another. We have found a classification made by Jeff Preshing [31] to be useful and will stick to it in this book.

According to it, the memory models can be divided into four categories, enumerated from the more relaxed ones to the stronger ones.

1. Really weak.

   In these models, any kind of memory reordering can happen (as long as the observable behavior of a single-threaded program is unchanged, of course).

2. Weak with data dependency ordering (such as hardware memory model of ARM v7).

   Here we speak about one particular kind of data dependency: the one between loads. It occurs when we need to fetch an address from memory and then use it to perform another fetch, for example,

   ```
   Mov rdx, [rbx]
   mov rax, [rdx]
   ```

   In C this is the situation when we use the ➤ operator to get to a field of a certain structure through the pointer to that structure.

   Really weak memory models do not guarantee data dependency ordering.

3. Usually strong (such as hardware memory model of Intel 64).

   It means that there is a guarantee that all stores are performed in the same order as provided. Some loads, however, can be moved around.

   Intel 64 is usually falling into this category.

4. Sequentially consistent.

This can be described as what you see when you debug a non-optimized program step by step on a single processor core. No memory reordering ever happens.

17.5 Reordering Example

Listing 17-4 shows an exemplary situation when memory reordering can give us a bad day. Here two threads are executing the statements contained in functions thread1 and thread2, respectively.

Listing 17-4. mem_reorder_sample.c

```
int x = 0;
int y = 0;

void thread1(void) {
    x = 1;
    print(y);
}

void thread2(void) {
    y = 1;
    print(x);
}
```

Both threads share variables x and y. One of them performs a store into x and then loads the value of y, while the other one does the same, but with y and x instead.

We are interested in two types of memory accesses: load and store. In our examples, we will often omit all other actions for simplicity.

As these instructions are completely independent (they operate on different data), they can be reordered inside each thread without changing observable behavior, giving us four options: store + load or load + store for each of two threads. This is what a compiler can do for its own reasons. For each option *six* possible execution orders exist. They depict how both threads advance in time relative to one another.

We show them as sequences of 1 and 2; if the first thread made a step, we write 1; otherwise the second one made a step.

1. 1-1-2-2

2. 1-2-1-2

3. 2-1-1-2

4. 2-1-2-1

5. 2-2-1-1

6. 1-2-2-1

For example, 1-1-2-2 means that the first process has executed two steps, and then the second process did the same. Each sequence corresponds to four different scenarios. For example, the sequence 1-2-1-2 encodes one of the traces, shown in Table 17-1:

Table 17-1. *Possible Instruction Execution Sequences If Processes Take Turns as 1-2-1-2*

THREAD ID	TRACE 1	TRACE 2	TRACE 3	TRACE 4
1	store x	store x	load y	load y
2	store y	load x	store y	load x
1	load y	load y	store x	store x
2	load x	store y	load x	store y

If we observe these possible traces for each execution order, we will come up with *24* scenarios (some of which will be equivalent). As you see, even for the small examples these numbers can be large enough.

We do not need all these possible traces anyway; we are interested in the position of load relatively to store for each variable. Even in Table 17-1 many possible combinations are present: both x and y can be stored, then loaded, or loaded, then stored. Obviously, the result of load is dependent on whether there was a store before.

Were reorderings not in the game, we would be limited: any of the two specified loads should have been preceded by a store because so it is in the source code; scheduling instructions in a different manner cannot change that. However, as the reorderings are present, we can sometimes achieve an interesting outcome: if both of these threads have their instructions reordered, we come to a situation shown in Listing 17-5.

Listing 17-5. mem_reorder_sample_happened.c

```c
int x = 0;
int y = 0;

void thread1(void) {
    print(y);
    x = 1;
}
```

```
void thread2(void) {
    print(x);
    y = 1;
}
```

If the strategy 1-2-*-* (where * denotes any of the threads) is chosen, we execute load x and load y first, which will make them appear to equal to 0 for everyone who uses these loads' results

It is indeed possible in case *compiler* reordered these operations. But even if they are controlled well or disabled, the memory reorderings, performed by CPU, still can produce such an effect.

This example demonstrates that the outcome of such a program is highly unpredictable. Later we are going to study how to limit reorderings by the compiler and by CPU; we will also provide a code to demonstrate this reordering in the hardware.

17.6   What Is Volatile and What Is Not

The C memory model, which we are using, is quite weak. Consider the following code:

```
int x,y; x = 1;
y = 2;
x = 3;
```

As we have already seen, the instructions can be reordered by the compiler. Even more, the compiler can deduce that the first assignment is the dead code, because it is followed in another assignment to the same variable x. As it is useless, the compiler can even remove this statement.

The volatile keyword addresses this issue. It forces the compiler to never optimize the writes and reads to the said variable and also suppresses any possible instruction reorderings. However, it only enforces these restrictions to one single variable and gives no guarantee about the order in which writes to different volatile variables are emitted. For example, in the previous code, even changing both x and y type to volatile int will impose an order on assignments of each of them but will still allow us to interleave the writes freely as follows:

```
volatile int x, y;
x = 1;
x = 3;
y = 2;
```

Or like this:

```
volatile int x, y;
y = 2;
x = 1;
x = 3;
```

Obviously, these guarantees are not sufficient for multithreaded applications. You cannot use volatile variables to organize an access to the shared data, because these accesses can be moved around freely enough.

To safely access shared data, we need two guarantees.

- The read or write actually takes place. The compiler could have just cached the value in the register and never write it back to memory.

  This is the guarantee volatile provides. It is enough to perform memory-mapped I/O (input/output), but not for multithreaded applications.

- No memory reordering should take place. Let us imagine we use volatile variable as a flag, which indicates that some data is ready to be read. The code prepares data and then sets the flag; however, reordering can place this assignment before the data is prepared.

  Both hardware and compiler reorderings matter here. This guarantee is not provided by volatile variables.

In this chapter, we study two mechanisms that provide both of the following guarantees:

- Memory barriers.

- Atomic variables, introduced in C11.

Volatile variables are used extremely rarely. They suppress optimization, which is usually not something we want to do.

17.7   Memory Barriers

Memory barrier is a special instruction or statement that imposes constraints on how the reorderings can be done. As we have seen in the Chapter 16, compilers or hardware can use many tricks to improve performance in the average case, including reordering, deferred memory operations, speculative loads or branch prediction, caching variables in registers, etc. Controlling them is vital to ensure that certain operations are already performed, because the other thread's logic depends on it.

In this section, we want to introduce the different kinds of memory barriers and give us a general idea about their possible implementations on Intel 64.

An example of the memory barrier preventing reorderings *by compiler* is the following GCC directive:

```
asm volatile("" ::: "memory")
```

The asm directive is used to include inline assembly code directly into C programs. The volatile keyword together with the "memory" clobber argument describes that this (empty) piece of inline assembly cannot be optimized away or moved around and that it performs memory reads and/or writes. Because of that, the compiler is forced to emit the code to commit all operations to memory (e.g., store the values of the local variables, cached in registers). It does not prevent the processor from performing speculative reads past this statement, so it is *not* a memory barrier for the processor itself.

Obviously, both compiler and CPU memory barriers are *costly* because they prevent optimizations. That is why we do not want to use them after each instruction.

There are several kinds of memory barriers. We will speak about those that are defined in the Linux kernel documentation, but this classification is applicable in most situations.

1. Write memory barrier.

   It guarantees that all store operations specified in code before the barrier will appear to happen before all store operations specified after the barrier.

   GCC uses asm volatile(""::: "memory") as a general memory barrier. Intel 64 uses the instruction sfence.

2. Read memory barrier.

   Similarly, it guarantees that all load operations specified in code before the barrier will appear to happen before all load operations specified after the barrier. It is a stronger form of data dependency barrier.

   GCC uses `asm volatile("":::  "memory")` as a general memory barrier. Intel 64 uses the instruction `lfence`.

3. Data dependency barriers.

   Data dependency barrier considers the dependent reads, described in section 17.4. It can be thus considered a weaker form of read memory barrier. No guarantees about independent loads or any kinds of stores are provided.

4. General memory barriers

   This is the ultimate barrier, which forces every memory change specified in code before it is committed. It also prevents all following operations to be reordered in a way they appear to be executed before the barrier.

   GCC uses `asm volatile("":::  "memory")` as a general memory barrier. Intel 64 uses the instruction `mfence`.

5. Acquire operations.

   This is a class of operations, united by a property called **Acquire semantics**. If an operation performs *reads* from shared memory and is guaranteed to not be reordered with the *following reads and writes* in the source code, it is said to have this property.

   In other words, it is similar to a general memory barrier, but the code that follows will not be reordered in a way to be executed before this barrier.

6. Release operations.

   Release semantics is a property of such operations. If an operation performs *writes* to shared memory and is guaranteed to not be reordered with the *previous reads and writes* in the source code, it is said to have this property.

   In other words, it is similar to a general memory barrier but still *allows* the more recent operations to be reordered in a position before the release operation.

Acquire and release operations, thus, are one-way barriers for reorderings in a way. Following is an example of a single assembly command `mfence`, inlined by GCC:

```
asm ("mfence" )
```

By combining it with the compiler barrier, we get a line that both prevents compiler reordering and also acts as a full memory barrier.

```
asm volatile("mfence" :::  "memory")
```

Any function call *whose definition is not available in the current translation unit* and that is *not an intrinsic* (a cross-platform substitute of a specific assembly instruction) is a *compiler memory barrier*.

17.8   Introduction to pthreads

POSIX threads (pthreads) is a standard describing a certain model of program execution. It provides means to execute code in parallel and to control the execution. It is implemented as a library pthreads, which we are going to use throughout this chapter.

The library contains C types, constants, and procedures (which are prefixed with pthread_). Their declarations are available in the pthread.h header. The functions provided by it fall into one of the following groups:

- Basic thread management (creating, destroying).

- Mutex management.

- Condition variables.

- Synchronization using locks and barriers.

In this section we are going to study several examples to become familiar with pthreads. To perform multithreaded computations you have the following two options:

- Spawn multiple threads in the same process.

  The threads share the same address space, so the data exchange is relatively easy and fast. When the process terminates, so do all of its threads.

- Spawn multiple processes; each of them has its own default thread. These threads communicate via mechanisms provided by the operating system (such as pipes).

  This is not that fast; also spawning a process is slower than spawning just a thread, because it creates more operating system structures (and a separate address space). The communication between processes often implies one or more (sometimes implicit) copy operations.

  However, separating program logic into separate processes can have a positive impact on security and robustness, because each thread only sees the exposed part of the processes others than its own.

Pthreads allows you to spawn multiple threads in a single process, and that is what you usually want to do.

17.8.1   When to Use Multithreading

Sometimes multithreading is convenient for the program logic. For example, you usually should not accept a network packet and draw the graphical interface in the same thread. The graphical interface should react to user actions (clicks on the buttons) and be redrawn constantly (e.g., when the corresponding window gets covered by another window and then uncovered). The network action, however, will block the working thread until it is done. It is thus convenient to split these actions into different threads to perform them seemingly simultaneously.

Multithreading can naturally improve performance, but not in all cases. There are CPU bound tasks and IO bound tasks.

- CPU bound code can be sped up if given more CPU time. It spends most of the CPU time doing computations, not reading data from disk or communicating with devices.

- IO bound code cannot be sped up with more CPU time because it is slowed by its excessive usage of memory or external devices.

Using multithreading to speed CPU bound programs might be beneficial. A common pattern is to use a queue with the requests that are dispatched to the worker threads from a thread pool–a set of created threads that are either working or waiting for work but are not re-created each time there is a need of them. Refer to Chapter 7 of [23] for more details.

As for how many threads we need, there is no universal recipe. Creating threads, switching between them, and scheduling them produces an overhead. It might make the whole program slower if there is not much work for threads to do. In computation-heavy tasks some people advise to spawn $n - 1$ threads, where n is the total number of processor cores. In tasks that are sequential by their own nature (where every step depends directly on the previous one) spawning multiple threads will not help. What we do recommend is to *always* experiment with the number of threads under different workloads to find out which number suits the most for the given task.

17.8.2   Creating Threads

Creating threads is easy. Listing 17-6 shows an example.

Listing 17-6. pthread_create_mwe.c

```c
#include <pthread.h>
#include <stdio.h>
#include <unistd.h>

void* threadimpl( void* arg ) {
    for(int i = 0; i < 10; i++ ) {
        puts( arg );
        sleep(1);
    }
    return NULL;
}

int main( void ) { pthread_t t1, t2;
    pthread_create( &t1, NULL, threadimpl, "fizz" );
    pthread_create( &t2, NULL, threadimpl, "buzzzz" );
    pthread_exit( NULL );
    puts("bye");
    return 0;
}
```

Note that the code that uses pthread library must be compiled with -pthread flag, for example,

```
> gcc -O3 -pthread main.c
```

That specifying -lpthread will not give us an esteemed result. Linking with the sole libpthread.a is not enough: there are several preprocessor options that are enabled by -pthread (e.g., _REENTRANT). So, whenever the -pthread option is available,[1] use it.

---

[1]This option is documented as platform specific, so it might be unavailable on some platforms.

Initially, there is only one thread which starts executing the main function. A pthread_t type stores all information about some other thread, so that we can control it using this instance as a handle. Then, the threads are initialized with pthread_create function with the following signature:

```
int pthread_create(
    pthread_t *thread,
    const pthread_attr_t *attr,
    void *(*start_routine) (void *),
    void *arg);
```

The first argument is a pointer to the pthread_t instance to be initialized. The second one is a collection of attributes, which we will touch later–for now, it is safe to pass NULL instead.

The thread starting function should accept a pointer and return a pointer. It accepts a void* pointer to its argument. Only one argument is allowed; however, you can easily create a structure or an array, which encapsulates multiple arguments, and pass a pointer to it. The return value of the start_routine is also a pointer and can be used to return the work result of the thread.[2] The last argument is the actual pointer to the argument, which will be passed to the start_routine function.

In our example, each thread is implemented the same way: it accepts a pointer (to a string) and then repeatedly outputs it with an interval of approximately one second. The sleep function, declared in unistd.h, suspends the current thread for a given number of seconds.

After ten iterations, the thread returns. It is equivalent to calling the function pthread_exit with an argument. The return value is usually the result of the computations performed by the thread; return NULL if you do not need it. We will see later how it is possible to get this value from the parent thread.

■ **Casting to void**   Constructions such as (void)argc have only one purpose: suppress warnings about unused variable or argument argc. You can sometimes find them in the source code.

However, the naive return from the main function will lead to process termination. What if other threads still exist? The main thread should wait for their termination first! This is what pthread_exit does when it is called *in the main thread*: it waits for all other threads to terminate and then terminates the program. All the code that follows will not be executed, so you will not see the bye message in stdout.

This program will output a pair of buzz and fizz lines in random order ten times and then exit. It is impossible to predict whether the first or the second thread will be scheduled first, so each time the order can differ. Listing 17-7 shows an exemplary output.

Listing 17-7. pthread_create_mwe_out

```
> ./main
fizz
buzzzz
buzzzz
fizz
fizz
buzzzz
fizz
buzzzz
fizz
```

---

[2]Remember to not return the address of a local variable!

```
buzzzz
buzzzz
fizz
buzzzz
fizz
buzzzz
fizz
buzzzz
fizz
buzzzz
fizz
```

As you see, the string bye is not printed, because the corresponding puts call is below the pthread_exit call.

■ **Where are the arguments located?**   It is important to note that the pointer to an argument, passed to a thread, should point to the data that stays alive until the said thread is shut down. Passing a pointer to stack allocated variable might be risky, since after the stack frame for the function is destroyed, accessing these deallocated variables yields undefined behavior.

Unless the arguments are guaranteed to be constant (or you intend to use them for synchronization purposes), do not pass them to different threads.

In the example shown in Listing 17-6, the strings that are accepted by threadimpl are allocated in the global read-only memory (**.rodata**). Thus passing a pointer to it is safe.

The maximum number of threads spawned depends on implementation. In Linux, for example, you can use ulimit -a to get relevant information.

The threads can create other threads; there is no limitation on that.

It is indeed guaranteed by the pthreads implementation that a call for pthread_create acts as a full compiler memory barrier as well as a full hardware memory barrier.

pthread_attr_init is used to initialize an instance of an opaque type pthread_attr_t (implemented as an **incomplete type**). Attributes provide additional parameters for threads such as stack size or address. The following functions are used to set attributes:

- pthread_attr_setaffinity_np–the thread will prefer to be executed on a specific CPU core.

- pthread_attr_setdetachstate–will we be able to call pthread_join on this thread, or will it be detached (as opposed to joinable). The purpose of pthread_join will be explained in the next section.

- pthread_attr_setguardsize–sets up the space before the stack limit as a region of forbidden addresses of a given size to catch stack overflows.

- pthread_attr_setinheritsched–are the following two parameters inherited from the parent thread (the one where the creation happened), or taken from the attributes themselves?

- pthread_attr_setschedparam–right now is all about scheduling priority, but the additional parameters can be added in the future.

- pthread_attr_setschedpolicy–how will the scheduling be performed. Scheduling policies with their respective descriptions can be seen in man sched.

- pthread_attr_setscope–refers to the contention scope system, which defines a set of threads against which this thread will compete for CPU (or other resources).

- pthread_attr_setstackaddr–where will the stack be located?

- pthread_attr_setstacksize–what will be the thread stack size?

- pthread_attr_setstack–sets both stack address and stack size.

All of them have their "get" counterparts (e.g., pthread_attr_getscope).

Question 357 Read man pages for the functions listed earlier.

Question 358 What will sysconf(_SC_NPROCESSORS_ONLN) return?

17.8.3 Managing Threads

What we have learned is already enough to perform work in parallel. However, we have no means of synchronization yet, so once we have distributed the work for the threads, we cannot really use the computation results of one thread in other threads.

The simplest form of synchronization is thread joining. The idea is simple: by calling thread_join on an instance of pthread_t we put the current thread into the waiting state until the other thread is terminated. Listing 17-8 shows an example.

Listing 17-8. thread_join_mwe.c

```c
#include <pthread.h>
#include <unistd.h>
#include <stdio.h>

void* worker( void* param ) {
    for( int i = 0; i < 3; i++ ) {
        puts( (const char*) param );
        sleep(1);
    }
    return (void*)"done";
}

int main( void ) {

    pthread_t t;
    void* result;

    pthread_create( &t, NULL, worker, (void*) "I am a worker!" );
    pthread_join( t, &result );
    puts( (const char*) result );
    return 0;
}
```

The thread_join accepts two arguments: the thread itself and the address of a void* variable, which will be initialized with the thread execution result.

Thread joining acts as a full barrier because we should not place before the joining any reads or writes that are planned to happen after.

By default, the threads are created joinable, but one might create a detached thread. It might bring a certain benefit: the resources of the detached thread can be released immediately upon its termination. The joinable thread, however, will be waiting to be joined before its resources can be released. To create a detached thread

- Create an attribute instance pthread_attr_t attr;

- Initialize it with pthread_attr_init(&attr);

- Call pthread_attr_setdetachstate(&attr, PTHREAD_CREATE_DETACHED); and

- Create the thread by using pthread_create with a &attr as the attribute argument.

The current thread can be explicitly changed from joinable to detached by calling pthread_detach(). It is impossible to do it the other way around.

17.8.4   Example: Distributed Factorization

We have picked a simple CPU bound program of counting the factors of a number. First, we are going to solve it using the most trivial brute-force method on a single core. Listing 17-9 shows the code.

Listing 17-9. dist_fact_sp.c

```c
#include <pthread.h>
#include <unistd.h>
#include <inttypes.h>
#include <stdio.h>
#include <malloc.h>

uint64_t factors( uint64_t num ) {
    uint64_t result = 0;
    for (uint64_t i = 1; i <= num; i++ )
        if ( num % i == 0 ) result++;
    return result;
}

int main( void ) {
    /* volatile to prevent constant propagation */
    volatile uint64_t input = 2000000000;

    printf( "Factors of %"PRIu64": %"PRIu64"\n", input, factors(input) );
    return 0;
}
```

The code is quite simple: we naively iterate over all numbers from 1 to the input and check whether they are factors or not. Note that the input value is marked volatile to prevent the whole result from being computed during the compilation. Compile the code with the following command:

```
> gcc -O3 -std=c99 -o fact_sp dist_fact_sp.c
```

We will start parallelization with a dumbed-down version of multithreaded code, which will always perform computations in two threads and will not be architecturally beautiful. Listing 17-10 shows it.

Listing 17-10. dist_fact_mp_simple.c

```
#include <pthread.h>
#include <inttypes.h>
#include <stdio.h>

int input = 0;

int result1 = 0;
void* fact_worker1( void* arg ) {
    result1 = 0;
    for( uint64_t i = 1; i < input/2; i++ )
        if ( input % i == 0 ) result1++;
    return NULL;
}

int result2 = 0;
void* fact_worker2( void* arg ) {
    result2 = 0;
    for( uint64_t i = input/2; i <= input; i++ )
        if ( input % i == 0 ) result2++;
    return NULL;
}

uint64_t factors_mp( uint64_t num ) {
    input = num;
    pthread_t thread1, thread2;

    pthread_create( &thread1, NULL, fact_worker1, NULL );
    pthread_create( &thread2, NULL, fact_worker2, NULL );

    pthread_join( thread1, NULL );
    pthread_join( thread2, NULL );

    return result1 + result2;
}
int main( void ) {
    uint64_t input = 2000000000;
    printf( "Factors of %"PRIu64": %"PRIu64"\n",
            input, factors_mp(input ));
    return 0;
}
```

Upon launching it produces the same result, which is a good sign.

```
Factors of 2000000000: 110
```

What is this program doing? Well, we split the range (0, *n*] into two halves. Two worker threads are computing the number of factors in their respective halves. Then when both of them have been joined, we are guaranteed that they have already had performed all computations. The results just need to be summed up.

Then, in Listing 17-11 we show the multithreaded program that uses an arbitrary number of threads to compute the same result. It has a better-thought-out architecture.

Listing 17-11. `dist_fact_mp.c`

```c
#include <pthread.h>
#include <unistd.h>
#include <inttypes.h>
#include <stdio.h>
#include <malloc.h>

#define THREADS 4

struct fact_task {
    uint64_t num;
    uint64_t from, to;
    uint64_t result;
};

void* fact_worker( void* arg ) {
    struct fact_task* const task =  arg;
    task-> result = 0;
    for( uint64_t i = task-> from; i < task-> to; i++ )
        if ( task->num %  i ==  0 ) task-> result ++;
    return NULL;
}

/* assuming threads_count < num */
uint64_t factors_mp( uint64_t num, size_t threads_count ) {

    struct fact_task* tasks = malloc( threads_count * sizeof( *tasks ) );
    pthread_t* threads = malloc( threads_count * sizeof( *threads ) );

    uint64_t start = 1;
    size_t step = num / threads_count;

    for( size_t i = 0; i < threads_count; i++ ) {
        tasks[i].num = num;
        tasks[i].from = start;
        tasks[i].to = start + step;
        start += step;
    }
    tasks[threads_count-1].to = num+1;

    for ( size_t i = 0; i < threads_count; i++ )
        pthread_create( threads + i, NULL, fact_worker, tasks + i );
```

```
    uint64_t result = 0;
    for ( size_t i = 0; i < threads_count; i++ ) {
        pthread_join( threads[i], NULL );
        result  +=  tasks[i].result;
    }

    free( tasks );
    free( threads );
    return result;
}
int main( void ) {
    uint64_t input = 2000000000;
    printf( "Factors of %"PRIu64": %"PRIu64"\n",
            input, factors_mp(input, THREADS ) );
    return 0;
}
```

Suppose we are using *t* threads. To count the number of factors of *n*, we split the range from 1 to *n* on *t* equal parts. We compute the number of factors in each of those intervals and then sum up the results.

We create a type to hold the information about single task called struct fact_task. It includes the number itself, the range bounds to and to, and the slot for the result, which will be the number of factors of num between from and to.

All workers who calculate the number of factors are implemented alike, as a routine fact_worker, which accepts a pointer to a struct fact_task, computes the number of factors, and fills the result field.

The code performing thread launch and results collection is contained in the factors_mp function, which, for a given number of threads, is

- Allocating the task descriptions and the thread instances;

- Initializing the task descriptions;

- Starting all threads;

- Waiting for each thread to end its execution by using join and adding up its result to the common accumulator result; and

- Freeing all allocated memory.

So, we put the thread creation into a black box, which allows us to benefit from the multithreading. This code can be compiled with the following command:

```
> gcc -O3 -std=c99 -pthread -o fact_mp dist_fact_mp.c
```

The multiple threads are decreasing the overall execution time on a multicore system for this CPU bound task.

To test the execution time, we will stick with the time utility again (a program, not a shell builtin command). To ensure, that the program is being used instead of a shell builtin, we prepend it with a backslash.

```
> gcc -O3 -o sp -std=c99 dist_fact_sp.c && \time ./sp
Factors of 2000000000: 110
21.78user 0.03system 0:21.83elapsed 99%CPU (0avgtext+0avgdata 524maxresident)k
0inputs+0outputs (0major+207minor)pagefaults 0swaps
```

```
> gcc -O3 -pthread -o mp -std=c99 dist_fact_mp.c && \time ./mp
Factors of 2000000000: 110
25.48user 0.01system 0:06.58elapsed 387%CPU (0avgtext+0avgdata 656maxresident)k
0inputs+0outputs (0major+250minor)pagefaults 0swaps
```

The multithreaded program took 6.5 seconds to be executed, while the single-threaded version took almost 22 seconds. That is a big improvement.

In order to speak about performance we are going to introduce the notion of speedup. **Speedup** is the improvement in speed of execution of a program executed on two similar architectures with different resources. By introducing more threads we make more resources available, hence the possible improvement might take place.

Obviously, for the first example we have chosen a task that is easy and more efficient to solve in parallel. The speedup will not always be that substantial, if any; however, as we see, the overall code is compact enough (could be even less would we not take extensibility into account—for example, fix a number of threads, instead of using it as a parameter).

Question 359   Experiment with the number of threads and find the optimal one in your own environment.

Question 360   Read about functions: `pthread_self` and `pthread_equal`. Why can't we compare threads with a simple equality operator `==`?

17.8.5   Mutexes

While thread joining is an accessible technique, it does not provide means to control the thread execution "on the run." Sometimes we want to ensure that the actions performed in one thread are not being performed before some other action in the other threads are performed. Otherwise, we will get a situation where the system is not always working in a stable manner: its output will become dependent on the actual order in which the instructions from the different threads will be executed. It occurs when working with the mutable data shared between threads. Such situations are called **data races**, because the threads compete for the resources, and any thread can win and get to them first.

To prevent such situations, there is a number of tools, and we will start with mutexes.

Mutex (a shorthand for "mutual exclusion") is an object that can be in two states: locked and unlocked. We work with them using two queries.

- Lock. Changes the state from unlocked to locked. If the mutex is locked, then the attempting thread waits until the mutex is unlocked by other threads.

- Unlock. If the mutex is locked, it becomes unlocked.

Mutexes are often used to provide an exclusive access to a shared resource (like a shared piece of data). The thread that wants to work with the resource locks the mutex, which is exclusively used to control an access to a resource. After the work with the resource is finished, the thread unlocks the mutex.

Mutex locking and unlocking acts as both a compiler and full hardware memory barriers, so no reads or writes can be reordered before locking or after unlocking.

Listing 17-12 shows an example program which needs a mutex.

Listing 17-12. `mutex_ex_counter_bad.c`

```c
#include <pthread.h>
#include <inttypes.h>
#include <stdio.h>
#include <unistd.h>

pthread_t t1, t2;

uint64_t value = 0;

void* impl1( void* _ ) {
    for (int n = 0; n < 10000000; n++) {
        value += 1;
    }
    return NULL;
}

int main(void) {
    pthread_create( &t1, NULL, impl1, NULL );
    pthread_create( &t2, NULL, impl1, NULL );

    pthread_join( t1, NULL );
    pthread_join( t2, NULL );
    printf( "%"PRIu64"\n", value );
    return 0;
}
```

This program has two threads, implemented by the function `impl1`. Both threads are constantly incrementing the shared variable `value` 10000000 times.

This program should be compiled with the optimizations disabled to prevent this incrementing loop from being transformed into a single `value += 10000000` statement (or we can make `value volatile`).

```
gcc -O0 -pthread mutex_ex_counter_bad.c
```

The resulting output is, however, not 20000000, as we might have thought, and is different each time we launch the executable:

```
> ./a.out
11297520
> ./a.out
10649679
> ./a.out
13765500
```

The problem is that incrementing a variable is not an atomic operation from the C point of view. The generated assembly code conforms to this description by using multiple instructions to read a value, add one, and then put it back. It allows the scheduler to give the CPU to another thread "in the middle" of a running increment operation. The optimized code might or might not have the same behavior.

375

To prevent this mess we are going to use a mutex to grant a thread a privilege to be the sole one working with value. This way we enforce a correct behavior. Listing 17-13 shows the modified program.

Listing 17-13. mutex_ex_counter_good.c

```c
#include <pthread.h>
#include <inttypes.h>
#include <stdio.h>
#include <unistd.h>

pthread_mutex_t m; //

pthread_t t1, t2;

uint64_t value = 0;

void* impl1( void* _ ) {
    for (int n = 0; n < 10000000; n++) {
        pthread_mutex_lock( &m );//

        value += 1;

        pthread_mutex_unlock( &m );//
    }
    return NULL;
}

int main(void) {
    pthread_mutex_init( &m, NULL );      //

    pthread_create(  &t1, NULL, impl1, NULL );
    pthread_create(  &t2, NULL, impl1, NULL );

    pthread_join( t1, NULL );
    pthread_join( t2, NULL );
    printf( "%"PRIu64"\n", value );

    pthread_mutex_destroy( &m ); //
    return 0;
}
```

Its output is consistent (although takes more time to compute):

```
> ./a.out
20000000
```

The mutex m is associated *by the programmer* with a shared variable value. No modifications of value should be performed outside the code section between the m lock and unlock. If this constraint is satisfied, there is no way value can be changed by another thread once the lock is taken. The lock acts as a memory barrier as well. Because of that, value will be reread after the lock is taken and can be cached in a register safely. There is no need to make the variable value volatile, since it will only suppress optimizations and the program is correct anyway.

Before a mutex can be used, it should be initialized with `pthread_mutex_init`, as seen in the `main` function. It accepts attributes, just like the `pthread_create` function, which can be used to create a recursive mutex, create a deadlock detecting mutex, control the robustness (what happens if the mutex owner thread dies?), and more.

To dispose of a mutex, the call to `pthread_mutex_unlock` is used.

■ **Question 361** What is a recursive mutex? How is it different from an ordinary one?

17.8.6 Deadlocks

A sole mutex is rarely a cause of problems. However, when you lock multiple mutexes at a time, several kinds of strange situations can happen. Take a look at the example shown in Listing 17-14.

Listing 17-14. `deadlock_ex`

```
mutex A, B;

thread1 () {
    lock(A);
    lock(B);
    unlock(B);
    unlock(A);
}

thread2() {
    lock(B);
    lock(A);
    unlock(A);
    unlock(B);
}
```

This pseudo code demonstrates a situation where both threads can hang forever. Imagine that the following sequence of actions happened due to unlucky scheduling:

- Thread 1 locked *A*; control transferred to thread 2.

- Thread 2 locked *B*; control transferred to thread 1.

After that, the threads will try to do the following:

- Thread 1 will attempt to lock *B*, but *B* is already locked by thread 2.

- Thread 2 will attempt to lock *A*, but *A* is already locked by thread 1.

Both threads will be stuck in this state forever. When threads are stuck in a locked state waiting for each other to perform unlock, the situation is called **deadlock**.

The cause of the deadlock is the different order in which the locks are being taken by different threads. It leads us to a simple rule that will save us most of the times when we need to lock several mutexes at a time.

■ **Preventing deadlocks**   Order all mutexes in your program in an imaginary sequence. Only lock mutexes in the same order they appear in this sequence.

For example, suppose we have mutexes A, B, C, and D. We impose a natural order on them: $A < B < C < D$. If you need to lock both D and B, you should always lock them in the same order, thus B first, D second.

If this **invariant** is kept, no two threads will lock a pair of mutexes in a different order.

■ **Question 362**   What are Coffman's conditions? How can they be used to diagnose deadlocks?

■ **Question 363**   How do we use Helgrind to detect deadlocks?

17.8.7   Livelocks

Livelock is a situation in which two threads are stuck but not in a waiting-for-mutex-unlock state. Their states are changing, but they are not really progressing. For example, pthreads does not allow you to check whether the mutex is locked or not. It would be useless to provide information about the mutex state, because once you obtain information about it, the latter can already be changed by the other thread.

```
if ( mutex is not locked ) {
    /* We still do not know if the mutex is locked or not.
       Other thread might have locked or unlocked it
       several times already.  */
}
```

However, pthread_mutex_trylock is allowed, which either locks a mutex or returns an error if it has already been locked by someone. Unlike pthread_mutex_lock, it does not block the current thread waiting for the unlock. Using pthread_mutex_trylock can lead to livelock situations. Listing 17-15 shows a simple example in pseudo code.

Listing 17-15. livelock_ex

```
mutex m1, m2;

thread1() {
    lock( m1 );
    while ( mutex_trylock m2 indicates LOCKED ) {
        unlock( m1 );
        wait for some time;
        lock( m1 );
    }
    // now we are good because both locks are taken
}
```

```
thread2() {
    lock( m2 );
    while ( mutex_trylock m1 indicates LOCKED ) {
        unlock( m2 );
        wait for some time;
        lock( m2 );
    }
    // now we are good because both locks are taken
}
```

Each thread tries to defy the principle "locks should always be performed in the same order." Both of them want to lock two mutexes m1 and m2.

The first thread performs as follows:

- Locks the mutex m1.

- Tries to lock mutex m2. On failure, unlocks m1, waits, and locks m1 again.

This pause is meant to provide the other thread time to lock m1 and m2 and perform whatever it wants to do. However, we might be stuck in a loop when

1. Thread 1 locks m1, thread 2 locks m2.

2. Thread 1 sees that m2 is locked and unlocks m1 for a time.

3. Thread 2 sees that m1 is locked and unlocks m2 for a time.

4. Go back to step one.

This loop can take forever to complete or can produce significant delays; it is entirely up to the operating system scheduler. So, the problem with this code is that execution traces exist that will forever prevent threads from progress.

17.8.8 Condition Variables

Condition variables are used together with mutexes. They are like wires transmitting an impulse to wake up a sleeping thread, waiting for some condition to be satisfied.

Mutexes implement synchronization by controlling thread access to a resource; condition variables, on the other hand, allow threads to synchronize based upon additional rules. For example, in case of shared data, the actual value of data might be a part of such rule.

The core of condition variables usage consists of three new entities:

- The condition variable itself of type pthread_cond_t.

- A function to send a wake-up signal through a condition variable pthread_cond_signal.

- A function to wait until a wake-up signal comes through a condition variable pthread_cond_wait.

These two functions should only be used between a lock and unlock of the same mutex.

It is an error to call pthread_cond_signal before pthread_cond_wait, otherwise the program might be stuck.

Let us study a minimal working example shown in Listing 17-16.

Listing 17-16. condvar_mwe.c

```c
#include <pthread.h>
#include <stdio.h>
#include <stdbool.h>
#include <unistd.h>

pthread_cond_t condvar = PTHREAD_COND_INITIALIZER;
pthread_mutex_t m;

bool sent = false;
void* t1_impl( void* _ ) {
    pthread_mutex_lock( &m );
    puts( "Thread2 before wait" );

    while (!sent)
        pthread_cond_wait( &condvar, &m );

    puts( "Thread2 after wait" );
    pthread_mutex_unlock( &m );
    return  NULL;
}

void* t2_impl( void* _ ) {
    pthread_mutex_lock( &m );
    puts( "Thread1 before signal" );

    sent = true;
    pthread_cond_signal( &condvar );

    puts( "Thread1 after signal" );
    pthread_mutex_unlock( &m );
    return NULL;
}

int main( void ) {
    pthread_t t1, t2;

    pthread_mutex_init( &m, NULL );
    pthread_create( &t1, NULL, t1_impl, NULL );
    sleep( 2 );
    pthread_create( &t2, NULL, t2_impl, NULL );

    pthread_join( t1, NULL );
    pthread_join( t2, NULL );

    pthread_mutex_destroy( &m );
    return 0;
}
```

Running this code will produce the following output:

```
./a.out
Thread2 before wait
Thread1 before signal
Thread1 after signal
Thread2 after wait
```

Initializing a condition variable can be performed either through an assignment of a special preprocessor constant PTHREAD_COND_INITIALIZER or by calling pthread_cond_init. The latter can accept a pointer to attributes of type pthread_condattr_t akin to pthread_create or pthread_mutex_init.

In this example, two threads are created: t1, performing instructions from t1_impl, and t2, performing ones from t2_impl.

The first thread locks the mutex m. It then waits for a signal that can be transmitted through the condition variable condvar. Note that pthread_cond_wait also accepts the pointer to the currently locked mutex.

Now t1 is sleeping, waiting for the signal to come. The mutex m becomes immediately unlocked! When the thread gets the signal, it will relock the mutex automatically and continue its execution from the next statement after pthread_cond_wait call.

The other thread is locking the same mutex m and issuing a signal through condvar. pthread_cond_signal sends the signal through condvar, unblocking at least one of the threads, blocked on the condition variable condvar.

The pthread_cond_broadcast function would unblock all threads waiting for this condition variable, making them contend for the respective mutex as if they all issued pthread_mutex_lock. It is up to the scheduler to decide in which order will they get access to the CPU.

As we see, condition variables let us block until a signal is received. An alternative would be a "busy waiting" when a variable's value is constantly checked (which kills performance and increases unnecessary power consumption) as follows:

```
while (somecondition == false);
```

We can of course put the thread to sleep for a time, but this way we will still wake up either too rarely to react to the event in time or too often:

```
while (somecondition == false)
    sleep(1); /* or something else that lets us sleep for less time */
```

Condition variables let us wait just enough time and continue the thread execution in the locked state.

An important moment should be explained. Why did we introduce a shared variable sent? Why are we using it together with the condition variable? Why are we waiting inside the while (!sent) cycle?

The most important reason is that the implementation is permitted to *issue spurious wake-ups to a waiting thread.* It means that the thread can wake up from waiting on a signal not only after receiving it but at *any time*. In this case, as the sent variable is only set before sending the signal, spurious wake-up will check its value and if it is still equal to false will issue the pthread_cond_wait again.

17.8.9 Spinlocks

A mutex is a sure way of doing synchronization. Trying to lock a mutex which is already taken by another thread puts the current thread into a sleeping state. Putting the thread to sleep and waking it up has its costs, notably for the context switch, but if the waiting is long, these costs justify themselves. We spend a little time going to sleep and waking up, but in a prolonged sleep state the thread does not use the CPU.

What would be an alternative? The active idle, which is described by the following simple pseudo code:

```
while ( locked == true ) {
    /* do nothing */
}
locked = true;
```

The variable `locked` is a flag showing whether some thread took the lock or not. If another thread took the lock, the current thread will constantly poll its value until it is changed back. Otherwise it proceeds to take the lock on its own. This wastes CPU time (and increases power consumption), which is bad. However, it can increase performance in case the waiting time is expected to be very short. This mechanism is called **spinlock**.

Spinlocks only make sense on multicore and multiprocessor systems. Using spinlock in a single core is useless. Imagine a thread enters the cycle inside the spinlock. It keeps waiting for other thread to change the `locked` value, but no other thread is executing at this very time, because there is only one core switching from thread to thread. Eventually the scheduler will put the current thread to sleep and allow other threads to perform, but it just means that we have wasted CPU cycles executing an empty loop for no reason at all! In this case, going to sleep right away is always better, and hence there is no use for a spinlock.

This scenario can of course occur on a multicore system as well, but there is also a (usually) good chance, that the other thread will unlock the spinlock before the time quantum given to the current thread expires.

Overall, using spinlocks can be beneficial or not; it depends on the system configuration, program logic, and workload. When in doubt, test and prefer using mutexes (which are often implemented by first taking a spinlock for a number of iterations and then falling into the sleep state if no unlock occurred).

Implementing a *fast* and correct spinlock in practice is not that trivial. There are questions to be answered, such as the following:

- Do we need a memory barrier on lock and/or unlock? If so, which one? Intel 64, for example, has `lfence`, `sfence`, and `mfence`.

- How do we ensure that the flag modification is atomic? In Intel 64, for example, an instruction `xchg` suffices (with `lock` prefix in case of multiple processors).

`pthreads` provide us with a carefully designed and portable mechanism of spinlocks. For more information, refer to the `man` pages for the following functions:

- `pthread_spin_lock`

- `pthread_spin_destroy`

- `pthread_spin_unlock`

17.9 Semaphores

Semaphore is a shared integer variable on which three actions can be performed.

- Initialization with an argument N. Sets its value to N.

- Wait (enter). If the value is not zero, it decrements it. Otherwise waits until someone else increments it, and then proceeds with the decrement.

- Post (leave). Increments its value.

Obviously the value of this variable, not directly accessible, cannot fall below 0.

Semaphores are *not* part of pthreads specification; we are working with semaphores whose interface is described in the POSIX standard. However, the code that uses the semaphores should be compiled with a -pthread flag.

Most UNIX-like operating systems implement both standard pthreads features and semaphores. Using semaphores is fairly common to perform synchronization between threads.

Listing 17-17 shows an example of semaphore usage.

Listing 17-17. semaphore_mwe.c

```c
#include <semaphore.h>
#include <inttypes.h>
#include <pthread.h>
#include <stdio.h>
#include <unistd.h>

sem_t sem;

uint64_t counter1 = 0;
uint64_t counter2 = 0;

pthread_t t1, t2, t3;

void* t1_impl( void* _ ) {
    while( counter1 < 10000000 ) counter1++;
    sem_post( &sem );
    return NULL;
}

void* t2_impl( void* _ ) {
    while( counter2 < 20000000 ) counter2++;
    sem_post( &sem );
    return NULL;
}

void* t3_impl( void* _ ) {
    sem_wait( &sem );
    sem_wait( &sem );
    printf("End: counter1 = %" PRIu64 " counter2 = %" PRIu64 "\n",
            counter1, counter2 );
    return NULL;
}

int main(void) {
    sem_init( &sem, 0, 0 );

    pthread_create( &t3, NULL, t3_impl, NULL );

    sleep( 1 );
    pthread_create( &t1, NULL, t1_impl, NULL );
    pthread_create( &t2, NULL, t2_impl, NULL );
```

```
    sem_destroy( &sem );
    pthread_exit( NULL );
    return 0;
}
```

The `sem_init` function initializes the semaphore. Its second argument is a flag: 0 corresponds to a process-local semaphore (which can be used by different threads), non-zero value sets up a semaphore visible to multiple processes.[3] The third argument sets up the initial semaphore value. A semaphore is deleted using the `sem_destroy` function. In the example, two counters and three threads are created. Threads `t1` and `t2` increment the respective counters to 1000000 and 20000000 and then increment the semaphore value `sem` by calling `sem_post`. `t3` locks itself decrementing the semaphore value twice. Then, when semaphore was incremented twice by other threads, `t3` prints the counters into `stdout`.

The `pthread_exit` call ensures that the main thread will not terminate prematurely, until all other threads finish their work.

Semaphores come up handy in such tasks as

- Forbidding more than n processes to simultaneously execute a code section.

- Making one thread wait for another to complete a specific action, thus imposing an order on their actions.

- Keeping no more than a fixed number of worker threads performing a certain task in parallel. More threads than needed might decrease performance.

It is not true that a semaphore with two states is fully analogous to a mutex. Unlike mutex, which can only be unlocked by the same thread that locked it, semaphores can be changed freely by any thread.

We will see another example of the semaphore usage in Listing 17-18 to make two threads start each loop iteration simultaneously (and when the loop body is executed, they wait for other loops to finish an iteration).

Manipulations with semaphores obviously act like both compiler and hardware memory barriers. For more information on semaphores, refer to the man pages for the following functions:

- `em_close`

- `sem_destroy`

- `sem_getvalue`

- `sem_init`

- `sem_open`

- `sem_post`

- `sem_unlink`

- `sem_wait`

■ **Question 364** What is a named semaphore? Why should it be mandatorily unlinked even if the process is terminated?

---

[3]In this case, the semaphore itself will be placed in the shared page, which will not be physically duplicated after performing the `fork()` system call

17.10   How Strong Is Intel 64?

Abstract machines with relaxed memory model can be tough to follow. Out of order writes, return values from the future, and speculative reads are confusing. Intel 64 is considered to be usually strong. In most cases, it guarantees quite a few constraints to be satisfied, including, but not limited to, the following:

- Stores are not reordered with older stores.

- Stores are not reordered with older loads.

- Loads are not reordered with other loads.

- In a multiprocessor system, stores to the same location have a total order.

There are also exceptions, such as the following:

- Writing to memory bypassing cache with such instructions as movntdq can be reordered with other stores.

- String instructions like rep movs can be reordered with other stores.

A full list of guarantees can be found in volume 3, section 8.2.2 of [15].

However, according to [15], "reads may be reordered with older writes to different locations but not with older writes to the same location." So, do not be fooled: memory reorderings do occur. A simple program shown in Listing 17-18 demonstrates the memory reordering done by hardware. It implements an example already shown in Listing 17-4, where there are two threads and two shared variables x and y. The first thread performs store x and load y, the second ones performs store y and load x. The compiler barrier ensures that these two statements are translated into assembly in the same order. As section 17.10 suggests, the stores and loads into independent locations can be reordered. So, we cannot exclude the hardware memory reordering here, as x and y are independent!

Listing 17-18. reordering_cpu_mwe.c

```c
#include <pthread.h>
#include <semaphore.h>
#include <stdio.h>
#include <inttypes.h>
#include <stdint.h>
#include <stdlib.h>
#include <time.h>

sem_t sem_begin0, sem_begin1, sem_end;

int x, y, read0, read1;

void *thread0_impl( void *param )
{
    for (;;) {

        sem_wait( &sem_begin0 );

        x = 1;
        // This only disables compiler reorderings:
        asm volatile("" ::: "memory");
```

```
        // The following line disables also hardware reorderings:
        // asm volatile("mfence" ::: "memory");
        read0 = y;

        sem_post( &sem_end );
    }

    return NULL;
};

void *thread1_impl( void *param )
{
    for (;;) {

        sem_wait( &sem_begin1 );

        y = 1;
        // This only disables compiler reorderings:
        asm volatile("" ::: "memory");
        // The following line disables also hardware reorderings
        // asm volatile("mfence" ::: "memory");
        read1 = x;

        sem_post( &sem_end );
    }
    return NULL;
};

int main( void ) {

    sem_init( &sem_begin0, 0, 0);
    sem_init( &sem_begin1, 0, 0);
    sem_init( &sem_end, 0, 0);

    pthread_t thread0, thread1;
    pthread_create( &thread0, NULL, thread0_impl, NULL);
    pthread_create( &thread1, NULL, thread1_impl, NULL);

    for (uint64_t i = 0; i < 100000; i++)
    {
        x = 0;
        y = 0;
        sem_post( &sem_begin0 );
        sem_post( &sem_begin1 );

        sem_wait( &sem_end );
        sem_wait( &sem_end );

        if (read0 == 0 && read1 == 0 ) {
            printf( "reordering happened on iteration %" PRIu64 "\n", i );
            exit(0);
        }
    }
}
```

```
        puts("No reordering detected during 100000 iterations");
        return 0;
}
```

To check it we perform multiple experiments. The main function acts as follows:

1. Initialize threads and two starting semaphores as well as an ending one.

2. x = 0, y = 0

3. Notify the threads that they should start performing a transaction.

4. Wait for both threads to complete the transaction.

5. Check whether the memory reordering took place. It is seen when both load x and load y returned zeros (because they were reordered to be placed before store s).

6. If the memory reordering has been detected, we are notified about it and the process exits. Otherwise it tries again from step (2) up to the maximum of 100000 attempts.

Each thread waits for a signal to start from main, performs the transaction, and notifies main about it. Then it starts all over again.

After launching you will see that 100000 iterations are enough to observe a memory reordering.

```
> gcc -pthread -o ordering -O2 ordering.c
> ./ordering
reordering happened on iteration 128
> ./ordering
reordering happened on iteration 12
> ./ordering
reordering happened on iteration 171
> ./ordering
reordering happened on iteration 80
> ./ordering
reordering happened on iteration 848
> ./ordering
reordering happened on iteration 366
> ./ordering
reordering happened on iteration 273
> ./ordering
reordering happened on iteration 105
> ./ordering
reordering happened on iteration 14
> ./ordering
reordering  happened  on  iteration 5
> ./ordering
reordering happened on iteration 414
```

It might seem magical, but it is the level lower than the assembly language even that is seen here and that introduces rarely observed (but still persistent) bugs in the software. Such bugs in multithreaded software are *very* hard to catch. Imagine a bug appearing only after four months of uninterrupted execution, which corrupts the heap and crashes the program 42 allocations after it triggers! So, writing high-performance multithreaded software in a lock-free manner requires tremendous expertise.

So, what we need to do is to add `mfence` instruction. Replacing the compiler barrier with a full memory barrier `asm volatile( "mfence":::"memory");` solves the problem and the reorderings disappear completely. If we do it, there will be no reorderings detected no matter how many iterations we try.

17.11 What Is Lock-Free Programming?

We have seen how we can ensure the consistency of the operations when working in a multithreaded environment. Every time we need to perform a complex operation on shared data or resources without other threads intervening we lock a mutex that we have associated to this resource or memory chunk.

We say that the code is **lock-free** if the following two constraints are satisfied:

- No mutexes are used.
- The system cannot be locked up indefinitely. That includes livelocks.

In other words, it is a family of techniques that ensure safe manipulation with the shared data without using mutexes.

We almost always expect only a part of the program code to satisfy the lock-free property. For example, a data structure, such as a queue, may be considered lock-free if the functions that are used to manipulate it are lock-free. So, it does not prevent us from locking up completely, but as far as we are calling functions such as enqueue or dequeue, progress will be made.

From the programmer's perspective, lock-free programming is different from traditional mutex usage because it introduces two challenges that are usually covered by mutexes.

1. Reorderings. While mutex manipulations imply compiler and hardware memory barriers, without them you have to be specific about where to place memory barriers. You will not want to place them after each statement because it kills performance.

2. Non-atomic operations. The operations between mutex lock and unlock are safe and atomic in a sense. No other thread can modify the data associated with the mutex (unless there are unsafe data manipulations outside the lock-unlock section). Without that mechanism we are stuck with very few atomic operations, which we will study later in this chapter.

On most modern processors reads and writes of naturally aligned native types are atomic. Natural alignment means aligning the variable to a boundary that corresponds to its size.

On Intel 64 there is no guarantee that reads and writes larger than 8 bytes are atomic. Other memory interactions are usually non-atomic. It includes, but is not limited to,

- 16-byte reads and writes performed by SSE (Streaming SIMD Extensions) instructions.
- String operations (`movsb` instruction and the like).
- Many operations are atomic on a single-processor system but not in a multiprocessor system (e.g., `inc` instruction).

Making them atomic requires a special `lock` prefix to be used, which prevents other processors from doing their own read-modify-write sequence between the stages of the said instructions. An `inc <addr>` instruction, for instance, has to read bytes from memory and write back their incremented value. Without `lock` prefix, they can intervene in between, which can lead to a loss of value.

Here are some examples of non-atomic operations:

```
char buf[1024];
uint64_t* data = (uint64_t*)(buf + 1);

/* not atomic: unnatural alignment */
*data = 0;

/* not atomic: increment can need a read and a write */
++global_aligned_var;

/* atomic write */

global_aligned_var = 0;

void f(void) {
/* atomic read */
int64_t local_variable = global_aligned_var;
}
```

These cases are architecture-specific. We also want to perform more complex operations atomically (e.g., incrementing the counter). To perform them safely without using mutexes the engineers invented interesting basic operations, such as compare-and-swap (CAS). Once this operation is implemented as a machine instruction on a specific architecture, it can be used in combination with more trivial non-atomic reads and writes to implement many lock-free algorithms and data structures.

CAS instruction acts as an atomic sequence of operations, described by the following equivalent C function:

```
bool cas(int* p , int old, int new) {
    if (*p != old) return false;
    *p = new;
    return true;
}
```

A shared counter, which you are reading and writing back a modified value, is a typical case when we need a CAS instruction to perform an atomical increment or decrement. Listing 17-19 shows a function to perform it.

Listing 17-19. cas_counter.c

```
int add(int* p, int add ) {
    bool done = false;
    int value;
    while (!done) {
        value = *p;
            done = cas(p, value, value + add );
    }
    return value + add;
}
```

This example shows a typical pattern, seen in many CAS-based algorithms. They read a certain memory location, compute its modified value, and repeatedly try to swap the new value back if the current memory value is equal to the old one. It fails in case this memory location was modified by another thread; then the whole read-modify-write cycle is repeated.

Intel 64 implements CAS instructions `cmpxchg`, `cmpxchg8b`, and `cmpxchg16b`. In case of multiple processors, they also require a `lock` prefix to be used.

The instruction `cmpxchg` is of a particular interest. It accepts two operands: register or memory and a register. It compares `rax`[4] with the first operand. If they are equal, `zf` flag is set, the second operand's value is loaded into the first. Otherwise, the actual value of the first operand is loaded into `rax` and `zf` is cleared.

These instructions can be used as a part of implementation of mutexes and semaphores.

As we will see in section 17.12.2, there is now a standard-compliant way of using compare-and-set operations (as well as manipulating with atomic variables). We recommend sticking to it to prevent non-portable code and use atomics whenever you can. When you need complex operations to be performed atomically, use mutexes or stick with the lock-free data structure implementations done by experts: writing lock-free data structures has proven to be a challenge.

■ **Question 365**   What is the ABA problem?

■ **Question 366**   Read the description of `cmpxchg` in Intel docs [15].

17.12   C11 Memory Model

17.12.1   Overview

Most of the time we want to write code that is correct on every architecture. To achieve that, we base it on the memory model described in the C11 standard. The compiler might implement some operations in a straightforward manner or emit special instructions to enforce certain guarantees, when the actual hardware architecture is weaker.

Contrary to Intel 64, the C11 memory model is rather weak. It guarantees data dependency ordering, but nothing more, so in the classification mentioned in section 17.4 it corresponds to the second one: weak with dependency ordering. There are other hardware architectures that provide similar weak guarantees, for example ARM.

Because of C weakness, to write portable code we *cannot assume* that it will be executed on an usually strong architecture, such as Intel 64, for two reasons.

- When recompiled for other, weaker architecture, the observed program behavior will change because of how the hardware reorderings work.

- When recompiled for the same architecture, compiler reorderings that do not break the weak ordering rules imposed by the standard might occur. That can change the observed program behavior, at least for some execution traces.

17.12.2   Atomics

The important C11 feature that can be used to write fast multithreaded programs is atomics (see section 7.17 of [7]). These are special variable types, which can be modified atomically. To use them, include the header `stdatomic.h`.

---

[4]Or `eax, ax, al`–depending on operand size

Apparently, an architecture support is needed to implement them efficiently. In the worst-case scenario, when the architecture does not support any such operation, every such variable will be paired with a mutex, which will be locked to perform any modification of the variable or even to read it.

Atomics allow us to perform thread-safe operations on common data in some cases. It is often possible to do without heavy machinery involving mutexes. However, writing data structures such as queue in a lock-free way is no easy task. For that we highly advise using such existing implementations as "black boxes."

C11 defines a new _Atomic() type specifier. You can declare an atomic integer as follows:

```
_Atomic(int) counter;
```

_Atomic transforms the name of a type into the name of an atomic type. Alternatively, you can use the atomic types directly as follows:

```
atomic_int counter;
```

A full correspondence between _Atomic(T) and atomic_T direct type forms can be found in section 7.17.6 of [7].

Atomic *local* variables should *not* be initialized directly; instead, the macro ATOMIC_VAR_INIT should be used. It is understandable, because on some architectures with fewer hardware capabilities each such variable should be associated with a mutex, which has to be created and initialized as well. Global atomic variables are guaranteed to be in a correct initial state. ATOMIC_VAR_INIT should be used during the variable declaration coupled with initialization; however, if you want to initialize the variable later, use atomic_init macro.

```
void f(void) {
    /* Initialization during declaration */
    atomic_int x = ATOMIC_VAR_INIT( 42 );
    atomic_int y;

    /* initialization later */
    atomic_init( &y, 42 );
}
```

It is your responsibility to guarantee that the atomic variable initialization ends before anything else is done with it. In other words, concurrent access to the variable being initialized is a data race.

Atomic variables should only be manipulated through an interface, defined in the language standard. It consists of several operations, such as load, store, exchange, etc. Each of them exists in two versions.

- An explicit version, which accepts an extra argument, describing the memory ordering. Its name ends with _explicit. For example, the load operation is

  ```
  T atomic_load_explicit( _Atomic(T) *object, memory_order order );
  ```

- An implicit version, which implies the strongest memory ordering (sequentially consistent). There is no _explicit suffix. For example,

  ```
  T atomic_load( _Atomic(T) *object );
  ```

17.12.3   Memory Orderings in C11

The memory ordering is described by one of enumeration constants (in order of increasing strictness).

- memory_order_relaxed implies the weakest model: any memory reordering is possible as long as the single thread program's observable behavior is left untouched.

- memory_order_consume is a weaker version of memory_order_acquire.

- memory_order_acquire means that the load operation has an acquire semantics.

- memory_order_release means that the store operation has a release semantics.

- memory_order_acq_rel combines acquire and release semantics.

- memory_order_seq_cst implies that no memory reordering is performed *for all operations that are marked with it*, no matter which atomic variable is being referenced.

By providing an explicit memory ordering constant, we can control how we want to allow the operations to be *observably* reordered. It includes both compiler reorderings and hardware reorderings, so when the compiler sees that compiler reorderings do not provide all the guarantees we need, it will also issue platform-specific instructions, such as sfence.

The memory_order_consume option is rarely used. It relies on the notion of "consume operation." This operation is an event that occurs when a value is read from memory and then used afterward in several operations, creating a data dependency.

In weaker architectures such as PowerPC or ARM its usage can bring a better performance due to exploitation of the data dependencies to impose a certain ordering on memory accesses. This way, the costly hardware memory barrier instruction is spared, because these architectures guarantee the data dependency ordering without explicit barriers. However, due to the fact that this ordering is so hard to implement efficiently and correctly in compilers, it is usually mapped directly to memory_order_acquire, which is a slightly stronger version. We do not recommend using it. Refer to [30] for additional information.

The **acquire** and **release semantics** of these memory ordering options correspond directly to the notions we studied in section 17.7.

The memory_order_seq_cst corresponds to the notion of sequential consistency, which we elaborated in section 17.4. As all non-explicit operations with atomics accept it as a default memory ordering value, C11 atomics are sequentially consistent by default. It is the safest route and also usually faster than mutexes. Weaker orderings are harder to get right, but they allow for a better performance as well.

The atomic_thread_fence(memory_order order) allows us to insert a memory barrier (compiler and hardware ones) with a strength corresponding to the specified memory ordering. For example, this operation has no effect for memory_order_relaxed, but for a sequentially consistent ordering in Intel 64 the mfence instruction will be emitted (together with compiler barrier).

17.12.4   Operations

The following operations can be performed on atomic variables (T denotes the non-atomic type, U refers to the type of the other argument for arithmetic operations; for all types except pointers, it is the same as T, for pointers it is ptrdiff_t).

```
void atomic_store(volatile _Atomic(T)* object, T  value);
T atomic_load(volatile _Atomic(T)* object);

T atomic_exchange(volatile _Atomic(T)* object, desired);
```

```
T atomic_fetch_add(volatile _Atomic(T)* object, U operand);
T atomic_fetch_sub(volatile _Atomic(T)* object, U operand);
T atomic_fetch_or (volatile _Atomic(T)* object, U operand);
T atomic_fetch_xor(volatile _Atomic(T)* object, U operand);
T atomic_fetch_and(volatile _Atomic(T)* object, U operand);

bool atomic_compare_exchange_strong(
    volatile _Atomic(T)* object, T * expected, T desired);
bool atomic_compare_exchange_weak(
    volatile _Atomic(T)* object, T * expected, T desired);
```

All these operations can be used with an `_explicit` suffix to provide a memory ordering as an additional argument.

Load and store functions do not need a further explanation; we will discuss the other ones briefly.

`atomic_exchange` is a combination of load and store: it replaces the value of an atomic variable with `desired` and returns its old value.

`fetch_op` family of operations is used to atomically change the atomic variable value. Imagine you need to increment an atomic counter. Without `fetch_add` it is impossible to do since in order to increment it you need to add one to its old value, which you have to read first. This operation is performed in three steps: reading, addition, writing. Other threads may interfere between these stages, which destroys atomicity.

`atomic_compare_exchange_strong` is preferred to its weak counterpart, since the weak version can fail spuriously. The latter has a better performance on some platforms.

The `atomic_compare_exchange_strong` function is roughly equivalent to the following pseudo code:

```
if ( *object == *expected )

    *object = desired;
else
    *expected = *object;
```

As we see, this is a typical CAS instruction that was discussed in section 17.11.

`atomic_is_lock_free` macro is used to check whether a specific atomic variable uses locks or not.

Remember that without providing explicit memory ordering, *all* these operations are assumed to be sequentially consistent, which in Intel 64 means `mfence` instructions all over the code. This can be a huge performance killer.

The Boolean shared flag has a special type named `atomic_flag`. It has two states: set and clear. It is guaranteed that operations on it are atomic without using locks.

The flag should be initialized with the `ATOMIC_FLAG_INIT` macro as follows:

```
atomic_flag is_working = ATOMIC_FLAG_INIT;
```

The relevant functions are `atomic_flag_test_and_set` and `atomic_flag_clear`, both of which have `_explicit` counterparts, accepting memory ordering descriptions.

Question 367   Read man pages for `atomic_flag_test_and_set` and `atomic_flag_clear`.

17.13 Summary

In this chapter we have studied the basics of multithreaded programming. We have seen the different memory models and the problems that emerge from the fact compiler and hardware optimizations mess with the instruction execution order. We have learned how to control them, placing different memory barriers, we have seen why `volatile` is not a solution to problems that emerge from multithreading. Then we introduced `pthreads`, the most common standard of writing multithreaded applications of Unix-like systems. We have seen thread management, used mutexes and condition variables, and learned why spinlocks only have meaning on multicore and multiprocessor systems. We have seen how memory reorderings should be taken into account even when working on an usually strong architecture such as Intel 64 and have seen the limits of its strictness. Finally, we have studied the atomic variables—a very useful feature of C11 that allows us to get rid of explicit mutex usage and in many cases boost performance while maintaining correctness. Mutexes are still important when we want to perform complex manipulations on non-trivial data structures.

Question 368   Which problems emerge from multithreading usage?

Question 369   What makes multiple threads worth it?

Question 370   Should we use multithreading even if the program does not perform many computations? If yes, give a use case.

Question 371   What is compiler reordering? Why is it performed?

Question 372   Why does the single-threaded program have no means to observe compiler memory reorderings?

Question 373   What are some kinds of memory models?

Question 374   How do we write the code that is sequentially consistent with regard to manipulation of two shared variables?

Question 375   Are `volatile` variables sequentially consistent?

Question 376   Show an example when memory reorderings can lead to very unexpected program behavior.

Question 377   What are the arguments against usage of volatile variables?

Question 378   What is a memory barrier?

Question 379   What kinds of memory barriers do you know?

Question 380   What is acquire semantics?

Question 381   What is release semantics?

Question 382   What is a data dependency? Can you write code where data dependency does not force an order on operations?

Question 383   What is the difference between `mfence`, `sfence`, and `lfence`?

Question 384   Why do we need instructions other than `mfence`?

■ **Question 385**   Which function calls act as compiler barriers?

■ **Question 386**   Are `inline` function calls compiler barriers?

■ **Question 387**   What is a thread?

■ **Question 388**   What is the difference between threads and processes?

■ **Question 389**   What constitutes the state of a process?

■ **Question 390**   What constitutes the state of a thread?

■ **Question 391**   Why should the `-pthread` flag be used when compiling with `pthreads`?

■ **Question 392**   Is `pthreads` a static or dynamic library?

■ **Question 393**   How do we know in which order the scheduler will execute the threads?

■ **Question 394**   Can one thread get access to the stack of the other thread?

■ **Question 395**   What does `pthread_join` do and how do we use it?

■ **Question 396**   What is a mutex? Why do we need it?

■ **Question 397**   Should every shared constant variable be associated with a mutex?

■ **Question 398**   Should every shared mutable variable which is never changed be associated with a mutex?

■ **Question 399**   Should every shared mutable variable which is changed be associated with a mutex?

■ **Question 400**   Can we work with a shared variable without ever using a mutex?

■ **Question 401**   What is a deadlock?

■ **Question 402**   How do we prevent deadlock?

■ **Question 403**   What is a livelock? How is it different from a deadlock?

■ **Question 404**   What is a spinlock? How is it different from a livelock and a deadlock?

■ **Question 405**   Should spinlocks be used on a single core system? Why?

■ **Question 406**   What is a condition variable?

■ **Question 407**   Why do we need condition variables if we have mutexes?

■ **Question 408**   Which guarantees does Intel 64 provide for memory reorderings?

■ **Question 409**   Which important guarantees does Intel 64 not provide for memory reorderings?

■ **Question 410**   Correct the program shown in Listing 17-18 so that no memory reordering occurs.

■ **Question 411**   Correct the program shown in Listing 17-18 so that no memory reordering occurs by using atomic variables.

■ **Question 412** What is lock-free programming? Why is it harder than traditional multithreaded programming with locks?

■ **Question 413** What is a CAS operation? How can it be implemented in Intel 64?

■ **Question 414** How strong is the C memory model?

■ **Question 415** Can the strength of the C memory model be controlled?

■ **Question 416** What is an atomic variable?

■ **Question 417** Can any data type be atomic?

■ **Question 418** Which atomic variables should be initialized explicitly?

■ **Question 419** Which memory orderings does C11 recognize?

■ **Question 420** How are the atomic variables manipulation functions with _explicit suffix different from their ordinary counterparts?

■ **Question 421** How do we perform an atomic increment on an atomic variable?

■ **Question 422** How do we perform an atomic XOR on an atomic variable?

■ **Question 423** What is the difference between weak and strong versions of `compare_exchange`?

PART IV

Appendices

CHAPTER 18

■ ■ ■

Appendix A. Using gdb

The debugger is a very powerful instrument at your disposal. It allows executing programs step by step and monitoring their state, including register values and memory contents. In this book we are using the debugger called gdb. This appendix is an introduction aimed to ease your first steps with it.

Debugging is a process of finding bugs and studying program behavior. In order to do that, we usually perform single steps observing a part of the program's state that is of interest to us. We can also run the program until a certain condition is met or a position in code is reached. Such position in the code is called **breakpoint**.

Let us study a sample program shown in Listing 18-1. We have already seen it in Chapter 2. This code prints the rax register contents into **stdout**.

Listing 18-1. print_rax_2.asm

```
section .data
codes:
db        '0123456789ABCDEF'

section .text
global _start
_start:
mov rax, 0x1122334455667788

mov rdi, 1
mov rdx, 1
mov rcx, 64
.loop:
push rax
sub rcx, 4
sar rax, cl
and rax, 0xf

lea rsi, [codes + rax]
mov rax, 1

push rcx
syscall
pop rcx
```

© Igor Zhirkov 2017
I. Zhirkov, *Low-Level Programming*, DOI 10.1007/978-1-4842-2403-8_18

```
pop rax
test rcx, rcx
jnz .loop

mov     rax, 60          ; invoke 'close' system call

xor rdi, rdi
syscall
```

We are going to compile an executable file `print_rax` from it and launch gdb.

```
> nasm -o print_rax.o -f elf64  print_rax.asm
> ld -o print_rax print_rax.o
> gdb print_rax
...
(gdb)
```

gdb has its own command system and the interaction with it happens through these commands. So whenever gdb is launched and you see its command prompt (gdb), you can type commands and it will interact accordingly.

You can load an executable file by issuing `file` command and then typing the filename, or by passing it as an argument.

```
(gdb) file print_rax
Reading symbols from print_rax...(no debugging symbols found)...done.
```

The `<tab>` key functions in the gdb command prompt perform autocompletion hints. Many commands also have shorthands.

The two most important commands are

- `quit` to quit gdb.

- `help cmd` to show help for the command cmd.

The `~/.gdbinit` file stores commands that will be automatically executed when gdb starts. Such a file can be created in the current directory as well, but for security reasons this feature is disabled by default.

■ **Note**   To enable loading the .gdbinit file from any directory, add the following line to the `~/.gdbinit` file in your home directory:

```
set auto-load safe-path /
```

By default, gdb uses AT&T assembly syntax. In our book we stick to Intel syntax; to change gdb's default preferences regarding assembly syntax, add the following line to `~/.gdbinit` file:

```
set disassembly-flavor intel
```

Other useful commands include the following:

- `run` starts program execution.

- `break x` creates a breakpoint near the label x. When performing `run` or `continue` we will stop at the first breakpoint hit, allowing us to examine the program state.

- `break *address` to place a breakpoint at a specified address.

- `continue` to continue running program

- `stepi` or `si` to step by one instruction;

- `ni` or `nexti` will execute one instruction as well, but will not enter functions if the instruction was `call`. Instead it will let the called function terminate and break at the next instruction.

Let us do the following actions:

```
(gdb) break _start
Breakpoint 1 at 0x4000b0
(gdb) start
Function "main" not defined.
Make breakpoint pending on future shared library load? (y or [n]) n
Starting program: /home/stud/test/print_rax

Breakpoint 1, 0x00000000004000b0 in _start ()
```

We stopped at the breakpoint that we have placed at the `_start` label. Let us switch into pseudo graphical mode using commands:

```
layout asm
layout regs
```

The result is shown in Figure 18-1. The layout is composed of three windows:

- The top part shows registers and their current values.

- The middle part shows the disassembly code.

- The bottom part is an interactive prompt.

- One of these windows is focused at the time. `Ctrl-X` and `Ctrl-O` let you switch between them.

- Arrow keys can be used to scroll up and down the current window.

- `print /FMT <val>` allows to look up register contents or memory values. Register names are prefixed with dollar signs, for example: `$rax`.

- `x /FMT <address>` is another very useful command to check memory contents. Unlike `print`, it expects an indirection level, so, it accepts a pointer.

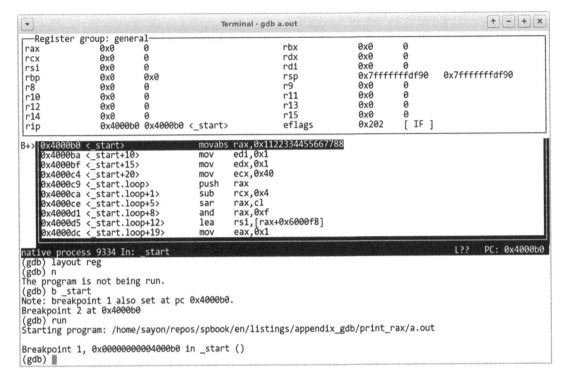

Figure 18-1. gdb *user interface:* asm + regs *layout*

FMT (used by print and x commands) is an encoded format description. It allows us to explicitly choose the data type to interpret the memory contents correctly.

FMT consists of a format letter and a size letter. The most useful format letters are

- x (hexadecimal)

- a (address)

- i (instruction, tries to perform disassembly)

- c (char)

- s (null-terminated string)

The most useful size letters are b (byte) and g (giant, 8 bytes).

To take an address of a variable, use the & symbol. The examples will show when it is handy.

Following are some examples based on the program shown in Listing 18-1:

- Displaying rax contents:

  ```
  (gdb) print $rax
  $1 = 1234605616436508552
  ```

- Displaying codes's first character:

  ```
  (gdb) print /c codes
  $2 = '0'
  ```

- Disassembling an instruction at address _start:

```
(gdb) x /i &_start
   0x4000b0 <_start>:    movabs rax,0x1122334455667788
```

- Disassembling current instruction:

```
(gdb) x /i $rip
=> 0x4000e9 <_start.loop+32>:   jne    0x4000c9 <_start.loop>
```

- Checking the contents of codes. The /FMT part of x command can start with the elements count. In our case, /12cb stands for "12 characters one byte each."

```
(gdb) x /12cb &codes
0x6000f8 <codes>:    48 '0' 49 '1' 50 '2' 51 '3' 52 '4' 53 '5' 54 '6'
55 '7'
0x600100:        56 '8' 57 '9' 65 'A' 66 'B'
```

- Examine the top 8 bytes of the stack:

```
(gdb) x /x $rsp
0x7fffffffdf90: 0x01
```

- Examine the second qword stored in the stack:

```
(gdb) x/x $rsp+8
0x7fffffffdf98: 0xc1
```

■ **Question 424**   Study the output of help x command.

To use gdb with C programs productively, remember to always use the -ggdb compiler option. It generates additional information that gdb can use, such as **.line** section or symbols for local variables.

An appropriate layout to work with C code is src; type layout src to switch to it. Figure 18-2 depicts this layout.

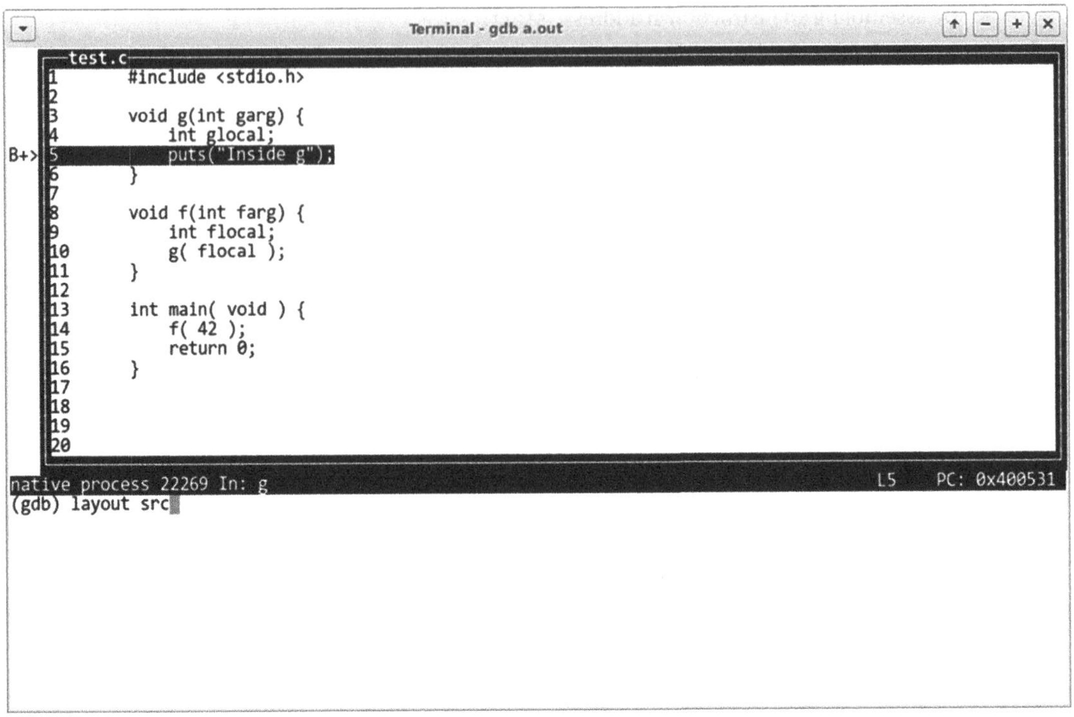

Figure 18-2. *gdb user interface:* src *layout*

Another useful option consists of studying and navigating a call stack. Each time any function is called, it uses a part of a stack to store its local variables. To demonstrate navigation we are going to use a simple program shown in Listing 18-2.

Listing 18-2. call_stack.c

```c
#include <stdio.h>

void g(int garg) {
    int glocal = 99;
    puts("Inside  g");
}

void f(int farg) {
    int flocal = 44;
    g( flocal );
}

int main( void ) {
    f( 42 );
    return 0;
}
```

We are going to compile the program and launch gdb on it as follows:

```
> gcc -ggdb call_stack.c -o call_stack
> gdb call_stack
```

Then we place a breakpoint at the function g and run the program as follows:

```
(gdb) break g
Breakpoint 1 at 0x400531: file call_stack.c, line 5.
(gdb) run
Starting program: .../call_stack

Breakpoint 1, g (garg=0) at call_stack.c:5
5        puts("Inside g");
```

We are free to issue layout src if we wish.

The program will run and stop at line 4 where the function g starts. We can explore local variables or arguments using the print command. gdb will deduce the correct types for us most of the time.

```
(gdb) print garg
$1  = 44
```

We want to see which functions are currently launched. The backtrace command is the way to do it.

```
(gdb) backtrace
#0    g (garg=44) at call_stack.c:4
#1    0x0000000000400561 in f (farg=42) at call_stack.c:10
#2    0x0000000000400572 in main () at call_stack.c:14
```

There are three stack frames that gdb is aware of, and we can switch between them using the frame <idx> command.

Our state right now is depicted in Figure 18-3. We are sure that the function f has launched function g as the backtrace says, so that instance of f should have a local variable flocal. We want to know its value. If we try to print it right away, gdb complains that such variable does not exist. However, if we select the appropriate stack frame using the frame 1 command first, we will gain access to all its local variables. Figure 18-4 depicts this change.

```
(gdb) print farg
No  symbol "farg" in current context.
```

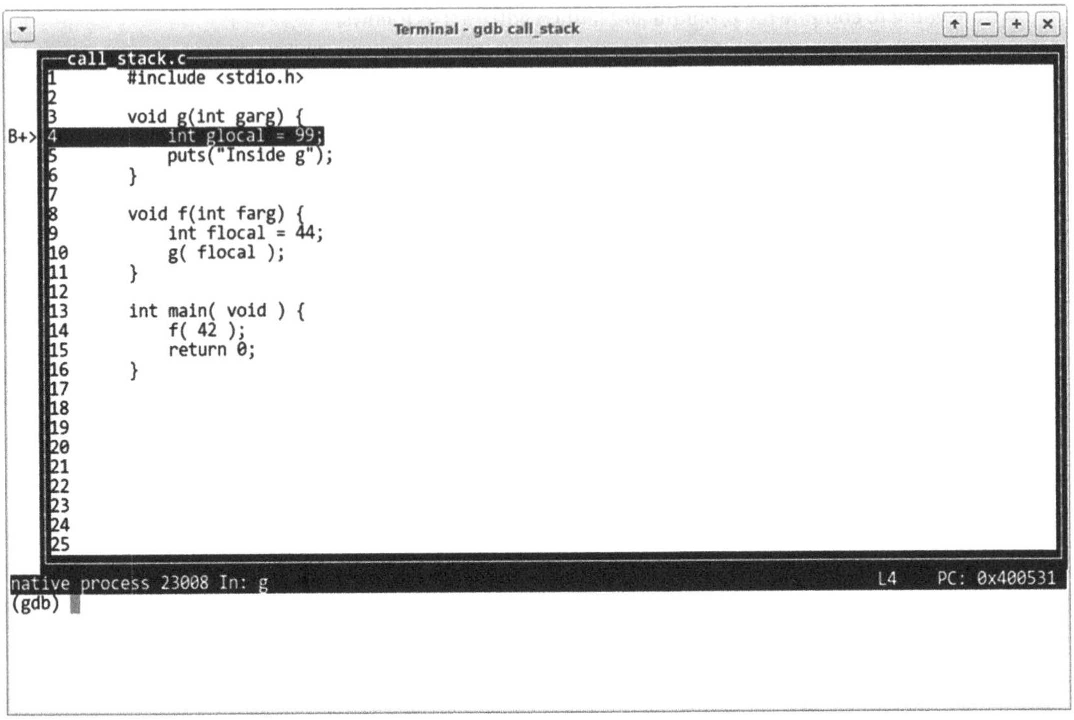

Figure 18-3. *Inside function g*

```
(gdb) frame 1
#1  0x0000000000400561 in f (farg=42) at call_stack.c:10
(gdb) print farg
$3  =  42
```

■ **Question 425** What does `info locals` do?

Other than that, gdb supports evaluating expressions with common arithmetic operations, launching functions, writing automation scripts in Python and much more.

For further reading, consult [1].

```
                           Terminal - gdb call_stack                    ↑  −  +  ×
   ┌─call_stack.c─────────────────────────────────────────────────────────────────
   │1        #include <stdio.h>
   │2
   │3        void g(int garg) {
B+ │4            int glocal = 99;
   │5            puts("Inside g");
   │6        }
   │7
   │8        void f(int farg) {
   │9            int flocal = 44;
 > │10           g( flocal );
   │11       }
   │12
   │13       int main( void ) {
   │14           f( 42 );
   │15           return 0;
   │16       }
   │17
   │18
   │19
   │20
   │21
   │22
   │23
   │24
   │25
native process 23008 In: f                                      L10    PC: 0x400561
No symbol "farg" in current context.
(gdb) frame 1
#1  0x0000000000400561 in f (farg=42) at call_stack.c:10
(gdb) print farg
$3 = 42
(gdb)
```

Figure 18-4. *Inside function f*

CHAPTER 19

Appendix B. Using Make

This appendix will introduce you to the most basic notions of writing Makefiles. For more information refer to [2].

To build a program you might need to perform multiple actions: launch compiler with the right flags, probably for each source file, and use linker. Sometimes you have to launch scripts written to generate source code files as well. At times the program consists of several parts written in different programming languages!

Moreover, if you changed only a part of the program, you might not want to rebuild everything but only those parts that depend on the source file changed. Huge programs can take hours of CPU (central processing unit) time to build!

In this book we are going to use GNU Make. It is a common tool used to control the generation of artifacts such as executable files, dynamic libraries, resource files, etc.

19.1   Simple Makefile

When you write a program, you should write a special Makefile for it, so that it is possible to use Make to build it. This text file describes the source files and the dependencies between them in a declarative manner. Then make will choose the right order in which the files should be worked so that when each file is being processed, its dependencies are already processed.

To start the building process, execute make in the directory where Makefile is created. It is usually a root directory of your project.

You can explicitly select another Makefile by providing -f flag, for example: make -f Makefile_other.

The basic Makefile is composed of the following blocks, each of them is called **rule**:

```
<target> : <prerequisites>
[tab] <recipe>
```

A rule describes how to generate a specific file, which is the rule's <target>. <prerequisites> describe which other targets should be generated first.

A recipe consists of one or many actions to be carried out by make. Every recipe line should be preceded by [tab] character!

Let us say, we have a simple program consisting of two assembly files: main.asm and lib.asm. We want to produce the object file for each of them and then link these into an executable program.

Listing 19-1 shows an example of a simple Makefile.

© Igor Zhirkov 2017

I. Zhirkov, *Low-Level Programming*, DOI 10.1007/978-1-4842-2403-8_19

Listing 19-1. `Makefile_simple`

```
program: main.o lib.o
    ld -o program main.o lib.o

lib.o: lib.asm
    nasm -f elf64 -o lib.o lib.asm

main.o: main.asm
    nasm -f elf64 -o main.o main.asm

clean:
    rm main.o lib.o program
```

When the `Makefile` with these contents is created, executing `make` in the same directory will launch the recipe for the first target described. If a target named `all` is present, its recipe will be executed instead. Otherwise, typing `make targetname` will execute the recipe for the target `targetname`.

The target `program` should produce the file `program`. To do it we should build files `main.o` and `lib.o` first. If we change the file `main.o` and launch `make` again, only `main.o` will be rebuilt before refreshing `program`, but not `lib.o`. The same mechanism forces rebuilding `lib.o` when `lib.asm` is changed.

So, the recipe is launched when there is no file corresponding to the target name or this file should be changed (because one of its dependencies has been updated).

Traditionally, every `Makefile` has a target named `clean` to get rid of all produced files, leaving only the sources. The targets such as `clean` are called **Phony Targets**, because they do not correspond to a certain file. It is best to enumerate them in a separate recipe corresponding to a special `.PHONY` target as follows:

```
clean:
    rm -f *.o

help:
    echo 'This is the help'

.PHONY: clean help
```

19.2   Throwing in Variables

It is not very appropriate to duplicate a lot of text in Makefiles. As soon as there are many source files that are compiled alike, we grow tired of repeatedly copying the same compile options. The variables solve this problem.

The variables are declared as follows:

```
variable = value
```

They are *not* the same thing as environmental variables such as PWD. Their values are substituted using a dollar sign and a pair of parentheses as follows:

```
$(variable)
```

Now, we are going to use the variables in at least the following cases:

- To abstract the compiler (we will be able to easily switch between Clang, GCC, MSVC, or whatever else compiler as long as they support the same set of flags).

- To abstract the compilation flags.

Traditionally, in case of C, these variables are named

- CC for "C compiler."

- CFLAGS for "C compiler flags."

- LD for "link editor" (linker).

- AS as "assembly language compiler."

- ASFLAGS as "assembly language compiler flags."

An additional benefit is that whenever we want to choose compilation flags we only need to do it in one place. Listing 19-2 shows the modified Makefile.

Listing 19-2. Makefile_vars

```
AS = nasm
LD = ld
ASFLAGS = -f elf64

program: main.o lib.o
    $(LD) -o program main.o lib.o

lib.o: lib.asm
    $(AS) $(ASFLAGS) -o lib.o lib.asm

main.o: main.asm
    $(AS) $(ASFLAGS) -o main.o main.asm

clean:
    rm main.o lib.o program

.PHONY: clean
```

A variable can be left empty, and it will be expanded to an empty string:

```
EMPTYVAR  =
```

A variable can include other variables' values:

```
INCLUDEDIR  = include
CFLAGS      = -c -std=c99 -I$(INCLUDEDIR) -ggdb -Wno-attributes
```

Target names support the wildcard symbol %. There should be only one such wildcard in a target name. The substring that % matches is called the **stem**. The occurences of % in prerequisites are replaced with exactly the stem. For example, this rule

```
%.o : %.c
    echo "Building an object file"
```

specifies how to build any object file from a .c file with the matching name. However, right now we do not know how to use these rules, because once we try to write a command to compile the file we face a problem: we do not know the exact names of the files involved, and the stem is inaccessible inside the recipe. The automatic variables solve this problem.

19.3 Automatic Variables

Automatic variables are a special feature of make. They are computed afresh for each rule that is executed, and their values depend on the target and its prerequisites. They can only be used within the recipe itself, not inside prerequisites or inside the target itself.

Imagine you want to compile each .c file into an .o file with the same flags. Should we really duplicate all the rules? No, we can use the wildcards in conjunction with automatic variables.

There are many automatic variables, but the most commonly used are

- $* The stem.

- $@ The file name of the target of the rule.

- $< The name of the first prerequisite.

- $^ The names of all the prerequisites separated by spaces.

- $? The names of all the prerequisites that are newer than the target.

Listing 19-3 shows an exemplary Makefile which uses all knowledge from this tutorial.

Listing 19-3. makefile_autovars

```
CC = gcc
CFLAGS = -std=c11 -Wall
LD = gcc

all: main

main: main.o lib.o
    $(LD) $^ -o $@

%.o: %.c %.h
    $(CC) $(CFLAGS) -c $< -o $@

clean:
    rm -f *.o main

.PHONY: clean
```

It assumes the following project tree:

```
.
 lib.c
 lib.h
 main.c
 main.h
 Makefile
0 directories, 8 files
```

A clean make will execute the following commands:

```
> make
gcc -std=c11 -Wall -c main.c -o main.o
gcc -std=c11 -Wall -c lib.c -o lib.o
gcc  main.o lib.o -o main
```

Refer to the well-written GNU Make Manual [2] for further instructions.

413

CHAPTER 20

Appendix C. System Calls

Throughout this book we have used several system calls. We gather the information about them in this appendix.

Note It is always a good idea to read the man pages first, for example, man -s 2 write.

The exact flag and parameter values vary from system to system and should never be used in the immediate form. If you write in C, use the relevant headers (shown in man pages for the system call of interest). If you write in assembly, you will have to use LXR or another online system with annotated kernel code or look through these C headers yourself and create your own, corresponding %define's.

The values provided are valid for the following system:

```
> uname -a
Linux 3.16-2-amd64 #1 SMP Debian 3.16.3-2 (2014-09-20) x86_64 GNU/Linux
```

Issuing a system call in assembly is simple: just initialize the relevant registers into correct parameter values (in any order) and execute syscall instruction. If you need flags, you should define them on your own first; we provided you with their exact values.

Remember, that NASM can also compute constant expressions, such as O_TRUNC|O_RDWR.

Issuing a system call in C is usually done like calling a function, whose declaration is provided in some include files.

Note In C, never use the flags values directly, like, substituting O_APPEND with 0x1000. Use the defines provided in the header files, because they are both more readable and portable. Since we will have no corresponding assembly headers, we have to define them by hand in the assembly files.

20.1   read

```
ssize_t read(int fd, void *buf, size_t count);
```

Description Read from a file descriptor.

rax	rdi	rsi	rdx	r10	r8	r9
0	int fd	void* buf	size_t count			

20.1.1   Arguments

1. fd   File descriptor by which we read. 0 for **stdin**; use open system call to open a file by name.

2. buf   The address of the first byte in a sequence of bytes. The received bytes will be placed there.

3. count   We will attempt to read that many bytes.

Returns rax = number of bytes successfully read, -1 on error.
Includes to use in C:

```
#include <unistd.h>
```

20.2   write

```
ssize_t write(int fd, const void *buf, size_t count);
```

Description Write to a file descriptor.

rax	rdi	rsi	rdx	r10	r8	r9
1	int fd	const void* buf	size_t count			

20.2.1   Arguments

1. fd   File descriptor by which we write. 1 for **stdout**, 2 for **stderr**; use open system call to open a file by name.

2. buf   The address of the first byte in a sequence of bytes to be written.

3. count   We will attempt to write that many bytes.

Returns rax = number of bytes successfully written, -1 on error.
Includes to use in C:

```
#include <unistd.h>
```

20.3   open

```
int open(const char *pathname, int flags, mode_t mode);
```

Description Opens the file with a given name (null-terminated string)

rax	rdi	rsi	rdx	r10	r8	r9
2	const char* filename	int flags	int mode			

20.3.1   Arguments

1. `filename`   Name of the file to be opened (null-terminated string).

2. `flags`   Are described below. They can be combined using |, for example, `O_CREAT| O_WRONLY|O_TRUNC`.

3. `mode`   Is an integer number encoding user, group, and all others' permissions. They are similar to ones used by `chmod` command.

Returns `rax` = new file descriptor for the given file, -1 on error.
Includes to use in C:

```
#include <sys/types.h>
#include <sys/stat.h>
#include <fcntl.h>
```

20.3.2   Flags

- `O_APPEND = 0x1000`

  Append to a file on each write.

- `O_CREAT = 0x40`

  Create a new file.

- `O_TRUNC = 0x200`

  If the file already exists and is a regular file and the access mode allows writing it will be truncated to length 0.

- `O_RDWR = 2`

  Read and write.

- `O_WRONLY = 1`

  Write only.

- `O_RDONLY = 0`

  Read only.

20.4   close

```
int close(int fd);
```

Description Close the file with a given name (null-terminated string)

rax	rdi	rsi	rdx	r10	r8	r9
2	const char* filename	int flags	int mode			

20.4.1   Arguments

1. `fd`   a valid file descriptor that should be closed.

Returns rax = zero un success, -1 on error. Global variable `errno` holds the error code.
Includes to use in C:

```
#include <unistd.h>
```

20.5   mmap

```
void *mmap(
    void *addr, size_t length,
    int prot, int flags,
    int fd, off_t offset);
```

Description Map pages in virtual address space to something. It can be anything that lies behind a "file" (devices, files on disk, etc.) or just physical memory. In the latter case, the pages are anonymous, they bear no correspondence to anything present in file system. Such pages hold the heap and stacks of a process.

rax	rdi	rsi	rdx	r10	r8	r9
9	void* addr	size_t len	int prot	int flags	int fd	off_t off

20.5.1   Arguments

1. `addr`   A hint for the starting virtual address of the freshly mapped region. We try to map at this address, and if we can't, we let the operating system (OS) choose it. If 0, will always be chosen by OS.

2. `len`   Length of a mapped region in bytes.

3. `prot`   Protection flags (see below). They can be combined using |.

4. `flags`   Behavior flags (see later). They can be combined using |.

5. `fd`   A valid file descriptor for the file to be mapped, ignored if MAP_ANONYMOUS behavior flag is used.

6. `off`   Starting offset in the file `fd`. We skip all bytes prior to this offset and map the file starting with it. Ignored if MAP_ANONYMOUS behavior flag is used.

Returns rax = pointer to the mapped area, -1 on error.
Includes to use in C:

```
#include <sys/mman.h>
```

20.5.2   Protection Flags

- PROT_EXEC = 0x4   Pages may be executed.

- PROT_READ = 0x1   Pages may be read.

- PROT_WRITE = 0x2   Pages may be written.

- PROT_NONE = 0x0   Pages may not be accessed.

20.5.3   Behavior Flags

- MAP_SHARED = 0x1   Pages can be shared between processes.

- MAP_PRIVATE = 0x2   Pages are not shared with other processes.

- MAP_ANONYMOUS = 0x20   Pages do not correspond to any file in the filesystem.

- MAP_FIXED = 0x10   Do not interpret addr as a hint but as an order. If we cannot map pages starting at this address, fail.

■ **Note**   To be able to use MAP_ANONYMOUS flag you might need to define _DEFAULT_SOURCE flag immediately before including the relevant header file, as follows:

```
#define _DEFAULT_SOURCE
```

```
#include <sys/mman.h>
```

20.6   munmap

```
int munmap(void *addr, size_t length);
```

Description Unmaps a region of memory of a given length. You can map a huge region using mmap and then unmap a fraction of it using munmap.

rax	rdi	rsi	rdx	r10	r8	r9
11	void* addr	size_t len				

20.6.1   Arguments

1. addr   Start of the region to unmap.

2. length   Length of the region to unmap.

Returns rax = zero un success, -1 on error. Global variable errno holds the error code.
Includes to use in C:

```
#include <sys/mman.h>
```

20.7 exit

```
void _exit(int status);
```

Description Exit process.

rax	rdi	rsi	rdx	r10	r8	r9
60	int status					

20.7.1 Arguments

1. `status`   Exit code. It is stored into $? environmental variable.

Returns Nothing.

Includes to use in C:

```
#include <unistd.h>
```

CHAPTER 21

Appendix D. Performance Tests
Information

All performance tests were conducted on the following system:

```
> uname -a
```

```
Linux perseus 3.16-2-amd64 #1 SMP Debian 3.16.3-2 (2014-09-20) x86_64 GNU/Linux
```

```
> cat /proc/cpuinfo
```

```
processor       : 0
vendor_id       : GenuineIntel
cpu family      : 6
model           : 69
model name      : Intel(R) Core(TM) i5-4210U CPU @ 1.70GHz
stepping        : 1
microcode       : 0x1d
cpu MHz         : 2394.458
cache size      : 3072 KB
physical id     : 0
siblings        : 1
core id         : 0
cpu cores       : 1
apicid          : 0
initial apicid  : 0
fpu             : yes
fpu_exception   : yes
cpuid level     : 13
wp              : yes
flags           : fpu vme de pse tsc msr pae mce cx8 apic
sep mtrr pge mca cmov pat pse36 clflush dts mmx fxsr sse
sse2 ss syscall nx pdpe1gb rdtscp lm constant_tsc arch_perfmon
pebs bts nopl xtopology tsc_reliable nonstop_tsc aperfmperf
pni pclmulqdq ssse3 fma cx16 pcid sse4_1 sse4_2 x2apic movbe
popcnt aes xsave avx f16c rdrand hypervisor lahf_lm ida arat
epb pln pts dtherm fsgsbase smep
```

```
bogomips        : 4788.91
clflush size    : 64
cache_alignment : 64
address sizes   : 40 bits physical, 48 bits virtual
power management:

processor       : 1
vendor_id       : GenuineIntel
cpu family      : 6
model           : 69
model name      : Intel(R) Core(TM) i5-4210U CPU @ 1.70GHz
stepping        : 1
microcode       : 0x1d
cpu MHz         : 2394.458
cache size      : 3072 KB
physical id     : 2
siblings        : 1
core id         : 0
cpu cores       : 1
apicid          : 2
initial apicid  : 2
fpu             : yes
fpu_exception   : yes
cpuid level     : 13
wp              : yes
flags           : fpu vme de pse tsc msr pae mce cx8 apic
sep mtrr pge mca cmov pat pse36 clflush dts mmx fxsr sse
sse2 ss syscall nx pdpe1gb rdtscp lm constant_tsc arch_perfmon
pebs bts nopl xtopology tsc_reliable nonstop_tsc aperfmperf
pni pclmulqdq ssse3 fma cx16 pcid sse4_1 sse4_2 x2apic movbe
popcnt aes xsave avx f16c rdrand hypervisor lahf_lm ida arat
epb pln pts dtherm fsgsbase smep
bogomips        : 4788.91
clflush size    : 64
cache_alignment : 64
address sizes   : 40 bits physical, 48 bits virtual
power management:

> cat /proc/meminfo

MemTotal:        1017348 kB
MemFree:          516672 kB
MemAvailable:     565600 kB
Buffers:           32756 kB
Cached:           114944 kB
SwapCached:        10044 kB
Active:           376288 kB
Inactive:          49624 kB
Active(anon):     266428 kB
Inactive(anon):    12440 kB
Active(file):     109860 kB
```

```
Inactive(file):      37184 kB
Unevictable:             0 kB
Mlocked:                 0 kB
SwapTotal:          901116 kB
SwapFree:           868356 kB
Dirty:                  44 kB
Writeback:               0 kB
AnonPages:          270964 kB
Mapped:              43852 kB
Shmem:                 648 kB
Slab:                45980 kB
SReclaimable:        29016 kB
SUnreclaim:          16964 kB
KernelStack:          4192 kB
PageTables:           6100 kB
NFS_Unstable:            0 kB
Bounce:                  0 kB
WritebackTmp:            0 kB
CommitLimit:       1409788 kB
Committed_AS:      1212356 kB
VmallocTotal:  34359738367 kB
VmallocUsed:        145144 kB
VmallocChunk:  34359590172 kB
HardwareCorrupted:       0 kB
AnonHugePages:           0 kB
HugePages_Total:         0
HugePages_Free:          0
HugePages_Rsvd:          0
HugePages_Surp:          0
Hugepagesize:         2048 kB
DirectMap4k:         49024 kB
DirectMap2M:        999424 kB
DirectMap1G:             0 kB
```

CHAPTER 22

■ ■ ■

Bibliography

[1]   *Debugging with gdb*. Available: `http://sourceware.org/gdb/current/onlinedocs/gdb/`. 2017.

[2]   *Gnu make manual*. Available: `www.gnu.org/software/make/manual/`. 2016.

[3]   *How initialization functions are handled*. Available: `https://gcc.gnu.org/onlinedocs/gccint/Initialization.html`. 2017.

[4]   *Using ld, the gnu linker*. Available: `www.math.utah.edu/docs/info/ld_3.html`. 1994.

[5]   *What is map-reduce?* Available: `www-01.ibm.com/software/data/infosphere/hadoop/mapreduce/`. 2017.

[6]   Jeff Andrews. *Branch and loop reorganization to prevent mispredicts*. Available: `https://software.intel.com/en-us/articles/branch-and-loop-reorganization-to-prevent-mispredicts`. May 2011.

[7]   C11 language standard—committee draft. `www.open-std.org/jtc1/sc22/wg14/www/standards`. April 2011.

[8]   Luca Cardelli and Peter Wegner. On understanding types, data abstraction, and polymorphism. *ACM Comput. Surv.* 17(4):471–523. December 1985.

[9]   Ryan A. Chapman. *Linux 3.2.0-33 syscall table, x86 64*. `www.cs.utexas.edu/~bismith/test/syscalls/syscalls64_orig.html`.

[10] Thomas H. Cormen, Clifford Stein, Ronald L. Rivest, and Charles E. Leiserson. *Introduction to algorithms*. New York: McGraw-Hill Higher Education, 2nd ed., 2001.

[11] Russ Cox. *Regular expression matching can be simple and fast*. `https://swtch.com/~rsc/regexp/regexp1.html`. November 2007.

[12] Ulrich Drepper. *What every programmer should know about memory*. `https://people.freebsd.org/~lstewart/articles/cpumemory.pdf`. November 2007.

[13] Ulrich Drepper. *How to write shared libraries*. `https://software.intel.com/sites/default/files/m/a/1/e/dsohowto.pdf`. December 2011.

[14] Jens Gustedt. *Myth and reality about inline in c99*. `https://gustedt.wordpress.com/2010/11/29/myth-and-reality-about-inline-in-c99/`. 2010.

© Igor Zhirkov 2017

I. Zhirkov, *Low-Level Programming*, DOI 10.1007/978-1-4842-2403-8_22

[15] Intel Corporation. Intel® 64 and IA-32 architectures software developer's manual. Available: `www.intel.com/content/dam/www/public/us/en/documents/manuals/64-ia-32-architectures-software-developer-manual-325462.pdf`. September 2014.

[16] Intel Corporation. *Intel® 64 and IA-32 architectures optimization reference manual.* Available: `www.intel.com/content/www/us/en/architecture-and-technology/64-ia-32-architectures-optimization-manual.html`. June 2016.

[17] David Kanter. *Intel's Haswell CPU microarchitecture.* Available: `www.realworldtech.com/haswell-cpu/1`.

[18] Brian W. Kernighan. *The C Programming Language.* Prentice Hall Professional Technical Reference, 2nd edition, 1988.

[19] Petter Larsson and Eric Palmer. Image processing acceleration techniques using intel streaming simd extensions and intel advanced vector extensions. January 2010.

[20] Doug Lea. *A memory allocator.* `http://g.oswego.edu/dl/html/malloc.html`. 2000.

[21] Michael E. Lee. *Optimization of computer programs in c.* Available: `http://leto.net/docs/C-optimization.php`.

[22] Lomont, Chris. "Fast inverse square root." Tech-315 nical Report (2003): 32. February 2003.

[23] Love, Robert. Linux Kernel Development (Novell Press). Novell Press, 2005.

[24] Michael Matz, Jan Hubicka, Andreas Jaeger, and Mark Mitchell. System V Application Binary Interface. AMD64 Architecture Processor Supplement. Draft version 0.99.6, 2013.

[25] McKenney, Paul E. "Memory barriers: a hardware view for software hackers." Linux Technology Center, IBM Beaverton (2010).

[26] Pawell Moll. How do debuggers (really) work? In *Embedded Linux Conference Europe*, October 2015. `http://events.linuxfoundation.org/sites/events/files/slides/slides_16.pdf`.

[27] *The netwide assembler: NASM manual.* Available: `www.nasm.us/doc/`.

[28] N. N. Nepeyvoda and I. N. Skopin. *Foundations of programming.* RHD Moscow-Izhevsk, 2003.

[29] Benjamin C. Pierce. *Types and programming languages.* Cambridge, MA: MIT Press, 1st ed. 2002.

[30] Jeff Preshing. *The purpose of memory order consume in c++11.* `http://preshing.com/20140709/the-purpose-of-memory_order_consume-in-cpp11/`. 2014.

[31] Jeff Preshing. *Weak vs. strong memory models* `http://preshing.com/20120930/weak-vs-strong-memory-models/`. 2012.

[32] Brad Rodriguez. *Moving forth: a series on writing Forth kernels.* `http://www.bradrodriguez.com/papers/moving1.html`. The Computer Journal #59 (January/February 1993).

[33]   Uresh, Vahalia. *"UNIX Internals: The New Frontiers."* (2005). Dorling Kindersley
        Pvt. Limited. 2008.

[34]   Anthony Williams. *C++ concurrency in action: practical multithreading.*
        Shelter Island, NY: Manning. 2012.

[35]   Glynn Winskel. *The formal semantics of programming languages: an
        introduction.* Cambridge, MA: MIT Press. 1993.

Index

A

Abstract machines, 3
Abstract syntax tree, 230–231
Accessing code
    header files, 187–188
Addressing, 23–24, 30–31, 36
    base-indexed with scale and displacement, 31
    direct, 31
    immediate, 23, 31
    indirect addressing, 23
Address space, 48
Address space layout randomization (ASLR), 285
Alignment, 235–239
Address translation process
    DEP and EXB, 55
    page table entry, 55
    PML4, 53
    segmentation faults, 55
    TLB, 55
Array, 147, 153–158, 160, 162–169, 179, 209–210
    defined, 153
    initializers, 154
    memory allocators, 153
    summation functionality
        bug, 163
        const qualifiers, 166
Assembly code
    dictionary implementation, 87–89
    dynamic library, 307–308
    GCC and NASM, 308
Assembly language, 4
    constant precomputation, 30
    endianness, 28–29
    function calls, 25–28
    instruction
        mov, 20–21
        syscall, 20–21
    label, 19
    output register
        local labels, 23
        rax value, 22–23
    relative addressing, 23–24
    pointer, 30
    string length computation, 32–33
    strings, 29
Assembly preprocessor, 64–73
    conditionals, 66–69
    %define, 64–67, 69–70
    macros with arguments, 65–66, 68–69
Assertions, 251

B

Backus-Naur form (BNF), 222
Binutils, 77
BitMaP (BMP) format, 256–257
BNF (Backus-Naur form), 222
Booleans, 150
Branch prediction, 338
Breakpoint, 399

C

C
    C89, 130
    compilation, 130
    control flow
        fibonacci series, 138
        for, 135–136
        switch, 137–138
        while, 135
    dangling else, 134
    data types, 132–133
    Duff's device, 137
    expressions, 139, 141–142
    function, 142–144
    main function, 156–157
    preprocessor, 144–145
        block, 143–144
        #define, 144–145
        #endif, 144
        #ifndef, 144
        #include, 144–145

I. Zhirkov, *Low-Level Programming*, DOI 10.1007/978-1-4842-2403-8

■ X, Y, Z

Get the eBook for only $5!

Why limit yourself?

With most of our titles available in both PDF and ePUB format, you can access your content wherever and however you wish—on your PC, phone, tablet, or reader.

Since you've purchased this print book, we are happy to offer you the eBook for just $5.

To learn more, go to http://www.apress.com/companion or contact support@apress.com.

Apress®

Printed in the United States
By Bookmasters